THE MOST TRUSTED NAME IN TRAVEL

Frommer's®

PARIS 2026

11th Edition

By Anna Brooke

FrommerMedia LLC

Frommer's Paris 2026, 11th Edition

Published by:
FrommerMedia LLC

Copyright © 2026 by FrommerMedia LLC. All rights reserved. No part of this publication may be reproduced, stored in a retrieval system, or transmitted in any form or by any means, electronic, mechanical, photocopying, recording, scanning or otherwise, except as permitted under Sections 107 or 108 of the 1976 United States Copyright Act, without the prior written permission of the Publisher. Requests to the Publisher for permission should be addressed to support@frommermedia.com.

Frommer's is a registered trademark of Arthur Frommer. FrommerMedia LLC is not associated with any product or vendor mentioned in this book.

ISBN 978-1-62887-643-7 (paper), 978-1-62887-644-4 (e-book)

Editorial Director: Pauline Frommer
Editor: Elizabeth Heath
Production Editor: Kelly D. Henthorne
Cartographer: Andrew Dolan

Photo Editor: Meghan Lamb
Indexer: Kelly D. Henthorne
Compositor: Heather Pope
Cover Design: Dave Riedy

Front cover: City street view in Paris, France with the Sacré-Cœur Basilica.
Title page: Roman sculpture of Diana the Huntress in the Hall of the Caryatids in the Louvre Museum.

For information on our other products or services, see www.frommers.com.

FrommerMedia LLC also publishes its books in a variety of electronic formats. Some content that appears in print may not be available in electronic formats.

Manufactured in Malaysia

5 4 3 2 1

HOW TO CONTACT US

In researching this book, we discovered many wonderful places—hotels, restaurants, shops, and more. We're sure you'll find others. Please tell us about them, so we can share the information with your fellow travelers in upcoming editions. If you were disappointed with a recommendation, we'd love to know that, too. Please write to: Support@FrommerMedia.com

FROMMER'S HEART RATINGS SYSTEM

Every hotel, restaurant and attraction listed in this guide has been ranked for quality and value. Here's what the hearts mean:

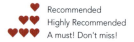

♥ Recommended
♥♥ Highly Recommended
♥♥♥ A must! Don't miss!

AN IMPORTANT NOTE

The world is a dynamic place. Hotels change ownership, restaurants hike their prices, museums alter their opening hours, and buses and trains change their routings. And all of this can occur in the several months after our authors have visited, inspected, and written about these hotels, restaurants, museums, and transportation services. Though we have made valiant efforts to keep all our information fresh and up-to-date, some few changes can inevitably occur in the periods before a revised edition of this guidebook is published. So please bear with us if a tiny number of the details in this book have changed. Please also note that we have no responsibility or liability for any inaccuracy or errors or omissions, or for inconvenience, loss, damage, or expenses suffered by anyone as a result of assertions in this guide.

CONTENTS

LIST OF MAPS v

1 THE BEST OF PARIS 1

2 SUGGESTED ITINERARIES & NEIGHBORHOODS 12

Iconic Paris in 1 Day 12
Iconic Paris in 2 Days 16
Iconic Paris in 3 Days 18
An Itinerary for Families 19
Paris for Romantics 22
City Layout 23
Neighborhoods in Brief 24

3 PARIS IN CONTEXT 37

The Making of Paris 37
Paris Today 48
Calendar of Events 50

4 WHERE TO STAY 57

What to Expect 57
Practical Matters 58
The Right Bank 59
The Left Bank 82
Alternative Lodgings 97

5 WHERE TO DINE 99

Practical Matters 100
The Right Bank 102
The Left Bank 134
The Top Tearooms 151
The Top Cafes 153

6 EXPLORING PARIS 157

The Right Bank 157
The Left Bank 206

Organized Tours & Classes 225
Especially for Kids 233
Active Paris 236

7 SHOPPING 241

Shopping by Area 241
Department Stores & Malls 245
Markets: Food & Flea 247
Recommended Stores 249

8 ENTERTAINMENT & NIGHTLIFE 265

Theater 265
Landmark Multiuse Venues 266
Opera & Classical Music 268
Cabaret & Chanson 270
Movies 271
Live Rock, Jazz, Electro & More 272
The Bar Scene 278
The Gay & Lesbian Scene 283
Spectator Sports 284

9 DAY TRIPS FROM PARIS 286

Versailles 286
Chartres 293
Giverny 298
Fontainebleau 301
Disneyland Paris 304
Parc Astérix 306

10 WALKING TOURS OF PARIS 308

Walking Tour 1: Montmartre 308

Walking Tour 2: The Marais 315

11 PLANNING YOUR TRIP TO PARIS 324

Getting There 324

Getting Around 327

Fast Facts: Paris 334

12 USEFUL TERMS & PHRASES 343

Basic Vocabulary 343

Basic Menu Terms 347

INDEX 349

LIST OF MAPS

Paris Neighborhoods 14
Right Bank West Hotels 62
Right Bank East Hotels 65
Montmartre Hotels 75
Left Bank Hotels (Eiffel Tower Area) 83
Left Bank Hotels (Latin Quarter, St-Germain, Montparnasse) 84
Right Bank West Restaurants 104
Right Bank East Restaurants 107
Montmartre Restaurants 123
Left Bank Restaurants (Eiffel Tower Area) 135
Left Bank Restaurants (Latin Quarter, St-Germain, Montparnasse) 136
Right Bank Attractions 158
Louvre 169
Père-Lachaise Cemetery 201
Left Bank Attractions 208
Métropole du Grand Paris 287
Versailles 289
Chartres Cathedral 295
Montmartre Walking Tour 309
The Marais Walking Tour 317

ABOUT THE AUTHOR

British-born **Anna Brooke** moved to Paris in 2000 and hasn't looked back since. A versatile journalist and storyteller, she juggles life between travel writing and authoring children's books. She is the writer of seven travel guides for Frommer's and has contributed to publications such as the UK's *Financial Times*, *The Times*, and *The Sunday Times*, where she is a long-standing expert on Paris and France. Her fiction includes the award-winning *Monster Bogey* and *Monster Stink* books for kids aged 7 and up and *Two Little Dicky Birds* and *HELP!* for younger readers.

ABOUT THE FROMMER TRAVEL GUIDES

For most of the past 65 years, Frommer's has been the leading series of travel guides in North America, accounting for as many as 24% of all guidebooks sold. I think I know why.

Though we hope our books are entertaining, we nevertheless deal with travel in a serious fashion. Our guidebooks have never looked on such journeys as a mere recreation, but as a far more important human function, a time of learning and introspection, an essential part of a civilized life. We stress the culture, lifestyle, history, and beliefs of the destinations we cover, and urge our readers to seek out people and new ideas as the chief rewards of travel.

We have never shied from controversy. We have, from the beginning, encouraged our authors to be intensely judgmental, critical—both pro and con—in their comments, and wholly independent. Our only clients are our readers, and we have triggered the ire of countless prominent sorts, from a tourist newspaper we called "practically worthless" (it unsuccessfully sued us) to the many rip-offs we've condemned.

And because we believe that travel should be available to everyone regardless of their incomes, we have always been cost-conscious at every level of expenditure. Though we have broadened our recommendations beyond the budget category, we insist that every lodging we include be sensibly priced. We use every form of media to assist our readers, and are particularly proud of our feisty daily website, the award-winning Frommers.com.

I have high hopes for the future of Frommer's. May these guidebooks, in all the years ahead, continue to reflect the joy of travel and the freedom that travel represents. May they always pursue a cost-conscious path, so that people of all incomes can enjoy the rewards of travel. And may they create, for both the traveler and the persons among whom we travel, a community of friends, where all human beings live in harmony and peace.

Arthur Frommer
(1929–2024)

A foreword TO THIS GUIDE TO PARIS
BY
ARTHUR FROMMER

It always happens. Toward the end of every TV, radio, or newspaper interview, I am asked, "If you could vacation in only one place in the world, where would it be?" And I disappoint the questioner by responding not with an exotic or colorful choice—such as New Guinea or Montevideo—but simply with the city of Paris. And while the deflated interviewer changes the subject, I go babbling on about how Paris never fails to enchant.

Let Me Count the Ways

It's true—I can never get enough of the City of Light. To me, Paris is on the frontier, the leading edge, of every touristic activity. It rules the roost not only in cuisine—who could deny that?—but also in art and museums; in concerts, dance, and opera; in political discourse and intellectual debate (scan the newspaper headlines if you doubt that); in monuments and history (from the Panthéon to the Tomb of Napoleon); in fashion and shopping; in its cafes and bars (where you can spend the entire afternoon sipping a single glass of wine and not be asked to move on); in the availability of its civic services (get sick and a roaming ambulance with a doctor on board will almost instantly be at your side); in its luscious-looking open-air markets; in the excitement of its student life; in literature and economics (its resident novelists, philosophers, scientists, and scholars are legendary); and in every other field and endeavor I can name. Return to it for the second time or even the fiftieth—it still seems new.

So obviously, a guidebook series such as ours must have an important volume devoted to Paris. And this one, by Brit-turned-Parisienne Anna Brooke, is surely among the leading examples.

Anna came to Paris some 25 years ago and fell in love with it during a study abroad year. She moved straight back after her studies, thinking she'd stay a year or two, and here she still is! While enjoying the delights of her adopted city, she proceeded to carve out a career as a distinguished travel journalist, whose writings have appeared in numerous prestigious newspapers and magazines. Anna also composes music and lyrics for film and the stage and writes fiction for children.

Although her *Frommer's Paris* devotes more-than-sufficient space to organized commercial tours of Paris (including the fabled Bateaux-Mouches riverboats), it's clear from the text that she primarily regards Paris as a walking city, to be explored on your own, often while wandering at random. Here, after all, is a metropolis so built to human scale, so lovely in its architectural design, so lined with small shops with their dynamic proprietors, that there is never an uninteresting block in it. Let me repeat: *You can walk its ancient streets for hours and you will never be uninterested.*

I hope that your decision to carry a light-and-manageable Frommer's guide will greatly assist you in your enjoyment of Paris, and that Anna's own special perspectives will make your visit full of joy—and memorable.

Cordially,

Arthur Frommer
(1929–2024)

THE BEST OF PARIS

1

Paris is a magnificent city, worthy of all the superlatives that have been heaped upon it for centuries. Its graceful streets, soaked in history, really are as elegant as they say. Its monuments and museums really are extraordinary, and a slightly world-weary *fin-de-siècle* grandeur really is part of day-to-day existence. But Paris is so much more than a beautiful assemblage of buildings and monuments. It is the pulsing heart of the French nation.

When you look beyond its beautiful facade, however, you'll see that this is a city where flesh-and-blood people live and work and a place with a palpable urban buzz. Not only is Paris the nation's capital; it and its suburbs (known collectively as Le Grand Paris) are home to about 20% of the country's population and is the source of most French jobs. For the best in art, culture, and business, all roads lead to Paris.

Not all that long ago, Paris was not only the navel of France but also the shining beacon of Europe. All the continent's greatest minds and talents clamored to come here: The city seduced Nietzsche, Chopin, Picasso, and Wilde, and then in the 1920s it drew Hemingway and the Lost Generation of American writers and artists. After World War II, it became the iconic backdrop of a new form of cinema: La Nouvelle Vague (the French New Wave), with many cineastes engaging with the political and social unrest of the time.

From before the French Revolution to the terrorist attacks of 2015, Paris has played center stage to turmoil—much of it romanticized (think *Les Misérables*), some of it too recent to properly put into perspective. But one thing is certain: Upheaval has always been as much a part of its urban makeup as the Seine—which is why Paris's coat of arms features a boat and the motto FLUCTUAT NEC MERGITUR ("She is tossed by the waves but does not sink"), a reminder that no matter what happens, Paris will prevail and protect those within her walls.

And it's true. Despite the heartache of recent years, the Covid-19 pandemic included, Paris is still a bastion of the best of French culture. It hosted the 2024 Olympics and Paralympics splendidly. And its culinary legacy alone is enough to fill several books. You can eat your way to nirvana in the city's restaurants, gourmet food stores, and bakeries. The architecture ranges from the lavish opulence of **Place Vendôme** (p. 171) to the contemporary quirkiness of the **Fondation Louis Vuitton** (p. 184). The city is also home to some of the world's greatest museums, including the legendary **Louvre** (p. 166). And let's not even get into its concert halls, nightspots, parks, gardens, and cafes—at least not just yet. Even if you have time to see only a fraction of what you'd like to see, in the long run, it really won't matter. What counts is that you'll have been to Paris, sampled its wonders, and savored the experience—and that counts for a lot.

Views of Paris from TOO Hôtel rooftop bar.

THE best AUTHENTIC PARIS EXPERIENCES

- **Seeing the city from above:** Whether it's from the top of the **Eiffel Tower** (p. 217) or in front of the **Sacré-Coeur** (p. 194), seeing the city from aloft will make your heart sing. In recent years, a multitude of hotels and restaurants have opened their rooftops, too, so you can marvel at the monuments poking out above Haussmann's elegant buildings, drink and food in hand. One of the best views is from the top of the **TOO Hôtel** (p. 88) in the emerging 13th arrondissement.
- **Strolling across the Pont Neuf:** The view from here is dramatic. To one side, you'll see the **Île de la Cité,** and to the other, the **Eiffel Tower** and the **Louvre.** It's a little like standing in the navel of the Parisian universe, and, in fact, you are: The island that this bridge straddles dates back to the city's earliest beginnings.
- **Walking along the Seine at night:** Paris is beautiful in the daytime, but at night, when many of the monuments are lit up, it's positively bewitching. An evening stroll along the banks of the Seine is about as romantic as it gets. A **nighttime boat cruise** (p. 225) is another great way to enjoy the magic.
- **Sipping an apéro at a sidewalk cafe at sunset:** After work or before play, Parisians love to meet up to have an *apéritif,* usually a light alcoholic drink like a glass of wine, a French beer, or—an enduring trend—a spritz (a sparkling wine cocktail made with Italian bitter orange Aperol) on a cafe terrace. Join the locals in this early evening ritual and feel like a real Parisian.

o **Soaking up the atmosphere at a street market:** All kinds of Parisians frequent the city's many **covered and open-air markets** (p. 247), which sell fresh fruits, vegetables, meats, cheeses, and oodles of other delicious goodies. Don't be afraid to plunge into these noisy places; you'll be participating in a tradition that goes back centuries. Just ask before you touch the merchandise; the vendors do the selecting and the bagging here.

o **Riding a bike:** Ever since the advent of the **Vélib'** low-cost bike-rental program (p. 331) in 2007, Paris has been evolving into a two-wheeler city, a phenomenon catalyzed by the 2024 Olympics and Paralympics, when even more bike lines and rental bikes were added. Now multiple companies offer rental schemes similar to Vélib'. Download one of the apps (p. 332) to buzz around like a local.

PARIS'S best ARCHITECTURAL LANDMARKS

o **Best monuments to La Gloire (the glory of France):** The **Arc de Triomphe**—the world's largest triumphal arch (p. 183)—is about as grandiose as it gets, at least until you arrive at the magnificent **Place de la Concorde** (p. 193), another flamboyant national gesture. If that's not enough, the church of **La Madeleine** (p. 187) was originally meant to be a

An open-air street market in the Bastille district.

temple to military glory, and the **Panthéon** (p. 211) is a church made into a crypt for the nation's intellectual heroes.

o **Best monuments to spiritual glory:** Despite the French obsession with keeping the Republic secular, the capital harbors some of the world's most exquisite churches. No matter what your views are on religion, you'll be bowled over by the soaring towers of the **Cathédrale de Notre-Dame** (p. 160), the stained glass of **Sainte-Chapelle** (p. 172), or the superb rood screen at **St-Etienne-du-Mont** (p. 212).

o **Best monuments to human ingenuity:** Extraordinary engineers and architects have spent time in this city, leaving behind some amazing buildings in their wake. Most famously, the **Eiffel Tower** (p. 217) gracefully reaches for the sky, while exerting minimal pressure on the ground. The land under the Belle Epoque wonder that is the **Palais Garnier** (p. 176) is stabilized by the man-made underground lake that inspired Gaston Leroux's *Phantom of the Opera* story. Modern architects also have made their mark, mostly on the city's museums, be it the inside-out structure of the **Centre Pompidou** (p. 177) or the spaceship-like aluminum shell of the **Philharmonie de Paris** (p. 269).

"Le Stryge" gargoyle at Cathédrale de Notre-Dame.

PARIS'S best RESTAURANTS

o **Best for romance:** Thinking of popping the question? Reserve a table at **La Tour d'Argent** (p. 134) and go for it. With its panoramic views over the Seine, legendary kitchen (and wine cellar), and elegant decor, there's no better setting. Or order gigantic sharing platters—think langoustines, snails and rib of beef—at **La Renommée** (p. 106), a beautiful Belle Epoque–style eatery with a cocktail boudoir in the basement.

o **Best for families:** At **Rosa Bonheur** (p. 133), inside Buttes Chaumont park (Thurs–Sun), parents can enjoy pizza and tapas on a large outdoor terrace while their kids play in the grass. French-fry freaks and their meat-eating parents will love **Le Relais de l'Entrecôte** (p. 143), where delicious steak frites (steak and french fries) with a special sauce is the only thing on the menu.

o **Best splurge:** The second floor of the Eiffel Tower has a restaurant where you can gorge on gastronomic French cuisine. After a refurb and a takeover by the talented chef, Frédéric Anton, the **Jules Verne** (p. 145) is a once-in-a-lifetime place to tuck into dishes like chicken poached with black truffles, and chocolate soufflé. Plus, there's the view: a magnificent bird's-eye sweep over the entire City of Light. Now sigh.

Escargot, a Parisian classic, at La Renommée.

o **Best value:** In a hidden garden on the site of a former distillery, **Laïa** (p. 126) is an unpretentiously classy Mediterranean restaurant specializing in robata-grilled delights. **Bouillon République** (p. 113) is where classic French dishes cost way less than what you'd pay for the same level of excellence elsewhere (think from 2.50€ for a starter and 9€ for a main course!).

o **Best classic brasserie:** White tablecloths, mural-clad walls, and a menu brimming with oysters, lobster, French onion soup, snails and slow-cooked pork belly? **Au Pied de Cochon** (p. 110) has got it all.

o **Best seafood:** Next door to the much-hyped neo-bistro **Septime** (p.125) is shellfish-centric **Clamato** (p. 125), an Eldorado for seafood lovers that serves plates of marinated sardines, fish *rillettes* (a sort of pâté), and smoked shrimp (not to mention excellent wine) in a beautifully toned-down dining room. Love oysters? Head to **Huîtrerie Régis** (p. 142); it serves the best in town, straight from Marennes-Oléron on France's west coast.

o **Best for gluten-free:** You don't need to suffer from gluten intolerance to appreciate the delicious home-cooked dishes at **Noglu** (p. 129), a snug little post in the trendy 11th arrondissement. Or try the delights at Chambelland, also in the 11th, where the flour is milled in the South of France and everything—cakes, bread, quiches—tastes delicious.

o **Best for wine enthusiasts:** If what's in your glass is just as important as what's on the plate, saunter over to **Frenchie Bar à Vins** (p. 120) in the Sentier district, where hand-picked wines by *petits producteurs* (small producers) are served alongside ultra-gourmet, tapas-size plates of mussels in artichoke and chorizo sauce, homemade pâté, and roasted cauliflower with smoked yogurt.

PARIS'S best HOTELS

o **Best view:** You won't want to get up in the morning at **Hôtel Brighton**; you'll be happy just staying in bed and gazing at the panorama, which, depending on the room you stay in, might include the Louvre, Tuileries gardens, or Eiffel Tower. See p. 60.

o **Best for families:** Right by the **Bois de Vincennes** (the city's eastern park, an ideal spot for a family picnic; p.238), **Hôtel de la Porte Dorée** (p. 79) offers pretty rooms at very affordable rates and caters to kids with freebies

The Oscar Wilde suite at L' Hôtel.

like crayons, toys, and cots. **Maison Bréguet** (p. 79) offers cots, monitors, and loaner strollers, and has the added bonus of an indoor pool.

- **Best splurge:** In the iconic La Samaritaine building, and with a hip rooftop brasserie and a Dior spa, **Cheval Blanc Paris** is a glamorous spot indeed. Most rooms—decked in sophisticated nuances of cream and gold—have postcard-worthy views of the Seine, a rarity in Paris. See p. 60.
- **Most charming period piece:** **L'Hôtel** re-creates the ambience of Belle Epoque Paris, when the hotel's most famous resident, Oscar Wilde, was cavorting in the neighborhood until he died here in 1900. It's a bit of Old France right in the middle of the trendy St-Germain-des-Prés neighborhood. See p. 90.
- **Most eco-friendly:** Off the beaten track in the 11th arrondissement, **Eden Lodge Paris** uses solar panels for all its lighting, has high-tech self-cleaning floor tiles, and serves delicious organic breakfasts. It also overlooks one of the loveliest hidden residential gardens in town. See p. 78.
- **Best for a honeymoon:** A location on a typical Left Bank street (close to the famed **Le Bon Marché** department store; p. 246); Art Deco cruise ship–inspired rooms; a hidden basement speakeasy; and a candlelit brasserie bar serving truly delicious comfort food—**Hôtel des Grands Voyageurs** is a cozy, romantic spot for couples looking to cuddle up in style. See p. 90.
- **Best value:** Blessed with a prime location in the Marais next to a lovely and leafy square, **Hôtel Jeanne d'Arc Le Marais** is a terrific budget option. See p. 67.
- **Best for movie history:** Greta Garbo, Orson Wells, David Lynch, Adrien Brody and Elizabeth Taylor are just some of the stars who have stayed in the grand, private-mansion-like **Hôtel Lancaster,** off the Champs-Elysées in the 8th arrondissement. Even if you don't stay, come for the hip cocktail bar and hidden courtyard. See p. 68.

PARIS'S best MUSEUMS

- **Musée d'Orsay:** A breathtaking collection of pre-, post-, and just plain old Impressionists deck the walls of this museum, including Renoir, Van Gogh, Manet, Degas, Gauguin, and a slew of other masters of 19th-century art. Not only is the artwork incredible, but the building itself, a transformed Belle Epoque train station, is a delight. See p. 220.
- **Musée du Louvre:** One of the world's largest and best museums, this colossus of culture has its share of masterpieces, including the *Mona Lisa,* the *Venus de Milo,* and *Winged Victory.* But aside from these three famous ladies are mountains of other incredible works to see, from ancient Egyptian sculptures to Renaissance masters to stunning gems and jewelry. See p. 166.
- **Musée du Quai Branly:** This ultramodern museum gives center stage to artworks from traditional societies in Africa, Asia, and even North America. You'll find everything from a shaman's cloak from Papua New Guinea to Australian aboriginal art, as well as delicate carvings, intricate weavings, and other masterpieces. See p. 222.
- **Musée Jacquemart-André:** Set in a gorgeous 19th-century mansion, this small museum offers a chance to see exquisite art and also how the other half lived. Highlights include a beautiful winter garden, a collection of Italian Renaissance masters, and a magnificent tearoom with a Tiepolo on the ceiling. See p. 189.
- **Picasso-Paris:** This magnificent museum offers a fantastic survey of all things Picasso. Housed in a grandiose 17th-century *hôtel particulier,* the gallery explores the artist's many periods in a beautiful Marais setting and holds ever-changing temporary exhibitions. See p. 181.

Impressionists room at the Musée d'Orsay.

Picnicking in the Jardin du Luxembourg.

THE best FREE & DIRT-CHEAP PARIS

- **Attending a free concert:** Every summer, the Parc Floral (in the Bois de Vincennes) hosts a bevy of free concerts: first the Paris Jazz Festival in June and July and then Classique au Vert in August. See p. 239.
- **Picnicking in the Jardin du Luxembourg:** You couldn't get richer surroundings if you were at a three-star restaurant, and yet you only pay a few euros for a sandwich. Sometimes being cheap is the best revenge. See p. 213.
- **Seeing Paris from a city bus:** Take your own tour of Paris by bus—for the price of a Métro ticket. Some of the municipal bus lines' routes would put a professional tour bus to shame, like route nos. 63 and 87, which hit many of the city's major sites. Visit www.ratp.fr for route maps or download the RATP app. See p. 330.
- **Dawdling over a coffee in a cafe:** Okay, you might pay 2.50€ for an espresso, but that means you can sit for hours watching the world go by in an atmospheric cafe and have an authentically Parisian experience to boot. See p. 153.
- **Discovering artworks for zip:** Hit one of the City of Paris museums, most of which offer free entry to their permanent collections all year round. This means you can see monumental sculpture at the **Musée Bourdelle** (p. 225), visit a stately mansion filled with 18th-century art at the **Musée Cognacq-Jay** (p. 179), and trace the history of Paris in the palatial **Musée Carnavalet** (p. 178) without ever having to open your wallet. See p. 166.

THE best NEIGHBORHOODS FOR GETTING LOST

- **Montmartre:** If you get away from the crowds at Sacré-Coeur, this mythic neighborhood is a great place to wander up and down winding lanes, tilt at windmills, admire the view, and cafe-hop. See our Montmartre walking tour on p. 308.

- **The Latin Quarter:** Once again, the trick here is to ditch the crowds on rue de la Huchette and take off for the less-trampled corners of this historic student quarter, such as near the universities around rue Erasme or down by the delightful **Jardin des Plantes.** See p. 32.
- **The Marais:** Get lost in style in this trendy neighborhood, known as much for its delightful boutiques and hip restaurants as for its magnificent 17th- and 18th-century *hôtels particuliers,* or aristocratic mansions, many of which have been turned into terrific museums. See our Marais walking tour on p. 315.
- **Belleville:** You'll see another side of Paris in this diverse working-class district, where a mix of artists and immigrants have made it into one of the city's most vibrant neighborhoods. **Parc de Belleville** offers wonderful views of Paris; around **rue de Menilmontant,** you'll find cool bars and vintage shops. Farther east is the romantic **Père-Lachaise** cemetery (p. 200).

THE best UNEXPECTED PLEASURES IN PARIS

- **Sipping cocktails on a rooftop:** Watch the sun set over Paris's chimney pots at **La Fantaisie** (p. 71), a hip hotel with a rooftop cocktail bar and fab restaurant in the ever-trendifying 9th arrondissement.
- **Navigating a self-drive boat along Paris's canals:** You don't need a license to sail one of **Marin d'Eau Douce**'s electric boats, just a sense of adventure. From Bassin de la Villette in the 19th arrondissement, glide along the canals d'Ourcq and St-Martin, taking in the city from an unexpected angle (p. 227).
- **Drinking fizzy water from fountains in the street:** Paris has 17 *fontaines pétillantes* dotted about the city, each spouting cold, sparkling tap water—a luxury on a sunny day. Try the fountain at **Parc André Citroën** in the 15th arrondissement (fontaine.eaude paris.fr).
- **Watching weavers make tapestries:** At the **Manufacture Nationale des Gobelins** (p. 210), you can take a tour and see skilled artists at their giant looms creating magnificent woven works.
- **Sipping mint tea in a Moroccan tearoom:** Dream you're in the Kasbah at the tearoom at the **Mosquée de Paris** (p. 153), which is covered in beautiful mosaic tiles.

A Montmartre windmill.

Bar Sur Le Toi on the rooftop at La Fantaisie Hotel.

PARIS'S best OUTDOORS

o **The best gardens:** It's hard to choose between the grand geometry of the **Tuileries** (p. 164), the relaxed elegance of the **Jardin du Luxembourg** (p. 213), or the colorful palette of **Giverny,** Monet's gardens, an easy day trip away (p. 298).

o **The best parks:** The **Bois de Boulogne** (p. 237) has lakes, gardens, and even a small amusement park (the **Jardin d'Acclimatation;** p. 235) for your rambling pleasure. The **Bois de Vincennes** may not have an amusement park, but it does have a medieval castle, the **Château de Vincennes,** complete with ramparts and a keep (p. 239), as well as the **Parc Floral** (p. 239) and the **Parc Zoologique de Paris** (p. 198).

o **The best primrose promenade:** The **Promenade Plantée** (now called **Coulée verte René-Dumont;** p. 198) must be the world's skinniest garden: From this path atop a former train viaduct, you can stroll among the flowers and greenery from the Place de la Bastille all the way to the Bois de Vincennes.

Rowing in Bois de Boulogne park.

THE best OF HIP PARIS

- **The coolest culture:** The **Musée Yves Saint Laurent** (p. 191) traces the fashion mogul's world-famous creations and his creative process in his former HQ, a sumptuous Belle Epoque mansion by the Champs-Élysées. The City of Lights wears its name well at the **Atelier des Lumières** (p. 197), a digital art museum in a former iron factory offering immersive light shows that walk you through famous artworks, blown up to smother all walls, floors, and ceilings.
- **The funkiest street food: Ground Control** (p. 128) in a gigantic former SNCF hangar has Greek, Italian, and Taiwanese counters inside, and disused buses outside, hawking ever-changing themed food, like ham 'n cheese crepes and authentic British fish and chips.
- **The hippest bar:** Tucked behind a hidden door at the back of a taqueria, **Candelaria** (p. 281) opened in 2011 as the city's first speakeasy-style cocktail bar and is still its best.
- **The funkiest shop: Landline** (p. 258) is a general supply concept store in the trendy 11th arrondissement, with everything from cool household items and wooden toys to artisan wool vests and cosmetics.

Ground Control terrace in the former SNCF hangar.

SUGGESTED ITINERARIES & NEIGHBORHOODS

2

Paris is an embarrassment of riches—with so many wonderful things to see, it's hard to know where to begin. And while you are standing there thinking about it, the clock is ticking, and your precious time is shrinking. In this chapter, we offer up detailed itineraries so you can see the city's highlights in a short time without wearing yourself to a frazzle. A couple of custom tours for particular interests provide other options. We also give you an overview of the city layout and break down the neighborhoods one by one, so you can design an itinerary of your own.

ICONIC PARIS IN 1 DAY

If you have just 1 day in Paris, your biggest challenge will be trying not to spend the whole day wishing you had more time. Here's an itinerary that will give you at least a taste of the city and ideas for your next trip. ***Start:*** *The Champs de Mars, 7th arrondissement, Métro: Ecole Militaire, RER: Champs de Mars–Tour Eiffel.*

1 The Eiffel Tower ♥♥♥

Ideally, you've booked an early-morning time slot online beforehand, and it won't take too long to go through security and up to the second or top floor to get a gander at the awe-inspiring view of the city. If you've not bought an advance ticket, try your luck or skip the climb and cross the bridge (Pont d'Iéna) to head up to the esplanade at the **Palais de Chaillot ♥**, where you can admire the Iron Lady in all her splendor and take some iconic selfies. See p. 217.

If you haven't done so already, cross the bridge (Pont d'Iéna) and head up to the Palais de Chaillot and the Place du Trocadéro. Hop on the no. 63 bus (direction Gare de Lyon), which will cruise past Les Invalides and down boulevard St-Germain. Get off at stop St-Germain-des-Prés.

2 St-Germain-des-Prés ♥♥♥

First, head to **St-Germain-des-Prés church** ♥♥ (p. 213) and then cross the square to at least stroll by **Les Deux Magots** ♥ (p. 155) and the **Café de Flore** ♥ (p. 154), two legendary cafes that were the home base of Sartre and De Beauvoir and scores of other artists and intellectuals. The cafes are crowded and pricey for lunch, so here's another option:

A guided tour of the Eiffel Tower.

Lunch at Marché St-Germain ☕
If you wander a little farther down boulevard St-Germain and take a right on rue Mabillon, you'll find yourself at the Marché St-Germain, a covered market that is half shops and half market stalls filled with delectable goodies (closed Mon). Either pick up the fixings for a picnic here or try one of the dozens of restaurants on the streets that surround the market. My personal favorite is **Chez Fernand** (p. 142), which looks the part in red-and-white checkered tablecloths; it serves lip-smacking French classics like beef bourguignon and chocolate soufflé.

Walk back out to boulevard St-Germain and turn right, then continue to rue de l'Ancienne Comédie and turn left to Carrefour de Buci; then veer right on rue Dauphine and continue down to the Seine (admiring the galleries and antiques shops as you go). When you reach the river, cross the Pont Neuf.

3 Île de la Cité ♥♥

Admire the view from the **Pont Neuf** ♥ (p. 179), which straddles the island. Wander around the pretty, tree- and cafe-lined **Place Dauphine** ♥ (you'll find the entrance opposite the statue of King Henri IV on horseback) and stroll along the quays of this island, where some of the first Parisians set up camp. Dominating its eastern edge is glorious **Notre-Dame cathedral** (p. 160), open again after the devastating 2019 fire. If you opted for a picnic lunch, the tree-shaded **Square du Vert Gallant** (a park at the very tip of the island) is a lovely spot.

From Notre-Dame, cross over the Pont d'Arcole, turn left onto Quai de Gevres and walk to Place du Châtelet. If you are tired, you can take the no. 7 Métro from here to Palais-Royal–Musée du Louvre. Otherwise, you can walk another 10 minutes or so down the Quai de la Mégisserie and Quai du Louvre to the Louvre.

4 The Louvre ♥♥♥

The sheer enormity of the former royal palace has to be seen to be believed. Turn right onto rue de l'Amiral de Coligny and admire its eastern facade, framed by Claude Perrault's 1660s Colonnade, a classical French facade of Corinthian columns. Below the columns is a passageway through to the Louvre's Cour Carrée, a sumptuous Renaissance-era

Paris Neighborhoods

RIGHT BANK
1. Louvre & Île de la Cité (1st)
2. Opéra & Grands Boulevards (2nd & 9th)
3. The Marais (3rd & 4th)
4. Champs-Élysées, Trocadéro & Western Paris (8th, 16th & 17th)
5. Montmartre (18th)
6. République, Bastille & Eastern Paris (11th & 12th)
7. Belleville, Canal St-Martin & La Villette (10th, 19th & 20th)

LEFT BANK
8. Latin Quarter (5th and 13th)
9. St-Germain-des-Prés & Luxembourg (6th)
10. Eiffel Tower & Les Invalides (7th)
11. Montparnasse (14th & 15th)

14

courtyard. If the passage is open, enter here. If not, you'll have to turn left onto rue de Rivoli and walk to the main Cour Napoléon square (home to the museum's iconic glass pyramid) along the outside (entering at the first available passage). Save visiting the museum for the next trip and wander through to the **Tuileries Garden** ♥♥♥. See p. 166.

The Jardin des Tuileries, near the Louvre.

5 Tuileries Garden ♥♥♥

There are worse ways to spend a late afternoon than strolling through formal French gardens (p. 164) studded with statues by Rodin and Maillol. The Tuileries has play areas for children, cafes for grown-ups, and ponds that everyone can loll beside. And if you're desperate to see at least one famous artwork on your day, Monet's water lilies are housed at the **Musée de l'Orangerie** ♥♥ in the gardens' southwest corner. Reservations aren't required, but it can get busy, so plan ahead and pre-purchase a ticket online to get into the museum.

Stroll west through the gardens until you arrive at the Place de la Concorde.

6 Place de la Concorde ♥♥♥

From this vantage point, you can not only take in the Place itself (p. 193) but also peer down the **Champs-Élysées** ♥♥ and see the **Arc de Triomphe** ♥♥♥ (p. 183) in the distance.

If you still have energy in the evening, finish your visit with an **evening cruise** along the river (see "Boat Tours," p. 225), during which you can admire just about all of the above gussied up in elegant lighting effects.

ICONIC PARIS IN 2 DAYS

Now you have a little more space to breathe. This itinerary also starts at the Eiffel Tower, but then takes off in another direction. ***Start:*** *The Champs de Mars, 7th arrondissement, Métro: Ecole Militaire, RER: Champs de Mars–Tour Eiffel.*

Day 1

1 The Eiffel Tower ♥♥♥

You could just turn up, but advance ticket reservations (which gives you a time slot for both the lifts and stairs) are recommended here, so be prepared for a little forward planning. Once you've seen the second and top floors, make sure you stop for coffee in **Madame Brasserie** (p. 146) on the first-floor, where you can sip with the monument's graceful girders towering above you. See p. 217.

Walk an hour along the riverfront, or take the RER C (10-min ride) to St-Michel–Notre-Dame.

2 The Latin Quarter ♥♥♥
Admire the Place St-Michel and the Boul' Mich (boulevard St-Michel) and try to imagine it all filled with long-haired students throwing *pavés* (paving stones) during the heady days of May 1968, when protesters brought the country to a standstill. Then wander up the boulevard and consider stopping in at the **Musée de Cluny** ♥♥ (p. 210). After, continue up past the dome of **La Sorbonne** (one of France's oldest universities, founded in 1257) to the **Jardin du Luxembourg** ♥♥♥ (p. 213). Either picnic here or settle down at a nearby table:

Lunch near the Jardin du Luxembourg ☕
If you are hungry, enjoy a terrific, hearty meal at **La Ferrandaise** (p. 141), about a block away (closed Sun, also Mon lunch). If you just want something light, and/or La Ferrandaise is closed, stop in for a *croque-monsieur* (a French version of a grilled cheese sandwich) or a salad at **Le Rostand,** an old literary cafe with a lovely terrace just across the street from the gardens (6 pl. Edmond Rostand, 6th arrond.; lerostand.fr; ✆ **01-43-54-61-58;** RER: Luxembourg).

Walk up rue Soufflot toward the stunning domed Panthéon at the top of the hill.

3 Le Panthéon ♥♥
Marvel at the neoclassical proportions of this national mausoleum's magnificent interior dome, home to a Foucault pendulum, the device that first proved the Earth's rotation. See p. 211.

Back on rue Soufflot, turn right down rue Saint-Jacques, the city's old Roman road, and cross the Seine to Île de la Cité.

4 Notre-Dame ♥♥♥
Visit the cathedral, freshly reborn (quite literally) from the ashes of the 2019 fire. By the time you're reading this, you should be able to see all of its interiors (and take the stairs to admire the fabulous view from the towers) in all their former glory. Fun fact: The 500-kilo Olympic bell rung by the winning athletes in 2024 is now in hanging in the tribune above the altar and is sounded during mass. See p. 160.

Nave of the newly restored Cathédrale de Notre-Dame de Paris.

Walk across the Pont d'Arcole to the Right Bank and the Place de l'Hôtel de Ville.

5 The Marais ♥♥♥

By now you deserve a break from the city's icons and are ready to shop or just sit in a cafe in this trendy—and beautiful—neighborhood. If you are still hungry for culture, you could visit one of the many museums here, but if not, save them for another day/trip. Around sunset, stop by **Place des Vosges ♥♥♥** (p. 182) for a pre-dinner *apéritif* before you hunt down a restaurant (p. 109).

Day 2

1 The Louvre ♥♥♥

Reserve in advance to start your day as early as possible at this megamuseum (p. 166), which should keep you going until at least lunchtime, when you can either call it quits or simply take a nice long break and eat at one of the restaurants recommended on p. 102. If you are in a hurry to get back to the artwork, grab a sandwich from one of the lunch counters under the pyramid. After the Louvre, you can recover in the **Tuileries Garden ♥♥♥** (p. 166).

Le Nemours ☕

If you need refreshment after the Louvre (and who doesn't?), this slick cafe on the Place Colette sits elegantly below the Palais Royal's (p. 170) colonnades. Great pastries, too.

Stroll west through the Tuileries Garden until you arrive at the Place de la Concorde.

2 Place de la Concorde ♥♥♥

From this grandiose, traffic-clogged plaza (p. 193), you can look down the **Champs-Élysées ♥♥** and see the **Arc de Triomphe ♥♥♥** (p. 183) in the distance.

Take Métro line 12 (direction Mairie d'Issy) to Sèvres Babylone in the 6th arrondissement.

3 St-Germain-des-Prés ♥♥♥

End your day in this delightful Left Bank neighborhood, where you can visit two of the city's loveliest churches (**St-Germain-des-Prés,** p. 213; **St-Sulpice,** p. 216), check out famous literary cafes (**Les Deux Magots,** p. 155; **Café de Flore,** p. 154), or shop 'til you drop. Then find a restaurant (p. 141), after which you can explore the nearby nightlife.

ICONIC PARIS IN 3 DAYS

Now that you've seen all the absolute must-sees, you have time to explore some of the great stuff you've missed. Here is a third day of discovery. ***Start: Musée d'Orsay, Métro: Assemblée Nationale, RER: Musée d'Orsay.***

Day 3

1 Musée d'Orsay ♥♥♥

Reserve ahead to spend the morning enjoying this incredible collection of Impressionist and 19th-century artworks (p. 220), and then break for lunch at one of the museum's three restaurants (light snacks, chic cafeteria, or full-on Belle Epoque restaurant). If Impressionists aren't your thing, you could start the day looking at non-Western art at **Musée du Quai Branly** ♥♥♥ (p. 222).

Leave the museum and take the steps down to the banks of the Seine. If you are starting from Musée d'Orsay, turn left (west); if you are coming from Musée du Quai Branly, turn right (east).

2 Les Berges ♥♥♥

Weather willing, enjoy the restored riverbanks (p. 236), strolling westward. Once a busy roadway, this embankment is now a delight for pedestrians, with floating gardens, running lanes, and gourmet snack bars (May–Oct only).

At the Pont Alexandre III, go up the stairs and admire the winged horses hovering above before going down into the Métro Invalides and taking line 13 (direction Asnières or St-Denis) and changing to line 12 (direction Porte de la Chapelle) at Gare St-Lazare. Get off at Place des Abbesses. Take the elevator up (don't get smart and take the stairs; it's a looong way up with 176 steps).

3 Montmartre ♥♥♥

While away the rest of the afternoon on top of this scenic hill ("La Butte"), clambering around the cobbled streets and perhaps taking a walking tour (p. 308). Visit the **Musée de Montmartre** (p. 196) to lounge in its garden cafe and find out more about the artists and poets who made this neighborhood famous, and **Dalí Paris** (p. 195) to see France's only museum dedicated to the surrealist master, Salvador Dalí. Around sunset, take in the panorama in front of **Sacré-Coeur** (p. 194), then bid adieu to Paris with a drink on the roof of the famous **Moulin Rouge** cabaret (p. 270) where its nightclub, **Machine du Moulin Rouge** (p. 277), has a bar (open from 6pm) set behind the iconic red windmill.

AN ITINERARY FOR FAMILIES

Paris can be a challenge with kids, especially if they're in strollers (sidewalks are narrow and uneven, and the Métro is filled with stairs), and parents may grow frustrated because there are so many wonderful grown-up things to see and do. The trick is to admit to yourself that you just won't see as much as you'd like to, and to schedule lots of playtime. In the end, everyone will be less stressed out and happier, even if you didn't get to all 14 of those museums you dreamed of visiting. *Start: Jardin du Luxembourg, Métro: Notre-Dame des Champs or Odeon, RER: Luxembourg.*

You can grab a sandwich from one of the lunch counters under the pyramid at The Louvre.

Day 1

Spend the morning at the **Jardin du Luxembourg** (p. 213), where your offspring can go wild at the huge **playground, sail boats** in the fountain, **ride a pony** (Sat–Sun and Wed afternoons, weather permitting; daily during Paris school holidays; see animaponey.com, French only), or just run around and have fun. Depending on your situation, parents can take turns sneaking off to visit nearby attractions, such as the **Panthéon** (p. 211), **Musée Zadkine** (p. 215), and **St-Etienne-du-Mont** (p. 212), or find peace and quiet in a **Latin Quarter** cafe (p. 134). Then walk down to **St-Germain-des-Prés** (p. 213) and peek into the church before lunching at **Le Relais de l'Entrecôte** (p. 143). After lunch, walk to boulevard St-Germain and catch the no. 86 bus to the **Champs de Mars,** where you will cross a playground-filled park to the **Eiffel Tower** (p. 217). After that, everyone will be pooped. Thankfully, the **boat ride on the Seine** leaves just down by the river.

Day 2

Start your day at the **Jardin des Plantes** (p. 206), where you can choose between the **Museum National d'Histoire Naturelle** (p. 211), the **Ménagerie** (a small zoo; p. 207), and the little **playground.** There's also a fun boxwood **labyrinth** at the top of a little hill. Lunch at the nearby **Mosquée de Paris** (p. 153), a lovely tearoom attached to the Paris Mosque that has an outdoor enclosed patio. Then, if there are wannabe eggheads in your crew, hop on Métro line 5 to Jaurès and stroll along the Canal de l'Ourcq to the **Cité des Sciences et de l'Industrie** (p. 202), a hands-on science museum in **La Villette** (p. 200). The museum includes a section for young kids (the Cité des Enfants, with 90-min. play slots for 2- to 7-year-olds and 5 to 12s; reserve ahead), and the vast canal-side park outside is filled with play areas and grassy expanses. It's also right by the new **Boom Boom Villette** (boomboomvillette.com), a recreation mall for families, with a food court, a bowling alley, arcade games, laser games and a trampoline park. If you're with older kids, you could even rent an electric self-hire boat from **Marin d'Eau Douce** from the Bassin de la Villette (p. 227; no license required; by Métro Jaurès) and watch the sunset as you sail along the Canal de l'Ourcq.

Day 3

Kids may not appreciate the view at **Sacré-Coeur** (p. 194), but they will enjoy the ride in the **funicular** that you take to get there (follow the signs from the Abbesses Métro stop). Once there, you'll find lots of buskers for entertainment. After tooling around Montmartre, grab a quick bite to eat at **Maison Millie** (19 rue la Vieuville, 18th arrond.; maison-milie.com; © **09-53-02-92-60**), a kid-friendly cafe with crepes, bakery items, and all-day breakfast. Or, if you're with a toddler, stop by the **Musée de Montmartre** (p. 196) and pay 5€ (or visit the museum) to enter its walled garden, where a basic cafe serves quiches and cakes, and you can let your little one run around without having to worry about passing cars (though there is a little pond). It's off the beaten tourist track, too, thus offering a welcome respite from the clogged streets outside. After lunch, wander around the **covered passages** off the Grands Boulevards (see "Arcades," p. 243), where you can window shop to your heart's content and reward everyone's good behavior with a visit to **Choco Story** (p. 203), a fun, chocolate-themed museum by Bonne Nouvelle metro station, with plenty of tasting opportunities.

Grande Galerie de l'Evolution at the Museum National d'Histoire Naturelle.

PARIS FOR ROMANTICS

Paris must be the honeymoon capital of the world, and for good reason—it seems like every time you turn a corner you see something beautiful. Here is a 2-day itinerary for a romantic getaway, or just for hopeless romantics. *Start: Pont Neuf, in front of the statue of Henri IV, Métro: Pont Neuf or Cité.*

Day 1

This itinerary starts in front of a statue of one of France's great romantic (or depending how you look at it, playboy) kings, Henri IV, who was known for his good humor and love of wine, women, and song. Walk down the steps to the pretty **Square du Vert Galant,** a quiet garden at the very tip of the island where you can contemplate the fantastic view and/or make out without anyone bothering you (in general, make-out sessions are well-tolerated in public parks here). From here, you can walk to the **Louvre** (p. 166) and take in endless representations of people in love, from all eras. If you're into wine, a *plat du jour* (daily special) at quaint, cozy **Juveniles** wine bar, washed down with a crisp chardonnay, will do the trick (p. 106).

After lunch, drift over to the **Palais Garnier,** also known as the Opéra Garnier (p. 176), the city's most sumptuous opera house, where you can tour the building, and where a true romantic will have bought tickets to an evening ballet. Or for some quirky romance, sign up for a virtual reality flight over Paris at **FlyView** to soar through the air and see the city's monuments up close, including Notre-Dame as it was before the fire. When it's time to think about dinner, you're right by the Japanese Quarter, which covers several streets around rue Ste-Anne. Grab a tasty *okonomiyaki,* a Japanese savory pancake topped with sauce, at **Aki** (p. 108), or head back past the Louvre to **La Renommée** (p. 106) for ginormous sharing plates of classic French dishes and cocktails. As night falls, the obligatory romantic stroll is along the pedestrian-only **Pont des Arts** (p. 179), where you can take in the gorgeously illuminated monuments lining the Seine.

Day 2

After sleeping in, start your day with a late breakfast at **Le Petit Cler** (p. 148), an adorable cafe on, that's right, rue Cler. After, mosey over to the **Musée Rodin** (p. 222, where you can contemplate, and even imitate, Rodin's famous marble sculpture *The Kiss.* When you are done inside, amble about the beautiful gardens and enjoy other legendary works, such as *The Thinker.* If it's nice out, grab a **Vélib'** (p. 331) and cycle down to the remodeled banks of the Seine, **Les Berges** (p. 236), where you can cycle or stroll free and easy by the river below the Quai d'Orsay. If the weather doesn't suit a bike ride, take the no. 13 Métro up to Miromesnil and have tea at the beautiful **tearoom** at the **Musée Jacquemart-André**

Seine riverfront promenade.

(p. 152). Visiting the museum afterward is well worth an hour of your time (p. 189). Otherwise, it's time to start thinking about the evening's activities. Jazz lovers should head to **Duc des Lombards** (p. 273); others will be just fine with **La Bellevilloise** (p. 276) in trendy Ménilmontant, where you can eat, drink, and dance the night away. For late-night cocktails, hit **Poppy,** across the Seine, a speakeasy-like spot hidden in the basement of **Hôtel des Grands Voyageurs** (p. 90).

CITY LAYOUT

One of the nice things about Paris is that it's relatively small. It's not a vast megalopolis like Tokyo or London. Paris *intramuros,* or inside the long-gone city walls, measures about 87 sq. km (34 sq. miles), excluding the parks of Bois de Vincennes and the Bois de Boulogne (which both lie just beyond the edge of the center), and the city counts a mere 2.2 million inhabitants. The suburbs, on the other hand, are sprawling.

Getting around is not difficult, provided you have a general sense of where things are. The city is vaguely egg shaped, with the Seine cutting a wide, upside-down U-shaped arc through the middle. The northern half is known as the **Right Bank,** and the southern, the **Left Bank.** To the uninitiated, the only way to remember is to face west, or downstream, so that the Right Bank will be to your right, and the Left to your left.

The city is neatly split up into 20 official ***arrondissements,*** or districts, which spiral out from the center of the city. The lower the number of the arrondissement, the closer you'll be to the center. As the numbers go up, you'll head toward the outer city limits. The lower-numbered arrondissements also correspond to some of the oldest parts of the city, like the Louvre and the Île de la Cité (1st arrond.) or the Marais (3rd and 4th arrond.). Note that the arrondissements don't always correspond to historical neighborhoods.

If you are in the city for more than a few days, download the app created by the city's transit authority, the RATP. Called *Bonjour RATP,* this free app (available via ratp.fr as well as App Store and Google Play) will guide you around town on public transportation. You may also want to download such usable offline apps as CityMaps2Go, MAPS.ME, and Citymapper.

Paris is old, so the logic of its **streets and avenues** is often as contorted as the city's history. That said, some major boulevards function as reference points. On the Left Bank, boulevard St-Michel acts as a more or less north–south axis, with boulevard St-Germain cutting a vaguely east–west semicircle close to the city center and boulevard Montparnasse cutting a larger one farther out. On the Right Bank, boulevard de Sébastopol runs north–south, with rue de Rivoli crossing east–west near the river. As rue de Rivoli heads east, it turns into rue de St-Antoine; to the west, it jogs around the Place de la Concorde and becomes the Champs-Élysées. Farther north, a network of wide boulevards crisscrosses the area, including boulevards Haussmann, Capucines, and Lafayette.

Large avenues converge at several enormous star-shaped traffic roundabouts: On the Left Bank, Place Denfert-Rochereau and Place d'Italie are major convergence points; on the Right Bank, Place de la Bastille, Place de la Nation, and Place de la République reign to the east, and Place de Charles de Gaulle (also called Etoile), home of the Arc de Triomphe, commands to the west.

In terms of street numbers, odd and even numbers are found on different sides of the street, and numbers begin on the side of the street closest to the Seine (for streets running on a north–south axis) or in the east (for streets running east–west).

NEIGHBORHOODS IN BRIEF

Paris is a city for walkers. One lovely neighborhood after another unfolds along its sidewalks, punctuated by plazas and monuments that are best experienced at ground level. At every turn there seems to be an intriguing area that begs to be explored.

The Right Bank
LOUVRE & ÎLE DE LA CITÉ
Best for: *Museums, historic sights, architecture, transportation hubs*
What you won't find: *Evening entertainment, quiet streets*
Parameters of the neighborhood: *1st arrondissement & part of the 4th*

This is the heart of the city, and the oldest part of Paris, though you'd never know it to see it now. In the 19th century, Baron Haussmann, Napoleon's energetic urban planner, tore down almost all the medieval houses that once covered this area. The **Île de la Cité** is where the city first emerged after Gallic tribes started camping out here in the 3rd century B.C.E. By the 1st century C.E., the Romans were building temples, and by the Middle Ages, a mighty fortress sat across the river on the Right Bank. The fortress has long since

La Samaritaine department store.

been incorporated into the majestic buildings of the **Louvre** (p. 157), which along with the **Jardin des Tuileries** (p. 164) takes up a big chunk of the neighborhood. (You can see vestiges of it—the old stone foundations—in the **Carousel du Louvre,** an underground shopping mall set below the museum.) Today, the Île is mostly visited for the soaring **Cathédrale de Notre-Dame** (p. 160) and the gemlike **Sainte-Chapelle** (p. 172), along with the **Conciergerie,** a palace turned revolutionary prison (p. 163).

On the neighborhood's eastern edge, **Les Halles** (the city's former food market) is where Parisians go for shopping, particularly along the bustling **rue de Rivoli** and around the remodeled **Forum des Halles** mall and park (p. 167). When the covered food market was demolished and relocated to the suburban town of Rungis in the 1970s, Les Halles lost its charm—and unfortunately, despite its multimillion-euro refurbishment, it's still not particularly picturesque. It is, however, a hot spot for high-street boutiques and late-night bistros. And it's officially part of the "Golden Triangle of Les Halles," a vast, triangular-shaped area of gentrification that is home to three new hot spots: the **Pinault Collection,** a contemporary art museum in the former Bourse de Commerce stock exchange (p. 157); the revamped **Samaritaine** department store (p. 247); and the upmarket **Poste du Louvre** mall. During the day, the area's very safe—if overcrowded—but avoid its Châtelet-les-Halles underground RER station late at night, as troublemakers sometimes hang out. The same is true of the seedy rue St-Denis, just to the east, as this is one of Paris's red-light districts.

OPÉRA & GRANDS BOULEVARDS

Best for: Good restaurants, covered shopping arcades, boutiques
What you won't find: Monuments (with the exception of the Opéra Garnier) and museums, green spaces
Parameters of the neighborhood: 2nd & 9th arrondissements

When the Grands Boulevards were plowed through the city in the 19th century (see box, below), they created a new opportunity for stylish Parisians to stroll, see, and be seen, and theaters and cafes flourished. Times changed and so did fashion, and for decades this area was considered a has-been. In recent years, it's undergone a transformation, particularly in the 9th arrondissement, where cafes, boutiques, and restaurants have popped up in between the church

> ### Baron Haussmann: A Man with a Plan
>
> The Paris you see before you was radically transformed in the late 19th century by a pugnacious urban planner named Georges-Eugène Haussmann. Before Haussmann got his hands on it, Paris was a mostly medieval city of tiny streets and narrow alleyways—and major sanitation problems. Everyone agreed that something needed to be done to facilitate traffic and clean up the city, but no one managed to come up with a solution.
>
> Enter Baron Haussmann. Named prefect of the Seine by Napoleon III, Haussmann pushed through wide boulevards (Malsherbes, Haussmann, and Sébastopol, among others), demolished dozens of old neighborhoods, and encouraged promoters to build new buildings, following, of course, his strict rules on the style of the facades and the height of the structures. The result was the elegant Haussmannian architecture that lines most of the city's streets, as well as the system of central arteries that collect in star-shaped intersections at various points. The boulevards were strategically placed—one of the reasons for their creation was to make it easier to crush rebellions in the workers' quarters, and garrisons were set up at crucial intersections. Streets were also now too wide in most areas to be easily barricaded. Haussmann also accessorized his new neighborhoods and streets; the famous kiosks, benches, and lampposts you see around the city today date from this epoch.
>
> While there's no denying that his projects improved traffic, sanitation, and security and gave a pleasing architectural unity to the cityscape, Haussmann's take-no-prisoners approach has been criticized for having neutered the personality of entire neighborhoods (the Île de la Cité, for example, was almost entirely razed) and destroying important historical buildings.

of St-Georges and Place de Clichy, in an area that used to be known as "New Athens." Many artists of the 19th-century Romantic movement, like George Sand and Eugène Delacroix, lived and worked here; the quaint **Musée de la Vie Romantique** (p. 174) is worth an hour's visit, with beautiful trinkets, letters, and drawings that once belonged to Sand. Today, those in the know call it SoPi (South of Pigalle), as entrepreneurial Parisians have begun opening trendy bakeries, shops, and restaurants.

The 9th is also the home of the *grands magasins* (big-name department stores), which are located on boulevard Haussmann near Gare St-Lazare, as well as the grandiose **Palais Garnier** (p. 174), home of the Opéra de Paris. An important monument in the 2nd arrondissement is the neoclassical **Palais Brogniart,** built between 1808 and 1813 on Place de la Bourse to house the city's former **Bourse,** the French stock exchange. To the east, the trendy set descends on **rue Montorgueil,** a picturesque, cobbled market street, and the pedestrian area around **rue Etienne Marcel,** which has gained a reputation as a hip fashion district. To the west, the city's restaurant-filled **Japanese Quarter** is found on and around rue Ste-Anne. This also is the arrondissement where you'll find the greatest concentration of *passages,* the **18th- and 19th-century covered shopping arcades** that were the forefathers of today's shopping malls (but much prettier; see "Arcades," p. 243).

Rue Montorgueil in Les Halles district.

THE MARAIS

Best for: Restaurants, nightlife, window-shopping, 17th-century mansions, museums
What you won't find: Bargain shopping, iconic sights, open spaces
Parameters of the neighborhood: 3rd & 4th arrondissements

What was once marshy farmland (*marais* means "marsh" or "swamp") quickly became a seat of power when the Knights Templar decided to build a fortress here in the Middle Ages. Other religious orders followed suit, and after King Charles V built a royal residence here in the 14th century, the ensuing real-estate boom produced a slew of mansions and palaces. In the 17th century, King Henri IV created a magnificent square bordered by Renaissance-style town houses, today called the **Place des Vosges** (p. 182). If Marais real estate was in demand before, then after the Place des Vosges it was positively off the charts. Nobles and bourgeois pounced on the neighborhood, each one trying to outdo the other by constructing more and more resplendent *hôtels particuliers,* or private mansions.

By the time the Revolution flushed out all its aristocrats in the 18th century, the overstuffed quarter was already falling out of fashion. The magnificent dwellings were abandoned, pillaged, partitioned, and turned into stores, workshops, and even factories. The new residents were working class, with more immediate concerns than saving historic patrimony. The neighborhood fell into disrepair, and periodic attempts on the part of the city to "clean up" unfortunately resulted in the destruction of many architectural gems.

The area underwent a real renovation in the 1960s, and today several of the most **magnificent mansions** have been restored and are open to the public in the form of museums such as the **Musée Carnavalet** (p. 178), **Musée Cognacq-Jay** (p. 179), and the **Musée National Picasso-Paris** (p. 181). The architecturally odd **Centre Pompidou** (p. 177) is also located here, though you might not be able to see much of it; at time of writing in was set to close for renovations at the end of 2025 until 2030.

Today, the area is terribly *branché* (literally, "plugged in"), and you'll see some of the hippest styles in boutique windows here, as well as dozens of happening restaurants and bars lining the narrow streets. The neighborhood remains a mix, though—jewelry and clothing wholesalers bump up against stylish cafes and shops. The vibrant gay scene around rue Vielle du Temple intersects with what's left of the old Jewish quarter on **rue des Rosiers.**

Place des Vosges.

CHAMPS-ÉLYSÉES, TROCADÉRO & WESTERN PARIS

Best for: *Serious strolling (on the Champs-Élysées), museums, monuments, chic restaurants, and stores*
What you won't find here: *Affordable eateries or hotels, regular folk*
Parameters of the neighborhood: *8th, 16th & 17th arrondissements*

The **Champs-Élysées** cuts through this area like an asphalt river—it's the widest boulevard in Paris. Crossing the street here feels a bit like traversing a raging torrent (be sure to wait for the light). This epic roadway has its fans and foes. Some find its lights and glitz good clean fun, while others dismiss it as crass and commercial. I find it lacks a soul. But no matter how you may feel about the street itself, you're bound to be impressed by the **Arc de Triomphe** (p. 183), which lords over the boulevard from its western tip. To the south of the Champs are some of the most expensive stores, restaurants, and homes in the city, particularly around avenue Montaigne. This is also where you'll find the **Musée Yves Saint Laurent** (p. 191), dedicated to the couturier's life and career, the vast Belle Epoque **Grand Palais** (p. 185) and its sumptuous little sister, across the street, the **Petit Palais** (p. 192) fine arts museum. To the north, a largely residential area extends up to the beautiful **Parc Monceau** (p. 192), which is surrounded by some equally delightful museums, such as the **Musée Jacquemart-André** (p. 189) and the **Musée Nissim de Camondo** (p. 191).

To the west, the illustrious Seizième (sez-ee-*em;* 16th arrond.) is the most exclusive arrondissement of the city. Lying on the outer western edge of the city, this residential area is packed with magnificent 19th-century residences and apartment houses, as well as many fine parks and gardens. In fact, the

Arc de Triomphe.

arrondissement shares its western border with the **Bois de Boulogne** (p. 237), one of the city's two huge, wooded parks. While the 16th is not known for its liveliness, it is graced with a terrific array of museums. The **Palais de Chaillot** shelters the **Cité de l'Architecture** (p. 186), the **Musée National de la Marine** (p. 188), and the **Musée de l'Homme** (p. 188), and just down the street is the vast **Musée National des Arts Asiatiques Guimet** (p. 191). A little farther on are two modern art museums in the **Palais de Tokyo** (p. 192), not to mention a half-dozen others, like the **Musée Marmottan Monet** (p. 191), sprinkled around the arrondissement. And a stop at the esplanade on the **Place du Trocadéro** is a must. Between the two wings of the Palais de Chaillot is a superb view of the Eiffel Tower, which you can walk to by strolling down the hill through the **Jardins du Trocadéro.**

MONTMARTRE
Best for: Restaurants, nightlife, atmosphere
What you won't find here: Monuments (with the exception of the Sacré-Coeur), major museums, grand architecture
Parameters of the neighborhood: 18th arrondissement

Once a village overlooking the distant city, Montmartre is now as inseparable from Paris as the Eiffel Tower, which means it's a major target for the tour-bus crowd. And crowded it is, especially in the area immediately around the **Basilique du Sacré-Coeur** (p. 194) and the overdone **Place du Tertre.** Yet, if you wander around the cobbled streets that surround **Place des Abbesses,** you'll find plenty of hip boutiques and cute restaurants frequented by an upwardly arty crowd, who have also staked out territory in the working-class neighborhoods immediately east and north of the basilica. Two small museums are worth your time here: **Musée de Montmartre** (p. 196), which traces the area's artistic history and has a peaceful garden; and **Dalí Paris** (p. 195), a must for fans of surrealism, with more than 300 pieces of the artist's work.

RÉPUBLIQUE, BASTILLE & EASTERN PARIS
Best for: Nightlife, good restaurants, Revolutionary history, arty boutiques
What you won't find here: Major monuments and museums, high-end shops
Parameters of the neighborhood: 11th & 12th arrondissements

These two arrondissements were pretty much off the tourist radar until 1989, when the new **Bastille opera house** provoked an explosion of bars and restaurants in the surrounding streets. Though the shine has already worn off the **nightspots** of rue de Lappe and rue de la Roquette (just off the Place de la Bastille), the nocturnal life of the 11th arrondissement is far from dull, as new clubs and cafes have opened farther north on rue de Charonne and **rue Oberkampf.**

    Place de la Bastille, once the site of its namesake prison, has had a recent face-lift to make it pedestrian friendly and provide access to its centerpiece, the **Colonne de Juillet** (p. 200), a 50m (164-ft.) column with a crypt, which is accessible on guided tours. North of the **Place de la Bastille** is the vast, pedestrian-friendly **Place de la République.** To the east is the Faubourg St-Antoine, a historic workers' quarter inhabited by woodworkers and furniture

Gare de Lyon train station.

makers since the 13th century. After a few centuries, the density of underpaid, overburdened workers made St-Antoine a breeding ground for revolutionaries. The raging mob that stormed the Bastille prison in 1789 originated here, as did those of the subsequent uprisings of 1830, 1848, and the Paris commune.

In recent years, the area has become a magnet for foodies, as young chefs have opened some of the city's most exciting restaurants, like **Septime** (p. 125) on rue de Charonne. While the architecture here is nowhere near as grand as elsewhere in Paris, the neighborhood has retained an authenticity that's rarely found in the more popular parts of the city. A substantial number of furniture stores and ébénistes (woodworkers) are tucked into large interior courtyards accessible by covered passages off rue du Faubourg St-Antoine. Make a point of wandering down one of these; you'll be rewarded with a look at a way of life that has survived the centuries. This quarter extends all the way past the **Viaduc des Arts** (p. 243) and the **Gare de Lyon** train station (a magnificent example of Belle Epoque architecture) to **Bercy,** an area of former wine warehouses that is now home to the **Cinémathèque Française, Musée des Arts Forains** (p. 198), and the sprawling **Parc de Bercy** (p. 198). At the western end is the **Bois de Vincennes,** one of the city's two wooded parks.

BELLEVILLE, CANAL ST-MARTIN & NORTHEAST PARIS
Best for: Nightlife, restaurants, strolling (along the canal), arty boutiques
What you won't find here: Major monuments, museums, and architectural wonders
Parameters of the neighborhood: 10th, 19th & 20th arrondissements

For a long time, no one seemed to care about these arrondissements. They were too far from the center of the city, too working-class to be of interest to the trendy set, and too monument-less to appeal to tourists. Then, around 2000, with real estate skyrocketing, young professionals and artists began to move in. Suddenly, the forgotten **Canal St-Martin** was blooming with cafes and restaurants, and the streets around it were full of trendy shops. Then a handful of up-and-coming chefs arrived north of Bonne Nouvelle Métro station, kick-starting an exciting food scene with restaurants like **EELS** (p. 130). Artists looking for studio space discovered multi-ethnic **Belleville,** a cultural melting pot of immigrants from North Africa (both Jewish and Muslim), Asia (this is Paris's second-biggest Chinatown), and other parts of the world. The vast park and cultural venues of **La Villette** (p. 200) have also attracted new interest away from the center. Happily, these areas aren't really gentrified (yet), and parts are infused with a certain youthful energy that's hard to come by in other areas. Relatively tourist-free, these districts offer an opportunity to see a more local side of the city.

Aside from the **Parc de la Villette,** three other green havens are here: the **Parc de Belleville,** the **Parc des Buttes Chaumont** (p. 205), and the **Père-Lachaise cemetery** (p. 200), where the likes of Jim Morrison, Edith Piaf, Oscar Wilde, and Chopin are buried. Several good bars and music venues, like **La Bellevilloise** (p. 276) are around **Ménilmontant** to the north of the cemetery.

Père-Lachaise cemetery.

The Left Bank
LATIN QUARTER & THE 13TH ARRONDISSEMENT

Best for: *Affordable dining, student bars, art-house movie theaters, museums, botanical gardens*
What you won't find here: *Good shopping, quiet (at least not in the environs of Place St-Michel)*
Parameters of the neighborhood: *5th & 13th arrondissements*

Since the Middle Ages, when the **Sorbonne** and other academic institutions were founded, this has been a student neighborhood. (It earned its name as the "Latin" Quarter because back in the old days, all classes were taught in Latin.) Today, the area still harbors the highest number of colleges and universities in the city, and you'll certainly see plenty of students and professors hanging around the restaurants and cafes here. You'll also see lots of tourists, who tend to swarm the warren of tiny streets that lead off the Place St-Michel. Avoid rue de la Huchette (except for the great swing-dancing club, **Le Caveau de la Huchette;** p. 272), which is lined with garish restaurants of questionable quality. **Boulevard St-Michel,** a legendary artery once lined with smoky cafes filled with thinkers and rabble-rousers, has now fallen prey to chain stores. But it does harbor the **Musée de Cluny** (p. 210), a terrific collection of medieval art (including the famed *Lady and the Unicorn* tapestries) and Roman ruins.

For a more authentic taste of this neighborhood, wander east and upward, around the windy streets on the hill that leads to the **Panthéon** (p. 211), the church of **St-Etienne-du-Mont** (p. 212), and around rue Monge, toward the lovely **Jardin des Plantes** (p. 206). Surrounded by the city's **natural history museum,** this botanical garden is a wonderful place to relax. Down by the Seine, the museum of the **Institut du Monde Arabe** (p. 210) is housed in a spectacular building by architect Jean Nouvel.

South of here, in the 13th arrondissement, is Paris's main **Chinatown** (p. 140). Below rue de Tolbiac, high-rise apartment blocks house Chinese, Vietnamese, and Laotian restaurants and shops, lending a distinctly Asian vibe. In total contrast, the villagey streets around rue de la Butte-aux-Cailles make for a charming walk. You can take in its quaint houses, street art, hip bars and eateries, and even an Arts and Crafts–era swimming pool, **Piscine de la Butte-aux-Cailles** (5 pl. Paul Verlaine).

Vaulted ceiling and columns of the Paris Panthéon.

ST-GERMAIN-DES-PRÉS & LUXEMBOURG

Best for: Fine dining, historic cafes, shopping, parks (the Jardin du Luxembourg)
What you won't find here: Penniless intellectuals and artists, low prices
Parameters of the neighborhood: 6th arrondissement

The church of **St-Germain-des-Prés** (p. 213), the heart of this neighborhood, got its name (St. Germain of the Fields) because when it was built in the 11th century, it was in the middle of the countryside. What a difference a millennium makes. The church became the nucleus of a huge and powerful abbey, which would later constitute an autonomous mini-city complete with a hospital and a prison. The Revolution cut the church down to its current size, and an elegant collection of apartment houses, squares, and parks grew up around it, making it one of Paris's most appealing areas to live in (as real-estate prices will attest). If the neighborhood has always had aristocratic airs (it was a favorite haunt of the nobility during the 17th and 18th c.), during the last part of the 19th century up to the mid–20th century, it was also a magnet for artists and intellectuals, who hung out in legendary cafes like the **Café de Flore** (p. 154) and **Les Deux Magots** (p. 155).

Today, few struggling creative types can afford either the rents or the price of a cup of coffee around here, and young artists and thinkers have moved north and east to cheaper parts

The church of St-Germain-des-Prés.

Café de Flore.

of town. Though the ambience is decidedly bourgeois these days, the neighborhood is still dynamic, and the cafes and shops along the boulevard St-Germain are crowded with a mix of politicians, gallery owners, French celebrities, tourists, and editors. This is also a fun neighborhood for shopping—from 500€ pumps on chic rue des St-Pères to 30€ sundresses on the more plebian rue des Rennes. And when you've tired yourself out, you can stroll over to the magnificent **Jardin du Luxembourg** (p. 213) for a timeout by the fountains.

EIFFEL TOWER & LES INVALIDES

Best for: Iconic monuments, majestic avenues, grand vistas, museums
What you won't find here: Affordable restaurants or shopping, nightlife
Parameters of the neighborhood: 7th arrondissement

The **Eiffel Tower** (p. 217) reigns over this swanky arrondissement, where the streets that aren't lined with ministries and embassies are filled with elegant apartment buildings and prohibitively expensive stores and restaurants. A large portion of the neighborhood is taken up by the **Champs de Mars,** a park that stretches between the tower and the **Ecole Militaire,** and by the enormous esplanade in front of the **Invalides** (p. 219), which sweeps down to the Seine with much pomp and circumstance. Some of the city's best museums are around here, including the **Musée d'Orsay** (p. 220), the **Musée Rodin** (p. 222), and the **Musée du Quai Branly** (p. 222), whose wacky architecture has added some spice to this very staid area.

While this neighborhood certainly has a lot to see, it is a little short on human warmth—this is not the place to come to see regular Parisians in their natural habitat. Two exceptions are the area closest to St-Germain-des-Prés, where you'll find music icon Serge Gainsbourg's former home, the **Maison Gainsbourg** (p. 213), now a museum and piano bar, and the area around the pedestrian **rue Cler,** a market street that is home to many delightful small restaurants and food stores. Word is out about this cozy corner, however, so expect to see plenty of tourists when you go into that cute *boulangerie* for a couple of croissants.

MONTPARNASSE

Best for: Shopping, historic cafes, nightlife
What you won't find here: Extraordinary architecture, museums, monuments
Parameters of the neighborhood: 14th & 15th arrondissements

In the early 1970s, government officials decided the time had come to make Paris a modern city. They blithely put aside concerns for historic patrimony and architectural harmony, and the old Montparnasse train station and its immediate neighborhood were torn down; a 56-story glass tower and shopping complex was erected in its place. A new train station was constructed behind the tower, as well as a barrage of modern apartment buildings and offices. Fortunately, even ugly contemporary architecture didn't manage to kill the neighborhood—at the foot of the **Tour Montparnasse,** life goes on as it always has. A few steps away from the station, stores and cafes still line the

The bones of millions of Parisians rest in Les Catacombes de Paris.

tiny old streets; you'll also find many *crêperies* (crepe restaurants), an outgrowth of the large Breton (that is, from Brittany) community that still inhabits this area. Farther down boulevard Montparnasse are legendary brasseries such as **La Coupole** (p. 155) and **Le Select,** where Picasso, Max Jacob, and Henry Miller used to hang out in the 1920s. For a bit of calm, take a walk around the **Cimetiére du Montparnasse** (p. 223), where writers and artists such as Charles Baudelaire and Constantin Brancusi are buried. In the evenings, crowds pour into the many restaurants and movie theaters around the station.

To the south, the arrondissement takes a more residential turn, with the exception of rue Daguerre, a lively market street a block south of the cemetery. The 14th is also home to the fascinating and somewhat moving **Musée de la Libération** (p. 224) war museum, and **Les Catacombes** (p. 225), former limestone mines lined with the bones of millions of Parisians whose remains were moved here in the 18th century when the city's overcrowded graveyards became unhygienic. It makes for a spooky (and intriguing) visit.

PARIS IN CONTEXT

3

Before there was Paris, there was the Seine. Much wider than it is today, the river looped and curved through the region, and at one point, split into two branches. One branch dried up, leaving a wide band of marshlands to the north, while the other, sprinkled with islands, remained. This swampy bog offered little indication that it had potential for urban grandeur. Yet, one day it would become the lifeline of one of the world's greatest cities.

THE MAKING OF PARIS

Origins

Prehistoric Paris did have two things going for it: a river that led to the Atlantic and strategically placed islands, which offered both protection and shelter. The largest island, the core of what would one day become the **Île de la Cité,** attracted a tribe of Celtic people called the Parisii, who fished and traded along its banks somewhere around the 3rd century B.C.E. Though they weren't the first Parisians (traces of human habitations have been found dating back to Neolithic times), they were the first to firmly implant themselves in the area, and they made ample use of the river not only as a source of food, but as a trade link. Their island had the good fortune of being on the "Pewter Route," a trade route that stretched from the British Isles to the Mediterranean. As a consequence, the Parisii's wealth was such that by the 1st century B.C.E., they were minting their own gold coins.

Roman Rule (1st c. B.C.E. – 2nd c. C.E.)

No recorded history of Paris exists from before the Romans showed up in 52 B.C.E., but when Caesar and his boys marched in, the Parisii numbered several thousand, and the island bustled with activity. Soon thereafter, however, the Parisii's main activity would be trying to get rid of the Romans. Though they fought valiantly, the Parisii were massacred, and a new Roman town was built on the island and the Left Bank, on the slopes of the **Montagne St-Genevieve** (where the Panthéon now stands; p. 211). The new town, for reasons that remain unclear, was baptized Lutécia and ran along a ramrod-straight north to south axis; the line of this road survives in today's

rue St-Jacques. (The Parisii would eventually get their due, however, as the city would be renamed Civitas Parisiorum in the 4th c., which eventually was whittled down to Paris.) Though there were only around 8,000 inhabitants, by the 2nd century the town boasted three **Gallo-Roman baths** (you can see the ruins of the largest of these at the corner of bds. St-Michel and St-Germain in the Musée de Cluny; p. 210) and a vast amphitheater (the **Arènes de Lutèce,** just off rue Monge in the Latin Quarter).

Barbarian Invasions (3rd–5th c.)

By the 3rd century, the city was subject to waves of barbarian invasions. Most of the population took refuge on the Île de la Cité, which was then encircled by ramparts. Somewhere around this time, St-Denis was decapitated when he was martyred up on a nearby hill, which in time would be dubbed **Montmartre** (p. 308). Legend has it that the saint picked up his severed head and walked with it for several kilometers, preaching all the while; the **Basilica of St-Denis** (just north of Paris) was built on the place where he finally dropped. The event, which supposedly happened around C.E. 250, coincides with Christianity's first appearance on the Parisian scene. Another particularly pious Christian, a young nun named Geneviève, was credited with turning Attila the Hun away from Paris in 451. Alerted that the barbarians were approaching, the citizenry was in a state of panic; Geneviève reassured them, telling them that God was with them. In the end, the Huns didn't march on Paris, but on Orléans; the grateful population, convinced it was Geneviève's doing, made her into the city's patron saint. A church was raised in her honor on the hill that's now known as the **Montagne-Ste-Geneviève;** it was pulled down and replaced by a magnificent new one, commissioned by Louis XV in the 18th century, which was subsequently turned into a national mausoleum after the Revolution and renamed the **Panthéon** (p. 211).

Merovingian & Carolingian Dynasties (6th–10th c.)

At the end of the 5th century, the Franks (a Germanic people) invaded and established the Merovingian dynasty of kings; the first, Clovis, made Paris the capital of his new kingdom in 508. The Merovingians were ardent Catholics; under their rule the city sprouted dozens of churches, convents, and monasteries. Childebert I, the son of Clovis, inaugurated a small basilica that would soon be dubbed **St-Germain-des-Prés** after the saint was buried there in 576. Over time, this church would grow into a powerful abbey and intellectual center that would dominate much of the Left Bank up until the Revolution. Even after the abbey was dismantled, and many of its buildings burned, the church lived on, as did the name of the neighborhood. Though the city enjoyed a certain amount of prosperity during this time, it was short-lived; the Merovingians, known as the "do-nothing" kings, were eventually toppled, and by the 8th century, a new dynasty, the Carolingians, had replaced them.

The most famous member of this clan was Charlemagne, who went on to conquer Italy and was crowned emperor by the pope in 800. Arts and letters

The Panthéon, final resting place of several heroes of France.

thrived during this period, and the city began to build up on the Right Bank, around the church of **St-Gervais–St-Protais,** and the Port du Grève, where the **Hôtel de Ville** (p. 177) now stands. Starting in the mid–9th century, the city was periodically ravaged by Normans and Vikings, who would sack Paris on their way to plundering Burgundy. The Normans were particularly persistent; after a barricade was erected on the Seine to keep their boats from passing in 885, they laid siege to the city for an entire year. It was only after King Charles the Simple signed a treaty in 911 giving the Normans Normandy that life returned to normal, but by then Paris was in ruins. The age of the Carolingians was drawing quickly to a close.

The Founding of the Capetian Dynasty (11th c.)

In 987, Hugues Capet, the Count of Paris, was crowned king of France; his direct descendants ruled the country for 3½ centuries, and two branches of the Capetian dynasty, the Valois and Bourbons, would continue to rule (with a brief pause during the Revolution) until 1848. With the Capetians came stability, and Paris rebuilt and grew, particularly on the Île de la Cité and the Right Bank. The Left Bank, flattened by the Normans, was left as it was; little by little it was covered with fields and vineyards. The 12th century was a period of economic growth; it saw the birth of **Les Halles** (p. 167), the sprawling central market around which a new commercial quarter developed. In 1163, ground was broken on the **Cathédrale de Notre-Dame de Paris** (p. 160). Finished 200 years later, Notre-Dame remains one of the world's most exquisite examples of medieval architecture (even after the fire of 2019, which caused extensive damage to its roof and engulfed its emblematic spire).

The lower chapel of Sainte-Chapelle.

The mushy, marshy land on the Right Bank, known as the **Marais** ("swamp"), was partially drained and carpeted with farms. Philippe Auguste, before taking off on a crusade, had a sturdy rampart built around the newly extended city limits; fragments of this wall can still be seen today (see "Walking Tours of Paris," p. 308). Philippe's grandson, Louis IX (St. Louis), added another architectural jewel to the cityscape: the **Sainte-Chapelle** (p. 172), a small church whose upper-story walls are almost entirely made of stained glass. Louis had it built to house a treasure he bought from the debt-ridden Byzantine emperor: Christ's crown of thorns and some fragments of the holy cross (the relics were in Notre-Dame until the 2019 fire; they're now—at time of writing—in the Louvre).

Medieval Glory & Gore (12th–15th c.)

By the 12th century, Paris boasted a population of around 200,000, much larger than other European capitals, as well as a burgeoning reputation as an economic as well as intellectual center. Quality fabrics, leather goods, and metalwork were produced in Paris, as well as art objects. The University of Paris was slowly coming into being, and colleges were popping up all over the Left Bank; in 1257, Robert de Sorbon established the small theological college that became the **Sorbonne** university. The city seemed unstoppable.

But the 14th century would, in fact, put an end to this fruitful period. When the last Capetian king, Charles IV, died in 1328, the succession to the throne was disputed, in part because the closest descendant was Edward III, king of England, who also presided over a chunk of southwestern France. This and many other gripes exploded into the Hundred Years' War, which devastated France for over a century. Expansion in Paris came to an abrupt halt, the endless wars and riots wore down the populace, and in 1348 the Black Plague killed tens of thousands. In the early 1400s, Paris was hit by famine and a string of extremely cold winters. Between one disaster and another during this period, the city lost about half of its population. In 1420, the English occupied Paris; despite the efforts of Joan of Arc and Charles VII, who laid siege to the city in 1429, troops loyal to the Duke of Bedford (the English Regent) didn't leave until 1437. This same duke was responsible for having Joan burned at the stake in Rouen in 1431.

Renaissance Renewal (16th c.)

Slowly, the city came to life again. The population increased, as did commercial and intellectual activity. The invention of the printing press spread new ideas across Europe. After centuries of rejecting the texts and ideas of classical antiquity, scholars embraced the concept of Humanism, which would find a home in Paris. Great thinkers such as Erasmus and John Calvin were drawn to the city's universities. More colleges emerged from the academic landscape: In 1530, François I established a school that would become the prestigious **College de France,** and in 1570 Charles IX founded the **Académie Française.** If the Renaissance made its mark on the intellectual life of the city, it had little impact on its architectural legacy. The Renaissance kings liked Paris but lived and did their building elsewhere. François I, the most construction-happy among them, brought some of the greatest masters of the Italian Renaissance, like Leonardo da Vinci and Benvenuto Cellini, to France, but their genius was mostly displayed in François' châteaux on the Loire and at **Fontainebleau** (p. 301), not in the capital. The king's primary contribution to the cityscape was the remodeling of the **Louvre** (p. 166) and construction of the **Hôtel de Ville** (p. 177), designed by the Italian architect Boccador. The latter building was burned down in 1871 during the fall of the Paris Commune; the existing edifice is a fairly faithful copy erected in 1873. Two glorious churches, **St-Etienne-du-Mont** (p. 212) and **St-Eustache** (p. 173), also were built during this period; their decoration attests to the jubilant spirit of the times.

War once again interfered with the city's development when the bloody struggle between the country's Protestants and Catholics morphed into the Wars of Religion in 1557. Even the marriage of the future king, Henri of Navarre, a Protestant, to Marguerite de Valois, a Catholic, did not diffuse the conflict: A week after their wedding, August 24, 1572, the bells of **St-Germain l'Auxerrois** (p. 174) signaled the beginning of the St-Bartholomew's Day massacre, which resulted in the deaths of between 2,000 and 4,000 Parisian Protestants. When in 1589 Henri was declared King of France (as Henri IV), Parisians would not let the Protestant monarch enter the city. After 4 months of siege, the starving citizens relented and, in the end, to show his goodwill, the king converted, famously declaring that "Paris is worth a Mass."

Henri IV lived on to be an enormously popular king, whose structural improvements left a lasting mark on the city. He was the force behind the **Pont**

Neuf (p. 179), which straddles the Right and Left banks, as well as the Île de la Cité. To create the bridge, two small islets off the western tip of the Île de la Cité were filled in and made part of the larger island; the tranquil **Place Dauphine** was also created during this time. Henri also conceived the strikingly harmonious Place Royale (now called **Place des Vosges,** p. 182). The king would not live to see it finished; in 1610, when the royal carriage got stuck in a traffic jam on rue de la Ferronerie, he was stabbed by Ravaillac, a deranged Catholic who was convinced that Henri was waging war against the pope.

Place Dauphine.

The Age of Louis XIV (17th c.)

The 17th century saw a building frenzy among the aristocracy. Marie de Médicis built the Italian-style **Palais du Luxembourg** in 1615, around the same time that the **Marais** (p. 315) was inundated with splendid palaces and *hôtels particuliers,* or mansions. The new **Île St-Louis,** made from the joining of two previously uninhabited islets to the east of the Île de la Cité, was filled with stately mansions that only the rich could afford. After Marguerite de Valois moved into the neighborhood, the **St-Germain** quarter also became a place to see and be seen. Finally, in 1632 the powerful Cardinal Richelieu built a huge palace, now called the **Palais Royal** (p. 170), near the Louvre, which encouraged yet another new neighborhood to develop.

In 1643, a 5-year-old boy named Louis XIV acceded to the French throne, where he would stay for the next 72 years. One of the most influential figures in French history, Louis XIV spent his early years in Paris, under the protection of his mother, Anne of Austria. It was not a happy time: The city was writhing under a nasty rebellion called La Fronde, instigated by cranky nobles trying to wrest control back from the powerful prime minister, Cardinal Mazarin. The young monarch and his mother were chased from one royal residence to the next. When Louis grew up and things calmed down, he settled in at the **Louvre,** commanding his team of architects, led by Le Vau, to complete the **Cour Carrée** and other unfinished parts of the palace. The spectacular colonnade on the eastern facade dates from this period. Louis eventually decided to build his own castle, one that was far enough from the noise and filth of the capital and big enough to house his entire court—the better to keep a close eye on political intrigues. The result was the **Château of Versailles** (p. 290), a testament to the genius of Le Vau and that of master landscape architect André Le Nôtre.

Even if Louis XIV didn't live in the city, he certainly added to its architectural heritage. He was responsible for the construction of **Les Invalides** (p. 217), a massive military hospital, and two squares, **Place des Victoires** and Place Louis-le-Grand, today known as **Place Vendôme** (p. 171). Two gigantic entryways, celebrating Louis' military victories, were built at the city gates: the **Porte St-Denis** and the **Porte St-Martin**. Both triumphal archways still tower over parts of the 10th arrondissement, along boulevard St-Denis close to Métro Strasbourg–St-Denis, looking somewhat out of place in this working-class district.

From Enlightenment to Revolution (18th c.)

Paris continued to grow, and the population density increased. At the turn of the 18th century, some 500,000 Parisians were crammed into a vast network of narrow, mostly unpaved streets. Sewers were nonexistent, and clean drinking water was a luxury. While life in the rarified atmosphere of the aristocratic salons of the **Marais** was brimming with art, literature, and deep thought, down on the ground it was filled with misery. Poverty and want were the constant companions of the vast majority of Parisians. On an intellectual level, the city was soaring—under the reign of Louis XV, Paris became a standard-bearer for the Enlightenment, a school of thought that championed reason and logic and helped construct the intellectual framework of both the American and French Revolutions. Salons—regular meetings of artists and thinkers in aristocratic homes—flourished, as did cafes. Drawn in by the wildly popular new drink called coffee, these cafes were the ideal meeting place for philosophers, writers, and artists, as well as a new breed of politicians with some revolutionary ideas. Political debates were particularly passionate in the cafes in the galleries of the **Palais Royal** (p. 170), which had been filled with shops and opened to the public by Duke Louis Philippe d'Orléans.

Meanwhile, back in Versailles, the court of Louis XVI seemed to be utterly oblivious to the mounting discontent in the capital. As the price of bread skyrocketed and more and more Parisians found themselves on the street (there were more than 100,000 homeless people in the city in 1789, out of an overall population of between 600,000 and 700,000), the disconnect between the aristocracy and the common man threatened to rupture into a bloody conflict. Amazingly, Louis XVI and his wife, Marie Antoinette, continued to live their lives as if the civil unrest in the capital didn't concern them. A financial crisis in the royal treasury prompted a meeting of the Estates-General in Versailles in May 1789, a representative body that had not been convened since 1616. The assembly began demanding a more democratic system of taxation, and better representation of the Third Estate (the people). When the king tried to close down the proceedings, the group, which had renamed itself the National Assembly, dug in its heels and wrote a constitution. The royals kept dithering and trying to break up the assembly, until finally, the Revolution erupted on July 14, 1789, when an angry mob stormed the Bastille prison. There were only seven prisoners in the fortress, but no matter—the genie was out of the bottle, and the pent-up anger of the populace was unleashed.

The royal family was imprisoned and beheaded. After the initial euphoria faded and the high ideals were set down on paper, the Revolution's leaders began to squabble, and factional skirmishes became increasingly deadly. The events of the Revolution are too many to relate here, but within a few years, not only were aristocrats being sent off to the guillotine, but also was just about anyone who disagreed with the ruling powers, including many of the leaders who wrote the rules. Finally, Robespierre, who directed the bloodiest phase of the Revolution, known as "the Terror," had his turn at the guillotine, and a new government was set up. Called the Directory, this unsuccessful attempt at representational government met its end when a general named Napoleon Bonaparte staged a coup in 1799.

The Empire (early 19th c.)

Under Napoleon, who was crowned emperor in 1804, Paris slowly put itself back together. The economy restarted, and the emperor turned his attentions to upgrading the city's infrastructure, building bridges (**Pont St-Louis, Pont des Arts, Pont d'Iéna,** and **Pont d'Austerlitz**), improving access to water (the **Canal de l'Ourcq**), and creating new cemeteries like **Père-Lachaise** (p. 200) because the old ones were so crowded that they had become public health hazards. Napoleon was also responsible for the **rue de Rivoli,** a wide east-west boulevard, the first of several that would be laid down later in the 19th century. The collection of the **Louvre** was greatly enhanced by all the booty the emperor acquired during his many military campaigns. Napoleon's love of war would eventually be his undoing; after his defeat by the English at Waterloo, he was exiled to the isle of Ste-Helena, where he died in 1821. Paris holds huge monuments to his memory, in particular the **Arc de Triomphe** (p. 183), which honors the Imperial Army. His tomb lies in Les Invalides military complex and museum (p. 217).

The Restoration & Urban Renewal (mid–19th c.)

Incredibly, after all the blood that was spilled in the name of the Republic, Louis XVI's brother (Louis XVIII) became King of France in 1814. What's more, another brother, Charles X, became king after Louis XVIII's death. What both brothers had in common is that they tried to bring back the old days of absolute monarchy. The citizenry, though, had become accustomed to the reforms of the Revolution and the relatively benign rule of Napoleon. This, coupled with the continuing poverty of many Parisians, resulted in two serious uprisings: "Les Trois Glorieuses," the 3 "glorious" days in July 1830, and the Revolution of 1848. It is these two uprisings that are honored on the column in the **Place de la Bastille** (p. 199), the site of the infamous prison. After Charles, a republic was declared, and Napoleon's nephew, Louis-Napoleon, ran for and won the presidency. He liked being president so much that he didn't want to give up power at the end of his term, so he staged a coup and declared the birth of the Second Empire, calling himself Napoleon III.

Under Charles X, the unhygienic state of the city center started to cause serious alarm, particularly after a cholera epidemic in 1832 devastated the

Place de la Bastille.

population. Many residents fled to the outer limits of the city, away from the overcrowded quarters where many impoverished people lived, and where the filthy streets were often completely clogged with traffic. City administrators began to draft plans for new avenues, in particular the prefect, Rambuteau, who went ahead and started laying down wide boulevards, like the one named after him.

But it was Napoleon III who really changed the face of Paris when he gave urban planner Baron Haussmann free rein to "modernize" the city. Not only did Haussmann lay down wide boulevards that eased congestion and opened up vistas, but he also cleverly arranged them so that if ever there was yet another popular uprising, the boulevards would facilitate military maneuvers and make it tough for citizens to set up barricades. Over half of the city was ripped up and rebuilt; Haussmann instituted strict regulations for the height of the new buildings and the style of their facades. The result: the elegant buildings and boulevards you see today. On the plus side, the city finally got a decent sewage system and water access, and the squalid slums were knocked down. Several parks sprouted up, such as **Buttes Chaumont** (p. 205) and the **Bois de Boulogne** (p. 237), as well as grand plazas like the **Place de la République** (p. 197) and **Place du Trocadéro.** On the other hand, the character of the city was completely changed, and much of its social fabric was pulled down with the houses. Working-class Paris has been slowly disappearing ever since.

From the Commune to the Belle Epoque (late 19th c.)

The boulevards were put to the test during the Paris Commune of 1871, a brief but bloody episode that was yet another attempt of the French people to construct a democratic republic—though this time it was in the wake of the Franco-Prussian War. The boulevards did their job: The rebellion was crushed, and at least 20,000 Communards were executed. When the smoke cleared, a new government was formed, and to everyone's surprise, it was a republic. The National Assembly had intended to form a constitutional monarchy, but the heir to the throne had no interest in the word *constitutional.* As a stopgap measure, a temporary republic was set up—little did anyone know that it would last for 60 years.

There must have been an audible sigh of relief from Parisians, who would finally enjoy a little peace and harmony—or at least enough of a break from war and woe to have a good time. And so they did. During the "Belle Epoque," the years at the end of the 19th century and the beginning of the 20th, the arts bloomed in Paris. Groundbreaking art expositions introducing new movements like Impressionism (around 1874) and Fauvism (around 1905) changed people's ways of seeing painting. Up in **Montmartre,** an entire colony of artists and writers (Picasso, Braque, Apollinaire, and others) were filling cafes and cabarets in their off hours. The Lumière brothers and Léon Gaumont showed their newly hatched films in the city's first movie theaters.

Strolling through Montmartre.

The city hosted a number of World's Fairs including that of 1889, which created the **Eiffel Tower** (p. 217), and 1900, which left behind the **Pont Alexandre III bridge** (p. 179), as well as the **Grand Palais** (p. 185) and **Petit Palais** (p. 192). Another great moment in 1900 was the inauguration of the Paris Métro's first underground line.

The World Wars (early 20th c.)

The fun came to an abrupt halt in 1914 with the outbreak of World War I, which killed 1.4 million Frenchmen and wounded 4.2 million others. Calling all Parisians to arms, General Gallieni and his troops fought off the approaching German army (the Battle of the Marne) and saved Paris from occupation. The city did get bombarded, however; on Good Friday, 1918, the church of **St-Gervais–St-Protais** took a direct hit and more than 100 people died.

The city rebounded after the war, both economically and culturally, especially during the 1920s, *les années folles* ("the crazy years"). Paris became a magnet for artists and writers from all over. Americans, in particular, came in droves—F. Scott Fitzgerald, Henry Miller, Ernest Hemingway, and Gertrude Stein were some of the better-known names. They and other European expats like Marc Chagall, James Joyce, and George Orwell gathered in **Montparnasse** cafes like **Le Dôme, Le Select,** and **La Coupole.**

The 1930s brought economic depression and social unrest—a dreary backdrop for the approaching war. The Germans were re-arming, and Hitler was rising to power. In May 1940 Germany invaded the Netherlands, Luxembourg, and Belgium, and then broke through France's defensive Maginot line.

The Germans occupied Paris on June 14, and for 4 years the city would know hunger, curfews, and suspicion. The Vichy government, led by Marchal Pétain, in theory governed unoccupied France, but in fact, it collaborated with the Germans. One of the darkest moments of the occupation was in July 1942, when the French police rounded up 13,152 Parisian Jews, including 4,115 children, and parked them in a velodrome before sending them off to Auschwitz; only 30 survived. General Charles de Gaulle became the leader of the Free French and organizer of the Resistance. After the Allies landed in Normandy in 1944, Paris was liberated, and de Gaulle victoriously strode down the **Champs-Élysées** before a wildly cheering crowd. He would later become president of the country (1958–69).

Postwar Paris (mid–20th to early 21st c.)

Writers and artists filtered back to the cafes once the war was over (some had never left), and the **Café de Flore** (p. 154) and **Les Deux Magots** (p. 155) were headquarters for existential all-stars like Jean-Paul Sartre and Simone de Beauvoir. But the late 1940s was also the beginning of the end of French colonial rule, which was punctuated by violent clashes, including a revolt in Madagascar and a war in Indochina (mainland Southeast Asia) that would eventually entangle the United States. In North Africa, Morocco and Tunisia won their independence relatively peacefully, but France would not let go of

Café Le Dôme, a Montparnasse landmark.

Algeria without a long and bloody fight, its repercussions still being felt today. The war in Algeria led to the collapse of the French government; de Gaulle was asked to start a new one in 1958. Thousands of Algerian refugees flooded France, with many settling in the Paris region; Algeria finally gained its independence in 1962.

The writer André Malraux was de Gaulle's minister of cultural affairs from 1958 to 1969 and was responsible for protecting and restoring endangered historic districts like the **Marais**. Elsewhere, modern architects were putting their own questionable stamp on the city, like the doughnut-shaped **Maison de Radio France** in the 16th arrondissement, and the vaguely Y-shaped **Maison de UNESCO** in the 15th. The late 1960s also marked Paris in less concrete ways. In May 1968, students, hoping to reform the university system, joined a general workers' strike that was paralyzing the nation. The police invaded **La Sorbonne** to calm the protests, and students and sympathizers took to the streets. The confrontations became violent, with students attacking police with cobblestones—**boulevard St-Michel** was subsequently paved with asphalt. This was a period of profound social change; those who participated still proudly refer to themselves as *soixante-huitards* (68ers).

The 1970s was a period of architectural awkwardness—horrified by the idea of becoming a "museum city," then-president Georges Pompidou decided to modernize. One idea that thankfully never came to fruition was to pave over the Canal St-Martin to make way for a freeway that would cut through the center of the city. The dismal **Tour Montparnasse** dates from this period, as does the destruction of the old Les Halles marketplace, which was replaced with an underground shopping mall (**Forum des Halles,** which has been rebuilt and covered over by a massive glass canopy; see box, p. 167). Pompidou's one "success" is the nearby **Centre Pompidou** (p. 177), whose strange, inside-out design provoked howls of outrage when it was built but now has been accepted as part of the Parisian landscape. When François Mitterrand became president in 1981, he too wanted to leave an architectural legacy, and the list of his *grands projets* ("big projects") is lengthy. Fortunately, most were considerably more palatable than his predecessor's. It is to Mitterrand that we owe the **Musée d'Orsay,** the **pyramid** (and underground shopping complex) at the Louvre, and the ultra-modern **Bibliothèque National François Mitterrand,** as well as the **Institut du Monde Arabe** (p. 210) and the **Opéra Bastille** (p. 269). President Jacques Chirac was the force behind the excellent **Musée du Quai Branly** (p. 222), which opened in 2006.

PARIS TODAY

Recent decades have brought Paris long periods of relative calm, punctuated by seismic upheavals, like the Métro bombings and paralyzing strikes that both hit the city in 1995. More recently, the 2015 terrorist attacks on the satiric newspaper *Charlie Hebdo* and a kosher supermarket, followed by coordinated assaults on restaurant terraces, the Stade de France stadium, and the Bataclan concert hall, shook the city to its core.

In 2018 and 2019, Paris, like the rest of France, was also affected by the grassroots yellow vests (*gilets jaunes*) movement, an anti-elitist, sometimes violent crusade against a whole hodgepodge of issues (including climate-change problems and President Macron's tax reforms). And *then,* in April 2019, a dramatic fire engulfed its most visited monument, the glorious, medieval Cathédrale de Notre-Dame de Paris.

Not a year after that, it was the Covid-19 pandemic's turn to spread chaos. Paris, like most capital cities around the world, was a hotspot for the virus and was thrust into lockdown, with only vital shops and services staying open for most of 2020. (In true French style, wine shops were considered vital!) Then finally, after a late-starting but hefty vaccine campaign, the city (along with the rest of the country) reopened in 2021 with only a few restrictions. But random acts of terror, freak fires, worldwide pandemics, and Putin's war aside, Paris is, for now at least, still Paris, and then some.

The city has been looking slicker and cleaner in the last few years—particularly after the 2024 Olympics and Paralympics. Renovation of historic buildings is ongoing, and a vigorous anti-dog-doo campaign has even made some headway on cleaning up the notoriously messy sidewalks. Paris feels younger these days too, with refreshed public spaces, like the new and improved **Place de la République** (p. 197) and the delightfully pedestrianized **banks of the Seine** (see "The New Banks of the Seine & Paris Plage," p. 236), which now include floating gardens, picnic areas,

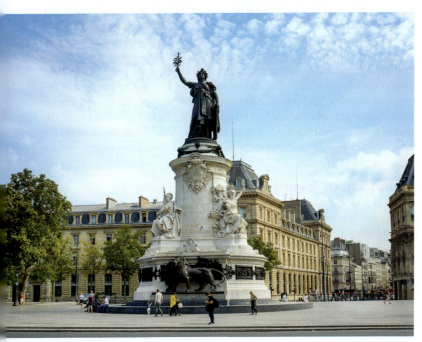

Place de la République.

and sports classes. The city is even home to both the world's largest startup campus, Station F, and Europe's biggest restaurant, the 1,000-seater La Felicità, both set in a converted 1920s industrial building known as the Halle Freyssinet.

The advent of the **Vélib' bike program** in 2007 (p. 331) has slowly transformed Paris into a bike-friendly place. There are now over 1,000km (621 miles) of bike lanes with more cyclists than car users at some times of the day. And the 2024 Paris Olympics saw the arrival of another 60km of new paths (nicknamed the Olympistes; "pistes" means "lanes"), which have now become permanent fixtures. By 2030 in the greater Paris region, there will also be another 750km (466 miles) of lanes linking the city and its suburbs. Other innovative initiatives include the ever-popular **Paris Plage**—an urban beach on the banks of the Seine—and **Nuit Blanche,** an annual all-night cultural party.

In 2014, the Socialist **Anne Hidalgo** was elected Paris's first female mayor. One of her top priorities is air pollution, which is an increasing problem in the capital, so much so that on particularly smoggy days, driving is restricted and the Métro is free. In 2021, she also instated a new speed limit of 30kmph (18mph) on most of Paris's streets to reduce noise pollution. It was under Hidalgo's watch that the city won the bid for the **2024 Olympics** too, which was the biggest event ever organized in France and deemed a huge success.

On the surface, at least, the capital seems to be in the pink of good health. Paris has managed to carefully conserve its architectural heritage and its traditional way of life while making a serious effort to enter the modern world. Paris is, after all, the capital of the second-largest economy in the European Union, and a certain dynamism comes with the territory—even if it is framed in Belle Epoque swirls and Mansard roofs. Yet even if the pulse of life in the capital ticks faster than it once did, it still allows for aimless intellectual discussions in cafes, leisurely Sunday strolls through leafy parks, and relaxed lunches over glasses of wine. And maybe it is exactly that gentle aesthetic that makes the city one of a kind. It is rare in today's turbulent world to find an urban center that so harmoniously mixes tradition and modernity, without enslaving itself to either.

Calendar of Events

Paris is an all-year-round kind of city, with great events in every season. No matter when you visit, you will have something to see beyond the traditional sights, be it a sports match, a cycle of museum concerts, or a movie festival. Here is a non-exhaustive list of the best events to look out for month by month. Dates may differ in 2026 and 2027, so always check the events' websites. The Tourist Office (parisjetaime.com) is also a good resource; in the menu bar, click "Events," then "Celebrations and Festivals in Paris."

Major holidays are New Year's Day (Jan 1), Easter Sunday and Monday (late Mar/Apr), May Day (May 1), VE Day (May 8), Ascension Thursday (40 days after Easter), Pentecost/Whit Sunday and Whit Monday (7th Sun and Mon after Easter), Bastille Day (July 14), Assumption Day (Aug 15), All Saints Day (Nov 1), Armistice Day (Nov 11), and Christmas Day (Dec 25).

JANUARY

International Circus Festival of Tomorrow. The annual International Circus Festival of Tomorrow at Paris's Pelouse de Reuilly (Métro: Liberté) offers the chance to catch the world's finest circuses under one roof. Young artists from such diverse schools as the Beijing Circus, the Moscow Circus, and France's own *Ecole Fratellini* compete at the festival in a bid to discover the stars of the future. Four days at the end of January. cirquededemain.paris.

FEBRUARY

International Agricultural Show. Every February, the *terroir* (France's countryside) comes to Paris for the International Agricultural Show at the Porte de Versailles. It's a real institution (even the French president makes an official call) with exhibits featuring the top models of the animal world, meaty gastronomic delicacies from 18 French regions, and leisure, hunting, and fishing displays. Late February. salon-agriculture.com.

Six Nations Rugby. France faces its European rivals (England, Scotland, Wales, Ireland, and Italy) in the Six Nations rugby union internationals at the humongous **Stade de France** (p. 267). The championship is the oldest rugby tournament in the world, having existed in one form or another since 1883. Since the advent of the Six Nations, France has been the most successful country, so come along and see whether they can be beaten on home territory. February and March. stadefrance.com or sixnationsrugby.com.

Chinese New Year. Paris celebrates this lively annual event in the 13th arrondissement and Belleville in the 20th, the city's Chinese quarters. Most of the action is on the 13th, where concerts and screenings are shown alongside the traditional dragon parade, which swirls through avenues such as d'Ivry and Choisy in a flurry of color and sparkle. One day in February.

MARCH

Banlieues Blues. This annual music festival, held in Paris's northern suburb of Pantin, brings top-notch jazz and blues names to the traditionally culture-hungry suburbs. It's a fine way to discover lesser-known theaters as your feet swing to the sound of top-notch international musicians. Mid-March to mid-April. banlieuesbleues.org.

Festival Chorus. Paris's Festival Chorus brings rock, pop, and French *chanson* to the Seine Musicale (p. 266) in the Hauts-de-Seine suburb of Boulogne-Billancourt, with over 50 different concerts over 5 days. It's a great way to get to know France's music scene as a whole. Five days late March to early April. chorus.hauts-de-seine.fr.

Foire du Trône. Europe's largest temporary funfair, the Foire du Trône at the Pelouse de Reuilly attracts around 5 million visitors every year. Though it has roots stretching back to the 12th century, since the 1950s the event has grown to epic proportions. With its flashing lights, pumping music, and greasy aromas, the Foire du Trône is a world away from the cultural clichés of the French capital, and sometimes that is the best thing about it. Late March to the end of April. foiredutrone.com.

L'Hippodrome en Famille. On most Sundays from April through November, the city's main horse racing stadiums, the Hippodromes de Longchamp and d'Auteuil, open for a family day out. There are children's activities and games galore, including pony rides, sack races, and pony-cycling (hybrid rocking horses that move like bikes), along with traditional horse races. End of March to mid-November. francegalop-live.com/evenement-p/hippodrome-en-famille.

Paris Carnival. The annual *Carnaval de Paris* goes by many names, including the *Pantruche Carnaval*, the *Saint-Fargeau*, and the *Promenade du Boeuf Gras* (Fat Cow Parade). Led by the Fat Cow herself (yes, an actual cow), it revives an age-old tradition begun in 1274. Cheerful Parisians, trumpeters, and other musicians parade through the capital's streets to the Place de la République in the 11th arrondissement. Usually early March. carnaval-paris.org.

APRIL

Paris Marathon. The Paris Marathon offers some 55,000 runners the chance to take in some of the city's most famous landmarks (cheered on by thousands of spectators),

The French Open at Le Stade Roland Garros.

including the Champs-Élysées, the Tuileries Garden, and Place de la Bastille. There's a special race for 7- to 10-year-olds too, the Marateens. One Sunday in April. www.schneiderelectricparismarathon.com.

MAY

Nuit Européenne des Musées. During the Nuit Européenne des Musées (Museum Night), the city's museums stay open until the wee hours, offering you a chance to see the Louvre, and hundreds more, for free. One Saturday in mid-May. nuitdesmusees.culture.gouv.fr.

St-Germain-des-Prés Jazz Festival. The Rive Gauche, Paris's traditional jazz quarter, swings as local and international musicians perform at this jazz festival. Playing everything from boogie-woogie to blues, free concerts are held in St-Germain square; ticketed concerts take place in local libraries, cafes, concert halls, and bars. One week in May. festivaljazzsaintgermainparis.com.

The French Open. For 2 weeks, the world's best tennis players battle it out on Roland Garros' clay courts. The event is one of France's biggest sports competitions; book in advance for a decent seat. The main matches are the most expensive, so if you want to save money, watch the unseeded players on the smaller courts: You could be watching the tennis stars of the future. Mid-May to early June. rolandgarros.com.

JUNE

Paris Jazz Festival. This annual summer event presents a program of free jazz concerts in the beautiful surroundings of the Parc Floral. Gigs take place every Saturday and Sunday throughout June and July. The concerts begin at 3 or 4pm and are free to all those who have paid the standard 5€ summer park entry fee. Arrive early to ensure that you get one of the seats available or pack a picnic and bask by the park's miniature lake. June to September. festivalsduparcfloral.paris.

Fête de la Musique. In Paris for the Fête de la Musique? Everywhere you go you'll hear music, from opera and jazz to techno and rock. The Fête unites big names at major venues with accordionists on street corners and choirs in church halls. All concerts are free; the website publishes a list of participating venues. June 21. fetedelamusique.culture.gouv.fr.

Solidays. Solidarité SIDA is France's main charity promoting the cause of those with HIV. Its annual festival, Solidays, held at Paris's Hippodrome de Longchamp, has fast become one of the city's hippest cultural events, attracting more than 100,000 visitors for a weekend of music and arts. Circus performers, fairground stalls, mime artists, and bungee jumpers create a festive atmosphere, but the real stars of the show are the big names from the international pop and rock scene. Late June. solidays.org.

Gay Pride (Marche des Fiertés). The flamboyant Paris Gay Pride parade has recently gone from Place de la Nation (11th/12th arrond.) to République, but final confirmation of the route is not usually given until the last minute. Paris has a large gay and lesbian population, with consequently one of the most liberal attitudes in France. Over the last few years, the march has grown into a huge carnival, and the big day itself is the culmination of a series of events, including debates and masked balls. Late June. gaypride.fr.

Fête des Tuileries. Every summer, the Jardin des Tuileries west of the Louvre turns its northern edge into a good old-fashioned funfair, with a big Ferris wheel, bumper cars, and a rather cheesy ghost train. For smaller kids, a 1900s-era carousel of wooden horses steals the show. The best bit? No tacky pop blasting through speakers. In fact, the fair is entirely music-free, so the relaxing atmosphere of the gardens stays intact. Late June to late August.

We Love Green. In the Bois de Vincennes, this is one of the best open-air music festivals of the year: Not only are the stages jam-packed with both international and French stars, performing anything from pop and rock to electro and rap, but there are also workshops and concerts just for kids. The festival is eco-responsible, being (among other things) partly powered by solar panels and offering programming and workshops that promote the environment. Early June. welovegreen.fr.

Nuit Blanche. See Paris as you've never seen it before, when museums, monuments, cinemas, parks, and swimming pools stay open from dusk to dawn (for 1 night only) as thousands of revelers celebrate Nuit Blanche. The Métro stays open later, and night buses serve all the main arteries until dawn. First weekend in June.

JULY

Bastille Day. France's national holiday commemorates the 1789 storming of the Bastille at the start of the French Revolution. Crowds line the Champs-Élysées for a military parade led by the president, during which jets fly in formation as top military brass bands march from the Arc de

Bastille Day parade along Champs-Élysées.

Touring the Grand Salon in Sorbonne University during the Journées du Patrimoine (Heritage Days).

Triomphe to the Place de la Concorde. Later, Parisians party until dawn as fireworks explode over the Trocadéro. Some of the best spots to watch the action at midnight are Paris's bridges. Try Pont d'Alma and Pont Bir-Hakeim. Or a rooftop bar. It'll be crowded, but not as much as elsewhere. July 14.

Paris Plage. Every summer, long, pedestrianized stretches of the Seine (from Sully Morland to Pont Neuf, on the Right Bank, and now also at Port de Solférino on the Left Bank) are turned into Paris Plage, a beach complete with golden sand and tanning beds. There are free sports, such as volleyball, and entertainment from comedy to hip-hop. A second stretch of beach, along the Canal de l'Ourcq, also draws crowds with yet more concerts, outdoor games, canoeing, and sand. July to August. paris.fr.

Open-Air Cinema at La Villette. Each summer, film fans converge on Paris's Parc de la Villette for its 4-week *Cinéma en plein air* (outdoor movie projections). Pack a picnic and watch movies with the locals. Some movies are dubbed or subtitled and are some "VO" (original language). Mid-July to mid-August. lavillette.com.

Lollapalooza. The great U.S. music festival has taken root in Paris too, at the Longchamp Racetrack in the Bois de Boulogne. Lineups are excellent—previous headliners have included Depeche Mode, Pearl Jam, and Twenty One Pilots—and the atmosphere is laid-back and good-humored. Music aside, the focus is on the nosh, with contemporary street food designed by some of the city's best chefs, many of them taking their signature dishes and adapting them for the festival's takeout system. Mid- to late July. lollaparis.com.

Classique au Vert. World-class classical musicians gather to serenade around 1,500 tourists and Parisians in the leafy Parc Floral (Métro: Château de Vincennes). Pack a picnic for a spot on the lawn while the sound fills the air; if you want a spot under the bandstand, get there around an hour before the concert. Weekends in late July, August, and early September. festivalsduparcfloral.paris/programmation/classique-au-vert.

AUGUST

Rock en Seine. This music festival, held in the Saint Cloud park just outside Paris (Métro: Boulogne Pont Saint-Cloud), offers a consistently excellent lineup of internationally renowned pop and rock stars, and its chilled-out atmosphere makes it a definite highlight of the city's musical calendar. Kids are welcome too, with a special "mini-rock" stage set aside for 6- to 10-year-olds, and a host of activities, from dressing up sessions and cooking classes to song-writing workshops. If you buy a festival pass, you can camp at the festival campsite (just bring your own tent). Late August. rockenseine.com/en.

SEPTEMBER

Techno Parade. The annual Techno Parade has been turning up the volume and quickening the pace on Paris's streets since 1998. Around 20 floats carrying 150 musicians, DJs, and performers turn out to dance their way along the 4.8km (3-mile) route. This huge event attracts 400,000 hardcore partygoers. Top DJs entertain the crowds with their mixing skills and decibel-defying sound systems. You can free your inner party animal afterward too, in numerous bars and clubs across the capital. Mid-September. technoparade.fr

Journées du Patrimoine (Heritage Days). France's Heritage Days give visitors the chance to peek behind the doors of around 17,000 buildings that are usually closed to the public. All over the country visitors can glimpse inside politicians' homes, private crypts and cellars, and the backstage of theaters; many museums open their doors for free as well. Paris has so many wonderful buildings to discover that this event often draws tremendous crowds, so expect to line up and be patient—the wait will be worth it. Late September. journeesdupatrimoine.culture.fr.

Paris-Versailles Walk. Walkers and runners have been taking part in the annual Paris-Versailles Walk, *Grande Classique*, since 1977. It starts on the quay in front of the Eiffel Tower and ends 16km (10 miles) away at the Château de Versailles. Changing rooms and refreshments are available all along the route. Anyone over the age of 16 is invited to enter, but French regulations dictate that you need to send in a medical certificate to prove you're up to the challenge. You'll also need to enroll online beforehand. Late September. parisversailles.com.

Paris Autumn Festival. Encompassing opera, film, dance, and performing arts, Paris's Autumn Festival (*Festival d'Automne*) incorporates more high-powered contemporary arts events than some other cities see in a whole year. Dip into this festival at any point and you'll discover the best productions Paris has to offer. Languages range from Japanese and Russian to French, German, and English (subtitled where necessary in French), so choose your productions wisely. September to January. festival automne.com.

Orchestra playing in Luxembourg Gardens during the Paris Autumn Festival.

OCTOBER

Qatar Prix de l'Arc de Triomphe. Paris's Hippodrome de Longchamp stages the Qatar Prix de l'Arc de Triomphe, the jewel in the crown of French horse racing, attended by around 48,000 onlookers. Part of the prestigious World Series Racing Championship, the Arc is popular with Brits, who cross the channel to watch the action. In addition to the race, expect a wonderful display of horses, hats, and enough champagne to sink a ship. First weekend of October. francegalop-live.com/evenement/qatar-prix-de-larc-de-triomphe.

Montmartre Grape Harvest Fest. The 5-day Montmartre Grape Harvest Festival (Fête des Vendages de Montmartre) celebrates the new Cuvée Montmartre vintage wine (produced on Montmartre's very slopes). Each year, thousands of revelers come to see short film screenings, listen to concerts, and drink vin. Stalls selling regional produce set up shop on the Butte (Montmartre's hill), and a colorful parade in honor of Bacchus fills the cobbled streets. Early to mid-October. fetedesvendangesdemontmartre.com.

Salon du Chocolat. The Salon du Chocolat, at Paris's Porte de Versailles, is heaven for thousands of chocolate lovers who come to devour the international ambrosia and learn how it's made. You can also discover the latest in industry trends from a series of chocolate tastings, demonstrations, and symposiums, and watch chocolatiers create their delicacies. This is a popular event, so buy your ticket online before you go. Late October. salon-du-chocolat.com.

NOVEMBER

Pitchfork Music Festival Paris. Paris's fabulous, week-long indie music festival takes place in multiple spots across the capital, attracting thousands of music fans with the promise of edgy bands and after-show DJ parties. The core of the action is usually around Bastille and the edgy 11th arrondissement. But you'll also find some concerts in prestigious halls, like Salle Pleyel not far from the Champs-Élysées. Early November. pitchforkmusicfestival.fr.

DECEMBER

Festival du Merveilleux. The Musée des Arts Forains (p. 198) is a magical ode to the Belle Epoque in Bercy's former wine warehouses. It is home to a vast collection of 19th- and early-20th-century fairground attractions, from carousels to pipe organs. For 10 days after Christmas, the museum hosts a magical festival that adds magicians, street performers, and musicians to its offerings. Late December to early January. arts-forains.com/en/visitors/le-festival-du-merveilleux.

New Year's Eve. The Champs-Élysées is the place to be (if you can stand the crowds) as the City of Lights lives up to its name with a great sound-and-light show at the Arc de Triomphe, starting about 11pm. Arrive by 9pm to grab a good spot. Alternatively, head to Montmartre, where the streets are full of partygoers, and watch midnight strike from the foot of the Sacré-Coeur with Paris at your feet. You might even be lucky enough to spot a few fireworks on the horizon.

Parade at the Montmartre Grape Harvest Fest.

WHERE TO STAY

Paris has more than 1,500 hotels, from palaces fit for a pasha to tiny, family-run operations whose best features are their warm welcome and personal touch. In theory, you should be able to find something in line with your budget, timeframe, and personal tastes.

WHAT TO EXPECT

Parisian lodgings can be many things: charming, opulent, cozy, homey, and even outrageous. But keep in mind the following: **Parisian hotel rooms tend to be small.** Why do I stress this? Because inevitably, guests who come from countries where hotel rooms are often staggeringly large are shocked when they check into tiny family hotels in ancient buildings.

Don't be too hard on the management, however; most historic Parisian buildings are protected by city regulations that make it difficult, if not impossible, to make structural changes. If you absolutely need room to stretch out, ask for a triple or even a quadruple room (if they're available). Otherwise, consider an international chain hotel, where space and extra amenities are usually not a problem, or an apartment rental.

Amenities

Unless you are staying in a hotel in our "expensive" category, you should be prepared for **minimal amenities.** Washcloths are scarce, toiletries can be few, and some smaller hotels don't have elevators (and when they do, they're often closet size). Assume that most guest rooms are large enough to sleep in comfortably, but you'll have to do your yoga workout somewhere else. All the rooms in the hotels listed below have in-room bathrooms with toilets, unless otherwise mentioned.

Now that we've prepared you for the worst, here's what Parisian hotels *do* have (besides charm and personality, *bien sûr*). Almost all have in-room TVs with cable channels and hair dryers in the bathrooms. Irons and hair dryers (if they are not in the room) can usually be found at the reception desk. Almost all have hotel-wide Wi-Fi. In more expensive hotels, equipment for making hot drinks is usually standard.

Most hotel rooms have air-conditioning, which can be a godsend, especially between July and September. Double-check if you're coming in summer; there's nothing worse than a room on a

> **Going Solo**
>
> Though the listings below show room rates for two people, single rooms are often available for solo travelers at reduced rates. The best tactic is to ask the hotel directly, since they don't always advertise their smallest rooms, even on their own websites.

non-air-conditioned top floor facing a noisy street, making it impossible to open the windows at night.

While a continental **breakfast** (juice, coffee, or tea, and a croissant and/or baguette) is still the traditional way to start the day, many hotels now also offer a generous buffet that may include various breads, sweet buns, fruit, yogurt, ham, cereal, juice, and sometimes eggs and bacon. A buffet breakfast might seem pricey at somewhere between 15€ to 30€, but keep in mind that a bare-bones continental version will usually cost at least 10€. If you are a light eater, you'll likely spend less and have more fun at the corner cafe. Romantics will appreciate the fact that at most hotels, you can have your breakfast delivered to your room for no extra charge.

PRACTICAL MATTERS
When & How to Reserve

First and foremost, make sure you understand the cancellation policy before you book. Most hotels take at least 1 night's stay as a deposit, which they will keep if you don't show up or cancel in time. What's more, cancellation policies vary depending on the type of rate or package you end up with. Like airlines, some of the very lowest hotel rates are non-refundable. You'll also need to comparision shop. While online travel-booking sites like Expedia, Booking.com, Hotelscombined.com, and Priceline are convenient for searching room rates, often the best place to look is the hotel's official website, particularly in the case of smaller, affordable hotels. Why? Those booking sites charge hotel fees as much as 20%, a percentage that many hotels feel obliged to pass on to the customer.

Perpetually fluctuating prices make it difficult to fix rates in guidebooks; the prices quoted here attempt to offer a realistic range. ***Note:*** Unless indicated, rates do not include breakfast.

High & Low Seasons

Parisian hotel rate fluctuations are a little like the weather—it's difficult to distinguish one season from the other. Everyone seems to agree that August is the lowest of low season. That's when most of France heads for the beach, and hotels are desperate for business. September

> **Parisian Hotels & Accessibility**
>
> Hotels in centuries-old buildings may be full of charm, but they also often feature narrow staircases and/or tiny elevators. If accessibility is a concern, be sure to check when you reserve. Parisian hotels are evolving: All hotels in the moderate and expensive categories are supposed to have at least one wheelchair-accessible room.

> ### Seeing Stars
>
> French hotels are graded by a government-regulated system that hands out 0 to 5 stars (plus "Palace" status for upper-end five-starred properties; see p. 71), which the hotels then must post at the entrance to their establishment. Unfortunately, palaces aside, the criteria used often have more to do with quantity than quality. Rooms are rated for size, number of beds, and the presence or absence of items like hair dryers and minibars—overall atmosphere and charm are not necessarily a factor. It's possible to end up in a darling three-star hotel that's much nicer than a four-star down the street with big rooms and a minibar but all the ambience of a rehab center. What's more, the addition of a fifth star prompted everyone to try to jump up a notch, so the most basic hotel might now have three stars. One thing is sure: The more stars it has, the more a hotel is allowed to charge. **Our advice:** Use the French star system as a rough estimate of quality, then do some homework on your own.
>
> By the way, the hearts beside the listings below are our own and have no relation to the French star system. You'll find our criteria at the front of the book.

and October are usually high season, while November and January are low season. Once spring arrives, prices tend to rise. December on the run-up to Christmas is also low, but the days around New Year's are high. The rest of the year is a free-for-all, heavily dependent on the scheduling of trade shows (over 420 a year) and Paris Fashion Week, when prices rise. For the nitty-gritty on trade show dates, visit the **Paris Tourist Office site** (parisjetaime.com) and click on "Events," then "Fairs and Trade Shows in Paris," where you can get a rundown on both trade shows and conventions.

THE RIGHT BANK
Louvre & Île de la Cité (1st Arrondissement)

It was here that Paris began, and it is here that you will still find a great number of the city's most famous sights—and the highest concentration of tourists. While the central location is tempting, this is not necessarily where you will find rows of cute neighborhood stores (shops tend to be expensive and geared to tourists) or a slice of typical Parisian life. What's more, the area is pretty dead at night. But, if you are in town for only 1 or 2 days, a central locale is key, since time will be of the essence. Plus, there are worse places to wake up than a few minutes' walk from the Louvre's bedazzling architecture.

price CATEGORIES

Expensive	320€ and up
Moderate	171€–319€
Inexpensive	Under 170€

EXPENSIVE

Cheval Blanc Paris ♥♥ Set within the iconic Samaritaine department store (p. 247) along the Seine, this ultra-refined spot is one of the only hotels in Paris to overlook the Seine—and not just any stretch of the river: the historic part, where the water flows gracefully around the islands, past Notre-Dame and the city's glorious tree-lined quays. If that's not romantic enough for you, romance oozes inside the hotel's Dior spa (home to a 30m/98-ft. pool and a hammam) and in its restaurants—especially the ultra-gastronomique Japanese eatery and the chic rooftop brasserie, which morphs into an all-day cocktail bar with 360° skyline views—perfect for a panoramic tête-à-tête. Rooms are an elegant mix of Art Deco and contemporary details, and many offer views over the Seine, the rooftops, and/or monuments like the Pompidou Center, the Eiffel Tower, and Montmartre. It's a mega-splurge to stay here, but even if you can't afford a night, stop by for the rooftop or a refined afternoon tea.

8 quai du Louvre, 1st arrond. chevalblanc.com. **01-40-28-00-00.** 72 units. 1,350€–2,200€ double; 2,200€ and up suite. Métro: Louvre-Rivoli or Châtelet. **Amenities:** Restaurant; bar; gym; spa; children's playroom; concierge; room service; free Wi-Fi.

MODERATE

Hôtel Brighton ♥♥♥ If you spring for a room with a view at this gracious hotel, you will not be disappointed. A splendid vista from the Louvre to the Tuileries Garden and the Eiffel Tower spreads before you as you loll in your bed. While not every room has the jackpot view, most in the "deluxe" and

Room with a view at Hôtel Brighton.

Lobby at Hôtel Thérèse.

"executive" categories do, and all have a subdued, sophisticated decor with elegant fabrics draping the windows and tasteful decorative touches. Top-notch bedding, plush bathrobes, and high thread counts are all part of the package. In short, this classy establishment belongs under the arcades of the rue de Rivoli. Rooms are spacious and airy, with roomy bathrooms and a mix of reproduction and real antique pieces. Understandably, rooms with views book up early.

218 rue de Rivoli, 1st arrond. paris-hotel-brighton.com. ✆ **01-47-03-61-61.** 61 units. 230€–600€ double; 286€–780€ suite (sleeps 2–4). Métro: Tuileries. **Amenities:** Restaurant; bar; concierge; laundry service; room service; tearoom; free Wi-Fi.

Hôtel Thérèse ♥♥♥ Just a few steps from the Palais Royal and a few more from the Louvre, these beautiful lodgings combine old-fashioned charm with modern chic. Comfy sofas invite you to relax in the lobby, whose decor includes lots of mirrors, bookcases, and unique lighting fixtures. The stylish yet comfortable vibe extends to the rooms, which feature soft grey/teal blues, subtle geometric patterns, upholstered headboards, and, on the third floor, very high ceilings. Despite its central location, the tiny street is very quiet, and light floods the building from both sides. Rooms are Parisian size, which means the least expensive are small; the rates go up with the dimensions.

5–7 rue Thérèse, 1st arrond. hoteltherese.com. ✆ **01-42-96-10-01.** 40 units. 180€–370€ double; 315€–450€ family room (up to 4). Métro: Palais Royal–Musée du Louvre or Pyramides. **Amenities:** Bar; bicycles; concierge; laundry service; loaner laptops; room service; free Wi-Fi.

INEXPENSIVE

Hôtel du Cygne ♥ Chock-full of exposed beams and stone walls (not to mention narrow stairways—there is no elevator), this 17th-century building has been carefully restored, and the simple lodgings receive ongoing tender loving care from Isabelle Gouge, the friendly owner. Most rooms are predictably small,

Right Bank West Hotels

Cheval Blanc Paris **13**	Hôtel Chopin **9**	Hôtel Thérèse **14**
Hôtel 34B **8**	Hôtel du Cygne **12**	The Hoxton **10**
Hôtel Arvor **6**	Hôtel La Fantaisie **7**	Monsieur George **2**
Hôtel Bachaumont **11**	Hôtel Lancaster **3**	New Orient Hôtel **5**
Hôtel Brighton **15**	Hôtel Passy Eiffel **1**	Le Pavillon des Lettres **4**

but are cheerfully decorated with fresh white walls, floral bedspreads, and the owner's personal touches. The reward for the climb to the top floor is a roomy suite that can sleep three. Because the hotel is near Les Halles and the Montorgueil neighborhood (very hip at night), staying on a Sunday is much cheaper than other nights. Some single rooms have bathrooms down the corridor and start at the unbeatable price of 13.50€ a night (yes, really!).

3–5 rue du Cygne, 1st arrond. hotelducygne.fr. **01-42-60-14-16.** 18 units. 81€–150€ double; 126€–200€ suite for up to 3 people. Métro: Etienne Marcel. RER: Les Halles. **Amenities:** Free Wi-Fi.

The Marais (3rd & 4th Arrondissements)

Centuries ago, this neighborhood was a swamp (*marais*), but now it's merely swamped with stylish boutiques and restaurants. Stunning 16th- and 17th-century mansions, which had fallen into disrepair, have been scrubbed down and fixed up over the past few decades, and they shine like pearls along the narrow streets of this fashionable area. The many excellent museums here include the **Picasso-Paris** (p. 181) and the **Musée Carnavalet** (p. 178). In short, this is a great area to stay in, but it's also a victim of its own success. You might not hear a lot of French in some of those cute cafes on rue Vielle du Temple. The northern Marais (in the 3rd arrond.) is generally quieter and less assailed by tourists.

EXPENSIVE

Pavillon de la Reine ♥♥♥   Just off the Place des Vosges, this "Queen's Pavilion" harkens back to when the magnificent square was the home of royalty. You certainly feel like a noble as you pass through an arcade into a small

Restaurant Anne in the courtyard garden at Pavillon de la Reine.

Right Bank East Hotels

Deskopolitan House Hotel Paris **11**
Le Citizen **2**
Eden Lodge Paris **10**
Generator Paris **1**
Hôtel Caron de Beaumarchais **6**
Hôtel de la Porte Dorée **12**
Hôtel Jeanne d'Arc Le Marais **7**
Hôtel Jules et Jim **3**
Hôtel Saint-Louis-en-L'Isle **5**
Maison Breguet **9**
Pavillon de la Reine **8**
The People—Paris Nation **11**
Sinner **4**

WHERE TO STAY | The Right Bank

formal garden and enter this elegant mansion. Despite its 56 rooms, the hotel feels small and intimate. The decor is a suave and subtle combination of modern and antique history: Dark period furniture blends with rich colors on the walls and beds, and choice objects and historic details abound. Several of the deluxe rooms are duplexes with a cozy sleeping loft. Guests have access to a full spa, offering sauna and fitness room, as well as massages and treatments. There's also a chic French restaurant, **Anne,** with a 79€ lunch menu and 190€ tasting menu that are worth staying in for (Wed–Sat lunch and dinner; Sun lunch only).

28 pl. des Vosges, 3rd arrond. pavillon-de-la-reine.com. **01-40-29-19-19.** 56 units. 450€–1,125€ double; 1,100€ and up suite. Métro: Bastille. **Amenities:** Bar; restaurant; concierge; fitness room; laundry service; room service; sauna; spa; free Wi-Fi.

Sinner ♥♥♥   Looking for a quirky splurge? Celebrated Parisian designer Tristan Auer has turned a standard Parisian building on rue du Temple into a joyously rebellious hotel with daring decor inspired by medieval religious iconography and the Templar knights who once lived in the area. Its dark hallways are lit by lanterns, stained-glass windows add pops of unexpected color, and each room is a different constellation of artwork and wood furnishings. There's even a concept store set in a dark crypt and a spa modeled on Roman baths. A hip cocktail lounge overlooks the restaurant, which has church-style paneling, cathedral ceilings, and a street food–inspired menu.

116 rue du Temple, 3rd arrond. sinnerparis.com. **01-42-72-20-00.** 43 units. 331€–800€ double; 1,200€ suite for up to 4 people. Métro: Rambuteau. **Amenities:** Restaurant; bar; spa; room service; laundry service; fitness equipment on request; free Wi-Fi.

The bar at Sinner Paris.

MODERATE

Hôtel Caron de Beaumarchais ♥♥♥   In the 18th century, Pierre Augustin Caron de Beaumarchais—author of *The Barber of Seville* and *The Marriage of Figaro*—lived near here, and this small hotel celebrates both the playwright and the magnificent century he lived in. The walls are covered in high-quality reproductions of period fabrics; rooms are furnished with authentic antique writing tables and chandeliers; and period paintings and first-edition pages of *The Barber of Seville* hang on the walls. The rooms are smallish, but the high ceilings (with exposed beams) and tall windows let in lots of light, making them feel spacious. Food stores, buses, and Métro stops are close by too, and it's a short walk to the Seine. *Note:* Some beds are not standard sizes.

12 rue Vieille-du-Temple, 4th arrond. carondebeaumarchais.com. **01-42-72-34-12.** 19 units. 170€–340€ double. Métro: St-Paul or Hôtel de Ville. **Amenities:** Free Wi-Fi.

Hôtel Jules et Jim ♥♥   The entrance to this gem of a hotel is so discreet you could walk right past it. Find your way inside and you're in for a treat: A cobbled courtyard with an outdoor fireplace merges into a low-key cocktail bar with vintage-inspired furniture, while the guest rooms—all ultra-comfortable—flaunt hip decor such as white walls with clever backlighting and beautiful wall art. Some have bathrooms with floor-to-ceiling windows; others, on the upper floors, provide panoramic rooftop views. The duplex suite is resplendent in dark woods and retro-chic furniture (but its staircase is not child-proof, so this isn't appropriate for families with toddlers).

11 rue des Gravilliers, 3rd arrond. hoteljulesetjim.com. ⓒ **01-44-54-13-13.** 23 units. 230€–450€ double; 400€ duplex for up to 4 people. Métro: Arts et Métiers. **Amenities:** Cocktail bar; free Wi-Fi.

Hôtel Saint-Louis en l'Isle ♥♥   Set on the tiny main drag of the tranquil Île Saint-Louis, this friendly place has a prime location on one of the city's most desirable pieces of real estate. The impeccable rooms are done up in a low-key modern style with historic touches: stone floors, dark wood furniture, and framed etchings of 17th- and 18th-century nobles. The street-side rooms are quiet but a little dark; if you want a lot of light, ask for a corner room or splurge on one of the rooms on the top floor. The elevators stop at landings between floors, so you'll have to be able to manage stairs here. A wheelchair-accessible room is on the ground floor.

75 rue St-Louis-en-l'Île, 4th arrond. saintlouisenlisle.com. ⓒ **01-46-34-04-80.** 20 units. 236€–300€ double; 245€–350€ triple. Métro: Pont Marie. **Amenities:** Free Wi-Fi.

INEXPENSIVE
Hôtel Jeanne d'Arc Le Marais ♥♥♥   Considering its prime location in the southern Marais, right next to the leafy Place du Marché Ste-Catherine, this cozy hotel is an incredible deal. Simple, tasteful rooms have textured wallpaper and contemporary lighting fixtures. Everything is impeccable, from the quality bedding to the spotless bathrooms. Families will be interested in the spacious and reasonably priced quads. Rooms book up months in advance, especially for fashion weeks (Feb, Mar, July, and Sept), so get in early if you can.

3 rue de Jarente, 4th arrond. hoteljeannedarc.com. ⓒ **01-48-87-62-11.** 34 units. 115€–320€ double; 142€–420€ quad. Métro: St-Paul. **Amenities:** Computer in lobby; free Wi-Fi.

Champs-Élysées, Trocadéro & Western Paris (8th, 16th & 17th Arrondissements)

Even grander than the 7th arrondissement on the Left Bank, the area around the Champs-Élysées is positively mythic. To the south of the boulevard, along avenues Montaigne and George V, are the most exclusive designer shops in the city; to the north, elegant buildings, shops, and expensive restaurants stretch up to Parc Monceau, which has excellent museum neighbors, including **Musée Nissim de Camondo** (p. 191). Affordable lodgings are scarce around here, especially near the Champs and the Arc de Triomphe, where the high prices often have more to do with location than accommodation quality. Ironically, the location is not particularly central; it's a 40-minute hike from here to Notre-Dame, but you will be well served by public transport.

EXPENSIVE

Hôtel Lancaster ♥♥♥   Beautiful artworks adorn much of this luxurious lodging, built in the classic Haussmann style in 1889, just off the Champs-Élysées. The whole place oozes class, yet feels very discreet—which is probably why movies stars and film directors have flocked here over the years (and still do). Rooms are spacious, with huge beds, high thread counts and typical period moldings and furniture. The ambience is classic and very French, with high ceilings and subtle colors. Things get more contemporary in the CopperBay cocktail bar downstairs—dressed up in blues and golds, and in the restaurant, Monsieur Lancaster, where France's regions are highlighted through an ever-changing menu that might include beef bourguignon (from Burgundy) and cassoulet (from the Southwest). You can eat and drink in the adjacent hidden courtyard too. Also tucked away is the tiny spa on the top floor, with a balcony overlooking the rooftops. Interesting historical fact: During WWII, the hotel was owned by Swiss hotelier, Emile Wolf, who managed to negotiate neutrality for the hotel during the Nazi Occupation. As a result, despite the omnipresence of the Nazis in Paris, not a single German soldier ever stepped foot on the premises.

7 rue de Berri, 8th arrond. hotel-lancaster.com. **01-40-76-40-76.** 56 units. 510€–800€ double; 1,000€ and up suite. Métro: George V. **Amenities:** Restaurant; bar; spa; babysitting; business center; dry cleaning; room service; concierge; free Wi-Fi.

Marlène Dietrich suite at Hôtel Lancaster.

An executive room at Monsieur George.

Monsieur George ♥♥♥ Steps from the Champs-Élysées, this hotel (named after George Washington) is as refined as its surroundings and has a lovely young staff to attend to your (almost) every need. Chic rooms in blacks, grays, and blues have a distinct Art Deco feel that continues in the bathrooms, where the marble sinks and gold taps wouldn't look amiss on a luxury 1920s ocean liner. Several rooms have small balconies, and a few even overlook the Sacré-Coeur or the Eiffel Tower; the all-white suites are fresh and airy. The garden suite is a duplex with its own garden courtyard. Guests have access to the hotel's spa and fitness space, set under vaulted ceilings. There's also a hip bar, a brasserie, and a one Michelin-star restaurant, **Galanga.**

17 rue Washington, 8th arrond. monsieurgeorge.com. © **01-87-89-48-48.** 46 units. 343€–650€ double; 670€ and up suite. Métro: Georges V. **Amenities:** Restaurant; bar; fitness center; spa; concierge; loaner smart devices; room service; laundry service; free Wi-Fi.

MODERATE

Hôtel Passy Eiffel ♥♥ These colorful lodgings are on a cute shopping street in Passy, previously its own village before it got gobbled up by the city. Rooms are individually decorated in lots of warm neutral colors, blues, and mauves, with most featuring patterned wallpaper. Everything is in tip-top condition, and double-paned windows keep out most street noise. If you are a light sleeper, ask for a courtyard room. For extra romance, request a room with an Eiffel Tower view. For a pre-dinner drink, make a beeline for the small garden courtyard, hidden away from the street.

10 rue de Passy, 16th arrond. passyeiffel.com. © **01-45-25-55-66.** 49 units. 190€–370€ double. Métro: Passy or La Muette. **Amenities:** Bar; concierge; free Wi-Fi.

Le Pavillon des Lettres ♥♥♥ Tastefully chic, this hotel is in the navel of the French political universe, being just across the street from the powerful Ministry of the Interior. The theme here, however, is literature. Each of the 26 exquisite rooms is designated by a different letter and linked to a famous author. If you are in room Z, for example, you might find a copy of Zola's *Nana* on the bedside table and some of the author's text on the wall. The room design is serenely hip, with handsome shades of gray, olive green, beige, and mauve. While the rooms are a little small, the ceilings are mostly high and bathrooms are spacious. Tapas are served at cocktail hour.

12 rue des Saussaies, 8th arrond. pavillondeslettres.com. ⓒ **01-49-24-26-26.** 26 units. 315€–420€ double; 400€–750€ junior suite. Métro: Madeleine. **Amenities:** Bar; bicycles; concierge; library; laundry service; room service; loaner iPads; free Wi-Fi.

INEXPENSIVE

New Orient Hôtel ♥♥♥   This lovely hotel offers comfortable rooms with high ceilings, 19th-century moldings, and colorful fabrics. While it may not be on top of the Champs-Élysées, it's not far, and it's close to stately Parc Monceau and a quick trot to the Saint Lazare train station. The friendly owners, who are inveterate flea-market browsers, have refinished and restored the antique furniture themselves. Rooms (many of which have small balconies) are small but in tip-top shape, and the bathrooms sparkle. Though the hotel has an elevator, you'll have to negotiate stairs to get to it. The best rates are on the hotel website.

16 rue de Constantinople, 8th arrond. hotelneworient.com. ⓒ **01-45-22-21-64.** 30 units. 160€–250€ double; 170€–300€ triple. Métro: Villiers, Europe, or St-Lazare. **Amenities:** Computer in lobby; concierge; free Wi-Fi.

A junior suite at Le Pavillon des Lettres.

Palace Hotels

The ultimate in upscale Parisian hospitality is the Palace Hotel, a rating given only to establishments able to symbolize "excellence and perfection, luxury and timelessness." It's here you'll find many of the Michelin-starred restaurants, spas, pools, and big bedrooms, as well as well-to-do Parisians looking for time out in sumptuous surroundings. Palaces usually occupy historically important buildings, like the **Peninsula** (peninsula.com), where George Gershwin wrote *An American in Paris* in 1928.

Our favorites are: **Le Bristol** (lebristolparis.com), for its enduring elegance, the best hot chocolate in town, and outstanding dining; **Le Crillon** (rosewoodhotels.com), for the James Bond–esque spa and pool, decorated with 17,600 gold scales, and the winter garden, which serves one of the best afternoon teas in town; **Le Lutetia** (hotellutetia.com), for its brasserie set under a sumptuous glass ceiling, and **La Réserve** (lareserve-paris.com), for its wonderful boutique feel, great restaurant, and luxury spa. Rooms in these establishments usually start at around 2,000€, but you can get a "more affordable" feel for the luxury by popping in for a cocktail at the bar (about 32€, but always served with nibbles) or an afternoon tea (expect to pay around 80€ per person).

The terrace of the Honeymoon Suite at Le Bristol.

Opéra & Grands Boulevards (2nd & 9th Arrondissements)

Grands Boulevards (those wide throughways that Baron Haussmann plowed through Paris in the 19th c.) and just below Montmartre is a lovely mix of hip bars and restaurants and old-time Paris, with a good sprinkling of small museums for a dose of culture. While you won't find too many big monuments around here, the area's upsides include lower room rates and a more neighborhood-y feel, at least away from the boulevards.

EXPENSIVE

Hôtel La Fantaisie ♥♥♥   This hip hotel has a lot going for it: Its location (on village-like rue Cadet lined with boutiques, cafes, and delis in a non-touristy part of the 9th) makes you feels like you're in "real" Paris; the decor (a savvy, retro-inspired mix of wicker, velvet, and kitschy knickknacks) wouldn't look amiss in a Wes Anderson movie; and the restaurant serves well-executed menu. As if that weren't enough, there's a lush garden, a rooftop bar, and a spa. Now sigh!

24 rue Cadet, 9th arrond. lafantaisie.com. ⓒ **01-55-07-85-07.** 73 units. 366€–690€ double; from 750€ suite. Métro: Cadet. **Amenities:** Restaurant; bar; rooftop bar; spa; concierge; room service; free Wi-Fi.

MODERATE

Hôtel Bachaumont ♥♥ Art Deco design gets a colorful, modern twist in this trendy little spot in the Montorgeuil district that draws Parisians as much as travelers, thanks to an excellent brasserie and a cocktail

Junior Suite Terrasse at Hôtel La Fantasie.

bar that serves inventive drinks with French ingredients (think cognac and Saint Germain, a liqueur made from elderberry flowers). Sit below the beautiful glass ceiling and tuck into delights like juicy steak in wine-rich Bordelaise sauce, and langoustines with sage potatoes. Then sleep it off in sleek, blue-toned rooms set with dark-wood retro furnishings. Standard rooms are larger than most (if you're a light sleeper, ask for a courtyard room overlooking the brasserie's atrium), while suites are downright big for Paris.

18 rue Bachaumont, 2nd arrond. hotelbachaumont.com. ⓒ **01-81-66-47-00.** 49 units. 199€–340€ double; 400€–600€ suite. Métro: Sentier or Etienne-Marcel. **Amenities:** Restaurant; bar; room service; massage room; fitness room; free Wi-Fi.

The Hoxton ♥♥♥   Set in a sumptuous 18th-century mansion, this place oozes class, from the cobblestone atrium and trendy brasserie to the cocktail bar dressed up in granny-tastic floral wallpaper. Rooms are just as lovely, mixing fun, midcentury-style furnishings with elegant classics such as chevron timber floors and typical Parisian moldings. Free breakfast is delivered to your room each morning and complimentary international calls. Oh, and you'll be staying in one of the city's most up-and-coming areas too, smack bang in the Sentier (a foodie hot spot) by Grands Boulevards, home to theaters and bars. *A word of warning:* A party vibe reigns here, and in warm weather, when the courtyards teem, noise can be an issue. Ask for a quiet room—or if you can't beat 'em, join 'em!

30–32 rue du Sentier, 2nd arrond. thehoxton.com/paris. ⓒ **01-85-65-75-00.** 172 units. 327€–600€ double. Métro: Bonne Nouvelle or Grands Boulevards. **Amenities:** Restaurant; cocktail bar; room service; minibar; free Wi-Fi.

INEXPENSIVE

Hôtel Arvor ♥♥   These spiffy lodgings are in the charming "New Athens" neighborhood, where 19th-century Romantics like George Sand and Frédéric Chopin lived and worked. Maybe that's why Mme. Flamarion, of the famous French publishing house, decided to open this arty yet relaxed hotel, where fresh white walls show off modern photography and art prints. Rooms are a little small, but simple and chic. Those on the upper floors have nice rooftop views, and some of the suites offer a glimpse of the far-off Eiffel Tower. The airy lobby, with large windows and shelves full of books, is an invitation to kick back and catch up on your reading.

8 rue Laferrière, 9th arrond. hotelarvor.com. © **01-48-78-60-92.** 30 units. 80€–260€ double; 160€–320€ suite. Métro: St-Georges. **Amenities:** Bar; room service; free Wi-Fi.

Hôtel Chopin ♥♥ Nestled at the back of the delightful Passage Jouffroy, this budget hotel has remarkably quiet rooms considering its location in the bustle of the Grands Boulevards. The staircase is a little creaky (you will have to climb a flight to get to the elevator), but the refreshed rooms are clean and colorful, and the bathrooms are spotless. Rooms on the upper floors get more light; many have nice views of Parisian rooftops. Across the street from the Passage Jouffroy is Passage des Panoramas, a maze of hip bistros and shops.

10 bd. Montmartre or 46 passage Jouffroy, 9th arrond. hotel-chopin.com. © **01-47-70-58-10.** 36 units. 100€–190€ double; from 170€ triple. Métro: Grands Boulevards or Richelieu-Drouot. **Amenities:** Free Wi-Fi.

Hôtel 34B ♥♥ In an upbeat, restaurant-rich part of town, this quirky, France-themed hotel offers comfortable lodgings at great prices. Rooms have modern decor, with cool headboards made to look like stripy French T-shirts or clusters of berets, and glass desks filled with fake turf and miniature French cars or bikes. Wallpaper in the corridors is a bold recreation of the French flag, a design mirrored on the facades overlooking the lobby atrium. Freebies

The atrium lobby at Hôtel 34B.

include breakfast for kids 12 and under, non-alcoholic minibar drinks, and afternoon soft drinks. There's also a fitness room and a sauna.

34 rue Bergère, 9th arrond. en.astotel.com/hotel/34b-en/overview. ⓒ **01-47-70-34-34.** 128 units. 81€–180€. Métro: Grands Boulevards. **Amenities:** Sauna; gym; free Wi-Fi.

Montmartre (18th Arrondissement)

If you're looking for a romantic setting, you can't do much better than Montmartre. Once you get away from the tourist hordes that invade Sacré-Coeur and Place du Tertre, you'll find lovely little lanes and small houses that harken back to the days when Picasso and the boys were at the Bateau Lavoir. Unfortunately, the pickings are a bit slim if you want to actually sleep here. If you are determined to stay up on the Butte, book early, as the few quality lodgings are generally in high demand.

EXPENSIVE

Hôtel Particulier Montmartre ♥♥ If your vision of Montmartre involves secret little cobbled lanes and old town houses with tree-filled gardens, this chic, arty hotel is for you. To get to it, you must buzz in from the street, then take a narrow, private path—Passage de la Sorcière (aka the "witch's alley")—to an elegant former mansion. Each of the five suites was designed by a different artist: One evokes a fancy bordello, with a riot of leopard print on all the walls; another has psychedelic floral wallpaper and stunning views over the garden; all are sumptuous. For extra pizzazz, the loft-like top-floor suite is awash in natural light and flaunts a glass roof with views over the city and the Eiffel Tower. The hotel's on-site restaurant, **Le Grand**

A themed room at Hôtel Particulier Montmartre.

Montmartre Hotels

B Montmartre **1**
Hôtel des Arts Montmartre **4**
Hôtel Particulier Montmartre **5**
Le Relais Montmartre **2**
Terrass" Hotel **3**

Salon, offers exquisite French dishes with a modern twist and has an old world–style courtyard—a glorious treat on a sunny day.

23 av. Junot (Pavillon D), 18th arrond. hotelparticulier.com. **01-53-41-81-40.** 5 units. 560€–900€ suite. Métro: Lamarck Caulincourt. **Amenities:** Restaurant; bar; garden; laundry service; room service; free Wi-Fi.

MODERATE

B Montmartre ♥♥♥   Just a 5-minute walk from the "Butte," off Place de Clichy, this lovely hotel has a hidden garden, an oasis of shrubbery and palm trees quite unlike anywhere else in the area. Many of the classic rooms—all relaxing beiges and browns—overlook it, as does the bar, and on warm days, breakfast is served there, too. Rooms are housed in two buildings: the original "town house" and a modern annex. The top-floor spaces have the best views, offering photogenic sweeps of the city's rooftops. If you're looking for extra pampering, ask for the room with a private hammam, or fork out for a suite, which comes with a balcony.

6 rue Lécluse, 17th arrond. b-montmartre.com. **01-42-93-35-77.** 36 units. 190€–270€; from 250€ suite. Métro: Place de Clichy. **Amenities:** Bar; free Wi-Fi.

Hôtel des Arts Montmartre ♥♥   On a narrow street just off lively rue des Abbesses, this unassuming hotel once hosted artists and sculptors and even a few dancers from the Moulin Rouge. It's currently run by the third generation of the Lameyre family. Today's guests enjoy the great rates, comfortable lodgings, and welcoming atmosphere. Rooms are small yet spotless, with funky decor, reminiscent of the '80s. A few have distant views of the Eiffel Tower over Parisian rooftops; the "Romantic" room comes with a bottle of champagne and has a small balcony. Montmartre's two remaining windmills, Moulin de la Galette and Moulin du Radet, are just up the street.

5 rue Tholozé, 18th arrond. arts-hotel-paris.com. © **01-46-06-30-52.** 50 units. 166€–300€ double. Parking 19€. Métro: Blanche or Abbesses. **Amenities:** Concierge; room service; free Wi-Fi.

Terrass" Hotel ♥   Most upper-floor rooms in this trendy hotel (once frequented by Dalí and Renoir) afford amazing cityscapes, from the steel-gray rooftops in the east to the filigreed silhouette of the Eiffel Tower in the west. Head to the rooftop bar-restaurant for cocktails and delicious seafood-inspired dishes. On some nights, live bands add to the atmosphere, playing everything from chanson to jazz. Or, after a busy day sightseeing, wind down in the hotel's Nuxe spa, with its massage rooms, hammam, sauna, and a rain shower. Another perk is the fitness center, where guests can sign up for weekend yoga,

The panoramic restaurant at Terrass" Hotel.

Hôtel Le Relais Montmartre.

Pilates, or even Kalon, which was created by former cabaret dancers and mixes yoga, Pilates, and bar work.

12 rue Joseph de Maistre, 18th arrond. terrass-hotel.com. © **01-46-06-72-85.** 100 units. 170€–285€ double; 770€ suite. Métro: Place de Clichy or Blanche. **Amenities:** Restaurant; bar; spa; fitness center; rooftop; room service; free Wi-Fi.

INEXPENSIVE

Le Relais Montmartre ♥♥   These comfortable lodgings include small but impeccable rooms decked out in light, warm colors and a stylish, classic decor of tasteful floral prints. The hotel is on a peaceful little side street, right around the corner from a delicious stretch of food shops on rue Lepic. Families can book into the adjoining rooms. In good weather, breakfast is served on a lovely little patio, with products brought in from the aforementioned gourmet shops. If you're in a hurry, or fancy a lighter breakfast, the 8€ option—juice, a pastry and a hot drink—is a very good value, costing roughly the same as in a cafe.

6 rue Constance, 18th arrond. hotel-relais-montmartre.com. © **01-70-64-25-25.** 26 units. 138€–200€ double. Métro: Blanche. **Amenities:** Concierge; laundry service; free Wi-Fi.

République, Bastille & Eastern Paris (11th & 12th Arrondissements)

Just north of the Marais, this shabby-chic, up-and-coming area offers low rates and proximity to the nightlife around rue Oberkampf. Nearby, the Faubourg St-Antoine area is an El Dorado for exciting restaurants and has nice lodging options; though it doesn't look central on the map, it has excellent public transport. This historic workers' neighborhood was where revolutionary fervor came to a head on July 14, 1789, when irate citizens stormed down the boulevard and took over the Bastille. Things have calmed down considerably since then, and outside of the festive bar and club scene around the Bastille and rue de Charonne, it's a pretty laid-back area.

MODERATE

Deskopolitan House Hotel Paris ♥♥ Want to see Paris's forward-thinking side? This high-concept hotel occupies a former distillery on a mini-campus that includes a fitness center, a fabulous Mediterranean restaurant, **Laïa** (p. 126), and a coworking space run by Deskopolitan, hence the hotel name. It's one of the city's only hotels to include unlimited time at a coworking desk for the price of the room—a godsend if you're mixing business and pleasure. Rooms are comfy and colorful, with a kitchenette and views over the courtyard garden, plus you're a short stroll from one of the foodiest streets in the 11th, **rue Paul Bert.** The hotel is tucked away from the street; you enter through large doors and walk to the back of a courtyard.

226 bd. Voltaire, 11th arrond. deskopolitan.com/hotel-deskopolitan-house. ⓒ **01-88-45-30-12.** 14 units. 183€–300€ double. Métro: Rue des Boulets. **Amenities:** Coworking access; free Wi-Fi.

Eden Lodge Paris ♥♥♥ Hidden from the street in the back of a beautiful garden, this modern wooden structure combines environmental awareness with extremely comfortable lodgings. There are only five rooms and breakfast is free, so some might call this a bed-and-breakfast instead of a hotel. Quality insulation, LED lighting, solar panels, and zero-carbon output give these lodgings their ecological cred. There's no skimping on comfort, though: Rooms are chic, warm, and minimalist, with vintage-esque furniture and high-tech Japanese toilets. A microwave and refrigerator are

An in-room kitchenette at Deskopolitan House Hotel Paris.

The leafy courtyard of Eden Lodge Paris.

available for guests in the breakfast room, which is open all day. Bicycles are on hand, as well as a 500-sq.-m (5,381-sq.-ft.) garden for communing with nature.

175 rue de Charonne, 11th arrond. edenlodgeparis.net. ☏ **01-43-56-73-24.** 5 units. 235€ double; 365€ suite. Rates include breakfast. Métro: Alexandre Dumas. **Amenities:** Bicycles; garden; free Wi-Fi.

Maison Breguet ♥♥♥ With its slick glass-roofed cocktail bar and a bistro serving modern versions of traditional French dishes, this hip five-star embodies the up-and-coming vibe of the 11th arrondissement. You can dine in the peaceful courtyard on sunny days, and the rooms are as cool as can be, with a classy retro-Scandinavian vibe and an earthy color palette. The other draw here (aside from the price, which is lower than most other five-starred properties) is the wellness area, with a lovely indoor pool, sauna, hammam, and gym. It's also a good one for families, with cots and loaner strollers.

8 rue Breguet, 11th arrond. maisonbreguet.com. ☏ **01-58-30-32-31.** 53 units. 240€–368€ double; from 384€ suite. Métro: Breguet Sabin or Chemin Vert. **Amenities:** Restaurant; bar; indoor pool; sauna; fitness rooms; hammam; free Wi-Fi.

INEXPENSIVE

Hôtel de la Porte Dorée ♥♥ True, it's a little out of the way, but these lovely lodgings are well worth the Métro fare. Soothing neutral tones, antique headboards, high ceilings, wood floors, and original curlicue moldings are all part of the package at this hotel, which is owned by a friendly Franco-American couple. The hotel goes the extra mile for both the environment (ecologically correct policies) and babies (toys, playpens, and even potty seats available). And you'll pay less for all this than you will for something utterly basic in the center of town. What's more, it is right next to the verdant **Bois de Vincennes,** where

Guest room in Hôtel de la Porte Dorée.

you can rent bikes, picnic, or visit the Paris zoo (p. 198). The nearby Métro will get you to the touristy part of the city center in about 15 minutes.

273 av. Daumensil, 12th arrond. hoteldelaportedoree.com. ✆ **01-43-07-56-97.** 43 units. 90€–184€ double; 135€ triple and up. Métro: Porte Dorée. **Amenities:** Babysitting; bicycles; free Wi-Fi.

The People – Paris Nation

♥♥ The area of Nation (just east of Bastille) is off the tourist radar, yet it's a great place to stay for a slice of real Parisian life. Métro lines 1, 2, 6 and 9, and RER A (direct to Disney) all pass here, so you can easily move around the city; not a single tourist is in sight in the cafés, and there's this place—The People—Paris Nation, a funky little hostel with a sought-after roof terrace and breathtaking views across Place de la Nation. Though a hostel per-se, with dorms for four to eight people, you can reserve private doubles too. All the modern rooms are spotless, and everything from the bed linens to the floor covering looks spanking new. Furthermore, the staff is friendly and helpful. The only downside is getting a spot on that terrace, which doubles as a pizzeria. It's popular, so reserve in

Dorm room in The People – Paris Nation.

advance—especially on Bastille day (July 14th), when you'll be in prime position to see the air force display fly over the Champs-Elysées in the distance to directly above the hostel (usually at 10am).

28 bis Place de la Nation, 12th arrond. thepeoplehostel.com/en/destinations/paris nation. ⓒ **09-78-36-20-28.** 39 units. 33€ dorms 4–8 people; 145€ double. Métro: Nation. **Amenities:** Restaurant; rooftop; free Wi-Fi.

Belleville, Canal St-Martin & La Villette (10th, 19th & 20th Arrondissements)

When historic arty neighborhoods like St-Germain and Montmartre became far too expensive for actual artists, many of them moved to these more proletarian neighborhoods, giving the area a bohemian feel. Though it's gentrifying, gritty Belleville is still known for artists' studios, while dozens of hip cafes and restaurants now line the Canal St-Martin and the Bassin de la Villette. The young and adventurous will appreciate this part of town, but you will need to use the Métro to get to the city's more central areas—though the Marais is just a 10-minute walk from the start of Canal St-Martin.

MODERATE

Le Citizen ♥♥   Maybe it's the smiling young staff in jeans or the ecological ethos, but there's something alternative about this adorable boutique hotel on the Canal St-Martin. While the rooms are on the small side, they are light and airy, with lots of blond wood, clean lines, and views out onto the tree-lined canal. Each floor has only two rooms, ranging from the snug "Cosy" to

Le Grande room at Le Citizen.

the spacious "Suite Familiale," a two-bedroom, two-bathroom apartment (without a kitchen) which can accommodate a couple with two children. On some floors, two rooms can be connected, for extra space.

96 quai de Jemmapes, 10th arrond. lecitizenhotel.com. ⓒ **01-83-62-55-50.** 12 units. 141€–220€ double; 250€–300€ suite; 283€–540€ apartment. Rates include breakfast. Métro: Jacques Bonsergent. **Amenities:** Bar; free Wi-Fi.

Generator Paris ♥♥ A 20-minute walk from Gare du Nord (the Eurostar terminal) and 5 minutes from the picturesque quays and bars of Canal St-Martin, this trendy establishment blurs the lines between hotel and hostel by offering both private rooms and dormitories (for 8 or 10 people). It also offers perks that many of the city's standard hotels can't provide, namely, a rooftop bar with views onto Sacré-Coeur and a Métro-themed basement "club" with a fab cocktail happy hour. Breakfast is served in a light-filled cafe overlooking a small urban garden. The bright dorms are filled with young, mostly English-speaking travelers, but the more expensive private rooms attract a more demanding set of mature clients with extras like terraces. Female-only dorms are available.

Generator Hostel's rooftop bar.

9–11 pl. du Colonel Fabien, 10th arrond. staygenerator.com/hostels/paris. ⓒ **01-70-98-84-00.** 199 units. 18€–50€ per person in dorms; 53€–120€ double; private dorms (4–10 beds) 118€–300€. Métro: Colonel Fabien. **Amenities:** Cafe; bar; in-room lockers; laundromat; towel rental; free Wi-Fi.

THE LEFT BANK
Latin Quarter (5th & 13th Arrondissements)

Central and reasonably priced, the Latin Quarter is a longtime favorite for travelers in search of affordable accommodations. As a consequence, a few corners of this famously academic neighborhood are overrun with tourists and trinket shops. The streets immediately surrounding Place St-Michel (especially around rue de la Huchette) are where you'll find the worst tourist traps, in terms of both hotels and restaurants. Better prices and quality are to be had in the quieter and more authentic areas around the universities (College de France, La Sorbonne, Faculté de Sciences), a little farther from Notre-Dame but still within easy walking distance.

Left Bank Hotels (Eiffel Tower Area)

Left Bank Hotels (Latin Quarter, St-Germain, Montparnasse)

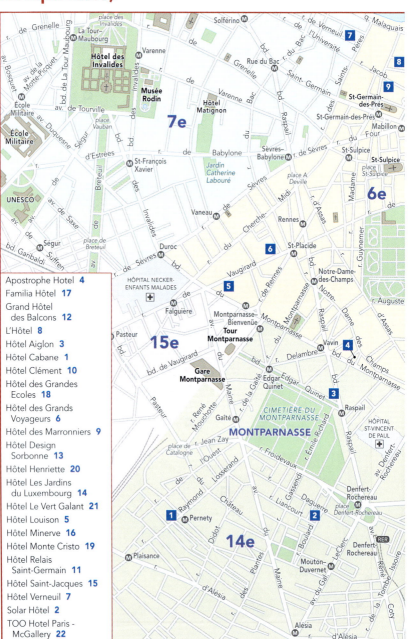

Apostrophe Hotel 4
Familia Hôtel 17
Grand Hôtel des Balcons 12
L'Hôtel 8
Hôtel Aiglon 3
Hôtel Cabane 1
Hôtel Clément 10
Hôtel des Grandes Ecoles 18
Hôtel des Grands Voyageurs 6
Hôtel des Marronniers 9
Hôtel Design Sorbonne 13
Hôtel Henriette 20
Hôtel Les Jardins du Luxembourg 14
Hôtel Le Vert Galant 21
Hôtel Louison 5
Hôtel Minerve 16
Hôtel Monte Cristo 19
Hôtel Relais Saint-Germain 11
Hôtel Saint-Jacques 15
Hôtel Verneuil 7
Solar Hôtel 2
TOO Hotel Paris - McGallery 22

85

EXPENSIVE

Hôtel Monte Cristo ♥♥♥ This hotel woos with wonderful decor themed around Alexandre Dumas' adventure novel *The Count of Monte Cristo*. Stunning hand-painted fabrics combine with antiques, paintings, and beautiful mirrors to create a plush and rather exotic setting. Bathrooms are a contemporary take on Napoleon III–style, with terrazzo tiles mixed with vintage-style porcelain. With a nod to Dumas' Caribbean roots, you can sample rum neat or in a lip-smacking cocktail at the rum bar. The Asian-themed indoor pool and sauna, rarities in this part of the city, are fab places to wind down after a day of sightseeing. Some room prices include exclusive 45-minute access to the pool. Note: While prices start low in low season, they can rise quickly, hence the hotel's position in the expensive category.

20–22 rue Pascal, 5th arrond. hotelmontecristoparis.com. **01-47-07-41-92.** 50 units. 229€–600€ double; 420€ and up suite. Métro: Censier-Daubenton or Les Gobelins. **Amenities:** Bar; indoor pool; sauna; free Wi-Fi.

MODERATE

Hôtel des Grandes Ecoles ♥♥♥ Tucked into a private garden on the slope of the Montagne Ste-Geneviève, this lovely hotel gives you the impression you have just walked out of Paris and into the countryside. A path leads to a flower-bedecked interior courtyard, where birds chirp in the trees; the reception area adjoins an inviting breakfast room with potted plants and an upright piano. The spotless rooms are filled with country-style furniture and papered in old-fashioned prints; quilted bedspreads and framed etchings

Garden at Hôtel des Grandes Ecoles.

complete the look. Views from most windows are of either the garden or surrounding trees. What's more, this unique ambience comes at a reasonable price. Rooms in the "Garden Building" are more modern, with newer bathrooms; families will appreciate the six suites that each sleep four.

75 rue de Cardinal-Lemoine, 5th arrond. hoteldesgrandesecoles.com. ⓒ **01-43-26-79-23.** 51 units. 182€–290€ double; 308€ and up family room. Parking 25€. Métro: Cardinal Lemoine or Place Monge. **Amenities:** Free Wi-Fi.

Hôtel Design Sorbonne ♥♥

In the thick of the student quarter facing La Sorbonne, this cozy boutique hotel combines comfort with unusual but classy decor. Period furniture is covered in lively green, pink, blue, and dark brown stripes; colorful wall fabrics put a modern spin on Victorian patterns, and excerpts from French literary classics are woven into the carpets. Each room has a desk with an iMac or a Mac mini for guests' use. As pretty as they are, the rooms are small, and some have tiny bathrooms. If you need space, opt for a deluxe with a bathtub or the large room on the top floor with a view of the Sorbonne and the Panthéon.

6 rue Victor Cousin, 5th arrond. hotelsorbonne.com. ⓒ **01-43-54-58-08.** 38 units. 172€–380€ double; 180€–400€ top-floor double. Métro: Cluny–La Sorbonne. RER: Luxembourg. **Amenities:** Free Wi-Fi.

Hôtel Les Jardins du Luxembourg ♥♥

Just around the corner from its glorious namesake and down the street from the university, these intimate lodgings are tucked away on a quiet cul-de-sac, making it a favorite with the professorial crowd. The building's claim to fame is that Sigmund Freud stayed here on his first visit to Paris. Today it exudes elegance, from the nature-themed wallpaper behind the beds to the glossy white tiles in the bathrooms. While the standard rooms are pretty, the superior rooms, which cost only a few euros more, have nicer views and small balconies.

5 impasse Royer-Collard, 5th arrond. hoteljardinsluxembourg.com. ⓒ **01-40-46-08-88.** 26 units. 207€–290€ double; 380€ suite. Métro: Cluny–La Sorbonne. RER: Luxembourg. **Amenities:** Bar; free Wi-Fi.

Hôtel Saint-Jacques ♥♥

The spacious rooms in this delightful hotel retain lots of architectural details from its Belle Epoque past. Most of the ceilings are adorned with masses of curlicues, and some have restored 18th-century murals. Modern reproductions of famous French paintings hang on the walls, and Second Empire–themed murals decorate the lobby and breakfast room. The romantic decor has a light, feminine feel, in shades of light blue, cream, and gray—considerably more inviting than when the hotel served as a set for the Audrey Hepburn/Cary Grant classic *Charade*. The best bit? The spa, with its hammam, sauna, ice room and massage menu. One wheelchair-accessible room is on the ground floor.

35 rue des Ecoles, 5th arrond. paris-hotel-stjacques.com. ⓒ **01-44-07-45-45.** 36 units. 247€–290€ double; 347€–408€ triple. Métro: Maubert-Mutualité. **Amenities:** Bar; babysitting; spa; free Wi-Fi.

TOO Hôtel Paris – McGallery
♥♥♥ Fancy going to sleep with the Eiffel Tower twinkling beyond your toes? It's possible in this slick hotel, set between the 17th and 25th floors of architect Jean Nouvel's 120m-tall (393-ft.) Tours Duo (two contemporary skyscrapers with tilted "heads" on the edge of the modern Avenue de France district). The views are, hands down, the best I've ever seen from a hotel bed—largely thanks to the rooms' picture windows and carefully calculated bed height. On the upper floors you'll find the TacTac, a rooftop cocktail spot with yet more of those views, and just below it, the TOO Restaurant, a glass-enclosed cube where chef Benjamin Six serves fantastic Asia-inspired dishes (from 33€). Book for about an hour before dusk, then watch the sun set over Paris's steely gray rooftops as you tuck in. It's easily one of the most exciting places to stay or eat in Paris right now, and perfect for those looking for a more modern take on city life.

The TOO Chill spa at TOO Hôtel.

65 rue Bruneseau, 13th arrond. toohotel.com/en. ✆ **01-47-07-41-92.** 139 units. 254€–500€ double; 480€ and up suite. Métro: Bibliothèque François-Mitterand. **Amenities:** Rooftop bar; restaurant; massages; sauna; hot tub; free Wi-Fi.

INEXPENSIVE
Familia Hôtel ♥♥ Perfectly located, close to rue Mouffetard but far from the maddening crowds, this is a budget hotel that doesn't feel like one. The rooms are snug and a little outdated, but every detail has been scrupulously considered, from the carved cherrywood headboards to the period fabrics on the windows to the top-quality mattresses on the beds. Some rooms have exposed beams, others have wall murals, and those on the second, fifth, and sixth floors have small balconies with lovely views of the Latin Quarter. If there's no room, try the slightly higher-end version of the Familia next door, **Hôtel Minerve** (parishotelminerve.com; ✆ **01-43-26-26-04**), with similar detailing and larger rooms (130€–320€ double; 320€ and up triple).

11 rue des Ecoles, 5th arrond. familiahotel.com. ✆ **01-43-54-55-27.** 30 units. 105€–170€ double; 180€–206€ triple. Métro: Jussieu or Cardinal Lemoine. **Amenities:** Free Wi-Fi.

Hôtel Henriette ♥♥♥ On a narrow, cobbled street that harks back to the Paris of yesteryear, this quaint hotel is made for those looking for a Parisian experience without the tourists. Room decor has a vintage slant, from bold, 1940s-style floral wallpaper to walls paneled with discreet 1970s natural wood. Downstairs, a lovely walled courtyard has wrought-iron furniture and plants creeping up old, crumbly walls. Breakfast is served buffet-style in a light-filled dining area and includes gluten-free and handy express options (coffee and pastries for just 8€). It's a real find.

9 rue des Gobelins, 13th arrond. hotelhenriette.com. ✆ **01-47-07-26-90.** 32 units. 129€–179€ double; 195€–250€ suite. Métro: Les Gobelins. **Amenities:** Room service; free Wi-Fi.

Hôtel Le Vert Galant ♥♥♥ In a quiet green corner near the Manufacture Nationale des Gobelins (p. 210), this lovely haven is only minutes away from rue Mouffetard and three Métro lines. Since it wraps around a small garden, all the rooms in this family-run operation look out on greenery, and the hotel has an

The courtyard garden at Hôtel Henriette.

unfussy, country feel. The recently renovated guest rooms feature rich red and brown colors, oak floors, and Italian tiled showers. The Basque restaurant next door, **Auberge Etchegorry,** is run by the same management and serves excellent dishes like foie-gras and *cassoulet* (sausage, duck, and white beans).

41 rue Croulebarbe, 13th arrond. vertgalant.com. ✆ **01-44-08-83-50.** 16 units. 82€–190€ double. Parking 20€. Métro: Corvisart, Gobelins, or Place d'Italie. **Amenities:** Restaurant; free Wi-Fi.

Guest room at Hôtel Le Vert Galant.

St-Germain-des-Prés & Luxembourg (6th Arrondissement)

Sleek boutiques and restaurants abound in this legendary (and expensive) neighborhood; historic cafes and monuments lend plenty of atmosphere. Unlike some other Parisian neighborhoods, this one is lively even late at night; it is also centrally located and within walking distance of many top sights. The highest concentration of noise and tourist traps is around boulevard St-Germain and Carrefour de l'Odéon; once you turn down a side street, things quiet down.

EXPENSIVE

Hôtel des Grands Voyageurs ♥♥♥   This lovely hotel (sister property to Hôtel des Arts Montmarte p. 76), just a stone's throw from the Le Bon Marché department store (p. 246), has a quirky transatlantic theme—a nod to its previous incarnation as a Holiday Inn, and an ode to French and American relations. Rooms feature wave-shaped moldings, and blue star-studded carpet inspired by the night sky as seen by boat, along with cabin-style wood paneling. Superior versions include a funky 1950s-style record player with vinyls by old American and French artists. The corridors have rope on the walls, like on a vintage cruise liner. The transatlantic concept continues in the wood-paneled brasserie and cocktail bar downstairs, where locals flock for classic, well-executed dishes. Post-dinner drinks can be sipped in Poppy, the secret basement speakeasy, lined with lithographs by Chagall. On Thursday evenings pop by for the hotel's free wine-tasting. It's not advertised on the website, so only those in the know attend.

92 rue de Vaugirard, 6th arrond. hoteldesgrandsvoyageurs.com. ⓒ **01-49-54-87-00.** 138 units. 196€–550€ double. Métro: St-Sulpice. **Amenities:** Bar; restaurant; gym; sauna; room service; free Wi-Fi.

Hôtel Relais Saint-Germain ♥♥♥   Fashioned out of three adjoining 17th-century town houses, this intimate hotel mixes old-world charm and jazzy modern ideas. Exposed beams abound in the spacious rooms, even the smallest of which is equipped with a comfortable sitting area. And yet there is nothing fussy or boring about the decor, which artfully blends period furniture with modern prints, like a Louis XV armchair covered in zigzagged leather. The effect is both stylish and deeply comforting. You'll want to fling yourself onto the king-size bed and just stare out the window at the lovely Carrefour de l'Odéon. There are some extra stairs between floors, so if you have mobility issues, make that clear when you reserve. Some rooms have a private in-bathroom hammam. Guests have priority at the hotel's restaurant, **Le Comptoir** (p. 143), where chef Yves Camdeborde kick-started France's 'bistronomie' movement in 2004, and which is still so popular that it doesn't otherwise accept reservations. Rooms book up far in advance here.

9 Carrefour de l'Odéon, 6th arrond. hotel-paris-relais-saint-germain.com. ⓒ **01-44-27-07-97.** 22 units. 210€–385€ double; 415€ and up suite. Rates include breakfast. Métro: Odéon. **Amenities:** Restaurant; babysitting; concierge; laundry service; room service; free Wi-Fi.

L'Hôtel ♥♥♥   The hotel where Oscar Wilde famously lived above his means and died in 1900 (on the ground floor) is now a gorgeous boutique hotel dressed up like a Belle Epoque boudoir. Each guest room is different, and all are set around a remarkable, six-story spiral staircase. Some rooms have fireplaces; some have fabric-covered walls; all come with lush period antiques, including one with a pair of gigantic, 19th-century Chinese vases. The Oscar Wilde room features a peacock-themed mural. The bijou cocktail bar (named after—you guessed it—Wilde) has live jazz every first Thursday of the month, while downstairs in the cellar, you'll find a hammam pool, a steam room, and a massage room.

13 rue des Beaux Arts, 6th arrond. l-hotel.com. © **01-44-41-99-00.** 20 units. 400€–515€ double; 795€–1,500€ suite. Métro: St-Germain-des-Prés. **Amenities:** Restaurant; bar; concierge; laundry service; room service; free Wi-Fi.

MODERATE

Hôtel des Marronniers ♥♥ If you are looking for old-fashioned Parisian charm, head for these cozy lodgings just a few minutes away from the church of St-Germain-des-Prés. Nestled in the back of a courtyard behind the galleries and antique stores of chic rue Jacob, rooms here feature rich fabrics, (mostly) high ceilings, warm colors, and reproduction antiques, as well as a dash of quirky *je ne sais quoi*. Rooms are so quiet it's hard to believe you are in the city center; those facing the garden get more light. The marble bathrooms offer Clarins' products—a chic touch. Guests are invited to have breakfast or just relax in the lush garden behind the hotel, which doubles as a tearoom during the day; if it's raining, you can do the same on the covered veranda. The triples and quads are particularly well laid out for families.

21 rue Jacob, 6th arrond. hoteldesmarronniers.com. © **01-43-25-30-60.** 36 units. 193€–250€ double; 320€–375€ triple; 350€–420€ quad. Métro: St-Germain-des-Prés. **Amenities:** Garden; laundry service; library; tearoom; free Wi-Fi.

Hôtel Louison ♥♥♥ Hovering on the invisible border between the Montparnasse and St-Germain neighborhoods, this adorable hotel is a quick walk to the **Luxembourg Gardens** (p. 213) and the delights of the **Le Bon Marché** department store (p. 246). While maintaining the original detailing and mood of this 19th-century building, the period decor is spiced up with contemporary colors and textures, like a gold and purple version of traditional *toile de jouy* wallpaper, or old-fashioned stripes cheered up with lush velvet pillows and contemporary headboards. There's also a fully equipped yoga room open 24/7. Connecting rooms are available, as well as a furnished apartment for rent by the week or the month.

105 rue de Vaugirard, 6th arrond. louison-hotel.com. © **01-53-63-25-50.** 41 units. 167€–329€ double; 260€–435€ triple. Parking 40€. Métro: Duroc or St-Placide. **Amenities:** Concierge; yoga room; laundry service; free Wi-Fi.

Hôtel Verneuil ♥♥♥ Both historic and chic, this intimate hotel has conserved the exposed beams and architectural details of the 17th-century building it inhabits. In a nod to the neighborhood's literary roots, manuscripts and scrolls are tucked into niches in the walls. Neutral colors and cozy period touches give it the feel of a private home—perhaps that of an eminent editor. While the hallways are painted in somber shades of brown and beige, the rooms are bright and friendly, if small. If you need to stretch out, go for the deluxe room, which has space for a desk and chairs; there are a few connecting rooms for families. ***Fun facts:*** Author James Baldwin used to live in the building, and the house/museum of music icon Serge Gainsbourg (p. 213) is just across the street (as the fan graffiti shows).

8 rue de Verneuil, 7th arrond. hotel-verneuil-saint-germain.com. ✆ **01-42-60-82-14.** 26 units. 206€–400€ double; 300€–500€ triple. Métro: St-Germain-des-Prés or Rue du Bac. **Amenities:** Bar; babysitting; business corner with printer; massages; laundry service; room service; free Wi-Fi.

INEXPENSIVE

Grand Hôtel des Balcons ♥   For the neighborhood, the rooms in this simple hotel are remarkably spacious, and very good value. Most have small balconies, and if you look up the street, you'll see the columns of the 18th-century Odéon theater. The roomy triples and quads are a good bet for families, and a wheelchair-accessible room is on the ground floor. The lobby has an Art Nouveau feel, and the well-kept rooms are impeccably clean, if not particularly stylish.

3 rue Casimir Delavigne, 6th arrond. balcons.com. ✆ **01-46-34-78-50.** 49 units. 169€–300€ double; 270€ triple; 290€ quad. Métro: Odéon. **Amenities:** Free Wi-Fi.

Hôtel Clément ♥♥   Facing the chic boutiques of Marché St-Germain, these charming and impeccably maintained rooms offer exceptional value about 2 blocks from St-Germain-des-Prés and a warren of restaurant-filled streets. Walls are covered in traditional *toile de jouy* prints, and beds are decked out in white quilted spreads. Doubles tend to be small, but the minisuites are good for families. The Marché is closed at night, so all is calm in the evenings; rooms on the upper floors enjoy views of Parisian rooftops. You'll need to be able to manage a few stairs to get to the elevator.

6 rue Clément, 6th arrond. hotel-clement.com. ✆ **01-43-26-53-60.** 28 units. 125€–190€ double; 180€–270€ triples and suites. Métro: Mabillon. **Amenities:** Babysitting; laundry service; room service; free Wi-Fi.

Eiffel Tower & Nearby (7th Arrondissement)

For some reason, many visitors to Paris clamor for hotels near the Eiffel Tower, perhaps under the impression that this is a central location. It isn't. Not only that, but the 7th arrondissement is also filled with government ministries and posh residences—not exactly the ideal spot to experience a typical slice of Parisian life. That said, this is undeniably a beautiful, quiet area, and there is something magical about wandering out of your hotel and seeing the Eiffel Tower looming in the background.

EXPENSIVE

Hôtel Signature St-Germain-des-Prés ♥♥♥   Run by the friendly Prigent family (also of the Hôtel de Londres Eiffel; see below), this stylish boutique hotel has a homey, retro charm. Bright colors on the walls blend harmoniously with subdued bedspreads and linens; vintage mid-20th-century reproduction furniture and faux antique phones take the edge off sleek modern lines. The "Prestige" rooms cost more but are especially roomy (30 sq. m/323 sq. ft.), a rarity even in upscale Parisian hotels. In addition to the attentive service, this hotel is blessed with an excellent location for shopping addicts: It's just down the street from Le Bon Marché (p. 246).

5 rue Chomel, 7th arrond. signature-saintgermain.com. © **01-45-48-35-53.** 26 units. 280€–490€ double; 360€–500€ triple; 440€–670€ 2-room connecting family suite. Métro: Sèvres-Babylone or St-Sulpice. **Amenities:** Concierge; free Wi-Fi.

MODERATE

Hôtel de L'Empereur ♥♥ All the rooms facing the street in this perfectly manicured hotel (run by the same meticulous management as the Hôtel Muguet; see below) have swell views of the nearby golden dome of Les Invalides, which hovers over the tomb of Napoleon (hence the name of the hotel). The best views are from the fifth and sixth floors. Larger rooms facing the courtyard get lots of light, have less street noise, and are less expensive. The hotel has connecting rooms for families.

2 rue Chevert, 7th arrond. hotelempereur.com. © **01-45-55-88-02.** 31 units. 180€–260€ double; 270€ triple; 420€ quad. Métro: Ecole Militaire. **Amenities:** Concierge; guest computer; free Wi-Fi.

Hôtel de Londres Eiffel ♥♥♥ From the moment you enter, you feel like you are in a private home, and you'll probably be greeted by the friendly owners, the Prigents. Knickknacks line the wood bookshelves in the neo-retro lobby, an old-fashioned yet cheerfully modern look that extends to the guest rooms. Walls are covered with tasteful printed fabrics featuring slightly kitsch 19th-century motifs, while the furniture harkens back to the 1940s, with lots of wood in soft shades of beige and brown. Two of the rooms have views of the Eiffel Tower (which is just steps away), but these book up early. For even more

A deluxe double room at Hôtel Signature St-Germain-des-Prés.

quiet and intimacy, request a spot in the Pavillon, a small, elevator-less building in the back with six rooms. Adjoining rooms are available for families.

1 rue Augereau, 7th arrond. hotel-paris-londres-eiffel.com. ✆ **01-45-51-63-02.** 30 units. 210€–400€ double; 300€–390€ triple; 370€–720€ quad. Métro: Ecole Militaire. **Amenities:** Free Wi-Fi.

Hôtel de Varenne ♥♥   This hotel maintains an atmosphere of refined serenity and caters to the ministerial crowd that frequents the area. Set back from the street, rooms are noiseless, and the pretty garden patio is perfect for breakfast alfresco in the warmer months. The decor is stately without being stuffy, with custom-made furniture inspired by the Louis XVI and Empire styles. Considering the quality of the lodgings and the self-importance of the neighborhood, rates are very reasonable. A wheelchair-accessible suite is on the ground floor.

44 rue de Bourgogne, 7th arrond. hoteldevarenne.com. ✆ **01-45-51-45-55.** 26 units. 210€–320€ double; 250€–380€ triple; 340€–590€ suite. Free breakfast when booking directly through the hotel's website. Parking 35€. Métro: Varenne or La Tour Maubourg. **Amenities:** Concierge; babysitting; laundry service; free Wi-Fi.

Hôtel du Champ de Mars ♥♥   An adorable and affordable little inn right around the corner from the food shops of rue Cler—what more could you ask for? The impeccably maintained rooms are tastefully decorated with the kind of care people generally reserve for their own homes: thick cotton bedspreads, framed etchings, and printed fabrics in warm colors on the walls

Oudinot Suite at Hôtel de Varenne.

View of the Eiffel Tower from Hôtel de Londres Eiffel.

IN impressionist FOOTSTEPS: A WORTHY NIGHT JUST OUTSIDE THE CENTER

Fancy a night in a hidden gem, away from the tourists, in verdant surroundings that inspired Impressionist painter Jean-Baptiste Camille Corot? Jump on a train from Gare Saint-Lazare to the suburb of Ville d'Avray (just a 15-min. ride to Sevres Ville d'Avray station), where hotel **Les Etangs de Corot,** 55 rue de Versailles, Ville d'Avray, overlooks one of the lakes the great artist painted. Bedrooms are classically chic, with a French country style and plenty of bold patterns. You can stroll Corot's lake at sunset, watching the sky turn from pastel blue to pink as herons fish for supper. Your dinner awaits in the Michelin-starred restaurant, dressed up like a contemporary hunting lodge; then it's cocktail time in the 19th-century *guinguette* (outdoor bar) on the water's edge. etangs-corot.com. ✆ **01-41-15-37-00.** 224€–350€ double; from 245€ family room; 350€–480€ suite.

and windows. Two rooms have a tiny courtyard, while those on the upper floors get lots of light.

7 rue du Champ de Mars, 7th arrond. hotelduchampdemars.com. ✆ **01-45-51-52-30.** 25 units. 195€–330€ double. Métro: Ecole Militaire. **Amenities:** Concierge; loaner laptop; free Wi-Fi.

Hôtel Muguet ♥♥♥ Known for its impeccable service and comfort level, this personable hotel is as classically chic as it is cozy. Modern wood headboards have a lily-of-the-valley (*muguet*) motif, and bright bathrooms have vintage-style washstands and Italian showers. Rooms are relatively large for Paris, and the triples are downright spacious. Five doubles have a great view of the Eiffel Tower, two others of Les Invalides; needless to say, they book up months in advance. The others, which are less expensive, look out on either the quiet street or the courtyard. Two wheelchair-accessible rooms on the ground floor face directly into a small but lush garden.

11 rue Chevert, 7th arrond. hotelparismuguet.com. ✆ **01-47-05-05-93.** 40 units. 191€–280€ double; 255€–360€ triple; 410€–850€ quad or quint. Métro: Varenne or La Tour Maubourg. **Amenities:** Computer and printer in lobby; concierge; free Wi-Fi.

Montparnasse & Nearby (14th & 15th Arrondissements)

Montparnasse is more centrally located than it might seem—it's right on the border of St-Germain and close to the Luxembourg Gardens. Also, the train station is a major transit hub for a bundle of Métro lines and bus routes. Though the utterly unaesthetic **Tour Montparnasse** now casts a shadow over this former writers' and artists' haunt (Henry Miller, Man Ray, Chagall, Picasso), eating in its top-floor restaurant, Ciel de Paris (p. 150), provides the some of the best views in the city, and the neighboring streets are still full of personality.

MODERATE

Apostrophe ♥♥   The intimate and rather kitschy "poem" hotel honors the neighborhood's literary history (Henry Miller wrote across the way at La Coupole, and Hemingway set up shop at Closerie des Lilas down the street). Each of the 16 rooms has a theme: "Calligraphie" has Chinese characters splashed on royal blue walls; "Musique" features stenciled sheet music, instruments, and giant piano keys; and "Paris–Paradis" pays homage to the city's skyline. The larger rooms include a Jacuzzi right in the room.

3 rue de Chevreuse, 6th arrond. apostrophe-hotel.com. ⓒ **01-56-54-31-31.** 16 units. 140€–270€ double with jet-massage shower; 200€–300€ double with Jacuzzi. Métro: Vavin. **Amenities:** Bar; free Wi-Fi.

INEXPENSIVE

Hôtel Aiglon ♥♥♥   Once upon a time, the likes of Jean-Paul Sartre, Luis Buñuel, and Albert Giacometti frequented this Art Deco hotel at the heart of what was once the city's most vibrant artistic scene. While the hotel has since had a makeover, it is still a favorite of artists, filmmakers, and writers. It's close enough to the train station to be convenient but well out of the shadow of the Tour Montparnasse, and south-facing rooms enjoy leafy views of the Montparnasse cemetery. While the rooms share a palette of discreet shades of gray, beige, and blue, each has a different custom-made mosaic in the bathroom, the works of a local artist. The hotel also offers 12 spacious family rooms that accommodate three to four people, as well as an apartment that sleeps five.

232 bd. Raspail, 14th arrond. paris-hotel-aiglon.com. ⓒ **01-43-20-82-42.** 46 units. 125€–240€ double; 155€–390€ triple; 270€–520€ quad; 210€–640€ apartment for 5. Parking: 35€/day. Métro: Raspail. **Amenities:** Concierge; laundry service; room service; portable Wi-Fi hotspot rental; free Wi-Fi.

Hôtel Cabane ♥♥♥   This hip and friendly hotel is one of the Left Bank's best deals. Room decor is understatedly elegant, with lots of creams, and browns, and wood accents that make you feel as though you're in a chic wood cabin (as the hotel's name suggests), and there are either garden views or vistas over the typically Parisian street below. If you're in Paris for romance, book La Cabane, a hidden wooden cabin with cool, rustic-chic decor, a two-person light-therapy shower, and its own garden terrace. The hotel bar serves excellent cocktails, and afternoon snacks for kids (5€ for homemade cake and a juice).

A woodsy guest room at Hôtel Cabane.

76 rue Raymond Losserand, 14th arrond. orsohotels.com/hotel-cabane. ⓒ **01-40-52-12-40.** 42 units. 122€–160€ double; from 225€ for La Cabane. Métro: Pernety. **Amenities:** Bar; free Wi-Fi.

Solar Hôtel ♥   Declaring itself "the first ecological, economical, and activist hotel," these basic lodgings feature energy-efficient lighting, water-saving measures, and composting and recycling. Breakfast, included in the low rate, is organic; bicycles are available for guests; and there is a nice garden for sipping a fair-trade tea. The bright rooms, though private, have a hostel-like feel, but the mattresses are firm and everything is clean and tidy. Just around the corner from rue Daguerre, a cute pedestrian market street, the hotel has two buildings. One has free Wi-Fi and small refrigerators in the rooms but no elevator; the other has an elevator but Wi-Fi only in the common areas.

22 rue Boulard, 14th arrond. solarhotel.fr. ✆ **01-43-21-08-20.** 34 units. 99€–199€ double. Rates include breakfast. Métro: Denfert-Rochereau. **Amenities:** Bicycles; free Wi-Fi.

ALTERNATIVE LODGINGS

Hotels are all very well and good, but for some, nothing beats staying in a private home or apartment, particularly if you are a family on a budget. Fortunately, travelers with an independent streak have several options, including short-term rentals, B&Bs, and "aparthotels."

Short-Term Rentals

The Internet is swimming in websites and agencies proffering hundreds of apartments smack in the center of the City of Light. Though the rates for two people can be close to what you'd pay at a hotel, the advantages include cooking some of your meals at home, saving yourself money. Other benefits are privacy, independence, and a chance to see what it's like to live like a Parisian, even if it's just for a week.

If your group includes more than two people, and especially if you are traveling *en famille,* the benefits can be huge. Family suites and/or adjoining rooms are rare in Parisian hotels (though I list a few places here), so you'll often end up paying for two doubles—somewhere around 250€ to 500€ per night—whereas you could rent a one-bedroom apartment with a foldout couch and/or extra bed for anywhere from 150€ to 350€ per night.

While agencies like the ones listed below come with more services and guarantees, rates also tend to be more expensive than Internet rental platforms like **Airbnb.com, Flipkey.com,** and **Vrbo.com,** as many of the rentals listed on these sites are done by the owners directly, so there's no middleman to pay. Agencies justify their costs by having cleaning staff, all-inclusive rates, and an office you can call when something goes wrong. They also can vet all their apartments to make sure they are legal and compliant with hygiene measures, and they can check that there is no funny business on the owners' side. That said, there is no denying that thousands of people happily use Airbnb and similar sites and find great accommodations for reasonable rates.

The problem is that hugely popular sites like Airbnb cannot check up on every owner, so you cannot be entirely sure that your rental is legal or indeed as good or clean as it looks in the photos. ***Bottom line:*** If you want to minimize risk and are willing to pay more for it, go with a well-established agency

A suite at 52 Clichy.

such as **Parisian Home** (parisianhome.com; ✆ **01-45-08-03-37**), **Paris Attitude** (parisattitude.com; ✆ **01-42-96-31-46**), or **Paris Appartements Services** (paris-appartements-services.com; ✆ **01-40-28-01-28**). **Apartments Actually** (apartmentsactually.com; sarahjpank@gmail.com) also has two stunning properties in the Marais. In most cases, you will deal directly with the agency (not the owners), and the minimum stay rules usually apply.

Bed & Breakfasts

Though bed-and-breakfasts (*chambres d'hôtes*) are common in the French countryside, in the big city, where privacy and anonymity are treasured, they are still relatively rare. Three B&Bs I wholeheartedly recommend are:

- **52 Clichy** (52clichy.com) in the new foodie quarter, the 9th arrondissement. Run by a British expat, Rosemary, there are two lovely spaces: One for two people (from 150€) and another (with a kitchen) for up to four people (from 250€); there's a 5-night minimum stay.
- **La Villa Paris** (la-villa-paris.com), occupying a 1920s villa in the residential 13th arrondissement. This place feels like a secret boutique hotel with five warmly decorated rooms and luxurious bathrooms, not to mention a leafy breakfast terrace (150€–200€).
- **Bonne Nuit Paris** (bonne-nuit-paris.com) in a 17th-century house in the hip end of the Marais (3rd arrond.). It's right by the Marché des Enfants Rouges food market, and the four rooms and an apartment all have a chic, old-world vibe (170€–275€).

Aparthotels

These utilitarian lodgings are a cross between a hotel and an apartment. Short on charm, *aparthotels* are decidedly practical: Units come with kitchenettes as well as hotel services like fresh towels, dry cleaning, and a concierge. Rates are generally higher than short-term rentals, but you are dealing with a large company with standardized apartments, organized websites, and customer service.

The best-known *aparthotel* company is **Citadines** (discoverasr.com/fr/citadines; ✆ **01-53-95-60-00;** eiffel@citadines.com;140€–350€), with its clean, comfortable units close to the Eiffel Tower. **Adagio** (adagio-city.com), has several locations in central Paris and offers bright, modern, fully equipped spaces (120€–380€ a night).

WHERE TO DINE

Everywhere you look in Paris, someone is doing their best to ruin your waistline. *Boulangeries* (bakeries) with buttery croissants and decadent pastries lurk on every street corner, open-air markets tempt the senses, and terrific restaurants with intriguing menus sprout up on every block.

In France, food is not a pastime; it's an art. Eating and drinking is a topic of serious discussion, the subject of radio shows, newspaper columns, and even feature films. It's not surprising that Paris, navel of the French universe, should boast some of the best food on the planet. Fortunately, you don't have to have a king-size budget to dine like royalty. But you do have to choose wisely. Once upon a time, you could wander into just about any restaurant in Paris and sit down to a good meal; today, this is no longer the case—especially as fast-food joints become increasingly ubiquitous.

Fortunately, the guardians of good food are fighting back—and not just in those world-famous, multi-starred restaurants that everyone has heard about, but in of the city's "**neo-bistros**" (modern Parisian bistros, often run by young chefs, where the accent is on high-quality eats that cost a fraction of what you would pay in a gourmet palace). One outgrowth of this movement is the obsession with "noble" ingredients—prime, regional products, often from a small-scale farm or artisan, often organic, and always in keeping with the oldest and best traditions.

As the cost of living continues to rise in Paris (like in other cities around the world), another recent trend is the return of the *bouillon*. Originally workers' restaurants in the 19th century offering decent food at modest prices, the concept has been revived more than 100 years later to promote good eating at lower prices (often 15€ to 20€ for three courses). It's a no-brainer and a hit—if the lines out of the bouillons' doors are any indication!

You will find a puzzling interest in American food though. Gourmet hamburgers are ubiquitous on bistro menus these days, fried chicken joints are on the rise, and you'll find bagels and smoked salmon at "le brunch," a relatively new meal (for the French) that is all the rage.

The coffeeshop movement has finally hit Paris too, and not just Starbucks (though you will, alas, find plenty of those). I'm talking American-style coffeeshops offering free Wi-Fi, and menus full of lattes and "le carrot cake." It's an inevitable part of globalization, and a welcome trend for both the city's freelance workers and visitors looking for familiar food and a sturdy Internet connection.

5

Plus, the city still has plenty of Belle Epoque beauties to feast your eyes on and fill your stomachs in.

This chapter offers a sampling of Paris's gourmet delights, including a list of the best cafes, tearooms, and other places to find sinful sweets at the end.

PRACTICAL MATTERS
Eating Hours & Annual Closings

In Paris, unless you see a sign that says SERVICE CONTINU, meals are usually restricted to set hours. This is one of the reasons it's a good idea to reserve if you can (the other is that dining rooms tend to be small). Don't expect to wander in someplace for a bowl of soup at 4pm. Lunch is generally served between noon and 2pm (sometimes 2:30pm), and dinner is from 7 to 10:30pm (sometimes 11pm). Many restaurants close on Sundays and/or Mondays, though some have started serving weekend brunch, generally from 11am to 3pm. Cafes and restaurants with a bar tend to stay open between mealtimes, serving drinks and coffee; if you are starving, you can usually order a light sandwich or a *croque-monsieur* (a French take on a grilled ham-and-cheese sandwich) and fries or salad. Some brasseries serve late into the night. For late-night dining options, see p. 110.

Many restaurants close in August (normally the first 2 weeks), and some shut down between Christmas and New Year's; see listings for details.

Tip: If you didn't reserve and you want to avoid waiting in line, try to arrive at the very beginning of the service, noon or around 7pm. Most French people eat later than that, so you'll have a better chance if you avoid the rush.

Reservations

Most restaurants in Paris are small, so if you have your heart set on eating at one in particular, reserving ahead, even if it is the same day, is essential. If you are looking to dine at one of Paris's hip neo-bistros or famous gourmet temples, you may have to reserve weeks in advance. Ask your hotel receptionist to help if you can't manage the telephone or try reserving online through thefork.com (which also offers discounts and is used by a lot of eateries). Otherwise, you can often reserve on the restaurant's site or via email.

> ### To Tip or Not to Tip?
>
> In France, waiting tables is a time-honored profession, one that comes with paid vacation and retirement benefits. That said, no one gets rich being a French waitperson. Tipping is not required or even expected, but it is a nice thing to do, especially if you've been at the table for several hours or enjoyed good service. While the price you see on the menu includes tax and service, if you feel so inclined, leave a small tip (about .50€ for drinks, a euro or two after meals in mid-range cafes or restaurants). Of course, no one will mind if you leave more.

> **Useful Websites for Foodies**
>
> o **The Fork** (thefork.com) allows you to reserve restaurants online for free and supplies a list of restaurant promotions—sometimes up to 50% off (check restrictions before you book).
> o **Le Fooding** (lefooding.com) compiles a list of the city's most innovative restaurants, including establishments that make up the *bistronomy* movement (gourmet comfort food). It's in French, however.
> o **David Lebovitz** (davidlebovitz.com) is a pastry chef and cookbook author with a rocking website that discusses everything from restaurants and recipes to shopping and travel tips.

One annoying trend that has appeared post-Covid is holding a deposit for your reservation at some (though fortunately not all) of the city's hippest restaurants (usually 50€). If you show up, the deposit won't be charged and you pay your final bill as usual. If you don't turn up, or you cancel less than 24 hours beforehand (or outside the timeframe specified upon reservation), then you lose the money. Apparently, it's to stop people making multiple reservations at the most sought-after restaurants, then choosing which one to go to at the last minute, leaving some tables empty.

Dejeuner sur l'Herbe (Picnics)

Although restaurants are all very well and good, there's a lot to be said for a quick and easy outdoor meal in one of Paris's many lovely parks and squares. Picking up picnic ingredients is a pretty easy affair, though you should familiarize yourself with a bit of terminology. For good takeout food, look for the nearest *charcutier* (these specialize in smoked meat, pâtés, and other pork products) or *traiteur* (a store that sells prepared takeout dishes and salads). At almost any *boulangerie* (bakery), you can find what may well be **the best lunch bargain in the city:** their lunch *formule* (set menu). For around 9€ to 12€, you can get a long sandwich (usually half a baguette), amply filled with chicken, ham, or tuna and *crudités* (tomato, lettuce, and other salad-like items), a drink, and a pastry. Often you can substitute a slice of quiche for the sandwich. *Formules* and sandwiches are usually only available from 11am to 2pm. **Eric Kayser** (maison-kayser.com) and **Paul** (paul.fr) are reliable bakery chains serving salads, sandwiches, and even hot dishes. But your best bet is to use your *nez* (nose) and find a place on your own. The telltale signs of a good bakery are an attractive window display and a queue at mealtimes.

Choosing a Restaurant

Below is a selective list of restaurants, wine bars, and tearooms that serve the type of excellent food you came specifically to Paris to try. But since the city has thousands of restaurants, you're bound to wander into something wonderful and unexpected on your own. Finding a good restaurant is extremely subjective, considering any number of variables and a good dose of what the French call *le feeling*.

That said, I recommend you take some precautions if you go beyond the suggestions in this guide. Unfortunately, Paris has many restaurants geared solely to tourists that shovel out food that is unmemorable at best, and indigestible at worst. Shun places that advertise English menus and look instead for places that are full of happy customers speaking French. And don't avoid places with lines out front (that's a *good* sign). And if there are delicious smells issuing from the kitchen, it's likely the food will be good (restaurants lacking in appetizing aromas may be relying on prepackaged foods and microwaves).

On a better note, many restaurants these days have at least one vegetarian option (see p. 111), and more than ever can cater to gluten-free needs, like the BigLove Caffé pizzeria-trattoria (p. 112).

THE RIGHT BANK
Louvre & Île de la Cité (1st Arrondissement)

Dining near the Louvre can be expensive and frustrating. Since almost every tourist visiting the city comes to this part of town, it's rife with overpriced, mediocre tourist restaurants (you can identify them by their menus printed in at least five languages). However, on some of the smaller streets away from the museum, you'll find more authentic eateries.

EXPENSIVE

Verjus ♥♥♥ MODERN FRENCH Okay, the chef's American, but that doesn't stop this nosh nirvana from being utterly Parisian, from the setting (an pale green-gray dining room, nestled at the top of a hidden staircase, with Art Deco–style furniture and views onto Théâtre du Palais Royal) to the food (contemporary takes on French classics). The dishes are served in tasting menus that list the ingredients in each dish—chicken, asparagus, and wild garlic or artichoke with caviar. But don't be fooled: On the plate, this simplicity translates to perfectly executed delicacies that may well be the highlight of your trip. Paris has few "gastronomique" restaurants where you can eat like a king for under 100€, and this, along with Pierre Sang in Oberkampf (p. 127) and Septime (at lunchtime; p. 125), is one of the best. Needless to say, the wine list is a treat, filled with biodynamic and organic wines. The 62€ wine pairing option is worth the splurge. Reservations required.

52 rue Richelieu, 2nd arrond. verjusparis.com. ✆ **01-42-97-54-40.** Tasting menu 98€. Mon–Fri 6:30–11pm. Closed 2 weeks in Aug. Métro: Palais Royal–Musée du Louvre or Pyramides.

price CATEGORIES

Expensive	Main dishes 35€ and up
Moderate	Main dishes 20€–34€
Inexpensive	Main dishes under 20€

MODERATE

Brasserie du Louvre–Bocuse

♥♥ MODERN BRASSERIE   Lyonnais cooking legend Paul Bocuse (nicknamed the "Pope of Gastronomy") passed away in 2018, but his legacy lives on in this vintage-chic brasserie on the ground floor of the Hôtel du Louvre. Tuck into wonderfully executed versions of his signature regional dishes, like hot pistachio-studded sausage (rolled in a soft brioche), sole meunière, and pike quenelle with Nantua (lobster) sauce, while admiring the views of the Comédie Française and Louvre through the bay windows or arcaded terrace. All the desserts are excellent, but I have a particular fondness for the crème brûlée—it's possibly the best in the city. *Note:* There are copious breakfast buffet options, too.

Baba au rhum at Brasserie du Louvre–Bocuse.

1 pl. du Palais Royal, 1st arrond. hyatt.com (then search for Hôtel du Louvre). ⓒ **01-44-58-37-21.** Main courses 21€–50€; fixed-price lunch (Mon–Fri) 31€. Daily 7am–10:30pm. Closed first 3 weeks of Aug. Métro: Palais-Royal–Musée du Louvre.

Clover Grill ♥♥♥ FRENCH/STEAKHOUSE

Grill restaurants are all the rage, but few can compete with this refined barbecue joint near Les Halles, which turns the concept of American-style grilling into something resolutely French: beech-smoked beef rib for two with mashed potato, fresh fish from *petit pêcheurs* (artisanal fishermen) with sauce *choron* (béarnaise sauce with tomatoes), and blue lobster with seasonal vegetables *en papillote*—all hands-down delicious. Even the fruit gets grilled, from brochettes of pineapple to apples in caramel sauce with Breton butter biscuits. Other desserts to look out for include the sticky pavlova, and fluffy *churros* (fried dough fingers) with chocolate. Chef Jean-François Piège is known for his playful approach to cooking, and the *churros* embody this, as he turns something simple into a gourmet dish.

6 rue Bailleul, 1st arrond. jeanfrançoispiege.com/clover-grill. ⓒ **01-40-41-59-59.** Main courses 20€–70€; fixed-price menu 74€. Tues–Wed 6–11pm; Thurs–Sat noon–3pm and 7–11pm. Métro: Louvre–Rivoli.

Côte de boeuf at Clover Grill.

Right Bank West Restaurants

Aki **13**	Chez Georges **17**	Frenchie Bar à Vins **23**	Lazare **9**
Angelina **10**	Clover Grill **19**	La Renommée **22**	Michi **16**
Boutique yam'Tcha **20**	Don Juan II **2**	Le Clarence **7**	Monte Carlo **3**
Brasserie du Louvre – Bocuse **18**	La Condesa **25**	Le Grand Restaurant **8**	Nell'Arte **26**
	La Nélie **6**	Juveniles **14**	Le Pantruche **24**
Café de la Paix **12**	Le Drugstore **4**	Ladurée **5**	Le Petit Rétro **1**

La Tour de Montlhéry–
Chez Denise 21
Public House 11
Verjus 15

105

Rude Waiters: Myth or Reality?

When people ask me about the legendary rudeness of Parisian waitstaff, I have to fight the urge to do the French shrug. It really depends. It is undeniable that Parisian customer service can be frosty, but here's how I see it: With Parisians, you are guilty until proven innocent. If you can weather the initial chilly blast and show them you are not easily flustered, they'll usually warm up—and they will be charming your socks off. Also, don't mistake cultural differences for rudeness. The ultimate faux pas in Paris is rushing you off your table, so if the waiters take forever to bring you your check, they're not being rude, they're saying "feel free to stay a little longer."

Juveniles ♥♥ WINE BAR   This lively wine bar has been around since 1987, and since the owner's daughter and son-in-law took over a decade ago, people have been coming just as much for the food as for the wine. You might start with scallops with Jerusalem artichoke puree and red-wine sauce, followed by roast duck with smoked chestnuts, and finish up with a salted caramel rice pudding, for example. Wash that down with a berry-rich Languedoc red or a light and fruity Beaujolais, and you've got yourself one memorable and gourmet meal. Prices are extremely reasonable, considering the close proximity to the chic Palais Royal. You can also buy wines to go, making this a great stop if you're picnicking. Reservations required for dining. Drinking at the bar is first-come, first-served.

47 rue de Richelieu, 1st arrond. juvenileswinebar.com. © **01-42-97-46-49.** Main courses 30€–38€. Tues–Sat noon–1:30pm and 7–9:30pm. Closed 2 weeks in Aug. Métro: Pyramides.

La Renommée ♥♥♥ FRENCH   Dressed up like a sumptuous 19th-century-style boudoir, with leather banquettes, stunning Belle Epoque paintings, and intricately carved wooden paneling, this is a glamorous spot for a meal. And that's just upstairs! Downstairs is a gorgeous velvet-clad cocktail bar, where you can sidle up to an armchair and sip negroni as you tuck into dessert. Food portions here are as huge as they are delicious, so while prices seem high (69€ for sole meunière; 125€ for a beef rib), dishes have been designed to share. Aside from those above, offerings might include garlicky snails, cockle linguini, and roast chicken with watercress salad. For an

Let's Do Lunch

Many restaurants in Paris serve a set-price menu at lunch that is considerably cheaper than the same food served at dinnertime. It is not unusual to find a two- or three-course lunch prix-fixe, also called a *formule*, or a menu for 18€ to 30€. The only downside is that your choice of dishes will usually be limited on the *formule*. If you plan to hit an expensive restaurant, going at lunchtime is a good way to experience the food without such a big bill. *Note:* Set-price lunches are usually only served Monday through Friday.

Right Bank East Restaurants

Les Arlots **1**
L'As du Fallafel **7**
Au Bascou **12**
Auberge Nicolas Flamel **4**
Aux Bons Crus **24**
Benoit **5**
Biglove Caffè **9**
Bob's Juice Bar **15**
Bouillon République **11**
Brasserie Martin **23**
Café des Musées **8**
Chez Michel **2**
Clamato **26**
L'Ebauchoir **28**
EELS **3**
ELMER **13**
Fulgurances **30**
Géosmine **21**
Ground Control **29**
Hôtel du Nord **17**
Laia **30**
Marché des Enfants Rouge **10**
MijoT **20**
Naam **19**
Noglu **25**
Pierre Sang in Oberkampf **22**
Le Potager du Marais **6**
Le Pure Café **27**
Rosa Bonheur **18**
Septime **26**
Le Verre Volé **16**
Zerda Café **14**

> ### Japantown, Paris-Style
>
> You are wandering around the streets near the Opéra, when you take a sharp turn onto the rue Ste-Anne. Suddenly, everything is in Japanese, with noodle shops everywhere! Plunge into a bowl at one of these restaurants:
>
> - **Udon Jubey,** 39 rue Ste-Anne, 1st arrond. (kintarogroup.com/udon-jubey; ✆ **01-40-15-92-54**; Métro: Pyramides), makes some of the best udon in town; slurp at the counter or grab one of the limited number of tables.
>
> - **Higuma,** 32 bis rue Ste-Anne, 1st arrond. (higuma.fr; ✆ **01-47-03-38-59**; Métro: Pyramides), features an open kitchen, ramen soups, and a long line out the front door.
>
> - **Aki Café,** 75 rue Ste-Anne, 1st arrond. (akiparis.fr; ✆ **01-40-41-95-27**), is a canteen with takeout service run by the same management as the restaurant (described below). It's the place to go for sweet Katsu curry and terrific Franco-Japanese pastries, such as adzuki bean tarts and matcha tea éclairs.

elevated version of a classic American side, try the macaroni cheese—gooey and flavorsome, and made with Mont d'Or cheese and black truffle! Desserts—veritable show pieces—are all big enough for four. Try the crème caramel if you can. It was hands down the best I've ever tasted.

95 rue St Honoré, 1st arrond. renommee.paris. ✆ **01-40-39-93-70.** Main courses 33€–126€. Daily 6-10:30pm. Métro: Louvre–Rivoli.

La Tour de Montlhéry–Chez Denise ♥♥ TRADITIONAL FRENCH/BISTRO

One of the last remnants of the bustling atmosphere that used to surround the old Les Halles central market, Chez Denise stays open until 12:30am and serves sturdy platters of snails, *côte de boeuf* (a giant rib steak), grilled marrow bones, and roast chicken served with some of the most delectable fries on the block. The long-aproned waiters are used to encountering English speakers, but that hasn't changed the vibe, which is local and lively. If you are not a carnivore, the menu has a few fish dishes, and you can always enjoy those homemade fries.

5 rue des Prouvaires, 1st arrond. ✆ **01-42-36-21-82.** Main courses 23€–34€. Daily noon–12:30am. Closed mid-July to mid-Aug. Métro: Les Halles.

INEXPENSIVE

Aki ♥♥ JAPANESE

The specialty here is *okonomiyaki*, a sort of grilled omelet topped with meat or seafood and a yummy sauce. Watch the cooks create yours on a griddle in the open kitchen before diving into your meal. You can also order excellent udon or soba noodles. Get here early or be prepared to stand in line. Just down the road at number 16 is their bakery-tearoom, **Aki Boulangerie,** an excellent spot for white bread and savory goodies. Also see Aki Café (above).

11 bis rue Ste-Anne, 1st arrond. akiparis.fr/pages/aki-restaurant. ✆ **01-42-97-54-27.** Main courses 12€–15€; fixed-price menu 14€–18€. Mon–Thurs 11am–10:45pm; Fri–Sat 11:30am–11pm. Métro: Pyramides.

Boutique yam'Tcha ♥♥♥ FRENCH-ASIAN STREET FOOD Book a table at renowned chef Adeleine Grattard's Michelin-starred restaurant yam'Tcha and you'll certainly have a fabulous meal (121 rue St-Honore, 1st arrond.; ⓒ **01-40-26-08-07;** tasting menu 190€; reservations at least 1 month in advance): Grattard works miracles with simple ingredients such as lobster, sea bass, truffles, and pork. But her second place near the Louvre—a dual take-out *bao* bar (steamed Taiwanese brioches) and tearoom—lets you taste her cooking for a fraction of the price. The bar section is a window open to the street, where foodies queue for *bao* buns filled with delectables such as smoked tofu or crab with vegetables, plus unexpected mixes like Stilton and cherries. In the tearoom, Grattard's Hong Kong–born husband, Chi Wah Chan (a veritable tea guru) will pair teas to your choice of *baos* and congee bowls.

4 rue Sauval, 1st arrond. yamtcha.com. ⓒ **01-40-26-06-06.** *Bao* buns 5€ each; main courses 15€–18€. Wed–Sat noon–7pm. Métro: Louvre–Rivoli.

Le Marais (3rd & 4th Arrondissements)

Between its working-class roots and its more recent gentrification, the Marais has a huge range of choices, from humble falafel joints to trendy brasseries. Unlike the shops here, which have become so hip it hurts, a good selection of midrange restaurants still attracts both the sleek set and just regular folks.

EXPENSIVE

Auberge Nicolas Flamel ♥♥♥ MODERN FRENCH This gastronomique destination is set in the oldest house in Paris, a medieval gem, dating from 1407, and the former home of Nicolas Flamel, the real-life

Restaurants in Le Marais district.

After-Hours Dining

Not many restaurants stay open until the wee hours of the night, but a few stalwarts are around Les Halles. Brasserie **Le Tambour**, 41 rue de Montmartre, 2nd arrond. (menuonline.fr/letambour; ⓒ **01-42-33-06-90**; Métro: Les Halles), serves reliable dishes like steak frites (main courses 14€–23€) from 7am to 2am (until 5am Fri–Sat) in a dining room filled with kitschy Paris memorabilia. Nearby, **Au Pied de Cochon**, 6 rue Coquillière, 1st arrond. (pieddecochon.com; ⓒ **01-40-13-77-00**; Métro: Les Halles), is a late-night brasserie (open 8am–5am) specializing in pork and more pork (fixed-price menu from 19.50€; main courses 19.50€–40.50€). Au Pied de Cochon also has some good seafood dishes, and a restorative onion soup is ideal after a night on the town. For a midnight beef fix, head to **La Tour de Montlhéry–Chez Denise** (p. 108; usually open until 12:30am), where the steak is as juicy as it is huge.

Au Pied de Cochon.

historical figure behind the sorcerer's stone character in Harry Potter. Legend has it that Flamel managed to turn metal into gold right here in the building, and the magic continues today—albeit on the plate. Sidle up to a table in the beige and brown dining room (where original beams and stonework mingle with contemporary furniture) and prepare to be wowed by chef Alain Geaam's perfectly executed dishes—delights like scallops with cauliflower and caviar, mushrooms with a cress sauce, lobster with celeriac, a deeply satisfying chocolate dessert filled with chocolate cream and hazelnuts—all theatrically prepared in the open kitchen. As if that weren't enough, there are amuse-bouchées a go-go too (think foie-gras tarts, choux pastry stuffed with cheese, the most delectable brioche you may ever taste served with a little potato and carrot emulsion), and a fabulous wine list. Dishes are served as 3-, 5- or 7-course tasting menus; there's also a very good-value 48€ lunch menu. Reservations required.

51 rue de Montmorency, 3rd arrond. auberge.nicolas-flamel.fr. ⓒ **01-42-71-77-78**. Lunch menu 48€; tasting menus 78€–148€. Tues–Sat noon–1:30pm and 7:30–9:30pm. Closed 2 weeks in Aug. Métro: Etienne Marcel, Arts et Métiers or Rambuteau.

Benoit ♥♥ TRADITIONAL FRENCH   This historic restaurant had hosted a century's worth of Parisian notables when renowned chef Alain Ducasse took the helm in 2005. Mirrors, zinc, and tiles still line the venerable dining room, while the one-Michelin-star menu features beautifully executed bistro classics. *Escargots* (snails) in garlic butter and brill braised with Jura wine share the stage with homemade cassoulet and beef filet bordelaise. Save room for the profiteroles, puff pastry filled with ice cream and drizzled with chocolate sauce.

20 rue St-Martin, 4th arrond. benoit-paris.com. © **01-42-72-25-76.** Main courses 34€–56€; fixed-price lunch 32€–42€. Daily noon–2pm and 7:30–10pm. Closed between Christmas and New Year's and in Aug. Métro: Hôtel-de-Ville.

ELMER ♥♥♥ FRENCH BISTRO For an all-out neo-bistro experience, reserve a table at ELMER, a chic, Nordic-inspired restaurant, where modern French

The dining room at ELMER.

delights like lobster ravioli and suckling lamb are reeled out of the kitchen with real panache. The star here is the rotisserie, which roasts to perfection everything from the aforementioned lamb to pork from the Ventoux mountains and locally caught fish. But no matter what you choose, the accent here is on well-sourced products, so you won't be disappointed.

30 rue Notre-Dame de Nazareth, 3rd arrond. elmer-restaurant.fr. © **01-43-56-22-95.** Main courses 38€–58€; fixed-price lunch 32€–38€. Tues–Thurs 12:15–2:15pm and 7:30–10pm; Fri 12:15–2:15pm and 7:30–10:30pm; Sat 7–10:45pm. Métro: République or Arts et Métiers.

MODERATE

Au Bascou ♥♥♥ BASQUE Basque cuisine, like the province, is not entirely French. Using lots of tomatoes, onions, and sweet Espelette pepper, Basque dishes have a decidedly different tang to them. But while the name of this restaurant refers to Basque country, the menu covers the entire southwest. Traditional Basque dishes like *pipérade* (a tasty omelet loaded with peppers and onions) and *axoa* (a stew of veal shoulder, peppers, and onions) mingle with southwestern classics like duck foie gras and roast *palombe* (wood

---

Eating Vegetarian in Paris

Though the French still love their meat, times are a-changing, and an increasingly large number of Parisian restaurants now cater to vegetarians and sometimes vegans, offering at least a couple of appropriate dishes on the menu. Even basic cafes will usually serve *salades composées*, meal-size salads that often come in meat-free versions. If you eat fish, most restaurants offer at least one or two pescatarian selections, too. And, of course, Paris does have vegetarian restaurants. We've listed a few (**Bob's Juice Bar,** p. 132; **Le Potager du Marais,** p. 114; **Noglu,** p. 129). For more options, visit the **Happy Cow** (happycow.net), a veggie and vegan online network with extensive listings for Paris.

pigeon). Everything is handled with great care by the chef Renaud Marcille, who used to be the right-hand man of Alain Sederens.

38 rue Réaumur, 3rd arrond. au-bascou.fr. **01-42-72-69-25.** Main courses 18€–32€; fixed-price lunch 20€ and 26€; fixed-price dinner from 40€. Mon–Fri noon–2pm and 7:45–10:30pm. Closed between Christmas and New Year's and in Aug. Métro: Arts-et-Métiers.

Café des Musées ♥♥ TRADITIONAL FRENCH/BISTRO Weary culture vultures who've just finished the Picasso Museum will appreciate this bustling corner cafe with its appealing sidewalk tables. I recommend it not just for the atmosphere, however, but because the chef does

Historic Café des Musées.

terrific things with bistro classics, like steak frites with béarnaise sauce, or *andouillette* (tripe sausage), as well as lighter fare like seasonal vegetable casserole with basil oil. The cafe's also famous for its award-winning, five-hour-simmered *boeuf bourguignon.* Or come in the afternoon for tea and gateaux—from chocolate eclairs to strawberry tart.

49 rue de Turenne, 3rd arrond. lecafedesmusees.fr. **01-42-72-96-17.** Main courses 23€–33€; fixed-price lunch 26€. Daily 10am–10:30pm. Closed last 2 weeks of Aug. Métro: St-Paul or Chemin Vert.

INEXPENSIVE

BigLove Caffé ♥♥ ITALIAN Jars of preserved fruit line the walls, and hams hang from the ceiling—yes, you're still in Paris, but this place sure feels like Napoli. It tastes like it, too. For brunch, patrons tuck into pancakes with *bufflonne* ricotta and passion fruit, or eggs Benedict with 24-month-matured Parma ham. For lunch and dinner, pizza reigns supreme (the gluten-free versions are just as good), as does pasta. Whatever you choose, everything is made with only the choicest and freshest of

A brunch entree at BigLove Caffé.

ingredients, many of them direct from *petits producteurs* (small producers) in Italy. Set in a frighteningly hip part of the northern Marais, it is a popular place, so reserve ahead—especially on Saturday and Sunday when this neighborhood is a brunch hot spot.

30 rue Debelleyme, 3rd arrond. bigmammagroup.com. © **01-42-71-43-62.** Main courses 14€–22€. Mon–Thurs noon–2:15pm (until 2:30pm Thurs) and 6:45–10:45pm; Fri noon–3pm and 6:30pm–11pm; Sat–Sun 11am–3:30pm and 6:30–11pm (until 10:45pm Sun). Métro: Filles de Calvaire.

Bouillon République ♥♥♥ BISTRO/TRADITIONAL FRENCH Resplendent in original 1930s wood paneling, pretty tiles, and a carved staircase, Bouillon République (on the northern-most edge of the Marais) is one of those *bouillons* I mention in the intro (p. 99)—a great place for insanely cheap (and insanely scrumptious) dishes that remind you of the good old days, even if you're not that old. You might find comfortable classics like duck terrine with green peppercorns, a quarter chicken with fries, and French onion soup, not to mention desserts such as lemon meringue tart and chocolate mousse. Wine by the glass starts at as little as 3.80€, and there are many bottles from small wine producers. Not surprisingly, this place is popular, so book ahead or arrive by 6pm or after 10pm for dinner, and by about noon for lunch; it's open all day, so opt for an early meal and you'll walk straight in.

39 bd. du Temple, 3rd arrond. bouillonlesite.com/bouillon-republique. © **01-42-59-69-31.** Main courses 8.50€–13.40€. Daily noon–midnight. Closed 2 weeks in Aug. Métro: République.

L'As du Fallafel ♥♥ FALAFEL/ISRAELI This Marais institution offers, without a doubt, the best falafel in Paris. And they're kosher, too. True, falafel joints are scarce in this city, but that doesn't take away from the excellence of these overstuffed beauties, brimming with cucumbers, pickled turnips, shredded cabbage, tahini, fried eggplant, and those crispy balls of fried chickpeas and spices. Other arrangements of similar ingredients *sans* pita can be found in the *assiettes* (platters). Wash it down with an Israeli beer. Service is fast and furious, but basically friendly—just be prepared to deal with hordes of tourists and locals at lunch.

34 rue des Rosiers, 4th arrond. instagram.com/lasdufallafel. © **01-48-87-63-60.** Main courses 9€–21€. Sun–Fri 11am–11pm. Métro: St-Paul.

L'As du Fallafel in Le Marais district.

Dining on market fare at Marché des Enfants Rouge.

Le Potager du Marais ♥♥ VEGAN   The shoebox-size dining room fills up quickly, as Paris doesn't have many vegan eateries, so make sure you reserve in advance. But even omnivores enjoy the delicious veggie offerings here, which might include seitan *bourguignon*, mushroom pâté, and pumpkin Parmentier. Many items are gluten-free. Finish off with a simple but scrumptious apple compote or crème brûlée.

26 rue Saint-Paul, 4th arrond. instagram.com/lepotagerdumarais. ✆ **01-57-40-98-57.** Main courses 14€–20€. Wed–Sun noon–3pm and 7–10:30pm. Métro: St-Paul.

Marché des Enfants Rouge ♥♥♥ STREET FOOD   On rue de Bretagne, this quaint, 400-year-old food market (the oldest in Paris) is a bustling, fragrant labyrinth of ready-to-eat food stalls hawking everything from Caribbean curries to couscous, sushi, and pasta. A hugely popular spot is Alain Miam Miam's organic crepe stand, which serves made-to-order paninis and pancakes dripping in tasty cheese and ham. (If the lines are too long, try his shop around the corner at 26 rue Charlot.) The market's also where you'll find some of the best burgers in town: Burger Fermier makes the bread on-site, slathers the burgers in French cheese such as cider-infused Tomme, and only uses hand-picked beef from a farm in northern France. Come late afternoon and you can join the post-shopping crowd over a glass of wine. Each stall has its own opening times, but a good guide is as below.

39 rue de Bretagne, 3rd arrond. No phone. Main courses 7.50€–20€. Tues–Sat 8am–7:30pm; Sun 8:30am–2pm. Métro: Saint Sébastien-Froissart.

Champs-Élysées & Western Paris (8th, 16th & 17th Arrondissements)

Mobbed with tourists and oozing with opulence, the Champs-Élysées is a difficult place to find a good meal unless you are willing to spend a lot of money.

Mediocre chain restaurants abound on the grand avenue itself; kebab joints mingle with frighteningly expensive gourmet palaces on the side streets. Many two- and three-Michelin star restaurants are here too; before you splurge on a dinner table, remember that lunch in one of these same eateries often costs half the price.

EXPENSIVE

Don Juan II ♥♥♥ MODERN FRENCH   Imagine yourself floating down the Seine on an Art Deco boat, tucking into Michelin-starred cuisine as the city's sparking monuments flit past your window like moving postcards. Chef Frédéric Anton's 190-minute dinner cruise offers just this, and it's the stuff travel dreams are made of. The single, five-course dinner menu costs 240€, but it includes memorable dishes like curried crab with caviar, langoustine ravioli and venison with truffle-studded cabbage, the lot topped off with the best chocolate soufflé in town, served with pistachio ice cream. If Anton's name sounds familiar, it probably is. He's the chef at the Jules Verne on the Eiffel Tower, too (p. 145). Reservations are required. If you have a dietary requirement, the restaurant needs 48 hours' notice.

Yacht de Paris, 5 Port de Debilly (opposite the Eiffel Tower), 16th arrond. donjuan2.yachtsdeparis.fr. *©* **01-83-77-44-40.** Fixed-price dinner 240€. Tues–Sat 7:45–11pm. Métro: Iéna.

Le Grand Restaurant ♥♥♥ MODERN FRENCH   Chef Jean-François Piège is—in my humble opinion—the most exciting chef in France. His ultra-modern take on traditional "bourgeois" cuisine is playful, delicious, and wholly unlike anything you'll taste anywhere else. Book ahead for a table in his swank, gray dining room (decked in concrete walls and geometric ceiling

The Art Deco dinner boat *Don Juan II.*

panels that wouldn't look amiss in Kubrick's *2001: A Space Odyssey*), then sit back for a roller-coaster ride of haute cuisine (served in fixed-price menus): shellfish-stuffed potato with caviar, Parmesan-infused spaghetti with truffles and fall-off-your-fork pork, and a delightful bergamot-flavored custard cream to finish. Don't be fooled by the simplicity of the descriptions: Piège's cooking is as complex as it is satisfying, and the menu changes with the seasons. His place is near the Élysée palace, so you might spot politicians out for a business meal—though Piège's devoted fans are never far away.

Chef at Le Grand Restaurant.

7 rue d'Aguesseau, 8th arrond. jeanfrancoispiege.com. ☏ **01-53-05-00-00.** Fixed-price lunch 166€ and 286€; fixed-price dinner 286€–376€. Thurs–Fri 12:30–1:30pm and 7–10pm; Mon–Sat 7–10pm. Closed 3 weeks in Aug and last week in Dec. Métro: Concorde or Madeleine.

Le Clarence ♥♥♥ MODERN FRENCH   It's not every day you can dine in a restaurant owned by royalty! This sumptuous spot, set in a 19th-century mansion, belongs to HRH Prince Robert of Luxembourg, who also happens to own the famous wine estates of Château Haut-Brion and Château La Mission Haut-Brion in Bordeaux, and Château Quintus in Saint-Emilion. Needless to say, a meal here involves drinking some of the best wine in the world (the cellar has over 1,400 types), but the food (courtesy of head chef Chrisopher Pelé) is something uber-special too: a never-ending succession of innovative (sometimes disconcertingly so) bite-size concoctions like squid ink risotto with fried shrimp head, or lamb stew with capers and porcini mushrooms, not forgetting desserts like lemon cream with dill jelly (the four-course tasting menu includes about 18 such portions and though the descriptions sound simple, the flavors are rich and delicious, and complex). The three dining rooms are fit (quite literally in this case) for a king, dressed in sculpted wood paneling and bright toile de jouy, and the service is both impeccable and friendly. Even if you don't eat here, come by for the wine shop on the ground floor. This place will blow your mind and your taste buds.

31 av. Franklin D. Roosevelt, 8th arrond. le-clarence.paris. ☏ **01-82-82-10-10.** Fixed-price lunch 150€–380€; fixed-price dinner 280€–430€. Wed–Sat noon–1:30pm and 7:30–9pm. Métro: Champs-Élysées–Clémenceau.

MODERATE

Lazare ♥♥♥ MODERN BISTRO   Once upon a time at the Gare St-Lazare train station, about the only thing you could get to eat was a limp sandwich.

A clubby dining room at Le Clarence.

Today, you can eat like a king as you wait for your train to come in, and we're not talking Burger King. Eric Frechon, a three-Michelin-starred chef, is the great mind behind this gourmet enterprise, which serves as cafe, bar, and restaurant. The lofty ceilings, wood furnishings, and white walls give the place a relaxed air, as does the menu, which features French comfort food like *boeuf bourguignon,* cod *brandade* (a sort of fish shepherd's pie), and Toulouse sausage with mashed potatoes. A gaggle of young, intense cooks bustle about, preparing each dish with the best ingredients and designing each plate with care. Breakfast is served from 8 to 11am, and teatime is 3 to 7pm.

Inside the Gare St-Lazare shopping gallery, 8th arrond. lazare-paris.fr. ☏ **01-44-90-80-80.** Main courses 22€–39€; fixed-price lunch and dinner 48€. Mon–Fri 8am–10pm; Sat–Sun 11:45am–10pm. Métro: Gare St-Lazare.

Le Drugstore (Publicis) ♥♥ MODERN BRASSERIE   You won't find toothpaste at the Publicis "drugstore," whose name comes from a former 1950s incarnation that consisted of a warren of shops, restaurants, and services "à l'americaine." This ultramodern, oh-so-chic complex has replaced the funky original, keeping the multifunctional concept intact with shops, restaurants, and a cinema. The brasserie (incidentally, like Lazare above, run by Eric Fréchon) is a gourmet delight: a light-filled expanse with an incredible street-side view of the Champs-Élysées and the Arc de Triomphe, and high-end versions of casual dishes, like asparagus pasta, grilled fish, pork chops, and steak and mash. A long daily breakfast menu is available from 8 to 11:30am and on Sunday's, there's a copious 69€ brunch.

133 av. des Champs-Élysées, 8th arrond. restaurant-le-drugstore.com. ☏ **01-44-43-77-64.** Main courses 24€–58€. Daily 8am–11pm. Métro: Charles de Gaulle–Étoile.

Le Petit Rétro ♥♥ TRADITIONAL FRENCH   This gorgeous little restaurant, dolled up in original Art Nouveau tiles, a zinc bar, and vintage

Le Drugstore (Publicis).

wooden tables, captures the essence of Belle Epoque Paris, and not only in terms of decor. The menu harks back to days gone by with traditional dishes like cod in langoustine cream sauce and veal blanquette. Make sure you mop up all that sauce with some wildly delicious bread and butter. Dessert? You'll be hard-pressed to find a finer dark chocolate soufflé, all oozy and sticky in the middle.

5 rue Mesnil, 16th arrond. petitretro.fr. **01-44-05-06-05.** Main courses 24€–40€. Mon–Sat noon–2:30pm and 7:30–10:30pm. Closed 2 weeks in Aug. Métro: Victor Hugo.

INEXPENSIVE

Monte Carlo ♥♥ SELF-SERVICE/FRENCH   Hitting a self-serve canteen might not be your idea of Parisian dining, but if you're on a budget, don't dismiss this handy spot by the Arc de Triomphe. Monte Carlo has been a favorite with local police officers, office workers, and tourist bus drivers alike since the 1970s—largely because it serves food all day, but also because it's one of the cheapest spots around the Champs-Élysées. A mere 11.30€ gets you a main course like chicken in mushroom sauce or smoked sausage and lentils and there are cheap menus (that include dessert), too. This won't be the culinary highlight of your stay, but the food is well prepared and tasty, and I honestly cannot name anywhere else in the area with such a good quality/price ratio.

9 av. de Wagram, 17th arrond. monte-carlo.fr. **01-43-80-02-20.** Fixed-price menus 15.30€–19.40€. Daily 11am–10pm. Closed 2 weeks in mid-Aug. Métro: Charles de Gaulle–Étoile.

Opéra & Grands Boulevards (2nd & 9th Arrondissements)

Buzzing with cafes and theaters in the 19th century, the long-overlooked Grands Boulevards are finally coming back to life, especially where these wide avenues intersect with the Opéra and the hip and happening part of the 9th arrondissement that borders Montmartre, nicknamed SoPi (as in South of Pigalle). Less trendy, but also less expensive, the little streets around the Bourse (the French stock exchange) have a wide range of restaurant options, especially at lunchtime. The covered passages that crisscross parts of the 2nd arrondissement (p. 243), especially Passage des Panoramas, also harbor some excellent dining options.

EXPENSIVE

Chez Georges ♥♥ TRADITIONAL FRENCH A step back in time, this is how Parisian restaurants were before cuisine became nouvelle.

The traditional interior of Chez Georges brasserie.

The room is crowded and lively, the cooking old-fashioned and delicious. Many of the customers are regulars who work in nearby offices. The handwritten menu features beautifully executed classics like filet of sole, *pot-au-feu* (beef simmered with vegetables), and sweetbreads with morels. Save room for the profiteroles for dessert.

1 rue du Mail, 2nd arrond. facebook.com/chezgeorges1965. ⓒ **01-42-60-07-11.** Main courses 22€–47€. Mon–Fri noon–2:30pm and 7–10:30pm. Closed Aug and the last week of Dec. Métro: Bourse.

La Condesa ♥♥♥ MODERN BISTRO On an up-and-coming street in SoPi, this joint is emblematic of Paris's cosmopolitan dining scene: At the helm is a Mexican chef who trained at Lyon's legendary Institut Paul Bocuse, worked in three-star restaurants in Paris, whizzed off to learn more in Japan, then came back to launch his own restaurant, which has held one Michelin star since 2019. And what a restaurant it is: Green fabrics and natural wood provide a slick backdrop for beautifully executed dishes like celery granita, kombu-marinated veal, and yellow pollock with spiced pineapple. Take it

Elaborate fusion cuisine at La Condesa.

A WORD ABOUT kids IN RESTAURANTS

Many foreigners wonder how French people manage to make their kids behave so well in restaurants. While the ritual of long Sunday family lunches probably trains them to sit still at an early age, there's also the fact that childhood rowdiness is not well tolerated in eating establishments. If the kids can't sit still, the parents simply don't eat out with them. It's rare to find crayons, puzzles, and other kid-friendly items in Parisian restaurants, though they usually have high-chairs (*chaise-haute*, shehz-oht), if not booster seats (*réhausseur*, ray-hoh-sur). That said, by and large French people are kid-friendly, so small, family-owned restaurants will usually be pretty understanding, as long as you don't let your kids run wild. Ask if there's a children's menu (*menu enfant*). While french fries are not particularly nutritious, restaurants usually keep small ones busy with plenty of these treats. You might want to bring along your own kiddie-size forks and spoons, however, as they are never provided. Below is a short list of some restaurants that are particularly amenable to the kid contingent:

- **Le Relais de l'Entrecôte** (p. 143) Serving unlimited helpings of steak and fries, this lively place is a no-brainer for the kid set.
- **Rosa Bonheur** (p. 133) Located inside the Parc des Buttes-Chaumont, this cool cafe has a beautiful outdoor terrace where parents can nibble on tapas while watching their kids roll down the hill.
- **Ground Control** (p. 128) By Gare de Lyon, this vast multidisciplinary arts center has a street food court serving all sorts of dishes, from *frites* to pasta to burgers to meat and cheese platters, with enough space for the kids to literally run around in.

all in with wines from France and Italy, Mexican mezcal, and even Japanese whisky.

17 rue Rodier, 9th arrond. lacondesa-paris.com. **01-53-20-94-90.** Fixed-price lunch 68€ or dinner 85€–160€. Tues–Wed 6:30–10:30pm; Thurs noon–1:15pm and 6:30–10pm; Fri noon–1:15pm and 6–11pm; Sat 6–10:30pm. Closed 2 weeks in Aug. Métro: Anvers or Notre-Dame de Lorette.

MODERATE

Frenchie Bar à Vins ♥♥ WINE BAR   If you're looking for a quiet night of nibbles and wine, don't go to this wine bar in the up-and-coming Sentier district north of Les Halles. The sister establishment of chef Gregory Marchand's ultra-successful Frenchie restaurant (where you still have to reserve well in advance) is a raucous, crowded spot, where you'll be lucky to get a table unless you arrive at 6:30pm when it opens. But that's part of the fun. The wonderful reds, whites, and rosés are the perfect social lubricant for getting to know the tipsy locals spilling out onto the sidewalk. And the plates that fly out of the kitchen like wildfire—mussels with chorizo, chicken-pot-pie croquettes, and fish tacos—are pure delights (many cost around 13€). If you miss the 6:30pm start, come for a post-dinner drink after 10pm, when you can usually waltz straight in.

6 rue du Nil, 2nd arrond. frenchie-bav.com. **01-40-39-96-19.** Mains 8€–31€. Daily 6:30–11pm. Closed 2 weeks in Aug. Métro: Sentier.

Le Pantruche ♥♥ TRADITIONAL FRENCH/BISTRO The name is old-fashioned slang for Paris, but this little bistro has a decidedly modern feel to it. Maybe it's the mirrored column near the bar. In yet another case of runaway chefs from Michelin-starred restaurants, here you'll find flavorful updated bistro fare like braised sweetbreads with carrots in a licorice glaze, or suckling pig with pears, celery root, and chestnuts. It's hard to resist indulging in dessert when the Grand Marnier soufflé is on the menu. The fixed-price menus at lunch and dinner are a terrific value, and the tiny dining room fills quickly; definitely reserve ahead. Note that if you reserve for 7:30 or 7:45pm, a second service begins at 9:15pm, so you will not be allowed to tarry.

3 rue Victor Massé, 9th arrond. lapantruchoise.com/lepantruche ✆ **01-48-78-55-60.** Main courses 22€–27€; fixed-price lunch 23€ or dinner 48€. Mon–Fri 12:30–2:30pm and 7:30–9:30pm. Closed first 3 weeks of Aug. Métro: Pigalle.

Public House ♥♥ FRANCO-BRITISH What do you get when you mix a traditional English pub with a classic French brasserie? Why, Public House, of course—the new playground for British chef Calum Franklin (dubbed London's King of Pies by no less than Jamie Oliver), where the best of British and French cooking come together in dishes like leek and comté tart, dauphinoise potato and aged cheddar pie, and possibly the best sausage and mash in town. The pies—which also include fillings such as lobster and braised beef—are proper works of art, with intricate pastry decoration akin to sculpture. It's hard to resist indulging in the dessert when the sticky toffee pudding, and apple and ginger trifle are on the menu. The bar's a great spot, too, for beer, wine, and gin, with no less than 25 varieties on offer. Decor-wise, expect lots of tartan fabric and peach-colored walls (the British inspiration) with colorful floor tiles (the French part). In winter, ask for a table away from the door; it can get mighty frisky.

21 rue Daunou, 2nd arrond. publichouseparis.fr ✆ **01-77-37-87-93.** Main courses 19.50€–36.50€. Daily 9am–2am. Closed first 2 weeks of Aug. Métro: Opéra or Madeleine; RER Auber.

INEXPENSIVE

Nell'Arte ♥♥ PIZZA Sometimes all you want is pizza, and when you do, this hip eatery (where flowers cover the ceiling) hits the spot with generously topped pies featuring fresh ingredients like goat cheese, spinach, eggplant, and of course, ham and farm-fresh mozzarella. Fancy something unique? If it's on the menu and you like truffles, try the Tartufa, smothered in creamy truffle-infused

Braised beef pie at Public House.

sauce, whose earthy tang is offset by fresh arugula. There are traditional salads like Caesar salad on the menu, too. Delicious!

58 rue Marguerite de Rochechouart, 9th arrond. restaurantnellarte.com. ✆ **06-10-40-36-89.** Main courses 14€–25€. Daily noon–3pm and 7–11:30pm (until midnight Fri–Sun). Métro: Anvers or Poissoniere.

Michi ♥ JAPANESE So discreet is Michi's facade (on rue Ste-Anne, the hub of Paris's "Little Tokyo") that you'd be forgiven for walking past without so much as batting an eyelid. But miss it and you'll miss one of the best sushi joints in town, a tiny spot where fish is as fresh as it gets, and the chef works tirelessly to prepare every dish in front of a seven-seater counter, the best seat in the house if you can get it (there's also a basement). In addition to the sushi and sashimi, look out for delicacies like sea urchin. There's also a good choice of sake and Japanese beer.

58 bis rue Ste-Anne, 2nd arrond. ✆ **01-40-20-49-93.** Main courses 14€–22€; fixed-price menu 14€–23€. Tues–Sat noon–2pm and 7–10pm. Métro: Quatre-Septembre or Bourse.

Montmartre (18th Arrondissement)

When you get away from the tourist traps of Place du Tertre, you start to understand why people love this neighborhood, and why it's become a favorite with the arty-hipster set. To the north and west of the basilica is where you will find the villagey atmosphere you've heard so much about; to the east and south, Montmartre gives way to Barbès, a lively immigrant neighborhood where you are just as likely to see women donning headscarves and African prints as smart Parisian apparel. Either way, you're bound to come across good food.

MODERATE

Le Coq & Fils ♥♥♥ ROTISSERIE At the top of the Butte de Montmartre, this popular rotisserie is where renowned chef Antoine Westerman proves that poultry can go way beyond the nugget. When raised in the right conditions (in the open air, with space and nutritious food), poultry can be just as delicious as the finest cut of beef. On the menu are such delicacies as pigeon with preserved lemons, succulent whole duck from the Dombes region (to share), and tantalizingly juicy Challans chicken—the lot accompanied by crispy, hand-cut fries or macaroni and cheese. The desserts are worth leaving space for, too: lemon crumble, caramelized brioche with poached pears and beer ice cream, and one of the best chocolate *mille-feuille* (layers of pastry and chocolate) in town.

98 rue Lepic, 18th arrond. lecoq-fils.com. ✆ **01-42-59-82-89.** Main courses 28€–53€; whole birds to share for 4 people 139€–169€. Daily noon–2:30pm and 7–11:30pm. Métro: Abbesses or Lamarck-Caulincourt.

Wepler ♥♥ FRENCH BRASSERIE Picasso and Modigliani used to hang out at this venerable brasserie on Place de Clichy, as did writer Henry Miller, who made it his headquarters. "I knew it like a book," he wrote. "The faces of the waiters, the managers, the cashiers, the whores, the clientele, even the attendants in the lavatory, are engraved in my memory as if they were

Montmartre Restaurants

Bouillon Pigalle **3**
Le Coq & Fils **1**
Eté en Pente Douce **2**
Wepler **4**

illustrations in a book which I read every day." Today the atmosphere is quite sedate, but it's still a wonderful place to sit and watch the world go by, and the prices are accessible enough that it is still frequented by artists and writers. The restaurant even offers an annual literary prize. The classic brasserie menu (steak tartare, shellfish platters, poached haddock in *beurre blanc*) has a light, gourmet touch. For a smaller meal, ask for the less expensive cafe menu, which features delicate omelets, a *plat du jour,* and meal-size salads served on the covered terrace. There's handy kids' menu (sausage-fries, chocolate mousse…) here too, at just 10€.

14 pl. de Clichy, 18th arrond. wepler.com. **01-45-22-53-24.** Main courses 17€–50€; seafood platters from 40€; fixed-price lunch 27€ and 40€; fixed-price dinner 40€. Daily 7:30am–midnight (until 1am Fri and Sat). Métro: Place de Clichy.

INEXPENSIVE

Bouillon Pigalle ♥♥ TRADITIONAL FRENCH   You come to this new-fangled "bouillon" (19th-century worker's restaurant) to tuck into classics like leeks in vinaigrette, *boeuf bourguignon,* and chocolate eclairs at prices so low

123

(think 2.50€ for a starter, 10€ for a main, and less than 3€ for dessert) that you wonder how the place makes a profit. The menu covers a wide variety of traditional dishes like steak with fries or rum baba. Service is fast and furious, but it's all part of the atmosphere, which is something that belongs to another time and place. Reserve in advance or be prepared to wait—something upwards of an hour. There's a second branch, Bouillon République (p. 113).

22 bd. de Clichy, 18th arrond. bouillonlesite.com/bouillon-pigalle. © **01-42-59-69-31.** Main courses 10€–13€. Daily noon–midnight. Métro: Pigalle.

Escargot, a Parisian classic, at Bouillon Pigalle.

République, Bastille & Eastern Paris (11th & 12th Arrondissements)

With a mix of working-class families, hipsters, and *bobos* (bourgeois bohemians), the area between Bastille, République and Nation is diverse, young, and fun. It's also one of the most exciting places for food right now, with a plethora of young chefs opening restaurants that Parisians cross the city for.

EXPENSIVE

Geosmine ♥♥♥ MODERN FRENCH The bathrooms at this restaurant contain the coolest toilets in Paris. Water cascades into the tank from through a long, glass tube, making each flush an event. That might seem like a strange way to start a restaurant review, but it's indicative of the imaginativeness and creativity that's goes into every aspect of the dining experience at this young restaurant. The silverware looks like something the painter Gustave Klimt might have invented, and the food combinations read like impossibilities on the menu, but meld into new flavor profiles unlike any I've ever tasted

Amuse-bouches at Geosmine.

before. On my last visit to this two-story townhouse restaurant, these included a splendid smoked eel tart, made even richer by a layer of pistachio cream; a starter of mozzarella and melon taken to another level by the addition of kalamata olives; and, on the more traditional side, perfectly cooked beef bathed in the most flavorsome béarnaise sauce I've ever tasted. Also unusual: the kindliness of the waitstaff here, who seem genuinely invested in making sure each diner has a meal to remember.

71 rue de la Folie Mericourt, 11th arrond. geosmine.com. ⓒ **09-78-80-48-59.** Lunch a la carte 11€–42€; fixed-price lunch 80€–120€; fixed-price dinner 140€. Tues and Thurs 7:30–9pm; Wed, Fri–Sat 12:30–2pm and 7:30–9pm. Metro République or Parmentier.

Septime ♥♥♥ MODERN FRENCH With its seafood tapas bar next door (**Clamato**) and its tiny wine bar across the street (**Septime la Cave**), Septime has done more to gentrify this stretch of the 11th arrondissement than years of town planning ever could. With reservations made at least 3 weeks in advance, people cross the entire city for a table in Bertrand Grébaut's retro-chic neo-bistro. The progressive, seasonal dishes—anything from line-caught squid with mustard and leek sauce to pigeon with beetroot and Morello cherries—are consistently delicious, and the menus change daily according to what's freshest in the produce market. If you can't score a dinner reservation, try lunchtime. And if all else fails, nip next door to Clamato, where fabulous small plates of crab fritters, clams, or trout roe are washed down with lip-smacking wine that starts for as little as 6€ a glass. You won't be disappointed.

80 rue de Charonne, 11th arrond. septime-charonne.fr. ⓒ **01-43-67-38-29.** Fixed-price lunch 85€ (wine pairing 60€) or dinner 135€ (wine pairing 75€). Mon–Fri 12:15–2pm and 7:30–11pm. Closed 3 weeks in Aug. Métro: Charonne or Ledru-Rollin.

An artfully prepared dish at Septime.

MODERATE

Fulgurances ♥♥ BISTRO Fulgurances looks like any other hip neighborhood bistro: natural wood tables, open kitchen, and a quaint spiral staircase tucked away at the back. However, something exciting is afoot. This place is an "incubator," a testing ground for sous chefs looking to become head chefs and open their own restaurants. For a limited number of weeks, they get free run of the kitchen, concocting their own menus, honing their styles, and seeing diners' reactions just meters from the kitchen counter. Menus are limited to what the chef decides to cook that day, usually a choice of two starters, mains, and desserts at lunch, and an evening tasting menu. As this is a cooking "playground," your taste might not always fit with the chef's vision, but this is undoubtedly one of the most interesting dining experiences in the city. There's its wine bar across the road now, too, at number 5.

The dining room at Fulgurances.

10 rue Alexandre Dumas, 11th arrond. fulgurances.com. ✆ **01-43-48-14-59.** Fixed-price lunch 25€ and 30€ or dinner 75€. Thurs–Fri noon–2pm; Mon–Fri 7–10pm. Closed part of Aug. Métro: Rue des Boulets.

Laïa ♥♥♥ MEDITERRANEAN This wonderful Mediterranean restaurant is tucked away in a hidden garden along the tourist-free boulevard Voltaire, on the site of a former distillery. It's like a slice of urban paradise—just you, the flowers, and not a peep from the traffic—not to mention that you get some of the most competitive menus on the block: 21.50€ for a two-course lunch and 55€ for the fixed-price dinner. And boy, are the dishes delicious: marinated grilled chicken, beef with mint and blackberries, and barbecued octopus. In fact, much of the food is barbecued on a *robata* (a Japanese-Spanish grill), with herbs and vegetables from the restaurant's

Dining in the garden at Laïa.

rooftop garden. Classic cocktails are given a Mediterranean spin (from 12€). The service is relaxed yet ultra-attentive, and always with a smile. The place is open for coffee from 10am. There are some vegetarian and gluten-free options, too.

226 bd. Voltaire, 11th arrond. laia-restaurant.com. 09-75-65-27-21. Main courses 18€–35€; fixed-price lunch 21.50€; fixed-price dinner 55€. Mon–Sat 10am–midnight. Closed 2 weeks in Aug. Métro: Rue des Boulets or Voltaire.

Pierre Sang In Oberkampf ♥♥♥ BISTRO   Pierre Sang was a finalist in France's TV cooking competition *Top Chef,* yet there's nothing pretentious or showy about this restaurant. The open kitchen does provide entertainment, as Sang's chefs chop, sizzle, and steam all sorts of spice-infused delights that send fragrant scents wafting over the long, shared tables. Expect an inventive selection of Franco-Korean tapas made with whatever market-fresh ingredients have come in that week (though they'll cater for allergies obviously; tell them as soon as you arrive). This might include a tender chicken and tarragon terrine, a crispy herring tempura, or spicy shrimp with *gochujang* (Asian chili sauce). Reserve in advance; it's as popular as can be. If you can't get in, Sang owns two other restaurants on rue Gambey (the street the restaurant looks out onto): **On Gambey** is a slightly more upmarket version of "in Oberkampf" (dinner menus cost 55.50€–95.50€) with the **Pierre Sang Express** takeout bibimbap counter (from 10.90€) out front. Check the website for other Express addresses in Paris.

55 rue Oberkampf, 11th arrond. pierresang.com. 09-67-31-96-80. Fixed-price lunch 30.50€–45.50€; dinner 45.50€. Daily noon–2:15pm and 7–9:45pm. Closed part of Aug. Métro: Parmentier or Oberkampf.

INEXPENSIVE

Aux Bons Crus ♥♥♥ BISTRO   Back in the 1960s France was peppered with *Routiers,* roadside restaurants that catered to truck drivers and holidaymakers on their way from the cities to the coast or countryside. As the ancestor of the service station, Routiers were known for serving cheap, homemade food, hearty enough to get you through the long journey ahead. While most have disappeared, Aux Bons Crus at Voltaire is alive and kicking, sporting the Routiers famous red, white, and blue logo, and serving classics like steak in pepper sauce (albeit at Parisian prices) on checkered tablecloths. Today you're more likely to run into people pushing strollers and zipping around on electric scooters than you are truck drivers, but that doesn't detract from the authentic, old-time Paris feel you get as you tuck into beetroot salad, roast chicken, and chocolate profiteroles.

54 rue Godefroy Cavaignac, 11th arrond. auxbonscrus.fr. 01-45-67-21-13. Main courses 19€–27€. Daily noon–2:30pm and 7:30–10:30pm. Closed part of Aug. Métro: Voltaire.

Brasserie Martin ♥♥ BISTRO   If you don't reserve a week ahead, you'll have to wait in line for a table at this excellent brasserie. The draw? Excellently executed bistro classics, served at low, low prices—like a delicious starter of egg and mayo for 3€, a main of sausage and mashed potato for 14€, and soul-satisfying desserts like chocolate mousse and Paris-Brest (choux pastry with praline cream) for 8€. The menu has other delectable meat and fish dishes, as well as sharing plates and terrines, and service is with a smile. What more can you ask for?

24 rue St-Amboise, 11th arrond. nouvellegardegroupe.com/en/brasseriemartin. **01-48-05-34-36.** Main courses 14€–24€. Daily 9am–midnight. Métro: Saint-Amboise or Rue Saint-Maur.

Chefs in the open kitchen at Brasserie Martin.

Ground Control ♥♥ STREET FOOD There's an underground feel to this sprawling venue near Gare de Lyon, a vast multidisciplinary arts center with its own radio station, exhibition spaces, and a food hall set in disused SNCF hangars. The food court is the place to get delicious international grub—from Chinese and Mexican to Greek and Italian, depending on which restaurants are there at the time (they change regularly), plus coffee and cake for dessert. Outside, converted buses hawk everything from British fish and chips to ham-and-cheese crepes to fresh oysters, with seating at vintage benches and tables. Just make sure you get your drink before you order food.

Outdoor dining at Ground Control.

None of the stalls sell beverages, and it's annoying to have to leave your hot food tray for some water or beer.

81 rue du Charolais, 12th arrond. ground controlparis.com. No phone. Main courses 9€–17€. Wed–Thurs noon–midnight; Fri–Sat noon–1am; Sun noon–10:30pm (last entry 1 hr. before closing time). Métro/RER: Gare de Lyon.

L'Ebauchoir ♥♥♥ MODERN FRENCH Located in an unlikely corner of the 12th arrondissement, this atmospheric neighborhood hang-out offers a fab selection of modern bistro cooking at decidedly reasonable prices. The high ceilings, light walls, and wooden fixtures create a warm and friendly environment for vaguely Mediterranean-inspired dishes like roast lamb with sweet spices and Thai basil, or *magret* (breast) of duck with vanilla and pineapple. You can usually find a nice vegetarian option here, like a vegetable "cake" with sautéed shiitake mushrooms, asparagus, and hummus. With a two-course lunch deal at 17€, this place gets jammed at noon, so try to reserve.

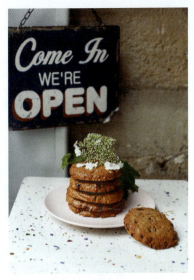

Vegan cookies at Noglu.

43 rue des Citeaux, 12th arrond. lebauchoir.com. ⓒ **01-43-42-49-31.** Main courses 24€–32€; fixed-price lunch 17€. Mon 7:30–9pm; Tues–Sat noon–2:30pm and 7:30–9pm. Closed 1 week mid-Aug. Métro: Faidherbe Chaligny or Reuilly Diderot.

Noglu ♥♥ GLUTEN-FREE This small restaurant is where gluten-intolerant people bring their friends because the home-cooked gluten-free food is so tasty you don't have to have a food allergy to appreciate it. Dishes might include cod with lentils, vegetable lasagna, and warm chocolate cake. Though not vegetarian per se, Noglu always has meat- and fish-free dishes on the menu. If you're in a hurry, everything can be made to take out. Like what you eat? There are now two other addresses on the Left Bank (69 rue de Grenelle, 7th arrond. and 62 rue de Vaugirard, 6th arrond.).

15 rue Basfroi, 11th arrond. noglu.fr. ⓒ **01-42-36-52-50.** Main courses 10€–22€; fixed-price breakfast 16.50€ and 21€. Mon–Fri 8:30am–6:30pm; Sat–Sun 9am–7pm. Closed 2 weeks in Aug. Métro: Voltaire, Charonne, or Ledru Rollin.

Belleville, Canal St-Martin & Northeast Paris (10th, 19th & 20th Arrondissements)

Between the two parks of Belleville and Buttes Chaumont and along the Canal St-Martin lie some of the city's most quirky and delightful restaurants. In one of the last strongholds of Paris's bohemian set, you can find both gourmet bistros and funky cheap eats, as well as a good number of wine bars that serve nibbles along with the fruit of the vine. One Thursday evening every month boulevard de Belleville morphs into a street food market where around 20 stands sell everything from Vietnamese *bò bún* (a beef and noodle salad) to Mexican street tacos (lefoodmarket.fr, p. 248).

MODERATE

Chez Michel ♥♥♥ BRETON/SEAFOOD Diners come from all over Paris, as well as from across the channel (via the nearby Eurostar train hub at Gare du Nord), to sample this institution's superb French cooking at affordable prices that have barely budged in a decade. The chef, Masahiro Kawai, improvises on classic French recipes, including roasted pigeon, and seafood dishes like pan-fried octopus and fresh crab salad. For dessert, try the bitter dark chocolate mousse with poached pear or the awe-inspiring crème-caramel with whipped cream.

Hearty Breton fish stew at Chez Michel.

10 rue de Belzunce, 10th arrond. restaurantchezmichel.fr. © **01-44-53-06-20.** Fixed-price lunch 40€–48€ or dinner 48€. Mon–Fri noon–1:30pm and 7–9:30pm. Closed Aug. Métro: Gare du Nord.

EELS ♥♥♥ BISTRO/SEAFOOD Foodies have been flocking to this fabulous seafood-oriented bistro, ever since it opened in 2017. And once you've tasted the namesake starter of smoked "eels" with apple, you'll understand why. Every single dish is a taste explosion—from the grilled sea trout with confit of fennel to the haunch of veal with caper leaves and the chocolate crisp with cardamom and pomegranate cream. At 39€, the three-course lunch menu is a steal. If you're up for an all-gourmet experience, the 89€, five-course tasting menu is a special experience.

27 rue d'Hauteville, 10th arrond. restaurant-eels.com. © **01-42-28-80-20.** Main courses 33€–344€; fixed-price lunch 32€–39€, fixed-price dinner 89€; wine pairing 54€. Tues–Sat 12:30–2pm and 7:30–10pm. Closed 2 weeks in Aug. Métro: Bonne-Nouvelle or Poissonnière.

Presenting an entree at EELS.

Les Arlots ♥♥♥ WINE BAR/BISTRO You'll need to reserve several days in advance to get a table in this tiny, noisy bistro by Gare du Nord, quite simply because it serves some of the best comfort cuisine in town—everything from langoustines in mayonnaise to foie gras–stuffed cabbage to perfectly cooked (that is, pink) veal with braised carrots. Locals wax lyrical about the homemade sausage and mash, and desserts are just as tempting: The cinnamon and orange is both creamy and tangy, the *fraisier* (strawberries, shortbread, and sour cream) has just the right crunch-to-cream ratio. Only the freshest products are used, so the menu changes regularly, but these are staples to look out for when the season's right. Wash them down with a crisp sauvignon blanc or a berry-red Syrah and you'll be smiling before you can say "bon appetit!"

136 rue du Faubourg Poissonnière, 10th arrond. facebook.com/lesarlots. ✆ **01-42-82-92-01.** Main courses 20€–34€; fixed-price lunch 32.50€. Tues–Sat noon–2pm and 7:30–10pm. Closed last 3 weeks in Aug and first week of May. Métro/RER: Gare du Nord or Métro Anvers, Poissonnière, or Barbès-Rochechouart.

MijoT ♥♥ MODERN FRENCH/BISTRO Tucked away on a narrow street, this tiny bistro feels like a secret, with mostly only locals in sight. The draw? Talented chef Isabelle Bouillon's delectable fare, which may include plates like carrot and orange soup, duck ravioli, and chocolate tart with thyme cream and champagne sorbet. Everything is made with ingredients sourced directly from local producers (except the duck, which is from the Nouvelle Aquitaine region), and proceeds go to a charity dedicated to feeding the poor. You can't say better than that.

Pulled pork, celery mousseline, Comté sauce, pea microgreens at MijoT.

6 rue Victor Letalle, 20th arrond. mijot.fr. ✆ **01-47-97-25-77.** Main courses 24€–29€. Tues–Sat 7–10:30pm. Closed part of August. Métro: Ménilmontant.

Zerda Café ♥♥ NORTH AFRICAN Intricately carved Moorish designs cover the walls of this friendly restaurant, which serves some of the best couscous in Paris. Zerda offers a choice of lamb, chicken, and *merguez* (spicy lamb sausage) versions; my favorite is the meltingly tender "lamb cooked in sauce," but all are good. If you prefer one of the scrumptious *tagines* (stews seasoned with such ingredients as dried fruits, olives, or preserved lemons), be patient: They take 20 minutes to prepare.

17 rue Rene Boulanger, 10th arrond. zerdacafe.fr. ✆ **01-42-00-25-15.** Main courses 18€–28€. Mon–Sat 4:30–11:30pm. Closed 2 weeks in Aug. Métro: République.

INEXPENSIVE

Bob's Juice Bar ♥ VEGETARIAN   People are tripping all over themselves to try "smoossies" (that is, smoothies) and juices these days, and some of the best can be found at this terrific vegetarian restaurant, which has become *the* place to sample muffins, bagels, soups, and other delicious vegetarian goodies. The brainchild of Marc Grossman (alias "Bob"), an erstwhile New Yorker, this may not be the most authentically French experience, but it certainly is a tasty one. You can sit down or take out. Also try **Bob's Bake Shop** in La Chapelle (Halle Pajol, 12 Espl. Nathalie Sarraute, 18th arrond.) or in the famous Shakespeare and Company bookshop cafe, 37 rue de la Bûcherie, 5th arrond. (p. 253).

15 rue Lucien Sampaix, 10th arrond. bobsjuicebar.com. © **09-50-06-36-18**. Smoothies and juices 6.50€–9€; main courses 9€–14€. Mon–Fri 8:30am–3pm. Métro: Jacques Bonsergent.

Hôtel du Nord ♥♥ FRENCH   Overlooking Canal St-Martin, just across from where Amélie threw pebbles in Jean-Pierre Jeunet's cult 2001 movie, this vintage bistro is a hip place for a meal. For casual dining, book the front section, reminiscent of a 1930s cafe with tiled floors and an Art Deco zinc bar; for something more sophisticated, the back section's red banquettes, white tablecloths, and mirrors create a boudoir-chic ambience. Wherever you sit, the food is good: classic dishes like beef carpaccio with fries, sausage-rich cassoulet, or vegetarian options such as ricotta and spinach ravioli. There is often live entertainment, too—everything from jazz nights to dancing to DJ sound.

102 quai de Jemmapes, 10th arrond. hoteldunord.org. © **01-40-40-78-78**. Main courses 17€–26€; fixed-price lunch 19€. Daily 7:30am–2am. Métro: Jacques Bonsergent.

Le Verre Volé ♥ WINE BAR/MODERN FRENCH   The sun is shining, the leafy trees are posing prettily along the Canal St-Martin, and you are walking one of the pretty footbridges that curve over the water. All that's missing is a table and a glass of wine. Luckily, this wine bar/restaurant is on hand with a vast selection of bacchic and gustatory delights. You could just share a plate of sliced smoked meats and sausage, the usual accompaniment to a glass of red, or

L Avant Comptior Hotel Du Nord Restaurant.

A cozy corner at Thai restaurant Naam.

you can explore the menu, which might include a slice of milk-fed veal or mullet ceviche. Then select a bottle of wine from the shelves that line the walls and enjoy it (for a nominal corkage fee; there are around 400 to choose between) in this informal, if crowded, setting.

67 rue de Lancry, 10th arrond. leverrevole.fr. **01-48-03-17-34.** Fixed-price lunch 21€–24€; main courses 18€–25€. Daily 12:30–2:30pm and 7:30pm–1am. Métro: Jacques Bonsergent.

Naam ♥♥♥ THAI Lovers of Thai cuisine flock to this restaurant high on the Belleville hillside. The reason? Chef Anne Coppin's lip-smacking Thai recipes that she spent years perfecting in Bangkok. And if the number of people of Thai origin in the dining room (a tiny space with dark turquoise paint and leafy wallpaper) is anything to go by, she's perfected it to a T. The minuscule kitchen has a big window out onto the street, so you can watch Anne cooking before you enter. Then once inside, sit back and tuck into such wow-worthy dishes as sweet and spicy *som tam* carrot with lemongrass sausage, *massaman* beef (a coconutty stew cooked for 5 hours and served with sweet potato), and green chicken curry. The 18€ lunch menu is a steal. There are only two starters and three main courses to choose between, but whatever you choose, you're guaranteed a taste explosion.

73 rue de Belleville, 19th arrond. instagram.com/naam_thaifood. **06-19-15-90-84.** Main courses 16€–23€; fixed-price menu 18€–22€. Tues–Thurs and Sun 7–10:30pm; Fri–Sat noon–2:30pm and 7–10:30pm. Métro: Pyrénées or Belleville.

Rosa Bonheur ♥ TAPAS This unconventional space is named after an unconventional 19th-century painter/sculptor. Yes, it's a tapas bar, but it's also a sort of off-the-wall community center, hosting various expositions and events, not to mention its own chorus and soccer team. Located in an old *buvette* (refreshment pavilion) inside the Parc des Buttes Chaumont that dates from the Universal Exposition of 1900, the restaurant boasts a sprawling terrace and one of the best panoramic views in town. Late afternoon, a huge crowd gathers to drink and nibble tapas both indoors and out. The ambience is relaxed and friendly; coming here is a good excuse to stroll through the lush Buttes Chaumont park. That park, plus an indoor play area and kids' menu, makes Rosa Bonheur a great family option. A second location is on a docked barge on the Seine, **Rosa Bonheur Sur Seine** (right near the Pont des Invalides on the Left Bank with outdoor seating and a pizza stand on the quay), a third, **Rosa à l'Est,** is in the Bois de Vincennes (p. 239) and there's a fourth, **Rosa à l'Ouest,** in the suburb of Asnières.

2 allée de la Cascade, 19th arrond. rosabonheur.fr. **01-42-00-00-45.** Tapas 7€–14€. Thurs–Fri 6pm–1am; Sat–Sun noon–1:30am. Closed first 2 weeks in Jan. Métro: Botzaris.

THE LEFT BANK
Latin Quarter (5th & 13th Arrondissements)

For more than 700 years, this lively neighborhood has been overrun with students, a population that is forever on the lookout for a good, cheap meal. As a result, the area is full of inexpensive snack shacks of varying quality, from souvlaki huts to Vietnamese noodle shops to Breton crêperies. Steer clear of the unbearably touristy area around rue de la Huchette, where you are bound to pay too much for a mediocre product, and be wary of rue Moufftard, which was once a good bet for good food but has since become a victim of its own success. If you want to eat well, you'll need to venture a little farther afield, where innovative restaurateurs have been cultivating a knowledgeable clientele of professors, professionals, and savvy tourists.

EXPENSIVE

La Tour d'Argent ♥♥♥ CLASSIC FRENCH Everyone from Queen Elizabeth II to Marilyn Monroe has dined in this venerable restaurant, famed for its history (a restaurant has stood here since 1582), its impeccable service, and its sweeping view of the Seine and Notre-Dame. In 2023, the place was given a huge makeover, adding a 1930s-inspired bar—Bar des Maillets d'Argent—on the ground floor and a rooftop for wine and cocktails. Inside the panoramic 6th-floor dining room, where you gaze out over Paris though huge windows, chef Yannick Franques woos well-dressed crowds with the promise of inventive French cuisine and the establishment's

View of the Seine from the rooftop of La Tour d'Argent.

Left Bank Restaurants (Eiffel Tower Area)

Left Bank Restaurants (Latin Quarter, St-Germain, Montparnasse)

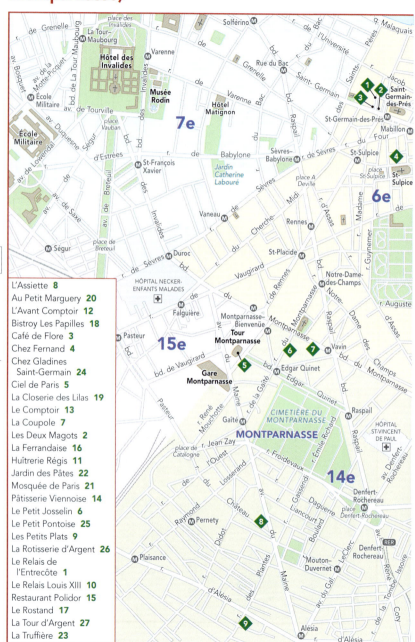

WHERE TO DINE — The Left Bank — 5

L'Assiette **8**
Au Petit Marguery **20**
L'Avant Comptoir **12**
Bistroy Les Papilles **18**
Café de Flore **3**
Chez Fernand **4**
Chez Gladines Saint-Germain **24**
Ciel de Paris **5**
La Closerie des Lilas **19**
Le Comptoir **13**
La Coupole **7**
Les Deux Magots **2**
La Ferrandaise **16**
Huîtrerie Régis **11**
Jardin des Pâtes **22**
Mosquée de Paris **21**
Pâtisserie Viennoise **14**
Le Petit Josselin **6**
Le Petit Pontoise **25**
Les Petits Plats **9**
La Rotisserie d'Argent **26**
Le Relais de l'Entrecôte **1**
Le Relais Louis XIII **10**
Restaurant Polidor **15**
Le Rostand **17**
La Tour d'Argent **27**
La Truffière **23**

136

coveted signature dish of pressed duck (each duck has been numbered since 1890). Five or six different waiters will visit your table at one time or another, accomplishing various tasks (opening wine bottles, pulling out your chair, and even leading you to the bathroom) with utmost professionalism and not a hint of snobbery. For something simpler and cheaper, check out the Rotisserie d'Argent (p. 140), just across the street—the Tour's gingham-clad sister establishment with a terrace that sprawls out onto the Tournelles bridge just outside in summer.

15–17 quai de la Tournelle, 5th arrond. latourdargent.com. 01-43-54-23-31. Main courses 109€–185€; fixed-price lunch 160€ or dinner 380€ and 450€. Tues–Sat noon–2pm and 7–9pm. Closed Aug. Métro: St-Michel or Maubert-Mutualité.

La Truffière ♥♥ CLASSIC FRENCH   An atmospheric 17th-century dining room near the Seine with exposed stone walls and wooden beams is the setting for the sort of French cuisine you crave when you think of Paris—langoustines, suckling lamb, ultra-ripe cheeses, and the "black diamonds" (truffles) that the restaurant takes its name from, prepared with panache by talented chef Quentin Maisonnobe. If you're into wine, you'll be hard-pressed to find a better restaurant: The menu has over 3,000 bottles. Thank goodness for the sommelier, who takes into account both your budget and the dishes you've ordered. Tasting menus cost 145€ in the evening, so the three-course 45€ lunch menu is a good deal.

4 rue Blainville, 5th arrond. la-truffiere.fr. 01-46-33-29-82. Main dishes 45€–85€; fixed-price lunch 30€–45€ or dinner 145€. Tues–Sat noon–1:30pm and 6:30–9:30pm. Closed Aug. Métro: Place Monge or Cardinal Lemoine.

Dining room in La Truffière.

A dining area at Bistroy Les Papilles.

MODERATE

Au Petit Marguery ♥♥ TRADITIONAL FRENCH/BISTRO This place has everything you always wanted in a French bistro: antique tile floors, banquettes, vested waiters, and a dark rose color scheme. The menu also reflects the traditions of yesteryear, with an emphasis on game dishes in autumn and fresh produce in summer. Appetizers include several different terrines, including homemade foie gras; main dishes feature meaty items like 7-hour lamb and lighter fare like sea bream with fennel and star anise. Top it all off with a Grand Marnier soufflé (a specialty of the house). The restaurant has a smaller and more relaxed version of itself next door, the **Comptoir Marguery** (comptoirmarguery.fr), where prices are lower and the menu is a little more basic.

9 bd. du Port-Royal, 13th arrond. petitmarguery.com. ✆ **01-43-31-58-59.** Mains 21€–36€; fixed-price lunch and dinner 31€–39€. Tues–Sat noon–2pm and 7–10:15pm; Sun noon–2pm. Métro: Gobelins.

Bistroy Les Papilles ♥♥ BISTRO/WINE BAR Lined with shelves upon shelves of delectable bottles, this bustling wine shop/bistro/gourmet grocery matches simple but excellent fare with terrific samples of the fruit of the vine. At lunchtime, the fixed-price menu offers great value—three courses for 45€—but few choices. If you don't want the menu, try the *marmite du marché*, the stew of the day served in a cast-iron pot (around 24€). Wine is available by the glass, but patrons are encouraged to choose a bottle from the nearby shelves and pay just a small corkage fee—a great way to try a good bottle without the usual restaurant markup on the wine.

30 rue Gay-Lussac, 5th arrond. lespapillesparis.fr. ✆ **01-43-25-20-79.** Main courses 24€–32€; fixed-price lunch 35€–45€. Tues–Sat noon–2pm and 6:30–10pm. Closed Aug and between Christmas and New Year's. RER: Luxembourg.

La Rotisserie d'Argent ♥♥

FRENCH/ROTISSERIE A great choice for roast chicken lovers, La Rôtisserie d'Argent (the sister brasserie of the *gastronomique* Tour d'Argent) serves some of the best half chickens in town—juicy and garlicky with piles of mashed potato. There are other birds too, namely pigeon and duck, with sides ranging from spinach and candied onions to delicious, crispy fries. Dessert-wise, expect creamy *île flottante* (meringue floating in custard cream) or a classic, vanilla-infused crème brûlée. The wine list is ample. A personal favorite (if available) is the 2020 Morgon Tradition by Domaine des Améthystes in the Beaujolais region in Burgundy, a light, lively red with notes of red fruits (42€).

Veal stew at Rôtisserie d'Argent.

19 quai de la tournelle, 5th arrond. rotisseriedargent.com. © **01-43-54-17-47.** Main dishes 28€–39€. Daily noon–2:15pm and 7–10:15pm. Closed 2 weeks in Aug. Métro: Maubert Mutualité, Cardinal Lemoine or Jussieu.

Le Petit Pontoise ♥ BISTRO

Looking for somewhere authentic and friendly in the tourist heart of the Latin Quarter? Le Petit Pontoise is just a 5-minute walk from Notre-Dame and even closer to the Seine, but it's coveted by locals who come for foie gras with figs, Provençal scallops, and honey-fried pigs' cheeks. The setting's lovely, too—all red leather banquettes and country-style wooden tables. Sample the luscious food with (many) glasses of great French wines, from golden-hued Sancerre white to light, fruity, organic Bourguil red. The place is packed in the evening, so get there early or reserve a table online beforehand.

9 rue Pontoise, 5th arrond. lepetitpontoise.fr. © **01-43-29-25-20.** Main dishes 27€–45€; fixed-price lunch 23€–35€. Wed–Mon noon–2:30pm and 6:30–10:30pm. Closed last week of Dec, first week of Jan, and 2 weeks in Aug. Métro: Maubert-Mutualité.

Chinatown, Paris-Style

Paris actually has two Chinatowns: the more established one, among the 1970s apartment towers between avenues d'Ivry and Choisy in the 13th arrondissement (about a 5-min. walk from Place d'Italie), and another newer one in Belleville in the 10th and 20th. Neither Chinatown is strictly Chinese—the population also includes communities from Vietnam, Cambodia, Laos and other Asian countries. The 13th's Chinatown has dozens of good restaurants. A couple of my favorites are **Imperial Choisy,** 32 av. de Choisy, 13th arrond. (imperialchoisy.fr/menu; © **01-45-86-42-40**) for Chinese food, and the Laotian restaurant **Lao Douang Chan,** 161 av. de Choisy, 13th arrond. (laodouangchan.fr; © **01-44-24-80-80**), for great noodle soup.

INEXPENSIVE

Chez Gladines Saint-Germain ♥ SOUTHWESTERN   Hungry? Come here for enormous and tasty portions of rib-sticking southwestern French specialties. That means crispy duck confit with sautéed potatoes; Basque-style chicken (with tomatoes and bell peppers); *pipérade* (a casserole of eggs with smoked ham, sliced and sautéed potatoes, bell peppers, and a bright tomato sauce); and the like. Even the salads are gargantuan, filled with goodies like bacon, goat cheese, smoked ham, and foie gras. The success of the original Gladines in the 13th arrondissement (30 rue des Cinq Diamants) has spawned two other locations: 11 bis rue des Halles, 1st arrond.; and 74 bd. des Batignolles, 17th arrond.

44 bd. St-Germain, 5th arrond. chezgladines-saintgermain.fr. ✆ **01-46-33-93-88.** Main courses 9.50€–15€. Mon–Thurs noon–11pm; Fri–Sat noon–11:45pm; Sun noon–11:30pm. Métro: Maubert-Mutualité.

Jardin des Pâtes ♥♥ PASTA/VEGETARIAN   This quaint restaurant by the Jardin des Plantes specializes in pasta. But this is no ordinary pasta—not only are the rice, wheat, rye, and barley noodles made fresh every day, but the organic flour that goes into them is ground daily on the premises. The focus on wholesome ingredients is menu-wide—even the ice cream is 100% natural. While you won't find the usual Italian sauces, you will find original creations like rye pasta with ham, cream, sweet onions, white wine, and Comté cheese or barley pasta with fresh salmon, leeks, seaweed, and crème fraîche. Vegetarians have ample choices here, and the relaxed atmosphere makes it a good place to bring (well-behaved) kids. Pastas are made to order, so don't be in a hurry. Reservations are advised, especially on weekends.

4 rue Lacépède, 5th arrond. ✆ **01-43-31-50-71.** Main courses 15€–25€. Daily noon–10:30pm. Métro: Place Monge.

St-Germain-des-Prés (6th Arrondissement)

St-Germain is a mix of expensive eateries that only the lucky few can afford and smaller bistros that bring back the days when intellectuals and artists frequented the Café de Flore. Overpriced tourist restaurants cluster around boulevard St-Germain near the Carrefour de l'Odéon; as you head south and north of this major boulevard, your choices will expand. Though the Marché St-Germain has been transformed into a type of mall, the restaurants hugging its perimeter offer a wide range of possibilities.

EXPENSIVE

La Ferrandaise ♥♥ TRADITIONAL FRENCH/BISTRO   Named after a particularly tasty breed of cow, this carnivore's paradise serves beef that comes direct from Puy du Dôme, the center of France's green heartland. The young chef is also a great believer in local products (all vegetables are local and/or organic) and authentic bistro cuisine. Menu highlights could include shoulder of lamb with spinach, or a juicy steak with sautéed carrots, but if meat is not your game, then equally delectable fish and poultry dishes are also on offer. To finish, try a fresh Auvergne cheese like Saint Nectaire or Fourme d'Ambert. Bring your appetite; portions are filling.

8 rue de Vaugirard, 6th arrond. laferrandaise.com. © **01-43-26-36-36.** Fixed-price lunch 38€–46€, fixed-price dinner 46€. Main courses 30€. Mon and Sat 7–11:30pm; Tues–Fri 11am–3pm and 7–11:30pm. Closed evenings in Aug. Métro: Odéon.

Le Relais Louis XIII ♥♥♥ TRADITIONAL FRENCH   In an ancient building on the site where Louis XIII was crowned back in 1610, this acclaimed restaurant pays homage not only to the monarch, but to traditional French cuisine at its most illustrious. No tonka beans or reduced licorice sauce here—Chef Manuel Martinez trains his formidable talents on classic sauces and time-honored dishes like sea bass *quenelles* and roast duck, though he's not opposed to topping off the meal with a little lemon-basil sherbet at dessert. Signature dishes include lobster and foie gras ravioli and braised sweetbreads with wild mushrooms. The dining room, crisscrossed with exposed beams and ancient stonework, makes you wonder if the Three Musketeers might not tumble through the doorway bearing your *mille-feuille* with bourbon vanilla cream.

8 rue des Grands-Augustins, 6th arrond. relaislouis13.fr. © **01-43-26-75-96.** Fixed-price lunch 80€–195€ or dinner 135€–195€. Tues–Sat 12:15–2:30pm and 7:15–10:30pm. Closed 1st week Jan, 1st week May, and all of Aug. Métro: Odéon or St-Michel.

MODERATE

Chez Fernand ♥♥ TRADITIONAL FRENCH/BISTRO   This neighborhood institution packs a flavorful punch. Red-checkered tablecloths provide a homey background for excellent bistro dishes like thick steak with a pepper sauce and creamy mashed potatoes, veal liver with caramelized onions, or the *boeuf bourguignon*, the specialty of the house. You could start with a nice, light sea bass tartare or a rich, grilled marrowbone. Whatever your choice, it will be executed with loving care and quality ingredients, which is why this restaurant has a devoted clientele.

13 rue Guisarde, 6th arrond. chezfernand-guisarde.com. © **01-43-54-61-47.** Main courses 24.90€–39.50€. Daily noon–2:30pm and 7–11pm (until midnight Fri and Sat). Métro: Mabillon.

Huîtrerie Régis ♥ OYSTERS/SEAFOOD   Like oysters on the half shell? Good, because that's pretty much all they have here: delicious bivalves that come straight from the Marennes-Oléron region on France's Atlantic coast. The brief and to-the-point menu gives you a choice of various sizes and grades of oysters, as well as sea urchins, clams, and shrimp. You'll have to order at least a dozen oysters to sit down in the tiny restaurant; considering the price, you may as well order a *formule*, or fixed-price menu, which includes various combinations of oysters, wine, and coffee. These oysters are fresh, oceany mouthfuls of flavor that deserve a good glass of Sancerre.

3 rue de Montfaucon, 6th arrond. huitrerie-regis.com. © **01-44-41-10-07.** Oysters per dozen 39€–49€; fixed-price lunch or dinner 39€–49€. Mon–Fri noon–2:30pm and 6:30–10:30pm; Sat noon–10:45pm; Sun noon–10pm. Closed mid-July to mid-Sept. Métro: Mabillon or St-Germain.

Le Comptoir ♥♥♥ TRADITIONAL FRENCH/BISTRO

The brainchild of super-chef Yves de Camdeborde, this small and scrumptious bistro set below the Relais Saint-Germain hotel (p. 90) is still bringing in the crowds more than a decade after its opening in 2005. Camdeborde is often credited with starting the bistronomy movement in the 1990s, when he walked out on the Crillon and opened his own bistro. He wanted to offer the French equivalent of "down home" cooking, using the best ingredients and charging affordable prices. During the day, Le Comptoir is a bistro, serving relatively traditional fare, like a slice of lamb with thyme sauce or *panier de cochonaille,* a basket of the Camdeborde family's own brand of sliced smoked ham, dried sausage, and other pork-based delectables. On weeknights, it's a temple to haute cuisine, with a tasting menu that includes as many as five different dishes. Reserve in advance for this fixed-price meal, which changes nightly. If you can't get a seat, try **L'Avant Comptoir,** the restaurant's adjacent wine bar/counter serving small plates of charcuterie, or if you're in the mood for seafood, its sister joint, just next door, **L'Avant Comptoir de la Mer** (tapas in both 7€–14€).

Le Comptoir, one of Paris's most beloved bistros.

9 carrefour de l'Odéon, 6th arrond. hotel-paris-relais-saint-germain.com. ⓒ **01-44-27-07-50.** Main courses 27€–39€; fixed-price dinner Mon–Fri 75€. Daily noon–11pm. Métro: Odéon.

Le Relais de l'Entrecôte ♥
TRADITIONAL FRENCH/STEAK
You won't have to trouble yourself with deciding what to eat here: The only thing on the menu is steak. Just tell the waiter how you want it cooked (*bien cuit* for medium-well, à point for medium-rare, or *saignant* for rare), and sit back and wait. First comes a fresh green salad, and then the main event: a giant silver platter of steak, doused in an addictive "secret sauce" and served with crispy golden fries. Expect to see your server return with a second helping once you've finished. Desserts, if you can find the

Steak is the only thing on the menu at Le Relais de l'Entrecôte.

strength, are classic and delicious, including profiteroles and crème brûlée. Get here early: You can't reserve, and a line snakes out the door. If the line looks too long, you can try one of the two other locations: 101 bd. Montparnasse in the 6th, or 15 rue Marbeuf in the 8th.

20 rue St. Benoît, 6th arrond. relaisentrecote.fr. © **01-45-49-16-00.** Daily noon–2:30pm and 7–11:30pm. Fixed-price lunch and dinner 29€. Métro: St-Germain-des-Prés.

INEXPENSIVE

Pâtisserie Viennoise ♥♥ BAKERY   Squeezed between two medical schools, this old-fashioned pastry shop gets its share of students and professors in need of a nosh. And this is a nosher's heaven: It has a huge selection of pastries, including Viennese classics like Linzer torte and strudel, and the hot chocolate is one of the best in the city (5.90€). It's thick and dark and bitter—sugar cubes are provided so you can adjust the sweetness—and if you ask for it à la viennoise, it will come with a dollop of real whipped cream. The tiny dining area looks like it hasn't changed in at least 50 years: a collection of wooden booths and small tables that might have been shipped in from Vienna. You can also lunch here on inexpensive quiches, salads, and pasta dishes, including some nice vegetarian choices.

8 rue de l'Ecole de Médecine, 6th arrond. © **01-43-26-60-48.** Main courses 7€–12€; pastries 4€–7.50€. Mon–Fri 8am–7:30pm. Closed mid-July through 3rd week of Aug. Métro: Odéon or Cluny La Sorbonne.

Restaurant Polidor ♥ TRADITIONAL FRENCH/BISTRO   An unofficial historic monument, Polidor is not so much a restaurant as a snapshot of a bygone era. The decor has not changed substantially for at least 100 years, when Verlaine and Rimbaud, the bad boys of French poetry, would come here for a cheap meal. The bistro would continue to be a literary lunchroom for decades: In the 1950s, it was dubbed "the College of Pataphysics" by a rowdy group of young upstarts that included Max Ernst, Boris Vian, and Eugene Ionesco; André Gide and Ernest Hemingway were reputed regulars. The menu features hefty bistro standbys like *boeuf bourguignon* and *blanquette de veau* (veal stew with white sauce), but if you look carefully, you'll also find lighter fare like salmon with basil and chicken breast with morel sauce. These days, the arty set has moved elsewhere; you'll probably be sharing the long wood tables with other tourists, along with a dose of locals and fans of Woody Allen's *Midnight in Paris,* as certain shots were filmed here. The food is not particularly memorable, but the ambience is unique.

41 rue Monsieur-le-Prince, 6th arrond. polidor.com. © **01-43-26-95-34.** Main courses 13.50€–19.90€; fixed-price lunch 15.50€, fixed-price dinner 25€. Daily noon–10:30pm. Métro: Odéon.

Eiffel Tower & Nearby (7th Arrondissement)

Crowded with ministries and important people, this neighborhood is so grand, you half expect to hear trumpets blowing each time you turn a corner. Eating here on a budget takes some skill, or at least a bit of insider knowledge.

Though this is a rather staid neighborhood, a few streets are fairly lively, namely rue Cler, a pretty market street, and rue St-Dominique, home to some of the best restaurants on this side of the Seine. You're likely to get fleeced if you insist on eating right next to the Eiffel Tower—that is, if you can find a restaurant, as the pickings are pretty slim in the Iron Lady's immediate vicinity. If it's a nice day, buy a sandwich at a bakery and have a picnic on the Champs de Mars, where you can't beat the price or the view.

EXPENSIVE

Divellec ♥♥ MODERN FRENCH/SEAFOOD Close your eyes and you're at the seaside, Deauville or Trouville perhaps (famed posh spots along the Normandy coast), for you can smell the salt as you step into this ultrachic, seafood-only restaurant near Les Invalides, where truffles and oysters top pillowy Saint Jacques scallops bathed in delicate watercress sauce. Fish, as is customary in France, comes with sauces—monkfish gets *ravigote* cream (herby, mustardy emulsion), sole gets walnut butter—but they never overpower the "pure" taste of the fish. The *navarin d'homard,* lobster in a creamy sauce, is possibly the best in town. Raw seafood is also popular here, with items like tuna in ponzu sauce or scallops with pink pepper. On a sunny day, reserve a terrace spot with a view of the tree-filled Esplanade des Invalides.

Navarin d'homard at Divellec Restaurant.

18 rue Fabert, 7th arrond. divellec-paris.fr. ⓒ **01-45-51-91-96.** Main courses 38€–85€. Daily noon–1:30pm and 7–9:30pm. Closed 3 weeks in Aug. Métro/RER: Les Invalides.

Jules Verne ♥♥♥ MODERN FRENCH Sometimes Paris is about embracing the clichés, and dining on the second floor of the Eiffel Tower is definitely a cliché worth embracing. Not only are the views magnificent, with the city's iconic rooftops undulating in graceful higgledy-piggledy-dom between Trocadéro, Les Invalides, and La Défense's skyscrapers, but now that award-winning chef

Jules Verne restaurant is located on the second floor of the Eiffel Tower.

Frédéric Anton has taken over the kitchen, the food is worth writing home about, too—especially since it was awarded a second Michelin star in 2024. Try wonders like langoustine ravioli in tarragon sauce, vanilla-salted pigeon, and a bitter chocolate soufflé—all beautifully presented to evoke (in the words of the chef) "the cogs, the nuts, and bolts" of the Eiffel Tower. The 160€ weekday three-course lunch menu is a good value, considering where you are. For an extra dose of romance, splurge at night when the city sparkles at your feet. Reservations are required at least 2 months in advance. *Note:* If you can't get a table, try **Madame Brasserie** on the 1st floor, where fixed-price meals start at 70€, though you'll still have to book online at least 3 weeks in advance. Alternatively, if you book an early ticket for the Eiffel Tower, you can just show up for breakfast between 10am and noon; croissants cost 5€.

2nd floor of the Eiffel Tower, av. Gustave Eiffel, 7th arrond. restaurants-toureiffel.com. **01-83-77-34-34.** Fixed-price lunch 180€ (Mon–Fri only); tasting menu (lunch and dinner) 290€ and 320€. Daily noon–1:30pm and 7–9pm. Métro: Bir-Hakeim or Trocadéro. RER: Champs de Mars Tour Eiffel. Closed July 14 dinner.

Restaurant Auguste ♥♥♥ MODERN FRENCH/SEAFOOD   It's not every famous chef who can call himself "Mr. Goodfish." Gael Orieux's love of the sea and everything in it has led him to become spokesperson for an association dedicated to protecting the oceans. Naturally, that means that what you see on your plate is not only delicious, but also ecologically correct. Let's hope he makes an impact on his clientele, many of whom are politicians taking a break from the nearby Assemblée Nationale. Aside from protecting fish, Orieux cooks it, serving some of the best seafood in town, and plates it with real flair. A dish of scallops with foie gras and enoki mushrooms might look like a Jackson Pollock abstract; a lacquered monkfish with lobster oil and nutmeg will be equally artistic. Meat eaters are taken care of with dishes like blackened lamb with cauliflower, and pigeon with nuts and sweet onion.

54 rue de Bourgogne, 7th arrond. restaurantauguste.fr. **01-45-51-61-09.** Main courses 54€–78€; fixed-price lunch 47€, or lunch and dinner 96€ and 120€ (with wine). Mon–Fri noon–2pm and 7:30–10pm. Closed 3 weeks in Aug. Métro: Varenne.

MODERATE

La Fontaine de Mars ♥♥ BISTRO/SOUTHWESTERN FRENCH   Red and white checks are everywhere at this old-school bistro: on the tablecloths, the wicker chairs, and even the curtains. A venerable institution that first opened in 1908, it continues to draw crowds with its classy, low-key decor and traditional menu. The kitchen turns out reliable and succulent southwestern dishes like cassoulet, foie gras, and duck breast with black cherry sauce. Starters include *escargots* (snails) and *oeufs au Madiran* (eggs baked with red wine and bacon). The dessert list is full of such classics as *île flottante* ("floating island," a puffy meringue floating on vanilla cream), crème brûlée, and dark chocolate mousse.

129 rue St-Dominique, 7th arrond. fontaine-de-mars.com. **01-47-05-46-44.** Main courses 21€–44€. Mon–Fri noon–3pm and 7–11pm; Sat–Sun noon–3:30pm and 7–11pm. Métro: École Militaire.

La Fontaine de Mars, serving guests since 1908.

Le Casse Noix ♥♥ TRADITIONAL FRENCH/BISTRO Chef Pierre-Olivier Lenormand brings his high-caliber food to a casual, affordable setting. The decor is nostalgic (note the nutcracker collection and vintage advertisements), and the traditional French cooking is sincere and generous. Perhaps a roast pork shoulder Ibaïona with olive purée will fit the bill? Or try a classic *petit salé* (lentils with smoky ham) followed by a crowd-pleasing dessert like *île flottante*. About a 10-minute walk from the Eiffel Tower, this is a good bet for those looking for a bit of authenticity in an otherwise very touristy neighborhood. Just make sure you have a loose belt buckle; the fixed-price menu is *obligatoire* so there is no a la carte ordering and portions are generous.

56 rue de la Fédération, 15th arrond. le-cassenoix.fr. **01-45-66-09-01.** Fixed-price lunch and dinner 42€. Mon–Fri noon–2pm and 7–10pm. Closed Aug and between Christmas and New Year's. Métro: Dupleix.

L'Escudella ♥♥♥ MODERN FRENCH This smart neo-bistro, dressed up in pretty turquoise, white, and red, is located on a quiet residential street between UNESCO and Les Invalides, and has a real locals' vibe, so you'll have no trouble imagining what life might be like if you lived in Paris. Its name means "plate" in Occitan—a nod to the restaurant's first owner who was from the Southwest. In the kitchen, with talented chef Rémi Poulin at the helm, the food mixes French classics with international ingredients. Dishes might include salmon with white asparagus and yuzu, or chicken stuffed with mushrooms and savory, and a glorious *île flottante* (meringue floating in vanilla cream) for dessert. The wine list is great, with bottles from all over France.

41 av. de Ségur, 7th arrond. escudella.fr. **09-82-28-70-70.** Fixed-price lunch 36€–40€, fixed-price dinner 62€, wine pairing 40€. Tues–Sat noon–2:30pm and 7–9:30pm. Métro: École Militaire or Saint François Xavier.

INEXPENSIVE

Chez Pippo ♥♥♥ ITALIAN/PIZZERIA   This down-to-earth, child-friendly Italian eatery is a handy address to have up your sleeve when visiting the Eiffel Tower or Musée du Quai Branly. Despite being in the heart of tourist central, it's well off the radar, drawing in-the-know locals (many from the American Library in Paris just around the corner) and just a handful of visitors. Pop by for a quick pizza (11€–26€)—the Miranda (Parma ham and olives) or Diavola (spicy sausage) are very good. Plus, the chef has three types of crust for you to choose between. If you're in the mood for something fancy, I recommend splurging on the Milanese-style veal escalopes (28€).

31 av. de la Bourdonnais, 7th arrond. chezpippo.com. **01-73-70-54-50.** Main courses 11€–32€. Daily 11:30am–11pm. Métro: École Militaire. RER: Gare du Pont de l'Alma.

Le Café du Marché ♥♥ TRADITIONAL FRENCH/BISTRO   Located on rue Cler, a pedestrian market street, this bustling cafe has one of the nicest sidewalk terraces in the area. You can do some serious people-watching here without inhaling excess car exhaust. The menu is nothing to shout about, but features pleasant bistro dishes like crispy duck confit, snails, and onion soup, as well as more modern turns like salmon brochettes with dill cream, and crowd pleasers like burgers. Meals are served "non-stop" all day.

38 rue Cler, 7th arrond. **01-47-05-51-27.** Main courses 16€–24€. Daily 7am–midnight. Métro: École Militaire.

Le Petit Cler ♥♥ TRADITIONAL FRENCH/BISTRO   This cute little cafe tumbles out onto the rue Cler pedestrian market street and serves high quality but simple food at very reasonable prices. While you won't find many red and white checks, you will find classic cafe fare (steaks with sautéed potatoes, omelets, open-faced grilled sandwiches, and the like) as well as a daily special, which might be roast chicken (Sun) or stuffed tomatoes (Mon). You can also get a complete breakfast (including eggs) for 15.50€, and (later in the day) cheese and cold meat platters (from 10.50€) to soak up all the wine on the menu.

29 rue Cler, 7th arrond. menuonline.fr/lepetitcler. **01-45-50-17-50.** Main courses 16€–24€. Daily 8am–midnight. Closed 2 weeks in Aug. Métro: École Militaire.

Montparnasse & Nearby (14th & 15th Arrondissements)

The famous cafes and brasseries (Café de Flore; Les Deux Magots; La Coupole [p. 153]; and Closerie des Lilas [p. 149], where struggling writers and artists like Picasso, Hemingway, and Chagall once hung out) make for atmospheric spots for a drink or meal. This is also the most Breton (that is, from Brittany) section of Paris. The trains from Brittany arrive and depart from Montparnasse, and the story goes that between the World Wars,

> ### Beaupassage: The Left Bank Food Arcade
>
> Though Paris is peppered with market streets and old-word *passages* (18th-c. precursors to today's shopping malls; see p. 243), Beaupassage in the chic 7th arrondissement is the city's first-ever arcade entirely dedicated to the glories of food. Opened in 2018 on the site of a former convent and a car showroom, it marries ultramodern design and contemporary art installations with restaurants and food shops run by the city's top chefs. Though the 7th is as chic as can be, and the chefs have multiple Michelin stars among them, you'll actually find food for all budgets—*breadmakis* (maki-style club sandwiches, rolled and cut into big slices) from 6.50€ in Thierry Marx's **Boulangerie** (thierrymarxbakery.fr); gourmet Japanese cuisine at **Isakaya Dassai** (run by the award-winning chef Yannick Alleno; lizakaya-alleno.com); and mussels, lobster rolls, and fish and chips at **Mersea** (famed for its seafood; merseaparis.com). Capping things off are a butcher, a cheese shop, an organic supermarket, and a gym. Beaupassage is at 53–57 rue du Grenelle, 7th arrond. (instagram.com/beaupassageparis; daily 7am–midnight).

fresh-off-the-train Bretons, not knowing where else to go, settled in the immediate vicinity—hence the high density of crêperies along rues du Montparnasse and d'Odessa (the crepe having its origins in Brittany). In recent years, the neighborhood has woken up, gastronomically speaking, and a bundle of new gourmet bistros are tantalizing local taste buds. Check out rue Daguerre, a quaint street by Denfert Rochereau Métro that's peppered with restaurants.

EXPENSIVE

Closerie des Lilas ♥♥♥ TRADITIONAL FRENCH/BRASSERIE This restaurant, brasserie, and piano bar was a favorite of Picasso and Gertrude Stein, not to mention Ernest Hemingway, who downed whiskey here so often that both the bar and a signature dish (panfried steak in creamy whiskey sauce) bear his name. With such history, you'd expect this to be on every tourist's radar, but the Closerie has managed to remain resolutely Parisian, drawing in locals with the promise of indulgent dishes like fresh seafood platters, panfried sweetbreads, and even caviar with steamed potatoes and cream. Literary fans will be pleased to learn that every year, the Closerie awards female writers with prestigious literary prizes, the Prix de la Closerie, Prix Lilas, and Lilas du Livre. Fare in the Brasserie is slightly less elaborate than the dishes in the main restaurant (hence the lower prices). But hit the restaurant part if you want to taste Hemingway's favorite dish: filet of steak flambéed at your table in Bourbon. It's 52€, but may well be the best beef you taste in the city.

161 bd. du Montparnasse, 6th arrond. closeriedeslilas.fr. **01-40-51-34-50.** Brasserie mains 20€–65€; seafood platters 50€–115€; Restaurant mains 50€–65€. Daily noon–2:15pm and 7–10:15pm; piano bar noon–12:30am. Closed Aug. Métro: Raspail or Vavin. RER: Port-Royal.

MODERATE

L'Assiette ♥♥ TRADITIONAL FRENCH
There's a whiff of the Belle Epoque in this old-fashioned dining room with its mirrors and ceiling ornaments. The menu appeals to culinary nostalgia as well, with dishes like homemade cassoulet and pike quenelles (long and delicate fish dumplings) with Nantua sauce, as well as *escargots* and homemade foie gras. For dessert, indulge in crème caramel made with salted butter or profiteroles with chocolate sauce.

181 rue du Château, 14th arrond. restaurant-lassiette.com. ℂ **01-43-22-64-86.** Main courses 34€–41€; fixed-price lunch 26€. Wed–Fri noon–2:30pm and 7–10:30pm. Closed Aug. Métro: Gaîté.

Le Ciel de Paris ♥♥ FRENCH
If you want to see the Eiffel Tower as you dine, this is the place to come. Set on the top of the Tour Montparnasse, it's one of the highest restaurants in Europe, with slick 1970s-inspired design and floor-to-ceiling windows that offer some of the best views of the Iron Lady in the city. Food-wise you won't be disappointed either. Chef Christophe Marchais' dishes are as flavorsome as they are pretty. If you don't want to dine, but fancy a cocktail, that's possible too, at the restaurant's panoramic 360 Bar, a coveted spot at night when the city and the Eiffel Tower sparkle at your feet. Breakfast is also served for 18€ between 8:30 and 10:45am. For all of the above, it's best to reserve ahead.

Tour Maine Montparnasse, 56th floor, 33 av. du Maine, 14th arrond. cieldeparis. com. ℂ **01-40-64-77-64.** Main courses 23€–48€; fixed-price lunch 35€–45€, fixed-price dinner 79€–145€. Daily 8:30am–12:30am. Métro: Montparnasse-Bienvenüe.

Floor-to-ceiling windows offer some of the best views of the Eiffel Tower at Le Ciel de Paris.

Les Petits Plats ♥♥ MODERN FRENCH/BISTRO
Not especially hungry but you still want to eat well? This friendly bistro offers all its main courses in full- or half-sizes (at full- and half-prices). The blackboard lists the day's offerings, which might include a juicy slab of Aubrac beef, lightly sizzled cod with compote of roasted fresh vegetables, or sautéed squid and scallops with black rice. Finish it off with a meltingly rich chocolate *mi-cuit* (a not-quite-cooked cake). The ambience is relaxed, and the young staff is downright charming. At dinner, a tasting menu of five different dishes costs 50€.

39 rue des Plantes, 14th arrond. ℂ **01-45-42-50-52.** Main courses 24€–34€; half-dishes 12€–17€; fixed-price lunch 22€. Tues–Sat noon–2pm and 7:30–10pm. Closed 3 weeks in Aug. Métro: Alésia.

INEXPENSIVE
Le Petit Josselin ♥♥ CRÊPERIE
Of the dozens of crêperies concentrated near the Montparnasse train station, this tiny dining room is one of the best. The *galettes* and crepes are perfectly cooked with lacy, crispy edges, and include fillings like bacon and egg, smoked salmon, and the can-do-no-wrong classic, ham and cheese. Plus, they make their own flour! Try to save room for a sweet crepe after—the salted caramel butter crepe is a wonder. Tradition demands that this meal be accompanied by a bowl of "brut" cider (low alcohol content, for adults only).

59 rue du Montparnasse, 14th arrond. creperielepetitjosselin.fr. **01-43-22-91-81**. Main courses 9€–19€. Mon–Fri noon–2:30pm and 6:30–11pm; Sat 11:30am–11pm. Métro: Edgar Quinet.

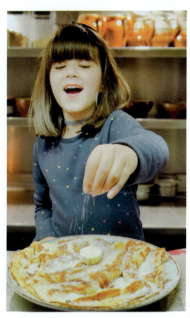

Banana crepes at Le Petit Josselin.

THE TOP TEAROOMS

It may surprise you to know that despite their famous cafe culture, many French people are closet tea fanatics. Thus, it is only fitting that some of the world's loveliest tearooms are in Paris.

Angelina ♥♥ TEAROOM This Belle Epoque beauty under the arcades on the rue de Rivoli was once frequented by Proust and Coco Chanel, among other notables. Famous for its hot chocolate and its chestnut-y Mont Blanc pastry, this is also a great (if not touristy) spot for a chic breakfast or lunch. Be prepared to wait in line to get in. Or try the separate take-out line, which goes much faster. Then hop across the road to the Tuileries garden to nibble your cake by one of the fountains.

226 rue de Rivoli, 1st arrond. angelina paris.fr. **01-42-60-82-00**. Main courses 18.50€–25.50€; fixed-price breakfast 23.50€–33.50€; brunch 45€. Mon–Thurs 7:30am–7pm; Fri 7:30am–7:30pm; Sat–Sun 8am–7:30pm. Métro: Tuileries.

Teatime at Angelina.

The City's Best Pastries

This is a particularly tough call, since new pastry shops open frequently, but here are a few classics where not even the snootiest gourmands will turn up their noses.

- **Arnaud Larher,** 93 rue de Seine, 6th arrond. (arnaudlarher.com; © **01-43-29-38-15**; Métro: Odéon or Mabillon), is a gâteaux and chocolate wiz, with everything made by hand. Try the chocolate éclair; it's a dream.
- **La Pâtisserie de Cyril Lignac,** 24 rue Paul Bert, 11th arrond. (lapatisseriecyrillignac.com; © **01-55-87-21-40**; Métro: Faidherbe-Chaligny or Rue des Boulets), is where cakes look like pieces of contemporary art. Try the Equinoxe, a gray, circular creation filled with vanilla cream and caramel.
- **Pierre Hermé,** 72 rue Bonaparte, 6th arrond. (pierreherme.com; © **01-45-12-24-02**; Métro: St-Sulpice), may look like a chic jewelry store, but the goods are edible here. Exquisite and fashionable pastries include the Ispahan series, based on lychee, rose, and raspberry flavors.
- **Sébastien Gaudard,** 1 rue des Pyramides, 1st arrond. (sebastiengaudard.com; © **01-71-81-24-70**; Métro: Pyramides), makes exquisite French cakes, from classic *mille-feuilles* (puff pastry layered with vanilla cream) to playful sharing cakes, like the cherry and chocolate *shirt*, with a marzipan collar and nuts crumbled on top like patterned fabric.
- **Stohrer,** 51 rue Montorgueil, 2nd arrond. (stohrer.fr; © **01-42-33-38-20**; Métro: Sentier or Les Halles), was opened by Louis XV's pastry chef in 1730. This is the place to sample the ultimate *baba au rhum*, the famous rum-soaked sponge cake; Stohrer invented it in the 18th century.

Le Nélie (Musée Jacquemart-André) ♥♥ TEAROOM

Peek up at the Tiepolo ceiling as you sip your tea in what was once the dining room of Edouard André and Nélie Jacquemart. This beautiful, newly-restored tearoom serves excellent teas and delicious pastries, as well as larger lunchtime dishes (think beef carpaccio, truffle-cream pasta, and salad laden with smoked salmon) There's brunch (Sat and Sun) from 11am to 2:30pm, and tea and pastries from 3 to 5:30pm. No reservations.

Musée Jacquemart-André, 158 bd. Haussmann, 8th arrond. musee-jacquemartandre.com. © **01-45-62-11-59.** Main courses 17.50€–27€; fixed-price lunch 20.50€–35€; brunch 39€. Mon–Thurs 10am–6pm; Fri 10am–10pm; Sat–Sun 11am–7pm. Métro: Miromesnil or Saint-Augustin.

Le Nélie tearoom at Musée Jacquemart-André.

Ladurée and its famed macarons.

Ladurée ♥ TEAROOM This luxury pastry shop has boutiques everywhere these days, but there's nothing quite like a cup of tea and macarons (Ladurée's famous light-as-air filled cookies) in one of its elegant Parisian tearooms. The rue Royale location, with its original 1862 *boiseries* (decorative wood paneling), and the grandiose Champs-Élysées site with its upstairs salon are the most impressive.

75 av. des Champs-Élysées, 8th arrond. laduree.fr. © **01-40-75-08-75.** Main courses 24€–42€. Daily 9am–9:30pm. Métro: George V.

Mosquée de Paris ♥ TEAROOM For an altogether different cup of tea, have a seat at the lovely tearoom attached to the grand Paris Mosque. Sip a glass of sweet mint tea and nibble on a *corne de gazelle* (a crescent-shaped, powdered-sugar-covered delight) on the patio or in the beautifully tiled tearoom and dream that you're in the Casbah. Couscous is served in the restaurant section too (from 18€). *Note:* The entrance is not the same as the one for the mosque; it's on the corner of rue Daubenton and rue Geoffroy St-Hilaire.

39 rue Geoffroy St-Hilaire, 5th arrond. la-mosquee.com. © **01-43-31-38-20.** Mint tea 2€; pastries from 2€; main courses 17€–34€. Daily 9am–midnight. Métro: Censier-Daubenton.

THE TOP CAFES

It would be a crime to come to Paris and not stop for a coffee (or other drink) in a cafe. Despite the onslaught of American-style coffee shops, classic cafe life is still an integral part of the Parisian scene, and it simply won't do to visit the capital without at least participating once. *Important note:* Cafes are not bars in the North American sense—though they generally serve alcohol, they are not places where people come to get smashed. They are places where people come to just "be," to sip a drink, to take a break, to read a book, or to simply watch the world go by. Most cafes open very early in the morning and close any time between midnight and 2am.

coffee TALK

Ordering a cup of coffee in Paris is not quite as simple as it sounds. Most any cafe has delightful caffeinated (and decaffeinated) java possibilities. Cappuccinos, by the way, are rare in Parisian cafes, and when you do get one, chances are it won't resemble anything you'd get in Italy. **Important tip:** Drinks at the bar (coffee or otherwise) can cost half what you will pay at a table—as little as 1€ for an espresso.

The following mini-glossary will help you navigate once your waiter makes it over to your table.

Café (ka-*fay*): Coffee. This is pure, black espresso, albeit lighter than the Italian version, served in a small demitasse cup. The equivalent of a "long shot," in Starbucks-speak.

Allongé (all-on-jay): Coffee. This is black espresso with a shot of hot water, served in a slightly bigger cup.

Décaf (*day-ka*): Decaf, or decaffeinated coffee. An unleaded version of the above.

Café serré (ka-fay sehr-ay): Though smaller in volume, packs a bigger punch. Resembles an Italian espresso.

Noisette (*nwa-zet*): Café with a dash of steamed milk (my favorite). You could also order an **Allongé Noisette** for a splash of milk in a longer coffee.

Café crème (crem): Café with an equal amount of steamed milk, served in a larger cup.

Café au lait (ka-fay oh lay): Virtually identical to the above, sometimes with a bit more milk. The biggest difference is the time of day; in the morning, they call it a *café au lait*, in the afternoon a *crème*.

Paris must have thousands of cafes. Though you could probably have a basic cafe experience in just about any corner operation, here are a few surefire options to choose from.

Historic Cafes

Café de Flore ♥♥ CAFE   A monument to the St-Germain quarter's intellectual past, Café de Flore is a must-sip on the cafe tour circuit. Seemingly every great French intellectual and artist has had his or her moment here: Poets Apollinaire and André Breton wrote here; artists Zadkine, Picasso, and Giacometti came to take refuge from Montparnasse; literary and theatrical stars came to preen; and of course, philosophers gathered to figure out the meaning (or nonmeaning) of life. During World War II, Simone de Beauvoir and Jean-Paul Sartre more or less moved in, and Sartre is said to have written his trilogy *Les Chemins de la Liberté* (*The Roads to Freedom*) here. The atmosphere now is less thoughtful and more showbiz, but it still may be worth an overpriced cup of coffee just to come in and soak it up.

172 bd. St-Germain, 6th arrond. cafedeflore.fr. ✆ **01-45-48-55-26.** Daily 7:30am–1:30am. Métro: St-Germain-des-Prés.

Café de la Paix ♥♥♥ CAFE   A Parisian institution ever since it was inaugurated by Empress Eugenie in 1862, this is the home of one of the most expensive cups of coffee in the city (7€; 11€ for a double expresso). Everyone from Emile Zola to Yves Montand has done time at this Second Empire marvel, whose gold leaf and curlicues have been meticulously renovated. Its outdoor terrace offers a magnificent view of the Palais Garnier—the perfect place for a drink before a night at the Opéra. It won't be cheap, but it will be memorable.

Corner of pl. de l'Opéra and bd. des Capucines, 9th arrond. cafedelapaix.fr. ⓒ **01-40-07-36-36.** Daily 7am–11pm. Métro: Opéra.

La Coupole ♥♥ CAFE/BRASSERIE   The artistic legacy of this café-cum-brasserie is almost as vast as its square footage: Marc Chagall, Josephine Baker, Henry Miller, Salvador Dalí, and Ernest Hemingway are just some of the stars that lit up this converted charcoal depot. One of the largest restaurants in France, this Art Deco mastodon first opened in 1927 and has been hopping ever since. Thirty-three immense painted pillars hold up the ceiling; huge murals and paintings cover the walls. The food here is very good (the lamb curry is the signature dish); but whatever you come for— just a drink or a snack—grab a table by the windows, and watch the world go by. It's also a fun place to have breakfast.

La Coupole cafe.

102 bd. du Montparnasse, 14th arrond. lacoupole-paris.com. ⓒ **01-43-20-14-20.** Daily 8am–midnight (until 11pm Sun and Mon). Métro: Vavin.

Les Deux Magots ♥♥ CAFE   After the war, de Beauvoir and Sartre moved from Café de Flore to this nearby artists' haunt, where they continued to write and think and entertain their friends for a good chunk of the rest of their lives. The literary pedigree here is at least as impressive as that of its neighbor: Poets Verlaine and Rimbaud camped out here, as did François Mauriac, André Gide, Paul Eluard, Albert Camus, and Ernest Hemingway. The outdoor terrace is particularly pleasant early in the morning before the crowds wake up.

6 pl. St-Germain-des-Prés, 6th arrond. lesdeuxmagots.fr. ⓒ **01-45-48-55-25.** Daily 7:30am–1am. Métro: St-Germain-des-Prés.

Cafes for People-Watching

Eté en Pente Douce ♥ CAFE   On a delightful corner facing the tranquil eastern side of Sacré-Coeur, this colorful cafe features a lovely sidewalk terrace where you can relax away from the tourist hordes. Don't bother with the food here, which is fair to middling; just order a *café* or a nice, cool beer, look

Soaking up the literary history at Les Deux Magots.

out on the greenery, and watch people huffing and puffing up the stairs to the basilica. You'll have to huff and puff a little yourself to get here.

23 rue Muller, 18th arrond. eteenpentedouce.com. © **01-42-64-02-67.** Daily noon–midnight (from 11am Sat–Sun). Métro: Anvers.

Le Pure Café ♥♥ CAFE   In the heart of the residential 11th arrondissement, this is a neighborhood cafe in the truest sense: With a small V-shaped terrace that looks out over a trio of relatively quiet roads (for Paris), it's the place to watch an odd assortment of local hipsters, pensioners, freelancers, and arty types slurp espressos and spritzes (a cocktail made with Aperol and prosecco). Indoors, it's Art Deco revisited with a huge zinc-topped, circular bar, turquoise metro tiles, and 1930s light fittings.

14 rue Jean Macé, 11th arrond. instagram.com/lepurecafeparis. © **01-43-71-47-22.** Daily 7am–1am. Métro: Faidherbe-Chaligny, Rue des Boulets, or Charonne.

Le Rostand ♥♥ CAFE   This quintessentially Parisian cafe has a swell terrace directly opposite the entrance to the Jardin du Luxembourg, and despite its touristy location, it draws oodles of chic locals. It's the ideal spot for a before- or after-promenade drink, a book-reading session, or just taking a load off after a visit to the park or the Panthéon.

6 pl. Edmond Rostand, 6th arrond. lerostand.fr. © **01-43-54-61-58.** Daily 8am–midnight. RER: Luxembourg.

Le Rostand cafe sits across from Jardin du Luxembourg.

EXPLORING PARIS

6

With more than 130 world-class museums to visit, scores of attractions to discover, extraordinary architecture to gape at, and wonderful neighborhoods to wander, Paris is an endless series of delights. The hardest part is figuring out where to begin. Fortunately, you can have a terrific time even if you don't see everything. Lolling on a park bench, dreaming over a drink at a sidewalk cafe, or noodling around an unknown neighborhood can be the stuff of your best travel memories.

The following pages will highlight the best that Paris can offer area by area, from iconic sights to quirky museums and hidden gardens, from 1,000-year-old castles to galleries celebrating the most challenging contemporary art, and from the must-sees to the only-if-you've-seen-everything-else. Just remember that it is always advisable to reserve advance tickets for the bigger attractions. You will not get into the Louvre without a pre-paid, time-stamped ticket, for instance. Here, then, are Paris's best attractions.

THE RIGHT BANK
Louvre & Île de la Cité (1st Arrondissement)

The city's epicenter, this area packs in a high density of must-see monuments and museums, but don't miss the opportunity for aimless strolling in the magnificent **Tuileries Gardens** or over the **Pont Neuf.** This section includes the entire Île de la Cité, though technically half of it lies in the 4th arrondissement.

Bourse de Commerce—Pinault Collection ♥♥ MUSEUM/ART GALLERY   At the western tip of the Les Halles gardens, the stunning former Chamber of Commerce building is the city's newest contemporary art space. This museum/art gallery houses the Pinault Collection, the personal 3,000-piece contemporary art

Right Bank Attractions

Arc de Triomphe 9
Atelier des Lumières 51
Basilique du Sacré-Coeur 23
Bourse du Commerce—Pinault Collection 33
Cathédrale de Notre-Dame 37
Centre Pompidou 39
Choco-Story 28
Cimetière du Père-Lachaise 51
Cité de l'Architecture et du Patrimoine 2
Cité des Sciences et de l'Industrie 53
Conciergerie 35
Coulée verte René-Dumont 50
Dalí Paris 21
Fondation Louis Vuitton 8
Grand Palais 13
Hôtel de la Marine 16
Hôtel de Ville 38
Jardin des Tuileries 19
MAD (Musée des Arts Décoratifs) 29
La Madeleine 15
Maison de Balzac 1
Maison de Victor Hugo 47
Musée d'Art et Histoire du Judaïsme 41
Musée d'Art Moderne de la Ville de Paris 6
Musée des Arts Forains 49
Musée Carnavalet 45
Musée Cognacq-Jay 44

Musée de la Chasse et de la Nature 42
Musée de l'Homme 3
Musée de Montmartre 22
Musée de la Musique 53
Musée de l'Orangerie 18
Musée de la Vie Romantique 24
Musée des Arts et Métiers 40
Musée du Louvre 31
Musée Grévin 27
Musée Gustave Moreau 25
Musée Jacquemart-André 12
Musée Marmottan Monet 3
Musée National de la Marine 1
Musée National des Arts Asiatiques Guimet 4
Musée National Picasso-Paris 43
Musée Nissim de Camondo 11
Musée Yves Saint Laurent 7
Opéra Garnier 26
Palais de Tokyo 5
Palais Royal 30
Parc de Bercy 49
Parc de la Villette 53
Parc des Buttes Chaumont 52
Parc Monceau 10
Parc Zoologique de Paris 50
Petit Palais 14
Philharmonie de Enfants 53
Place de la Bastille 48
Place de la Concorde 17
Place des Vosges 46
Place Vendôme 20
Sainte-Chapelle 36
St-Eustache 34
St-Germain l'Auxerrois 32

The 1607 Pont Neuf bridge is the oldest in Paris.

holding of billionaire François Pinault. The third-floor restaurant offers sweeping views over Paris's rooftops and St-Eustache church.

2 rue Viarmes, 1st arrond. pinaultcollection.com. © **01-83-75-10-00.** Admission 15€ adults (audio guide included), 10€ ages 18–25, free for children 17 and under. Wed–Sun 11am–7pm. Métro: Louvre-Rivoli or Les Halles. RER: Châtelet-des-Halles.

Cathédrale de Notre-Dame ♥♥♥ CATHEDRAL

One of France's most brilliant expressions of medieval architecture, this remarkably harmonious ensemble of carved portals, huge towers, and flying buttresses has survived close to a millennium's worth of French history and served as a setting for some of the country's most solemn moments. Even the vast fire that consumed its spire and gutted the entire roof in 2019 didn't bring it down (thanks to 400 firefighters). And the good news is, it reopened in 2024 (in keeping with the deadline set by President Emmanuel Macron), in a much-broadcasted event attended by a plethora of world leaders and royals

Napoleon crowned himself and Empress Joséphine here, Napoleon III was married here, and some of France's greatest generals (Foch, Joffre, Leclerc) had their funerals here. In August 1944, the liberation of Paris from the Nazis was commemorated in the cathedral, as was the death of de Gaulle in 1970.

The story of Notre-Dame begins in 1163, when Bishop Maurice de Sully initiated construction, which lasted over 200 years. (The identity of the architect who envisioned this masterpiece remains a mystery.) The building was relatively untouched up until the end of the 17th century, when monarchs started meddling with its windows and architecture. By the time the Revolutionaries decided to convert it into a "Temple of Reason," the cathedral was already in sorry condition—and the pillaging that ensued didn't help. The interior was ravaged, statues were smashed, and the cathedral became a shadow of its former glory.

Victor Hugo's novel *The Hunchback of Notre-Dame* drew attention to the state of disrepair, and other artists and writers began to call for the restoration of the edifice. In 1844, Louis-Phillipe hired Jean-Baptiste Lassus and architect/archaeologist/writer/painter Eugène Viollet-le-Duc to restore the cathedral, which they finished in 1864. Though many criticized Viollet-le-Duc for what they considered to be overly romantic and inauthentic excesses, he actually took extreme care to remain faithful to the historic Gothic architecture.

Over 1 billion euros were donated to the cathedral in the first week following the fire, so money for repairs wasn't—for once—lacking. Though some treasures were lost, the organ, Quasimodo's bell (the Bourdon), and relics such as the **Crown of Thorns** were saved and are now back on show. The city also gifted the 2024 Olympic Bell to the cathedral. It now hangs in the tribune, high above the altar, and sounds during mass (along with two smaller new bells, Carlos and Chiara, which are adorned with depictions of Notre-Dame's famous rosary window).

Excitement for Notre-Dame's reopening has been such that you now need to book for a free time slot on their reservation system, notredamedeparis.fr/en/visit/reservation. Begin your visit at **Point Zéro,** just in front of the building on the *parvis* (the esplanade). It is the official center of Paris and the point from which all distances relative to other French cities are calculated. Before you are three enormous **carved portals** depicting (from left to right) the Coronation of the Virgin, the Last Judgment, and scenes from the lives of the Virgin and St-Anne. Above is the **Gallery of the Kings of Judah and**

The newly restored west facade of the Cathédrale de Notre-Dame.

Israel—thought to be portraits of the kings of France, the original statues were chopped out of the facade during the Revolution; some of the heads were eventually found in the 1970s and now are in the Musée de Cluny (p. 210). Above this is the iconic **rose window,** over which soar the two bell **towers** of Quasimodo fame.

Upon entering the cathedral (via the central portal of the Last Judgement to follow the obligatory visitor's route from north to south), you'll be immediately struck by two things: the sheer beauty of the restorations—the stonework looks both simultaneously timeless and new, as if just created by our Gothic forefathers—and then, when you look up, the heavenly dimensions of the pillars holding up the solidly resurrected ceiling. Soaring upward, these delicate archways give the impression that the entire edifice is about to take off into the sky. Up there in the upper atmosphere are the three remarkable stained-glass **rose windows,** one for each of the west, north, and south ends of the church. Notre-Dame's most famous relic is without doubt the **Crown of Thorns** (brought back from Constantinople by Saint Louis in the 13th century). Saved during the fire, it is now on display in the apse of the central chapel (behind the choir), where it can be viewed along with a nail and a piece of the Holy Cross on the first Friday of the month in its stunning new cedar, stone and glass casing, reminiscent of a halo. For a detailed look at the cathedral, rent an **audioguide** for 6€ or download the Notre Dame de Paris app.

When you leave, be sure to take a stroll around the outside of the cathedral to admire the other portals and the famous flying buttresses.

Parvis Notre-Dame, place Jean-Paul II, 1st arrond. notredamedeparis.fr. No phone. Free admission. Mon–Fri 7:45am–7pm (until 10pm Thurs), Sat–Sun 8:15am–7:30pm. Métro: Hôtel-de-Ville, Cité or Saint-Michel. RER: Saint-Michel – Notre-Dame.

Notre-Dame's Towers

At time of writing, the cathedral's famed towers had not yet reopened (the vague schedule was "at some point in 2025"), so please refer to the following website for the latest information: tours-notre-dame-de-paris.fr. What is for sure is that once they do open, you'll be able to trudge up some 422 steps (along a narrow, winding staircase with a handrail—not for small children or anyone with mobility concerns) to be rewarded with a panorama that not only encompasses the Île de la Cité, the Eiffel Tower, and Sacré-Coeur, but is also framed by a collection of photogenic **gargoyles.** These fantastic monsters, composed of various portions of apes, birds, and even elephants, came directly from the imagination of Viollet-le-Duc, who placed them during the restoration of the cathedral. One of the most famous is the **Stryga**, a horned and winged beasty holding his head in his hands, pensively sticking his tongue out at the city below. Squeeze around the narrow first balcony to the entrance to the belfry, Quasimodo's old haunt; its massive wood beams hold up a 14-ton bell. On a cloudy day, the vista is beautifully moody, especially from the **south tower,** from which there is an endless view of Paris.

> ### Should You Pass on the Pass?
>
> Paris is a walkable city with numerous free museums and serendipitous experiences, so paying for its sightseeing pass, the **Paris Passlib'**, might not make sense. It comes down to math. The fully digitized pass is valid for a year and comes in three versions: **Discover** (59€ for three activities from 30 offered), **City** (109€ for five attractions from 50 offered), and **Explore** (179€ for six attractions from 65 offered). An activity is classed as anything from entry to a museum to an experience like a boat trip or a cabaret show, depending on the pass you choose. The passes save you some money, but only if you select the most expensive activities on the list. Take the Discover pass: If you use it to book a river cruise with Bateaux Parisiens (19€), a ticket to the Monnaie de Paris (12€), and the Musée Rodin (15€), the pass will cost you 13€ more than individual tickets. In short, don't dismiss the pass, but do your homework: Deciding which activities you'd like to experience and totting up the sums before you buy is a time-consuming activity, but worth it to save some cash. And don't forget that Paris has multiple museums that offer free entry (p. 166). For more information, visit parisjetaime.com.

Conciergerie ♥♥ HISTORIC SITE   Despite looking like a turreted, fairy-tale castle, the Conciergerie is in fact a relic of the darker side of the Revolution, where some of its most famous participants spent their final days before making their way to the guillotine. Danton, Desmoulins, Saint-Just, and Charlotte Corday passed through these doors, but perhaps its most famous guest was Marie Antoinette, who spent her time here in a dismal cell, reading and praying while she awaited her fate. After doing away with the monarchy, the Revolution began to eat itself alive; during the particularly bloody period known as the Terror, murderous infighting between the various revolutionary factions engendered panic and paranoia that led to tens of thousands of people throughout the country being arrested and executed. Eventually Robespierre, the main force behind the Terror and an ardent advocate for Marie Antoinette's execution, found himself in the cell next door to the one she stayed in.

Though it's been a prison since the 15th century, the building itself is actually what remains of a 14th-century royal palace built by Philippe le Bel. Even before the Revolution, the Conciergerie was notorious: Henry IV's murderer, Ravaillac, was imprisoned here before an angry crowd tore him apart alive. The enormous **Salle des Gens d'Armes,** with its 8.4m-high (28-ft.) vaulted ceiling, is an impressive reminder of the building's palatial past, and is where you begin your self-guided tour, courtesy of a Histropad, a smart tablet with augmented reality functions that lets you see parts of the building as it would have looked in the 14th century and during the Revolution. Standout areas include the **Cours des Femmes** (the women's courtyard), which virtually hasn't changed since the days when female prisoners did their washing in the fountain. A creation of **Marie Antoinette's cell** containing some original objects, is on display. Other worthwhile historical exhibits include a list of the names of all those guillotined during the Revolution, 2,780 in Paris alone. The

Conciergerie can be visited in conjunction with the **Sainte-Chapelle,** which lies along the same road (p. 172; joint tickets with time slots 20€ adults, free for children 17 and under.

2 bd. du Palais, 1st arrond. paris-conciergerie.fr. © **01-53-40-60-80.** Admission 13€ adults, free for children 17 and under. Daily 9:30am–6pm. Métro: Cité, Châtelet, or St-Michel. RER: St-Michel.

Jardin des Tuileries ♥♥♥ PARK   This exquisite park spreads from the Louvre to the Place de la Concorde. One of the oldest gardens in the city—and the first to be opened to the public—it's also one of the largest. In the Middle Ages, a factory here made clay tiles (*tuiles*), a word that was incorporated into the name of the palace that Catherine de Médicis built at the far end of the Louvre in 1564. Such a grand palace needed equally splendid Italian gardens; later in the mid-1600s, Louis XIV had master landscape artist André Le Nôtre—the man behind the gardens of Versailles—give them a more French look.

Though the Tuileries Palace burned down during the Paris Commune in 1871, the landscaping lived on. During World War II, furious fighting went on here, and many statues were damaged. Little by little in the postwar years, the garden was put back together. Seventeenth- and 18th-century representations of various gods and goddesses were repaired, and the city added new works by modern masters such as Max Ernst, Alberto Giacometti, Jean Dubuffet, and Henry Moore. Rodin's *The Kiss* and *Eve* are here, as well as a series of

The Conciergerie, the notorious prison on Île de la Cité.

Jardin des Tuileries, outside the Louvre.

18 of Maillol's curvaceous women, peeking out of the green **labyrinth** of hedges in the Carousel Gardens near the museum.

Pulling up a metal chair and sunning yourself on the edge of the large **fountain** in the center of the gardens (the **Grande Carrée**) is a delightful respite after a day in the Louvre.

Near pl. de la Concorde, 1st arrond. Free admission. Daily 7:30am–dusk. Métro: Tuileries or Concorde.

MAD (Musée des Arts Décoratifs) ♥♥ MUSEUM

Possessing some 150,000 items in its rich collection, this fascinating museum offers a glimpse of history through the prism of decorative objects, with a spectrum that ranges from medieval traveling trunks to Philippe Starck stools. The collection is organized by period and style, so on your journey you will pass by paintings from the First Italian Renaissance, through a room filled with exquisite 15th-century intarsia ("paintings" made out of intricately inlaid wood), before gaping at huge, intricately carved 17th-century German armoires. Other highlights include a tiny room covered in gilded woodwork from an 18th-century mansion in Avignon; a stunning Art Nouveau/Art Deco section; and fashion designer Jeanne Lanvin's decadent, purple Art Deco boudoir.

Two other worthy collections are the Publicité/Graphisme collection on the history of advertising and the Mode/Textile fashion displays. While the former will be of interest primarily to those who are in the biz, the latter hosts a terrific range from famous couture houses like Jean-Paul Gaultier and Dior. *Note:* Tickets can be combined with the Musée Nissim de Camondo (p. 191; 22€).

Palais du Louvre, 107 rue de Rivoli, 1st arrond. madparis.fr. **01-44-55-57-50.** Admission 15€ adults (audio guide included), free for ages 25 and under. Tues–Sun 11am–6pm (until 9pm Thurs for some temporary exhibitions only). Métro: Palais-Royal–Musée du Louvre or Tuileries.

> ### Museums for Free
>
> Most museums offer free entry to students and young adults ages 25 and under from the European Union with valid ID. If this is you, ask when you buy your ticket. Children, typically ages 17 and under, but sometimes only up to age 7, often get in for free, too. See the listings below for details. With only a few exceptions, all city museums are free (permanent collections only), all the time. That includes the following cultural cornucopias:
>
> - Musée d'Art Moderne de la Ville de Paris (p. 187)
> - Maison de Balzac (p. 187)
> - Musée Bourdelle (p. 225)
> - Musée Carnavalet (p. 178)
> - Musée Cognacq-Jay (p. 179)
> - Petit Palais (p. 192)
> - Maison de Victor Hugo (p. 178)
> - Musée Zadkine (p. 215), except during temporary exhibits
> - Musée de la Vie Romantique (p. 174)
>
> You can also get into all national museums free of charge on the first Sunday of every month (seasonal restrictions may apply). Expect even bigger crowds than your usual Sunday. National museums include
>
> - Musée du Louvre (below), October to March
> - Musée National des Arts Asiatiques Guimet (p. 191)
> - Musée National Eugène Delacroix (p. 215)
> - Musée de l'Orangerie
> - Musée d'Orsay (p. 220)
> - Musée Rodin (p. 222)
> - Musée National Picasso-Paris (p. 181)

Musée de l'Orangerie ♥♥ MUSEUM   Since 1927, this former royal greenhouse has been the home of Monet's stunning *Nymphéas,* or water lilies, which he conceived as a "haven of peaceful meditation." Two large oval rooms are dedicated to these masterpieces, in which Monet tried to replicate the feeling and atmosphere of his garden at Giverny. He worked on these enormous canvases for 12 years, with the idea of creating an environment that would soothe the "overworked nerves" of modern men and women.

The other highlight here is the Walter–Guillaume collection, an impressive assortment of late-19th- and early-20th-century paintings that once belonged to art collectors Jean Walter and Paul Guillaume. Renoir's glowing, idyllic *Femme Nu dans un Paysage* and Cézanne's rather dour-looking *Madame Cézanne.*

Jardin des Tuileries, 1st arrond. musee-orangerie.fr. ✆ **01-44-77-80-07.** Admission 12.50€ adults, 10€ ages 18–25, free for children 17 and under. Wed–Mon 9am–6pm (until 9pm Fri). Métro: Concorde.

Musée du Louvre ♥♥♥ MUSEUM   The best way to thoroughly visit the Louvre would be to move in for a month. Not only is it one of the largest museums in the world, with more than 35,000 works of art displayed over 60,000 sq. m (645,835 sq. ft.), but it's also packed with enough artistic masterpieces to make the Mona Lisa weep. Rembrandt, Reubens, Botticelli, Ingres, and Michelangelo are all represented here; subjects range from the grandiose (Antoine-Jean Gros's gigantic *Napoleon Bonaparte Visiting the Plague-Stricken in Jaffa*) to the mundane (Vermeer's tiny, exquisite *Lacemaker*). You can gape at a diamond the size of a golf ball in the gilded Galerie d'Apollon or marvel over exquisite bronze figurines in the vast Egyptian section. There's something for everyone here.

Today, the building is divided into three wings: Sully, Denon, and Richelieu, each one with its own clearly marked entrance, found under I. M. Pei's glass pyramid. There's no way to see it all; you'll be an instant candidate for early exhaustion if you try. Mercifully, the museum is well organized and has been very reasonably arranged into color-coded sections. There's also a handy app (the Louvre Museum Visitor Guide) you can download ahead of your visit to help you plan what to see. If you're really in a rush, or you just want to get an overall sense of the place, you can take the introductory "Welcome to the Louvre" guided tour in English (12€ on top of regular entry price or 31€ for entry, plus the tour; 1.5 hr.; times must be booked on the website or call ✆ **01-40-20-52-63**). Most important of all, reserve admission at least 14 days in advance. If you're traveling with children, head to the Information point under the glass pyramid and ask for a free "Louvre Passport"—leaflet with major works for the kids to tick off once they've seen them. It turns the museum visit into a fun activity, as they try to tick off the most works possible.

By the time this book is printerd, the museum's biggest star has to be *La Joconde,* otherwise known as the **Mona Lisa** (see "Men Have Named You . . . ," p. 170), will have an entire room to herself, making it easier to contemplate her enigmatic smile, despite her surprisingly small size. Another inscrutable female is the **Venus de Milo,** (room 345, Sully Wing) who was found on a Greek isle in 1820. Possibly the most photographed woman in the world, this armless marble goddess gives no hint of the original position of her limbs or her exact identity. Recently restored and lovelier than ever, the **Winged Victory of Samothrace** is the easiest to locate. Standing atop a majestic flight of stairs in the Denon wing, her powerful body pushing forward as if about to take flight, this headless yet magnificent Greek sculpture once guarded the Sanctuary of the Great Gods on the island of Samothrace.

Because a complete listing of the Louvre's highlights would fill a book, below is a decidedly biased selection of our favorite areas:

The "New" Les Halles

Famously called "the belly of Paris," **Les Halles** was the city's primary wholesale food market for 8 centuries. The smock-clad vendors, beef carcasses, and baskets of vegetables all belong to the past, as the market was relocated to the suburb of Rungis in the early 1970s. In a fit of modernity, all the pretty 19th-century pavilions were torn down, and in their place a weird, partly underground shopping mall was constructed: the **Forum des Halles,** 1–7 rue Pierre-Lescot, 1st arrond. Today, "the canopy," an immense, undulating sheet of glass and metal that floats over the Forum. Most Parisians complain that it's unattractive, but it does house a myriad of shops and restaurants, and it opens onto a wonderful, immense garden that sweeps across lawns and kids' play areas over to 16th-century **Eglise St-Eustache** (p. 173)—a masterpiece of Gothic architecture. For info, visit westfield.com/france/forumdeshalles.

The courtyard of the Louvre Museum.

13TH- TO 18TH-CENTURY ITALIAN PAINTINGS A few standouts in the immense Italian collection include Botticelli's delicate fresco **Venus and the Three Graces Presenting Gifts to a Young Woman,** Veronese's aforementioned and enormous **Wedding Feast at Cana,** and of course, the **Mona Lisa.** Once you've digested this rich meal, stroll down the endless Grande Galerie, past more da Vincis (*Saint John the Baptist, The Virgin of the Rock*), as well as works by Raphael, Caravaggio, and Artemisia Gentileschi.

GREEK & ROMAN SCULPTURE While the **Winged Victory of Samothrace** and the **Venus de Milo** are not to be missed, the Salle des Caryatides (the room itself is a work of art) boasts marble masterworks such as *Artemis* hunting with her stag and the *Sleeping Hermaphrodite,* an alluring female figure from behind—and something entirely different from the front.

THE GALERIE D'APOLLON Commissioned by Louis XIV, aka "the Sun King," every inch of this gallery is covered with gilt stucco sculptures and flamboyant murals invoking the journey of the Roman sun god Apollo. The main draw here is the collection of crown jewels. Among necklaces bedecked with quarter-sized sapphires and tiaras dripping with diamonds and rubies are the **jewel-studded crown** of Louis XV and the **Regent,** a 140-carat diamond that decorated his hat.

THE EGYPTIANS This is the largest collection outside of Cairo, thanks in large part to Jean-François Champollion, the 19th-century French scientist and scholar, who first decoded Egyptian hieroglyphs. Sculptures, figurines, papyrus documents, steles, musical instruments, and of course, mummies fill numerous rooms in the Sully wing, including the colossal **statue of Ramses II** and the strangely moving **Seated Scribe.** He gazes intently out of intricately crafted inlaid eyes: A combination of copper, magnesite, and polished rock crystal creates a startlingly lifelike stare.

Louvre

LARGE-FORMAT FRENCH PAINTINGS Enormous floor-to-ceiling paintings of monumental moments in history cover the walls in these three rooms. The overcrowded and legendary *Coronation of Napoléon* by Jacques-Louis David depicts the newly minted emperor crowning Joséphine, while the disconcerted pope and a host of notables look on. On the facing wall, *Madame Récamier* (also by David), one of Napoleon's loudest critics, reclines fetchingly on a divan. Farther on are several tumultuous canvases by Eugène Delacroix, including *Liberty Guiding the People,* which might just be the ultimate expression of French patriotism. In the painting, which evokes the events of the revolution of 1830, Liberty—breast exposed, a rifle in one hand, the French flag in the other—leads the crowd over a sea of dead bodies. High ideals and gore—it sort of sums up the French revolutionary spirit.

Note: When visiting the museum, **watch your wallets and purses**—there has been an unfortunate increase in pickpockets; thieves even use children to prey on unsuspecting art lovers. On a more positive note, the Louvre has made great strides in improving **accessibility for travelers with disabilities,**

MEN HAVE named YOU...

Everything about the *Mona Lisa* is mysterious—the identity of the sitter, how long it took to paint, and how it got into the French royal collection, among other things. Most scholars agree that it is a portrait of Lisa Gheradini, the wife of one Francesco del Giocondo, but Ms. Lisa could also be Isabella of Aragon (as suggested by the patterning of her dress) or simply an embodiment of beauty and happiness (hence the smile), as suggested by the Italian word *gioconda*.

In 2006, researchers found evidence of a fine, translucent veil around the subject's shoulders, a garment that women in Renaissance Italy wore when they were expecting, provoking an onslaught of speculation that her secret smile had to do with her being pregnant.

What's certain is that the painting created a sensation. The overall harmony of the composition, the use of a distant landscape in the background, the lifelike quality of the subject, had a huge impact on early-16th-century Florentine art. As Giorgio Vasari, a Renaissance painter and biographer, lamented, "It may be said that it was painted in such a manner as to make every valiant craftsman, be he who he may, tremble and lose heart."

The painting's history is action packed. One morning in 1911, an artist named Louis Béroud entered the museum to sketch a copy of the famous portrait and found a bare spot with four hooks in the wall. After a concerted effort, he convinced the lackadaisical guard to find out what happened. In fact, the *Mona Lisa* had been stolen. The thief had entered the museum posing as a visitor, hid in the building overnight, and in the morning disguised himself as a workman and made off with the painting while the guard went out to smoke a cigarette.

---

including special programs, ramps, free wheelchairs, and folding chairs. For more info, click "visit" and then "accessibility" at the top of the museum's website.

1st arrond. Main entrance in the glass pyramid, cour Napoléon. louvre.fr. ☏ **01-40-20-50-50.** Admission 22€ adults, free for children 17 and under. Wed–Mon 9am–6pm (until 9pm Fri). Métro: Palais-Royal–Musée du Louvre.

Palais Royal ♥♥ HISTORIC SITE/GARDEN   The gardens and long arcades of the Palais Royal are not only a delight to stroll through but were also witnesses to one of the most important moments in French history.

Built by Cardinal Richelieu, the lavish palace was left to the king upon his prime minister's death in 1642. It was subsequently occupied by a number of royal family members (including Louis XIV as a child) until it came into the hands of Duke Louis Philippe d'Orleans at the end of the 18th century. An inveterate spendthrift, the young lord soon found himself up to his ears in debt. To earn enough money to pay off his creditors, he came up with the shockingly modern idea of opening the palace gardens to development, building apartments on the grounds. The bottom floor of these lodgings, which make up three sides of the enclosure you see today, were let out as shops, cafes, and boutiques. Since the police had no power over these royal grounds, gambling houses and bordellos sprang up between the shops and cafes, and

Needless to say, panic ensued. There was a nationwide investigation, and the borders were sealed. What the police didn't realize was that the painting was at first hidden only a mile from the Louvre. There was a lot of criticism of the Louvre's lax security, in particular from the poet Apollinaire. He soon found himself arrested as a suspect, and his friend Pablo Picasso was also brought in for questioning after they were caught in possession of some other art objects of dubious origins. After they both broke down in tears before the bench, the judge let them go with a slap on the wrist.

After 2 years of false leads and bungled investigations, the *Mona Lisa* was finally found when the thief, Vincenzo Perugia, tried to sell it to an art dealer in Florence. What was the motive for the crime? It seems that Perugia, an Italian patriot who had once worked at the museum, simply felt that the *Mona Lisa* belonged in her country of birth, Italy.

The life of a superstar certainly isn't easy. With millions of admirers around the world, at least a couple are bound to have a few screws loose. Once she was back at the museum (under increased security), things calmed down until 1956, when a deranged visitor threw acid on the painting, severely damaging its lower half (restoration took several years). A few months later, someone threw a rock at her. The painting is now covered with bulletproof glass, and a full-time guard stands at the ready—though that didn't stop a man from smearing cake over the glass in an apparent protest about climate change in 2022 (the painting was untouched). So be patient with the lines and velvet ropes—if *Mona Lisa* gets the kind of security usually reserved for rock stars or heads of state, she has certainly earned it.

---

the gardens became the central meeting place for Revolutionaries. Things came to a head on July 12, 1789, when Camille Desmoulins stood up on a table in front of the Café de Foy and called the people to arms—2 days later, the mob would storm the Bastille, igniting the French Revolution.

The glory days of the Palais Royal would end abruptly in 1815, when a new Louis-Philippe showed up, decided this was not the way to treat the home of his ancestors, and kicked everyone out. Once the royals finally left in the 19th century, the palace was taken over by various government ministries, and the apartments in the galleries were let out to artists and writers, among them Collette and Jean Cocteau.

Today the shops in the arcades are a smattering of high-end designer clothes and a couple of pricey restaurants. The *cour d'honneur* on the south end is filled with black-and-white-striped columns by Daniel Buren; though most Parisians have now gotten used to this unusual installation, when it was unveiled in 1987 it caused almost as much of a stir as Camille Desmoulins.

Rue St-Honoré, 1st arrond. Free admission to gardens and arcades, buildings closed to public. Daily 7:30am–dusk. Métro: Palais-Royal–Musée du Louvre.

Place Vendôme ♥♥ SQUARE   In 1686, Louis XIV decided the time had come to design a magnificent square, at the center of which would stand a statue of His Royal Highness. This uber-elegant octagonal ensemble of

The Palais Royal gardens.

17th-century buildings is the home of the original Ritz Hôtel, as well as the world's most glitzy jewelry makers, including Cartier, Van Cleef and Arpels, and Boucheron. Though the statue is long gone, this is still one of the classiest squares in the city. The famous statue reigned over the square up until the Revolution, when it was melted down for scrap. When Napoleon took over, he decided it was the perfect place for a huge Roman-style column honoring his glorious army (yes, once again), this time documenting its victory at Austerlitz. A long spiral of bas-reliefs recounting the campaign of 1805 marches up the Colonne de la Grande Armée, which was crowned by a statue of the emperor himself. The original statue did not survive the regime; a few decades later, Napoleon III replaced it with the existing copy.

Enter by rue de Castiglione, 1st arrond. Métro: Tuileries or Concorde.

Sainte-Chapelle ♥♥♥ CHURCH   A wall of color greets visitors who enter this magnificent chapel. Stained-glass windows make up a large part of the walls of the upper level of the church, giving worshippers the impression of standing inside a jewel-encrusted crystal goblet. What isn't glass is elaborately carved and painted in gold leaf and rich colors: vaulting arches, delicate window casings, and an intricate wainscoting of arches and medallions. The 15 stained-glass windows recount the story of the Bible, from Genesis to the Apocalypse, as well as the story of Saint Louis, who was responsible for the chapel's construction. Back in the early 13th century, Louis IX spent 2 years bargaining with Emperor Badouin II of Constantinople for some of the holiest relics in Christendom: the Crown of Thorns and a piece of the Holy Cross. The relics were finally purchased for a princely sum, and Louis decided that they should be housed in an appropriately splendid chapel in the royal palace (the relics are currently at the Louvre Museum; p. 166). The record is not clear, but the architect may have been the illustrious Pierre de Montreuil, who worked on the cathedrals of St-Denis and Notre-Dame. Whoever it was, he was a speed demon; the chapel was built in record time for the Middle Ages, from 1241 to 1248. He was also quite brilliant; he managed to support the structure with arches and buttresses in such a way that the walls of the upper chapel are almost entirely glass.

The lower chapel, which was meant for the servants, has a low, vaulted ceiling painted in blue and red and gold and covered with fleur-de-lis motifs. Up a small staircase is the upper chapel, clearly meant for the royals. This masterpiece suffered both fire and floods in the 17th century and was pillaged by zealous Revolutionaries in the 18th. By the mid–19th century, the chapel was being used to store archives—2m (6½ ft.) of the bottom of each window was removed to install shelves. Fortunately, renewed interest in medieval art staved off plans for Sainte-Chapelle's demolition, and eventually led to a conscientious restoration by a team that was advised by master restorer Viollet-le-Duc. The quality of the work on the windows is such that it is almost impossible to detect the difference between the original and the reconstructed stained glass (which makes up about one-third of what you see).

The royal chapel of Sainte-Chapelle.

Sainte-Chapelle stages evening **concerts** March to November (15€–75€). And they're very popular (and sometimes come with tapas and wine), so I recommend reserving in advance online at classictic.com.

If you plan to visit the Conciergerie (p. 163), you can save money by buying a joint ticket with time slots: 20€ adults, free for children ages 17 and under.

Palais de Justice, 4 bd. du Palais, 1st arrond. sainte-chapelle.fr. **01-53-40-60-80.** 13€ adults, free for ages 25 and under. Daily Oct–Mar 9am–5pm; Apr–Sept 9am–7pm. Métro: Cité, St-Michel, or Châtelet–Les Halles. RER: St-Michel.

St-Eustache ♥♥ CHURCH

A Gothic church with Renaissance decor, St-Eustache is one of the largest in the city, at more than 105m long (344 ft.) and 43m wide (141 ft.). It was built from 1532 to 1640 along the plan of Notre-Dame. These dimensions result in excellent acoustics for the church's huge 8,000-pipe organ. The church's musical reputation stretches back centuries: Berlioz and Liszt both conducted their works here, among others. Before the Revolution, St-Eustache was a parish where both the nobility and working class came to worship—Cardinal Richelieu and Madame de Pompadour were baptized here, as was the playwright Molière. After the Revolution, it was turned into a temple to agriculture, and, like many Parisian churches, its interior suffered mightily. It has subsequently been restored to its former glory and is truly breathtaking, not least on the outside, where (if you stand in the new Les Halles gardens) you can see an unusual figure for a church, a giant stag's head. The story goes that a Roman general called Placidus was hunting deer when a stag appeared with a crucifix hanging between its antlers. The vision caused Placidus to convert to Christianity and change his name to Eustathios, or "Eustache," after whom the church is now named. You can hear the organ and the choir in action Sunday at 5pm before (and during) the 6pm Mass; other concerts are listed on the church's website.

2 impasse St-Eustache, 1st arrond. saint-eustache.org. **01-42-36-31-05.** Free admission. Mon–Fri 9:30am–7pm; Sat–Sun 9am–7pm (summer hours from 10am). Sun organ recitals 5pm. Métro: Les Halles.

St-Germain l'Auxerrois ♥ CHURCH This is a church with a checkered past. St-Germain was designated the royal church when the Valois moved in across the street at the Louvre in the 14th century, and kings, queens, and their entourages often attended Mass here. But its most infamous moment came at dawn on August 24, 1572, when the church's bells sounded the signal that began the Saint Bartholomew's Day massacre. Despite her erstwhile tolerance, Catherine de Médicis and her son Charles IX gave their blessing to a plot to slaughter the Huguenot (Protestant) leaders. The crowd murdered every Protestant in sight—between 2,000 and 4,000 were killed over the following 5 days.

The church has been rebuilt several times over the centuries, resulting in a mix of architectural styles. The 12th-century Romanesque tower hovers over a 15th-century Flamboyant Gothic porch embellished with human and animal figures. The vaulted interior is relatively simple and shelters some interesting works of art, among which are a monumental **sculpted wooden pew,** designed for the royal family in 1684 by Le Brun, and a 16th-century carved wood **retable** depicting scenes from the life of Christ.

2 pl. du Louvre, 1st arrond. saintgermainlauxerrois.fr. **01-42-60-13-96.** Free admission. Daily 9am–7pm. Métro: Louvre-Rivoli.

Opéra & Grands Boulevards (2nd & 9th Arrondissements)

The grandiose **Opéra Garnier** reigns over this bustling neighborhood, which teems with office workers, tourists, and shoppers scuttling in and around the *grands magasins* ("big stores") on boulevard Haussmann. The 2nd arrondissement has more outstanding retail experiences than cultural ones, but the hip 9th has a few small museums worthy of your time.

Musée de la Vie Romantique ♥♥ MUSEUM This quaint villa, with painted shutters and a fragrant rose garden, is where Romantic painter Ary Scheffer (1795–1858) once entertained such illustrious guests as Baronne Aurore Dupin (George Sand), Eugène Delacroix, Chopin, and Charles Dickens. Today, the tiny museum gives an inkling as to what life might have been like in the company of these iconic artists, with atmospheric period rooms, one of which is dedicated to George Sand and displays moving mementos from her life—jewelry, trinkets, paintings, and even a plaster cast of her right arm. In summer, the rose garden doubles as one of Paris's most charming tearooms. The museum is closed for renovations until March 2026.

16 rue Chaptal, 9th arrond. museevieromantique.paris.fr. **01-55-31-95-67.** Free admission to permanent collection except during certain temporary exhibits. Métro: Saint-Georges, Pigalle, or Blanche.

Musée Grévin ♥♥ MUSEUM This vast, kitsch cavern of wax figures—movie stars, historical figures, sports heroes, rock 'n' rollers,

The courtyard of the Museum of Romantic Life.

notables from the political scene—is a fun place to take the kids. If you're not up on French history or pop culture, you might not recognize some of the faces, but don't worry, Marilyn Monroe, Ryan Gosling, and Albert Einstein are here, too. Stars appear in their natural habitats: chic brasseries, cocktail parties, and fashion shows. Historical tableaus feature such scenes as Joan of Arc being burned at the stake and Louis XIV holding court at Versailles. *Tip:* If you're traveling as 2 adults and 2 children (ages 5–15), save money by buying the family ticket online from 14.50€ per person.

10 bd. Montmartre, 9th arrond. grevin-paris.com. **01-47-70-85-05.** Admission varies with the season, starting at 27.50€ adults, 19.50€ ages 6–17, free for children 5 and under. Daily 10am–6pm (hours vary with seasons; check website for exact times). Métro: Grands Boulevards.

Musée Gustave Moreau ♥♥♥ MUSEUM Symbolist painter Gustave Moreau was a contemporary of the Impressionists, but he worked against the grain, rejecting realism and naturalism to draw inspiration from the Bible, Greek mythology, Leonardo da Vinci, and Indian miniatures. This quaint museum, set in the elegant town house where he once lived and worked, has atmospheric period rooms that reveal Moreau's obsession for Second Empire and Restoration-era knickknacks and furniture. This ticket will give you a discount at the following museums: Musée d'Orsay (p. 220), Musée National des Arts Asiatiques Guimet (p. 191), and the Opéra Garnier.

14 rue de la Rochfoucauld, 9th arrond. musee-moreau.fr. **01-48-74-38-50.** Admission 8€ adults, 6€ students 18–25, free for children 17 and under. Wed–Mon 10am–6pm. Métro: Trinité.

Opéra Garnier ♥♥ OPERA HOUSE This splendid example of Second Empire architectural excess, built by architect Charles Garnier between 1862 and 1875, sits on the underground lake that inspired Gaston Leroux's 1911 novel, *The Phantom of the Opera*. Corinthian columns, loggias, busts, and friezes cover the facade of the building, which is topped by a flattened gold

175

dome. Seventy-three sculptors worked on the decoration, which includes symbolic representations of Music, Poetry, Drama, and Dance.

The interior is no less dramatic. The vast lobby, built in a spectrum of different colored marble, holds a spectacular double staircase that sweeps up to the different levels of the auditorium, as well as an array of glamorous antechambers, galleries, and ballrooms that make you wonder how the opera scenery could possibly compete. Mosaics, mirrors, gilt, and marble line these grand spaces, whose painted ceilings dance with fauns, gods, and nymphs. The largest room, the grand foyer, is drenched in gold leaf and hung with gigantic chandeliers, looking something like a real palace, which was, in fact, the effect

The grand staircase of the Opéra Garnier National de Paris.

Garnier was going for. The main event, of course, is the auditorium, which might seem a bit small, considering the size of the building. The horseshoe shape of the seating area ensures that viewers see both the stage and each other—19th-century operagoers were equally concerned with what was on the stage and who was in the house. The beautiful ceiling was painted by Marc Chagall in 1964 with colorful images from various operas and ballets.

All of this (with the exception of the Chagall ceiling) sprang from the mind of a young, unknown architect named Charles Garnier, who won a competition launched when Napoleon III decided the time had come to build himself an opera house. Though the first stone was laid in 1862, work was held up by war, civil unrest, and a change in regime; the **Palais Garnier** was not inaugurated until 1875. Some contemporary critics found it a bit much (one called it "an overloaded sideboard"), but today it is generally acknowledged as a masterpiece of the architecture of the epoch.

You can visit the building on your own (for a fee), but with so much history and so many good stories, you might want to take advantage of the **guided visits in English** (23€ adults, 16.50€ ages 10–25, 10€ children 9 and under; check website for times). Or simply **buy tickets to a show.**

Corner of rue Scribe and rue Auber, 9th arrond. operadeparis.fr. © **08-92-89-90-90** (.35€/min.). Admission 15€ adults, 10€ students and ages 12–25, free for children 11 and under. Daily Oct to mid-July 10am–5pm; mid-July to Sept 10am–6pm. Métro: Opéra.

Le Marais (3rd & 4th Arrondissements)

Home to royalty and aristocracy between the 14th and 17th centuries, the Marais still boasts remarkable architecture, some of it dating back to the

Middle Ages. One of the few neighborhoods that was not knocked down during Baron Haussmann's urban overhaul, its narrow streets are lined with magnificent *hôtels particuliers* (mansions) as well as humbler homes from centuries past. The **Pompidou Center** and **Musée National Picasso-Paris** are probably the biggest attractions, but the Marais also harbors a wealth of terrific smaller museums, as well as the delightful **Place des Vosges.** Remnants of the city's **historic Jewish quarter** can be found on rue des Rosiers, which has seen an influx of clothing shops in recent years. Nowadays, a larger Jewish neighborhood is in the 19th arrondissement.

Centre Pompidou ♥♥ MUSEUM   The bizarre architecture of this odd building provokes such strong emotions that it's easy to forget that there is something inside. Believe it or not, President Pompidou searched far and wide to find an architect. In 1971, an international design competition was held with entrants from 49 countries, and the winners were the Italo-British design team of Renzo Piano and Richard Rogers. Their concept was to put the support structure and transport systems on the outside of the building, thereby liberating space on the inside for a museum and cultural center. The result was a gridlike exoskeleton with a tubular escalator inching up one side, and huge multicolored pipes and shafts covering the other. To some, it's a milestone in contemporary architecture; to others, it's simply a horror. Either way, it's one of the most visited structures in France.

The Pompidou is much more than just an art museum. Its over 100,000 sq. m (1,076,390 sq. ft.) of floor space includes a vast **reference library,** a **cinema archive, bookshops,** and a **music research institute,** as well as a **photography** and **children's gallery,** a **performance hall,** and areas for educational activities. Even behemoths require renovations. At time of writing, the Centre Pompidou was set about to **close for renovations until 2030,** so many of its 120,000 works were set to go on show in multiple exhibitions all across France.

pl. Georges-Pompidou, 4th arrond. centrepompidou.fr. ✆ **01-44-78-12-33.** Métro: Hôtel de Ville. RER: Châtelet–Les Halles.

Hôtel de Ville ♥ HISTORIC SITE   No, it's not a hotel. This enormous neo-Renaissance wedding cake is Paris's city hall, and the only way to see the inside is to make friends with the mayor, though it does host regular art exhibits on subjects linked to Paris's history, usually for free (access is through the back entrance on rue Lobau). Even if you can't get inside, you can feast on the lavish exterior, which includes 136 statues representing VIPs of Parisian history. Since the 14th century, this spot has been an administrative seat for the municipality; the building you see before you dates from 1873, but it is an accurate copy of an earlier Renaissance version that was burned down in 1870 during the Paris Commune. The vast square in front of the building was once used for municipal festivals and executions. It was also the stage for several important moments in the city's history, particularly during the Revolution: Louis XVI was forced to kiss the new French flag here, and Robespierre was shot in the jaw and arrested here during an attempted coup. Today the square

Walking along the Seine.

hosts more peaceful activities: There's a merry-go-round, and in winter, an ice-skating rink is sometimes set up.

29 rue de Rivoli, 4th arrond. paris.fr. © **01-42-76-63-01.** Free admission to exhibits. Métro: Hôtel-de-Ville.

Maison de Victor Hugo ♥ MUSEUM   The life of Victor Hugo was as turbulent as some of his novels. Regularly visited by both tragedy and triumph, the author of *The Hunchback of Notre-Dame* lived in several apartments in Paris, including this one on the second floor of a corner house on the sumptuous Place des Vosges. From 1832 to 1848, he lived here with his wife and four children, during which time he wrote *Ruy Blas* and part of *Les Misérables;* met his lifelong mistress and muse, Juliette Drouet; was elected to the Académie Française; lost his 19-year-old daughter in a boating accident on the Seine; and entered the political arena. When Napoleon III seized power in 1851, this passionate advocate of free speech and social justice was distinctly unwelcome, particularly after he declared the new emperor a traitor of France. Hugo fled the country and lived in exile until 1870, when he triumphantly returned to France and was elected to the senate. By the time he died in 1885, he was a national hero; his funeral cortege through the streets of Paris is the stuff of legend, and his body was one of the first to be buried in the Panthéon (p. 211). The museum's collection charts this dramatic existence through the author's drawings, original manuscripts, notes, furniture, and personal objects, all displayed in small rooms that re-create the ambience and the spirit of the original lodgings.

6 pl. des Vosges, 4th arrond. maisonsvictorhugo.paris.fr. © **01-42-72-10-16.** Free admission to permanent collection except during certain temporary exhibits. Tues–Sun 10am–6pm. Métro: St-Paul, Bastille, or Chemin Vert.

Musée Carnavalet ♥♥♥ MUSEUM   Paris has served as a backdrop to centuries' worth of dramatic events, from Roman takeovers to barbarian

THE bridges OF PARIS

Despite its name (*neuf* means "new"), the **Pont Neuf** (Quai du Louvre to Quai de Conti) is the oldest bridge in Paris. The bridge was an instant hit at its inauguration by Henri IV in 1607 (its ample sidewalks made it a delight for pedestrians), and it still is. For a quiet picnic spot, take the stairs by the statue of Henri IV (in the center of the span) down to the **Square du Vert Galant.**

The **Pont des Arts** (Quai François Mitterrand to Quai de Conti) was originally constructed at the beginning of the 19th century. Delicately arching over the river, the iron pedestrian bridge is still the most romantic bridge in the city—with its splendid view of the Île de la Cité—in spite of the fact that overenthusiastic lovers attached so many locks to the railing that the barrier actually fell over and has now been replaced with plastic screens. It's best to avoid any symbolic gestures (like writing your names on a lock, attaching it to the railing, and throwing away the key) and opt for romantic selfies instead.

A modern way to get from the Left to the Right bank is via the **Passerelle Simone de Beauvoir** (Quai de Bercy to Quai François Mauriac). A graceful pedestrian passage, the bridge consists of two arching bands of oak and steel, which intertwine and cross the river without the support of a central pillar. The central lens-shaped structure was constructed by the Eiffel factory (founded by Gustave).

With its enormous pillars topped by gilded statuary, it's hard to miss the **Pont Alexandre III** (Cours de la Reine to Quai d'Orsay). Linking the vast esplanade of the Invalides with the glass-domed Grand Palais, this elegant bridge fits right in with its grand surroundings. The span was named after Czar Alexander III of Russia and inaugurated at the opening of the Paris Exposition of 1900.

Incredibly, the small and lovely **Pont Marie** (Quai des Célestins to Quai d'Anjou–Ile St-Louis), composed of three gentle arches, was once loaded down by some 50 houses. During a flood in 1658, the Seine washed away two of its arches and 20 houses fell into the water. The tragedy, which claimed 60 lives, got city officials to thinking, and finally, in 1769, homesteading on bridges was outlawed.

---

invasions, from coronations to decapitations to the birth of the modern French republic. These stories and others are told at this fascinating museum through objects, paintings, and interiors. The collection is displayed in two extraordinary 17th-century mansions—works of art in their own right. Starting with an eye-catching installation of old shop signs, the history of Paris is illustrated with items as diverse as Gallo-Roman figurines, Napoleon's toiletry kit, a portrait of Benjamin Franklin painted when he was the U.S. ambassador to France and even a prehistoric canoe from 4600 B.C.E. It's a fascinating place, with an outdoor summer cafe in its stunning landscaped garden, where you can sip tea among the pretty parterres before or after your visit.

16 rue des Francs-Bourgeois, 3rd arrond. carnavalet.paris.fr. **01-44-59-58-58.** Free admission to permanent collection except during certain temporary exhibits. Tues–Sun 10am–6pm. Métro: St-Paul or Chemin Vert.

Musée Cognacq-Jay ♥ MUSEUM   This bite-size museum offers a bite-size taste of the finer side of 18th-century France. Its founder, Ernest Cognacq, led a rags-to-riches life: At 12 years old, he was selling odds and ends as an

Musée d'Art et d'Histoire du Judaïsme–MAHJ.

itinerant merchant, and by the end of his life, he was the owner of a fabulously successful department store (today's La Samaritaine building) with a prodigious private art collection. His rich assortment of 18th-century art and furniture make up the contents of this small museum, which is housed in a lovely *hôtel particulier* (mansion). What's most impressive here is the furniture, such as the bed à la polonaise draped in blue damask and framed in gilt, or the exquisite Louis XVI–era writing table with geometric wood inlay.

8 rue Elzévir, 3rd arrond. cognacq-jay.paris.fr. **01-40-27-07-21.** Free admission to permanent collection except during certain temporary exhibits. Tues–Sun 10am–6pm. Métro: St-Paul or Chemin Vert.

Musée d'Art et d'Histoire du Judaïsme ♥♥ MUSEUM

Housed in the magnificent Hôtel de Saint Aignan, one of the many palatial 17th-century mansions that dot the Marais, this museum chronicles the art and history of the Jewish people in France and in Europe. It features a superb collection of objects of both artistic and cultural significance (a splendid Italian Renaissance Torah ark, a German gold and silver Hanukkah menorah, a 17th-c. Dutch illustrated Torah scroll, documents from the Dreyfus trial), which is interspersed with texts, drawings, and photos telling the story of the Jews and explaining the basics of both Ashkenazi and Sephardic traditions. The final rooms include a collection of works by Jewish artists, including Modigliani, Soutine, Lipchitz, and Chagall. Be prepared for airportlike security at the entrance.

71 rue du Temple, 3rd arrond. mahj.org. **01-53-01-86-60.** Admission 13€ adults, 9€ ages 18–25, free for children 17 and under. Tues–Fri 11am–6pm (Wed until 9pm); Sat–Sun 10am–6pm. Métro: Rambuteau or Hôtel de Ville.

Musée de la Chasse et de la Nature ♥ MUSEUM

If you can get over the fact that it's a museum dedicated to hunting, this small, freshly renovated museum makes for a pleasant outing. You'll find the expected taxidermy animals, but they are discreetly presented among an elegant collection of paintings, tapestries, sculptures, and even contemporary art. The emphasis is not so much on the kill as the symbolism behind each piece, and it's all rather intriguing. It reminds you that the relationship between humans and animals dates to well before there were naturalists and environmentalists, and if that relationship was filled with animosity and fear, it was also tinged with a sort of mystical respect.

62 rue des Archives, 3rd arrond. chassenature.org. *©* **01-53-01-92-40.** Admission 11€ adults, 9€ students, free for children 17 and under. Tues–Sun 11am–6pm (until 9:30pm Wed). Métro: Rambuteau.

Musée des Arts et Métiers ♥♥♥ MUSEUM   If you've read Umberto Eco's novel *Foucault's Pendulum,* you'll probably want to come here just to see Foucault's original pendulum swing in the church of St-Martin-des-Champs, but there are plenty of other reasons to spend a couple of hours at this temple of technology. The Musée harbors sterling examples of just about every discovery that made the mechanical world possible. True techies will linger over the many displays of gearboxes, steam engines, and other historic gizmos; the less technically inclined will probably prefer the first versions of telephones, movie cameras, and toasters. A lot of "firsts" are here, like the first omnibus (a "high-speed" steam vehicle built in 1873), and the Blériot XI (the first plane to cross the English Channel), as well as the earliest examples of phonographs, lightbulbs, and tape decks. Those "new" antiques—the typewriters, record players, and VCRs on display in those old wooden cases—drive home the fact that the technological revolution is ongoing, and today's wonders will be tomorrow's curiosities.

60 rue Réaumur, 3rd arrond. arts-et-metiers.net. *©* **01-53-01-82-00.** Admission 12€ adults, 9€ students, free for 25 and under. Tues–Sun 10am–6pm (until 9pm Fri). Métro: Arts et Métiers.

Musée National Picasso-Paris ♥♥♥ MUSEUM   This shrine to all things Picasso is in the stunning Hôtel Salé, a 17th-century mansion built by salt-tax farmer Pierre Aubert, whose position gave the mansion its name—*salé* means "salty." Some 400 carefully selected paintings, sculptures, collages, and drawings are presented in more or less chronological and thematic order, no small task when dealing with an artist who experimented with every style, from neoclassicism to surrealism to his own flamboyantly abstract inventions. Impressionist portraits (*Portrait of Gustave Coquiot,* 1901), Cubist explorations (*Man with Guitar,* 1911), mannerist allegories (*The Race,* 1922), and deconstructionist forms (*Reclining Nude,* 1932) make up only part of his oeuvre, which has been estimated to include some 50,000 works. Picasso often worked in wildly different styles during the same period, sometimes on the same subjects. For example, the rounded yet realistic lovers dancing in *La Danse des Villageois,* painted in 1922, hang next to two forms in a blaze of color representing *The Kiss,* painted in 1925. There's also a sampling of the somewhat disturbing portraits of the many women in his life, including

Musée National Picasso-Paris.

portraits of Dora Maar and Marie-Thérèse, both painted in 1937. On the top floor is Picasso's private collection, which includes works by artists he admired like Courbet and Cézanne, as well as paintings by his friends, who included Braque and Matisse. What you see on the walls is less than 10% of the 5,000 works in the collection; the presentation rotates every couple of years. *Note:* Families (1 or 2 adults, plus a child) also have reduced rates of 12€ per adult; the entry price also goes down to 12€ on the first Wednesday of the month for late-night opening.

5 rue de Thorigny, 3rd arrond. museepicassoparis.fr. **01-85-56-00-36.** Admission 16€ adults, free for children 17 and under. Tues–Fri 10:30am–6pm; Sat–Sun 9:30am–6pm (until 10pm 1st Wed of month). Métro: St-Paul or Chemin Vert.

Place des Vosges ♥♥♥ SQUARE Possibly the prettiest square in the city, the Place des Vosges combines elegance, greenery, and quiet. Nowhere in Paris will you find such a unity of Renaissance-style architecture; the entire square is bordered by 17th-century brick town houses, each conforming to rules set down by Henri IV himself. Arched arcades run under the houses. In the center is a garden with a geometric arrangement of lush lawns, fountains, and trees. At the epicenter is a huge equestrian statue of Louis XIII, during whose reign (1610–43) the square enjoyed a golden age of festivals and tournaments. But it was a tournament in a previous century that proved pivotal to the creation of this square. In the 16th century, a royal palace called the Hôtel des Tournelles stood on this site. In 1559, an organized combat was held there, during which the current monarch, feisty Henri II, defeated several opponents. Feeling pleased with himself, he decided to fight Montgomery, the captain of his guard. A badly aimed lance resulted in Henri's untimely death; his wife,

Catherine de Médicis, was so distraught that she had the palace demolished. His descendant, Henri IV, took advantage of the free space to construct a royal square. Today the homes are for the rich, as are many of the chic art galleries under the arcades, but the park, the fountains, and the children's playground are for everyone.

4th arrond. Métro: St-Paul.

Champs-Élysées, Trocadéro & Western Paris (8th, 16th & 17th Arrondissements)

Decidedly posh, this is one of the wealthiest parts of the city in both per capita earnings and cultural institutions. While the **Champs-Élysées** is more glitz than glory, the surrounding neighborhoods offer high-end shops and restaurants as well as some terrific museums and concert halls. This is also where you will find grand architectural gestures, like the **Arc de Triomphe** and the **Place de la Concorde,** which bookend the Champs, and the **Grand Palais** and **Petit Palais,** leftovers from the legendary 1900 Universal Exposition.

Arc de Triomphe ♥♥♥ MONUMENT   If there is one monument that symbolizes the glory of France, it is this giant triumphal arch. Crowning the Champs-Élysées, this mighty archway celebrates the victories of the French army and memorializes the sacrifices of its soldiers. Over time, it has become an icon of the Republic and a setting for some of its most emotional moments:

Aerial view of Arc de Triomphe.

the lying in state of the coffin of Victor Hugo in 1885, the burial in 1921 of the ashes of an unknown soldier who fought in World War I, and General de Gaulle's pregnant pause under the arch before striding down the Champs-Élysées to cheering crowds after the Liberation in 1944.

It took a certain amount of chutzpah to come up with the idea to build such a shrine, and sure enough, it was Napoleon who instigated it. In 1806, still glowing after his stunning victory at Austerlitz, the emperor decided to erect a monument to the Imperial Army, along the lines of a Roman triumphal arch. Architect Jean-François Chalgrin drew inspiration from Rome's Arch of Titus, though he abandoned the columns and made Napoleon's arch a whopping 50m (163 ft.) high and 45m (147 ft.) wide, the largest of its type on the planet. The defeat at Waterloo put an end to the Empire before the arch was finished, and construction came to an abrupt halt. It wasn't until 1823 that building got going again; it was finally finished in 1836 by Louis-Philippe.

The arch is covered with bas-reliefs and sculptures, the most famous of which is the enormous *Departure of the Volunteers* of 1792, better known as the Marseillaise, by François Rude, showing winged, female Liberty leading the charge of Revolutionary soldiers. Many smaller panels detailing Napoleonic battles—in this case, Aboukir. At the base of the arch is the Tomb of the Unknown Soldier, over which a flame is relit every evening at 6:30pm. The inscription, added after World War I, reads ICI REPOSE UN SOLDAT FRANÇAIS MORT POUR LA PATRIE, 1914–1918 ("Here lies a French soldier who died for his country").

Don't even think about crossing the traffic circle; instead take the underpass near the Champs-Élysées Métro entrance. You can visit the area under the arch free of charge, but if you want to enjoy the view from the rooftop terrace, you have to pay. You also have to climb 284 stairs to get there (only the very young, the very old, and those with disabilities get to use the elevator). Though you are not as high up as the viewing platforms on the Eiffel Tower, the panorama is quite impressive. Directly below, 12 boulevards radiate from the star-shaped intersection (hence the moniker "Étoile"), and out front is the long sweep of the Champs-Élysées, ending at the obelisk of the Place de la Concorde. You can pick out many of the most famous monuments, including Sacré-Coeur and the Eiffel Tower; to the west are the skyscrapers of La Défense, including the huge, hollowed-out Grande Arche, a modern version of the one you are standing on.

pl. Charles de Gaulle, 8th arrond. paris-arc-de-triomphe.fr. **01-55-37-73-77.** Admission 16€ adults, free for children 17 and under. Apr–Sept daily 10am–11pm (from 11am Tues); Oct–Mar daily 10am–10:30pm (from 11am Tues). Métro: Charles-de-Gaulle–Étoile.

Fondation Louis Vuitton ♥♥ MUSEUM In a building designed by mega-architect Frank Gehry, this stunning contemporary art museum is swathed in a mass of billowing "sails" of glass, giving the impression that it is about to sail off into the lush greenery of the Bois de Boulogne, a large park on the western edge of the city (p. 237). Once you've taken in the arty outside,

Fondation Louis Vuitton.

you have two choices: (1) see the sophisticated temporary collections of art (previous shows have included everything from early 20th-century Matisse to Modern pieces by Mark Rothko, and the relationship between Warhol and Basquiat), or (2) go explore the Bois de Boulogne's alleys, gardens, and lakes. If you are big on heady modern and conceptual art, it's a must; if not, stick to option number 2.

8 av. du Mahatma Gandhi, Bois de Boulogne, 16th arrond. fondationlouisvuitton. fr. **01-40-69-96-00.** 16€ adults, 10€ ages 18–26, 5€ artists and children 3–17, free for children 2 and under. Usually Sat–Mon and Wed 11am–8pm; Thurs–Fri 11am–11pm, but times vary, so check the website before you go. Métro: Les Sablons or Porte Maillot. Shuttle bus 1€ one-way from by pl. Charles de Gaulle–Etoile, 44 av. Friedland.

Grand Palais ♥ HISTORIC SITE/MUSEUM Built for the 1900 Universal Exhibition, this giant exhibition hall spans a total area of 72,000 sq. m (775,000 sq. ft.), with the biggest glass roof in Europe—an elegant lighting solution, since the building was constructed prior to electricity. After years of renovations, the Grand Palais finally re-opened in time for the 2024 Olympics, and is now back to its usual occupation of hosting a changing and impressive array of sporting and cultural events. The building also houses the Palais de la Découverte (palais-decouverte.fr), a science museum dedicated to children, with live experiments, a planetarium, and lots of interactive exhibits about our living world.

Place Clemenceau, 8th arrond. grandpalais. fr. **01-44-13-17-17.** Opening hours and admission prices vary according to the exhibitions and events. Métro: Champs-Élysées–Clémenceau.

Hôtel de la Marine ♥♥ MUSEUM Standing in the center of Place de la Concorde, with your back to the Seine, you can't miss three wonderful monuments: the Hôtel de Crillon (a palace hotel), the Madeleine church (p. 187) at the end of rue Royale, and the Hôtel de la Marine, the 18th-century neoclassical beauty

Grand Palais.

(the Crillon's twin) that once stored the king's furniture before becoming the naval ministry's HQ. Its history is fascinating: Here, in 1792, France's crown jewels—more than 10,000 gemstones of diamonds, topazes, rubies, emeralds, sapphires, and pearls—were stolen under the guards' noses. In 1848, it was here that minister François Arago abolished slavery in the colonies. It's now a museum, with period rooms showcasing 18th-century design and the Qatarian Al Thani Collection, an assembly of over 6,000 works of art, including the 17th-century Idol's Eye, the world's largest blue diamond. The museum's inner courtyard is open to the public from 9am to midnight and displays contemporary floor lights that at night make you feel as though you're walking on stars. *Note:* Part of the building now also hosts workshops for the Cordon Bleu cooking school (p. 232).

The golden gallery in Hôtel de la Marine.

2 pl. de la Concorde, 8th arrond. hotel-de-la-marine.paris. **01-58-51-52-00.** Admission 9€–23€ adults depending on which parts you visit, free for children 17 and under. Daily 10:30am–7pm (until 9:30pm on Fri). Métro: Concorde.

La Cité de l'Architecture et du Patrimoine ♥♥ INSTITUTE/MUSEUM   Created to promote French architecture and showcase evolving trends, this vast institution (located in the Palais de Chaillot) includes a museum, a research facility, and a top-notch school of architecture. On the ground floor, the enormous Galerie des Moulages with its vaulting skylights, exhibits casts of the gems of French architecture from the 12th to the 18th centuries. Commissioned in the late 19th century as a way of documenting France's architectural heritage, the project turned out to be an invaluable tool when it came to restoring the ravages of two world wars.

On the second floor, you'll dip into the cool waters of 20th- and 21st-century architecture, represented by intricate architectural models of structures like Piano and Rogers' Centre Pompidou (p. 177) and Rem Koolhaus' Maison Lemoine, a three-layer home built in Floriac, France, for a man who was paralyzed and his family. Don't miss clambering through a reconstruction of an apartment from Le Corbusier's Cité Radieuse, a shockingly (for the late 1940s) modern approach to urban housing.

1 pl. du Trocadéro, 16th arrond. citedelarchitecture.fr. **01-58-51-52-00.** Admission 9€ adults, 6€ ages 18–25, free for children 17 and under. Wed and Fri–Mon 11am–7pm; Thurs 11am–9pm. Métro: Trocadéro.

La Madeleine ♥♥ CHURCH   As you peer up the rue Royale from the Place de la Concorde, you'll see something that very closely resembles a Roman temple. In 1763, architect Pierre Constant d'Ivry laid the first stone of a church that would include a neoclassical facade with multiple columns. He didn't get very far. First the architect died, and then the Revolution broke out, during which construction ground to a halt. No one knew what to do with the site until Napoleon finally strode onto the scene and declared that it would become the Temple de la Gloire, to honor the victories of his army. He wanted something "solid" because he was sure that the monument would last "thousands of years." Unfortunately for him, military defeats and mounting debt would again delay construction. Once Napoleon was out of the picture for good, inertia took over the project again, and it wasn't until 1842, under the Restoration, that La Madeleine was finally consecrated.

The inside is pretty dark, thanks to a lack of windows (though it's lit by skylights and electric lights), but there are some interesting works of art here, if you can make them out. On the left as you enter is François Rude's *Baptism of Christ;* farther on is James Pradier's sculpture *La Marriage de la Vierge.*

pl. de la Madeleine, 8th arrond. lamadeleineparis.fr. *©* **01-44-51-69-00.** Free admission. Daily 9:30am–7pm. Métro: Madeleine.

Maison de Balzac ♥♥ MUSEUM   Fleeing his creditors in 1840, writer Honoré de Balzac rented this small house in what was then the village of Passy, where he lived for 7 years under an assumed name. He also worked like a demon: He was capable of writing for up to 20 hours a day for weeks at a time. The five rooms of Balzac's dwellings are hung with paintings and portraits of his family and friends, including several of Madame Hanska, whom he finally married after 18 years of passionate correspondence. There are also a few manuscripts and personal objects, including his turquoise-encrusted cane, which was the talk of Paris, and his monogrammed coffee pot, which kept him going through the marathon work sessions. In his office is the little table where he wrote *The Human Comedy,* "a witness," he wrote to Madame Hanska, "to my worries, my miseries, my distress, my joys, everything . . . my arm almost wore out its surface from taking the same path over and over again."

47 rue Raynouard, 16th arrond. maisondebalzac.paris.fr. *©* **01-55-74-41-80.** Free admission to permanent collection. Tues–Sun 10am–6pm. Métro: Passy or La Muette.

Musée d'Art Moderne de la Ville de Paris ♥♥ MUSEUM   Housed in a wing of the massive Palais de Tokyo, this municipal modern-art museum covers ground similar to that of the Pompidou Center but on a smaller scale. Picasso, Rouault, Picabia—the big names are all here, but the works are often lesser-known, making the museum a fab spot for discovering paintings you may never have seen before. Highlights include a room dedicated to surrealism (the personal collection of André Breton) and a series of paintings by Delaunay and Léger. The contemporary section, from 1960 on, covers seriously abstract movements like Fluxus and Figuration. The collection has acquired several new works from the 1980s on, but for the latest cutting-edge ideas, you are probably better off at the Palais de Tokyo museum (p. 192) in the wing next door. One huge room is covered with murals by Raoul Dufy (*La Fée Electricité*), as well as another vast room with two enormous versions of *La Danse* by Matisse.

11 av. du Président-Wilson, 16th arrond. mam.paris.fr. 📞 **01-53-67-40-00.** Free admission to permanent collections. Tues–Sun 10am–6pm (Thurs until 9:30pm during temporary exhibitions). Métro: Iéna or Alma-Marceau.

Musée National de la Marine ♥♥ MUSEUM   A steampunk-like metal diving suit from 1892 welcomes you to this fascinating, yet underrated maritime museum, set next-door to the Musée de l'Homme (p. 189) in the Chaillot palace. A must for naval lovers, you'll find all sorts of stunning model ships, from 20th-century warships to 17th-century galleons, along with a multitude of gigantic figureheads fished out of the sea from shipwrecks, and historical stern decor, including the heavily-gilded, cherub-speckled baroque stern made for the Sun King, Louis XIV, in the 17th century. For kids, there are several good interactive exhibits that let curious minds try out activities such as underwater archeology and even (thanks to a computer screen and joystick) open sea rescue.

17 place du Trocadéro, 16th arrond. musee-marine.fr. 📞 **01-53-65-69-48.** 11€ adults, 9€ ages 18–26, free for children 17 and under. Wed–Mon 11am–7pm (until 10pm Thurs) Métro: Trocadéro.

Musée National de la Marine.

Musée de l'Homme ♥♥

MUSEUM The African and Pacific art housed in this museum once inspired Picasso. Today, it is a state-of-the-art anthropology museum showcasing the richness of human culture and the evolution of mankind. In true existential Sartre fashion, this is where you come to reflect on the hard questions: What does it mean to be human? Where do we come from? And where are we headed—especially in the light of climate change? The answer is there's no one answer, but it's great thinking about it as you work your way around the exhibits—

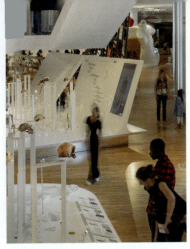

Galerie de l'Homme Sortie d'Afrique at the Musée de l'Homme.

everything from a Cro-Magnon skull to André Pierre Pinson's anatomical waxworks (fabulous, intricate examples of anatomy from the French Enlightenment) and a gallery of 19th-century busts designed to illustrate the diversity of human beings. The building itself is a showpiece. Set in the Passy wing of the Palais de Chaillot—built for the 1937 World's Fair on the site of the former 1878 Trocadéro Palace—it is an Art Deco treasure filled with natural light, with floor-to-ceiling windows that look out onto the Eiffel Tower. For the best tower views, head to **Café Lucy,** an ultra-modern cafeteria on the second floor and the **Café de l'Homme,** a chic brasserie with a terrace offering undisrupted vistas (cafedelhomme.com).

17 pl. du Trocadéro, 16th arrond. museedelhomme.fr. ⓒ **01-44-05-72-72.** Admission 15€ adults, free for ages 25 and under. Wed–Mon 11am–7pm. Métro: Trocadéro.

Musée Jacquemart-André ♥♥♥

MUSEUM The love child of a couple of passionate art collectors, Nélie Jacquemart and Edouard André, this terrific, bite-size museum takes the form of a 19th-century mansion filled with fine art and decorative treasures, including Botticelli's *Virgin and Child.* Because of its size, you can see a wide range here without wearing yourself to a frazzle.

At its inauguration in 1875, the marble Winter Garden with its spectacular double staircase was the talk of the town, and the awe-inspiring second floor—with works by masters such as Bellini, Uccello, and Mantegna—is like walking into a felt-lined jewel box. An impressive assortment of Louis XV– and Louis XVI–era decorative objects are also in evidence, as are the paintings of Fragonard, Boucher, and Chardin. The couple also amassed a number of 17th-century Dutch paintings, including a jaunty *Portrait of a Man* by Frans Hals and Rembrandt's shadowy and powerful *Supper at Emmaus,* where the figure of Christ is backlit and it is only the look on his tablemate's

An ornate hallway at Musée Jacquemart-André.

face that reveals the identity of the mysterious guest. The museum also has a looker of a tearoom, Le Nélie (p. 152).

158 bd. Haussmann, 8th arrond. musee-jacquemart-andre.com. © **01-45-62-11-59.** Admission 18€ adults, 9.50€ students and children 7–25, free for children 6 and under. Daily 10am–6pm (Fri until 10pm and Sat–Sun until 8pm during temporary exhibitions). Métro: Miromesnil or St-Philippe-du-Roule.

Musée Marmottan Monet ♥♥ MUSEUM   Boasting the world's largest collection of Monets, this museum offers an in-depth look at this prolific genius and some of his talented contemporaries. Among the dozens of canvases by Monet is the one that provided the name of an entire artistic movement. Pressed to give a name to this misty play of light on the water for the catalog for the 1874 exposition that included Cézanne, Pissarro, Renoir, and Degas, Monet apparently said, "Put 'impression.'" The painting, *Impression, Sunrise,* certainly made one, as did the show—thereafter the group was referred to as the Impressionists. Monet never stopped being fascinated with the interaction of light and water, be it in a relatively traditional portrait of his wife and daughter against the stormy sea in *On the Beach at Trouville,* or in an almost abstract blend of blues and grays in *Charing Cross Bridge.* Monet was also interested in light's transformation; he often painted the same subject at different times of the day. One of his famous series on the Cathedral of Rouen is here: *Effect of the Sun at the End of the Day.* The collection also includes dozens of paintings of his beloved garden in Giverny.

Paintings by Renoir, Sisley, Degas, Gauguin, and other contemporaries can also be seen in the light-filled rooms of this 19th-century mansion, which belonged to art collector Paul Marmottan. Upstairs is a room dedicated to the only female member of the group, Berthe Morisot, known for her intimate portraits and scenes of family life.

2 rue Louis-Boilly, 16th arrond. marmottan.fr. © **01-44-96-50-33.** Admission 14€ adults, 9€ students 25 and under and ages 8–18, free for children 7 and under. Tues–Wed and Fri–Sun 10am–6pm; Thurs 10am–9pm. Métro: La Muette. RER: Bouilainvilliers.

Musée National des Arts Asiatiques Guimet ♥♥ MUSEUM
Founded in 1889 by collector and industrialist Emile Guimet, this vast collection of Asian art is one of the largest and most complete in Europe. Here you'll find room after room of exquisite works from Afghanistan, India, Tibet, Nepal, China, Vietnam, Korea, Japan, and other Asian nations. You could spend an entire day here, or you could pick and choose regions of interest; the audio guide is a good bet for finding standouts and providing cultural context. Highlights include a marvelous Tibetan bronze sculpture (*Hevajra and Nairâtmya*) of a multiheaded god embracing a ferocious goddess with eight faces and 16 arms; a blissfully serene stone figure of a 12th-century Cambodian king (*Jayavarman VII*) who presided over a short-lived Khmer renaissance; and superb Chinese scroll paintings, including a magnificent 17th-century view of the Jingting Mountain in autumn.

6 pl. d'Iéna, 16th arrond. guimet.fr. ⓒ **01-56-52-53-00.** Admission to permanent collection 13€ adults, 10€ ages 18–25, free for children 17 and under. Wed–Mon 10am–6pm. Métro: Iéna.

Musée Nissim de Camondo ♥♥ MUSEUM Having made a fortune in his business ventures, in 1914 Count Moïse de Camondo built a mansion in the style of the Petit Trianon at Versailles and furnished it with rare examples of 18th-century furniture, paintings, and art objects. After the count's death in 1935, the house and everything in it was left to the state as a museum, named after the count's son, who was killed fighting in World War I. The family's troubles did not stop there—in 1945, the count's daughter and her family were deported and died at Auschwitz. The count's will stipulated that the house be left exactly "as is" when it was transformed into a museum; as a result, you can wander through a fully equipped kitchen, a gigantic tiled bathroom, and salons filled with gilded mirrors, inlaid tables, and Beauvais tapestries—all in the same configuration as when Camondo lived there. Be sure to pick up a free English audio guide. Tickets can be combined with the Musée des Arts Décoratifs (p. 165; 22€).

63 rue de Monceau, 8th arrond. madparis.fr. ⓒ **01-53-89-06-40.** Admission 13€ adults, free for ages 25 and under. Wed–Sun 10am–5:30pm. Métro: Villiers.

Musée Yves Saint Laurent ♥♥ MUSEUM This wonderful museum for fashion lovers is set in the sumptuous 19th-century mansion Yves Saint Laurent used as his headquarters from 1974 to 2002. The king of couture planned for a museum from the 1980s onward, marking important items with an M (for *musée*). There are some 5,000 in all, plus over 15,000 accessories—which are now part of the Fondation Pierre Bergé-Yves Saint Laurent (which he started with his partner Pierre Bergé in 2002). Though Saint Laurent died in 2008 and didn't see the opening of the museum (in 2017), he would undoubtedly have been happy with the result: Temporary retrospectives highlight both his career and his creative genius, resulting in rich and fascinating displays of game-changing outfits—like the Mondrian dress and the "smoking" tuxedo—as well as lesser-known pieces designed for the ballet and the theater. The spaces are beautiful, especially Saint Laurent's studio, filled with his books and sketches, unchanged, as if the great designer is about to come home.

5 av. Marceau, 16th arrond. museeyslparis.com. ✆ **01-44-31-64-00.** Admission 10€ adults, 7€ ages 10–18, free for children 9 and under. Tues–Sun 11am–6pm (until 9pm Thurs). Métro: Alma Marceau.

Palais de Tokyo ♥♥ MUSEUM/PERFORMANCE SPACE If you're traveling with cranky teenagers who've had enough of La Vieille France, or if you're also sick of endless rendezvous with history, this is the place to come for a blast of contemporary madness. This vast art space not only offers a rotating bundle of expositions, events, and other happenings but is also one of the only museums in Paris that stays open until 10pm. While some might quibble about whether or not the works on display are really art, there's no denying that this place is a lot of fun. You'll find a completely different crowd here, one that is generally young and intense. There's no permanent collection, just continuous temporary exhibits, installations, and events, such as live performances and film screenings. The center, whose mission includes nurturing, promoting, and providing studio space for emerging artists, is one of the largest sites devoted to contemporary creativity in Europe. Check the website for what's on during your visit. In warm weather, you can eat on the splendid terrace of its chic, neo–Art Deco brasserie, **Monsieur Bleu,** which has Eiffel Tower views, or sip cocktails in its restaurant/bar **Bambini.** Both stay open until 2am.

13 av. Du Président-Wilson, 16th arrond. palaisdetokyo.com. ✆ **01-81-97-35-88.** Admission 13€ adults, 9€ ages 18–25, free for children 17 and under. Wed–Mon noon–10pm (until midnight Thurs). Métro: Iéna.

Parc Monceau ♥♥ PARK/GARDENS Located in a posh residential neighborhood and ringed by stately mansions, this small park is the brainchild of the duke of Chartres (the future Philippe Egalité), who commissioned a fanciful garden in 1769 filled with *folies,* faux romantic ruins, temples, and antiquities inspired by exotic faraway places. Don't be surprised to stumble upon a minaret, a windmill, or a mini-Egyptian pyramid here; the most famous *folie* is the **Naumachie,** a large oval pond surrounded in part by Corinthian columns. A sizable **playground** is in the southwest corner, and there's a **merry-go-round** near the north entrance, where columns surround a **round pavilion;** the Duke of Chartres used to keep a small apartment on the second floor from which he could see the entire park.

35 bd. De Courcelles, 8th arrond. paris.fr/lieux/parc-monceau-1804. Free admission. 8am–sundown. Métro: Monceau or Villiers.

Petit Palais ♥♥ MUSEUM You may not see any world-famous works, but you will enjoy a wonderful and impressive mix of periods and artists at this bijou fine arts museum, set in a sumptuous "little" palace built for the 1900 Paris Exposition (opposite the ginormous, glass-roofed **Grand Palais,** p. 185). Its chronology stretches from the ancient Greeks to World War I, with paintings by Monet, Ingres, and Rubens, an Art Nouveau dining room by

Petit Palais.

Hector Guimard, and the exquisite multilayered glass vases of Emile Gallé. Those interested in earlier works will find Greek vases, Italian Renaissance majolica, and a small collection of 16th-century astrolabes and gold-and-crystal traveling clocks. Intricately carved ivory panels and delicately carved wood sculptures (including a grinning, long-locked Saint Barbara who looks like she is about to burst out in a fit of the giggles) stand out in the small medieval section, and a series of rooms dedicated to 17th-century Dutch painters like Steen and van Ostade is considered one of the best collections of its kind in France (after the Louvre). Refresh yourself after your visit at the Cafe 1902 in the gorgeous inner courtyard.

av. Winston Churchill, 8th arrond. petitpalais.paris.fr. **01-53-43-40-00.** Free admission to permanent collection. Tues–Sun 10am–6pm (Fri until 9pm during temporary exhibitions). Métro: Champs-Élysées–Clémenceau.

Place de la Concorde ♥♥♥ SQUARE

Like an exclamation point at the end of the Champs-Élysées, the Place de la Concorde is a magnificent arrangement of fountains and statues, held together in the center by a 3,000-year-old Egyptian obelisk. When it was inaugurated in 1763 during the reign of Louis XV, this vast plaza was on the outer edges of the city; today, though part of an urban landscape, it still gives the impression of open space. If it weren't for the cars hurtling around the obelisk, this would be a delightful spot for a breath of fresh air (if you feel compelled to cross to the obelisk and you value your life, find the stoplight and cross there).

It's hard to believe that this magnificent square was once bathed in blood, but during the Revolution, it was a grisly stage for public executions: King Louis XVI and his wife, Marie Antoinette, both bowed down to the guillotine here, as did many prominent figures of the Revolution, including Danton, Camille Desmoulins, and Robespierre. Once the monarchy was back in place, the plaza hosted less lethal public events like festivals and trade expositions.

In 1835 the *place* was given its current look: Two immense fountains, copies of those in St. Peter's Square in Rome, play on either side of the obelisk; 18 sumptuous columns decorated with shells, mermaids, sea horses, and other sea creatures each hold two lamps; and eight statues representing the country's largest cities survey the scene from the edges of the action. On the west side are the famous **Marly Horses,** actually copies of the originals, which were suffering from erosion and have since been restored and housed in the Louvre. On the north side of the square are two palatial buildings that date from the square's 18th-century origins: On the east side is the **Hôtel de la Marine** (p. 185), a vast art museum housing the Qatarian Al Thani Collection, and on the west side is the **Hôtel Crillon,** where on February 6, 1778, a treaty was signed by Louis XVI and Benjamin Franklin, among others, wherein France officially recognized the United States as an independent country and became its ally.

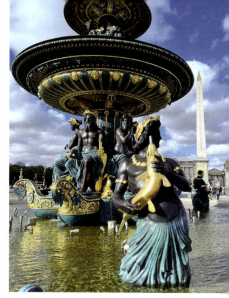

Fontaines de la Concorde and the Luxor Obelisk.

8th arrond. Métro: Concorde.

Montmartre (18th Arrondissement)

Few places in this city will fill you with the urge to belt out sappy show tunes like the *butte* (hill) of Montmartre. Admiring the view from the esplanade in front of the oddly Byzantine **Basilique du Sacré-Coeur,** you'll finally understand what all the fuss is about. Try to ignore the tour buses and crowds mobbing the church and the hideously touristy **Place du Tertre** behind you; instead, wander off into the warren of streets toward the **Place des Abbesses,** or up **rue Lepic,** where you'll eventually stumble across the **Moulin de la Galette** and **Moulin du Radet,** the two surviving windmills (of 30 that once stood on this hill). We have a walking tour on p. 308 that will lead you to these less-touristy gems and others.

Basilique du Sacré-Coeur ♥ CHURCH   Poised at the apex of the hill like a *grande dame* in crinolines, this odd-looking 19th-century basilica is one of the city's most famous landmarks. After France's defeat in the Franco-Prussian War, prominent Catholics vowed to build a church consecrated to the Sacred Heart of Christ as a way of making up for whatever sins the French may have committed that had made God so angry at them. Since 1885, prayers for humanity have been continually chanted here (the church is a pilgrimage site, so dress and behave accordingly). This multi-domed confection was inspired by the Byzantine churches of Turkey and Italy. Construction began in 1875, and the church was completed in 1914, though it wasn't consecrated until 1919 because of World War I. The white travertine stone was chosen for its self-cleaning capabilities: In the rain, it secretes a chalky substance that acts as a fresh coat of paint. The interior of the church includes a breathtaking mosaic ceiling, installed in the 1920s. Most visitors climb the 300 stairs to the dome, where the splendid view of the city extends over 48km (30 miles). *Note:* The crypt is generally closed to the public.

Parvis de la Basilique, 18th arrond. sacre-coeur-montmartre.com. ✆ **01-53-41-89-00.** Basilica free; ticket to the dome 8€ adults, 5€ ages 4–16, free for children 3 and under (though with 300 steps, it's not advisable). Basilica daily 6:30am–10:30pm; dome daily 10am–5:30pm. Métro: Abbesses; take elevator to surface and follow signs to funicular.

Dalí Paris ♥ MUSEUM   This tiny museum dedicated to the works of surrealist Salvador Dalí won't take more than 45 minutes to visit, but what a 45 minutes you'll spend! The space is littered with erotic engravings, dreamlike objects, and whimsical furniture, not to mention Dalí's theatrical sculptures, including a spindly-legged Space Elephant and several of his iconic soft watches, which seem to drip phantasmagorically to the floor. The man with the iconic moustache lived in Montmartre with his wife and muse Gala, in an apartment at 7 rue Becquerel. It was from here in 1956, following a commission for Dalí to illustrate Cervantes' novel *Don Quixote,* that the Catalan artist staged one of the *butte*'s most memorable artistic moments: the filming of him

Basilique du Sacré-Coeur in Montmartre.

Dalí Paris, a small museum dedicated to the surrealist artist.

creating the first engravings. Against a windmill backdrop rose forth a knight on horseback, and Dalí, true to form, used two rhinoceros' horns and bread dipped in ink to create the illustrations. You can see some engravings from the series alongside others from the Bible and *Alice in Wonderland.*

11 rue Poulbot, 18th arrond. daliparis.com. © **01-42-64-40-10.** Admission 16€ adults, 13€ ages 8–26, free for children 7 and under. Daily 10am–6pm. Métro: Anvers, Abbesses, or Lamarck-Caulincourt.

Musée de Montmartre ♥♥ MUSEUM   The main reason to visit this small museum is to get an inkling of what Montmartre really was like back in the days when Picasso, Toulouse-Lautrec, Van Gogh, and others were painting and cavorting up on the *butte.* While there are few examples of the artists' works here, plenty of photos, posters, and even films document the neighborhood's famous history, from the days when its importance was mainly religious to the glory days of the Paris Commune, and finally to the artistic boom in the 19th and 20th centuries. The 17th-century house that shelters the museum was at various times the home of Auguste Renoir and Raoul Dufy, as well as Susan Valadon and her son, Maurice Utrillo, whose studio can now be visited. Surrounded by gardens and greenery, the site offers a lovely view of the last scrap of the Montmartre vineyard. English-language audio guides are a big help here. On a sunny day, stop for coffee in the garden cafe—it's a heavenly setting and great for small kids to run around without you having to worry about traffic.

12 rue Cortot, 18th arrond. museedemontmartre.fr. © **01-49-25-89-39.** Admission garden only 5€; museum 15€ adults, 10€ ages 18–25, 7€ ages 10–17, free for children 9 and under. Daily 10am–6pm. Métro: Lamarck-Caulaincourt.

République, Bastille & Eastern Paris (11th & 12th Arrondissements)

While you can't really point to any major tourist attractions in this area, this part of town is seriously up-and-coming and has great nightlife and clothing stores, not to mention a booming restaurant scene. Some important historical sites are also here: The French Revolution was brewed in the workshops of the **Faubourg St-Antoine** and was ignited at the **Place de la Bastille.** The former stomping grounds of the medieval Knights Templar, the recently remodeled **Place de la République** is a potent symbol of the French Republic.

Atelier des Lumières ♥♥♥ IMMERSIVE MUSEUM If you've ever watched a light show projected onto the facade of a building, you'll know just how impressive they can be. But few shows can top this museum's offerings: Set in a converted foundry, the entire indoor space—floors, walls, and ceilings—is one monumental, moving canvas. Around 140 projectors and a high-tech sound system transport you smack-dab into famous paintings, as if you've shrunk and become part of the work. The first space covers the history of art, the second, smaller in size but no less impressive, is for today's emerging digital artists. Because of flashing lights and the overwhelming nature of the exhibits, people with epilepsy and kids ages 2 and under should not visit.

38 rue St-Maur, 11th arrond. atelier-lumieres.com. ✆ **01-80-98-46-00.** 18€ adults, 16€ students 12–25, 11€ ages 3–11. Times may vary, according to the exhibition, but it's mostly daily 10am–6pm (until 8 or 10pm Fri–Sat).

Atelier des Lumières offers an immersive light show.

Coulée Verte René-Dumont ♥ WALKING TRAIL Transformed from an unused train viaduct, this beautiful, elevated garden walkway (also known by its former name, the Promenade Plantée) runs from the Place de la Bastille to the Bois de Vincennes. The 4.5km (2.8-mile) pedestrian path traces flower gardens, tree bowers, rose trellises, and fountains, taking you over the 12th arrondissement, past the Gare de Lyon, and through the Reuilly Gardens (home to fizzy drinking-water fountains). At ground level along avenue Daumesnil, the archways now shelter the **Viaduc des Arts,** where galleries and workshops show off the work of highly skilled artisans.

Enter by the staircase on av. Daumesnil just past the Opéra Bastille, 12th arrond. paris.fr/lieux/coulee-verte-rene-dumont-1772.

Musée des Arts Forains ♥♥ MUSEUM This offbeat museum in Bercy's former wine warehouses is the largest of its kind in Europe, packed to the rafters with fairground memorabilia from the 19th and 20th centuries. It's a magical place, where Belle Epoque carousels populated by mermaids, horses, and fantastical carriages sit alongside weird and wonderful automated mannequins, Venetian carnival costumes, and even a hot-air balloon with an elephant-shaped basket. Light shows that make you feel you've stepped into a surreal version of the 2017 movie *The Greatest Showman* complete the offerings. English tours are during the summer only; tours are in French the rest of the year, but with English printouts, so you'll still be able to follow. Entrance is by tour only; reserving by phone or online is mandatory. Visitors with some disabilities should bear in mind that while the museum offers wheelchair access, there are no seats.

53 av. des Terroirs de France, 12th arrond. arts-forains.com. ✆ **01-43-40-16-22.** Admission 19€ adults, 13€ ages 4–11, free for children 3 and under. Usually Wed, Sat, and Sun, times vary (reserve beforehand). Métro: Cour Saint-Emilion.

Parc de Bercy ♥♥ PARK Sandwiched between the AccorHotels Arena and Bercy Village (shops and movie theaters in former wine warehouses), Parc de Bercy is well off most tourists' radar. However, it bursts with photogenic, tree-shaded walkways, pretty lakes where herons strut their stuff, and themed gardens of roses and color-coded flower beds. The area around the Maison du Jardinage, a quaint house assimilated into the greenery, makes you feel as though you're in the countryside. The carousel (2.5€ ticket; cash only) provides a bit of extra excitement for small kids.

128 quai de Bercy, 12th arrond. paris.fr/lieux/parc-de-bercy-grandes-pelouses-5. Free admission. Mon–Fri 8am to sundown; Sat–Sun 9am to sundown. Métro: Bercy or Cour Saint-Emilion.

Parc Zoologique de Paris ♥♥ ZOO Lush and ecologically correct, this animal reserve invites visitors to five regions of the world, from the plains of Sudan to Europe, via Guyana, Patagonia, and Madagascar. Going for quality instead of quantity, the zoo may not have room for elephants and bears, but

Giraffes at the Parc Zoologique de Paris.

it does introduce visitors to animals they might not be familiar with, like the fossa, a catlike carnivore from Madagascar, or the capybara, a giant South American rodent. There is also a good sampling of zoo favorites like lions, baboons, penguins, and a troupe of giraffes—if you are lucky, you can get an up-close look while the latter lunch in the giraffe house. The enclosures are well adapted to their inhabitants, so much so that at times it's hard to see them. But if you are patient, you'll spy wolves peeking out of the foliage, or a bright red tomato frog gripping a vine. Home to more than 1,000 animals in all, the zoo still manages to feel human-sized. Don't miss the huge aviaries, one of which is home to a large flock of flamingoes. In summer, the zoo stays open until 11:30pm on Thursdays, offering a great chance to catch the nocturnal animals at play.

Parc de Vincennes, 12th arrond. parczoologiquedeparis.fr. **01-44-75-20-10.** Admission 22€ adults, 17€ age 12–25 and children 3–11; free for children 2 and under. Mid-Oct to mid-Mar daily 10am–5pm; mid-Mar to mid-May and Sept to mid-Oct Mon–Fri 10am–6pm, Sat–Sun and school holidays 9:30am–7:30pm; mid-May to end Aug daily 9:30am–8:30pm and night hours Thurs 7–11:30pm. Métro: Porte Dorée.

Place de la Bastille ♥ SQUARE   The most notable thing about this giant plaza—aside from architect Carlos Ott's Opéra Bastille, a modern opera house opened in 1989—is the building that's no longer here: the Bastille prison. Now a revamped traffic circle with bike lanes and steps down to the Canal St-Martin, this was once the site of an ancient stone fortress that became a symbol for all that was wrong with the French monarchy. Over the centuries, kings and queens condemned rebellious citizens to stay inside the cold walls, sometimes with good reason, other times on a mere whim. By the time the Revolution started to boil, though, the prison was barely in use; when the angry mobs stormed the walls on July 14, 1789, only seven prisoners were left to set free. The Bastille came to be seen as the ultimate revolutionary moment; July 14 is still celebrated as the birth of the Republic. Surprisingly, the giant bronze column, the **Colonne de Juillet,** in the center honors the victims of a different revolution, that of 1830. Even more surprisingly, below the column is a crypt containing a mummy. Guided tours of the crypt are offered (in French) on Saturday and Sunday at 2:30 and 4:30pm (advance reservations at colonne-de-juillet.fr; 13€ adults, 6€ ages 7–18, free for ages 6 and under).

12th arrond. Métro: Bastille.

Place de la Bastille with the Colonne de Juillet monument.

Belleville, Canal St-Martin & La Villette (10th, 19th & 20th Arrondissements)

One of the most picturesque attractions in this area is the **Canal St-Martin** itself, which extends up to **La Villette,** a former industrial area that has been transformed into a gigantic park and cultural compound. Other intriguing outdoor attractions include the romantic **Père-Lachaise cemetery,** the resting place of France's most noteworthy notables, and the verdant **Buttes Chaumont park.** The Belleville neighborhood is home to one of the city's bustling Chinatowns, as well as many artists' studios.

Cimetière du Père-Lachaise ♥♥♥ CEMETERY   Cemeteries are not usually on the top of anyone's must-see list, but this is no ordinary cemetery. Romantic and rambling as a 19th-century English garden, this hillside resting place (open in 1804) is wonderfully green, with huge, leafy trees and narrow paths winding around the graves, which include just about every French literary or artistic giant you can imagine, plus several international stars. Proust, Apollinaire, Colette, Delacroix, Seurat, Modigliani, Bizet, and Rossini are all here, as well as Sarah Bernhardt, Isadora Duncan, Simone Signoret and Yves Montand (buried side by side, of course). Though some graves have simple tombstones, many are miniature architectural marvels, embellished with exquisite marble and stone figures, or even individually sized chapels, complete with stained-glass windows. Some of the standouts include:

Père-Lachaise Cemetery

Abélard & Héloïse **37**	Honoré de Balzac **16**	Alfred de Musset **21**
Guillaume Apollinaire **5**	Eugène Delacroix **15**	Edith Piaf **27**
Pierre-Auguste Beaumarchais **30**	Gustave Doré **14**	Camille Pissarro **38**
Hans Bellmer **24**	Isadora Duncan **6**	Marcel Proust **4**
Sarah Bernhardt **9**	Paul Eluard **26**	Gioacchio Antonio Rossini **22**
Georges Bizet **17**	Max Ernst **2**	Rothschild family plot **39**
Maria Callas **3**	Théodore Géricault **20**	Henri de Saint-Simon **31**
Frédéric Chopin **36**	Jean-Auguste-Dominique Ingres **13**	Georges Seurat **18**
Colette **23**	Jean La Fontaine **33**	Simone Signoret & Yves Montand **8**
Auguste Comte **34**	René Lalique **12**	Gertrude Stein & Alice B. Toklas **25**
Jean Baptiste Camille Corot **11**	Lefebvre Masséna **29**	Oscar Wilde **1**
Honoré Daumier **10**	Amedeo Modigliani **28**	Richard Wright **7**
Jacques-Louis David **19**	Molière **32**	
	Jim Morrison **35**	

201

Tomb of Oscar Wilde in Cimetière du Père-Lachaise.

- **Héloïse and Abélard:** These two legendary lovers actually existed, and their 12th-century remains were brought here in 1817, when the city built them this monument. It's covered by an openwork Gothic chapel taken from an abbey in southwestern France.
- **Molière and La Fontaine:** Although there was no romantic link, the celebrated playwright and noted fable writer were also brought here in 1817 and placed in nearby sarcophagi, both of which stand appropriately high on pillars. If the authenticity of the remains is in doubt, they still make a fitting memorial to these two brilliant talents.
- **Oscar Wilde:** This huge stone monument is topped with a winged figure that resembles an Aztec deity. It's an elegant homage to the brilliant writer, who died a pauper in Paris in 1900. For many years it was covered in lipstick kisses, which eroded the stone, hence today's protective barrier.
- **Jim Morrison:** Though the grave itself is unexceptional, the tomb of the 1960s rock star is possibly the most visited in the cemetery. Fans left behind so much graffiti, litter, and mind-altering substances that families of those buried nearby began to complain, and the tomb was surrounded by a fence.

Graves can be hard to find, so a map is essential. You can use the one in this book (p. 201) or the one on the Paris municipal site (paris.fr/pages/cimetiere-du-pere-lachaise-informations-17576). *Note:* Entry is via the gate opposite rue de la Roquette; the other entrances may be closed.

16 rue de Repos, 20th arrond. paris.fr/pages/cimetiere-du-pere-lachaise-informations-17576. Free admission. Mon–Fri 8am–6pm; Sat–Sun 8:30am–6pm (Nov to early Mar until 5pm). Métro: Père-Lachaise or Philippe Auguste.

Cité des Sciences et de l'Industrie ♥♥ MUSEUM   This gigantic and terrific science and industry museum was built upon the site of the city's former 19th-century slaughterhouse auction room. It includes a planetarium, a 4D IMAX movie theater, and a multimedia library, not to mention a real submarine and an entertainment mall (Boom Boom Villette, p. 247). The heart of the museum is its permanent collection, which flaunts huge floors of interactive exhibits and displays on subjects like sound, mathematics, and human genes. On the ground floor, parents will be delighted to find the **Cité des Enfants** (separate admission 13€ for a 90-min. session; see website for hours; reservations essential, particularly during French school vacations), which has separate programs for 2- to 7-year-olds and 5- to 12-year-olds. Kids get to explore the world around them in a series of hands-on activities and displays. If all this isn't enough, outside you can clamber into the *Argonaut,* a real submarine that was one of the stars of the French navy in the 1950s, or if the kids still have energy to burn, take them for a run around the adjacent Parc de la Villette (p. 204).

Mission Spatiale exhibit at Cité des Sciences et de l'Industrie.

Parc de La Villette, 30 av. Corentine-Cariou, 19th arrond. cite-sciences.fr. ⓒ **01-40-05-80-00.** Varied ticket packages 15€ adults, 12€ visitors 25 and under, free for children 2 and under. Tues–Sat 10am–6pm; Sun 10am–7pm. Métro: Porte de La Villette.

Choco Story ♥♥ MUSEUM   Now here's a place that would make Willy Wonka proud! A chocolate-themed museum that traces the history of the cacao bean—from its origins in Aztec and Mayan society thousands of years ago, to its appearance in the courts of Spain in the 16th century and the manufacture of an entire chocolate industry in the 19th-century—and lets you eat as much chocolate as you like along the way . . . for free! Needless to say, it's a hit with families, with regular live chocolate-making demonstrations by a crew of award-winning French chocolatiers, gigantic chocolate sculptures of Parisian monuments and cabinets dripping with all sorts of chocolate-themed curiosities. You could also reserve a 45-minute chocolate-making workshop (for anyone age 7 and over, from 50€), to dress up in a chef's gown before designing (and probably gobbling) your own chocolates.

28 boulevard de Bonne Nouvelles, 10th arrond. museeduchocolat.fr. ⓒ **01-42-29-68-60.** Admission 18€ adults, 16€ students, 10.80€ for children 3 to 11, free age 2 and under. Daily 10am–6pm. Métro: Bonne Nouvelle.

Musée de la Musique ♥♥ MUSEUM   Located on the north end of the Parc de la Villette, and part of the striking Philharmonie de Paris concert complex (p. 269), this museum has a permanent collection of over a thousand instruments, sculptures, paintings, and other objects that recount the history of music in

The Canal St-Martin

The pretty Canal St-Martin waterway connects the Seine, near Bastille, to the Canal de l'Ourcq, near the Villette in the 19th arrondissement. When Parisians talk about *le canal*, they are usually referring to the popular stretch of the quays Jemmapes and Valmy, which begins just above République and runs up to Jaurès Métro. Canal St-Martin was listed as a historic monument in 1993, and today its tree-lined banks and arched bridges make it a delightful place to stroll, especially on Sundays when the east side is closed to cars. You can take a boat tour with **Paris Canal** (pariscanal.com; © **01-42-40-29-00**) or **Canauxrama** (p. 226) or explore in a self-drive boat with **Marin d'Eau Douce** (p. 227) on the Canal de l'Ourcq.

Europe from the 16th to 20th centuries. Study a beautiful and rare 17th-century guitar with ivory inlay, a clutch of Stradivarius violins, or a concert piano that Franz Liszt once played on. A separate section on world music includes another 700 objects, mostly from Africa and Asia. As you wander about, you will probably come across live demonstrations by local musicians.

In the Cité de la Musique, 221 av. Jean-Jaurès, 19th arrond. philharmoniedeparis.fr. © **01-44-84-44-84.** Admission 8€ adults, 6€ ages 26–28, free for visitors 25 and under. Tues–Fri noon–6pm; Sat–Sun 10am–6pm. Métro: Porte de Pantin.

Parc de la Villette ♥♥♥ PARK   This vast complex, which includes a park, museums, concert halls, and other cultural institutions, was built on the site of the city's slaughterhouses, abandoned since the mid-1970s. The park harbors **Musée de la Musique** (p. 203) and **Cité des Sciences et de l'Industrie** (p. 202)—two excellent museums—as well as the **Zénith** (p. 274) and **Cabaret Sauvage** (p. 273) concert halls, not to mention the **Philharmonie de Paris** (p. 269). As far as the green spaces go—well, let me put it this way: If it is possible for a park to have a sense of humor, this one definitely has one. Eleven themed gardens are dotted with 25 red *folies*—oddball contemporary structures that sometimes house a drink stand or an information

The Geode in the Parc de la Villette is a 3D-IMAX cinema.

booth, and sometimes are just there for the heck of it. The gardens range from the sublime to the silly; a few are strictly reserved for children (who can bring along their parents).

From mid-July to mid-August the **Cinéma en Plein Air** takes place Tuesday to Sunday at sundown, presenting classic movies for free.

19th arrond. villette.com. 🕾 **01-40-03-75-75.** Daily 6am–1am. Métro: Porte de Pantin or Porte de la Villette.

Parc des Buttes Chaumont ♥♥ PARK

Up until 1860, this area was home to a deep limestone quarry, but thanks to Napoleon III, the gaping hole was turned into an unusual park, full of hills and dales, rocky bluffs, and cliffs. It took 3 years to make this romantic garden; over 1,000 workers and 100 horses dug, heaped, and blasted through the walls of the quarry to create green lawns, a cool grotto, cascades, streams, and even a small lake. By the opening of the 1867 World's Fair, the garden was ready for visitors. The surrounding area was, and still is, working-class; the emperor built it to give this industrious neighborhood a green haven and a bit of fresh air. **Pony rides** are available for the kids on weekends and Wednesdays (3–6pm; animaponey.com); the park also has a **puppet theater,** a **carousel,** and **two playgrounds.** The *guinguette*-style (open-air) bar/cafe—**Rosa Bonheur** (p. 133), named after the 19th-century feminist artist—is a bucolic spot for drinks and snacks, staying open even after the park has closed.

Rue Botzaris, 19th arrond. Daily 7am–dusk. Métro: Botzaris or Buttes Chaumont.

Philharmonie des Enfants ♥♥♥ MUSEUM

Within the Philharmonie building and accessed—somewhat strangely—by a door below its concrete arches, this is one of the best kids' museums in Paris. While the Musée de la Musique (p. 203) in the same building takes a more adult approach to music, this place is aimed at 4- to 10-year-olds, and feels like a big sound lab, teaching kids about music through five genuinely fun, interactive themed sections. For example, the first, the "Forest of Sounds," looks at noise and melody, and shows that you don't just hear with your ears—that you can pick up on sound vibrations through other parts of your body. The fifth, my favorite, called "Music This Way," lets you add sound effects to a choice of movies. You'll need to reserve a time slot in advance, then arrive 15 minutes beforehand, so staff can set you up with a "time beeper"; you have 75 minutes to go around the space. Leave your email address in one of the machines, and the museum will take your picture as you perform some of the activities, then send you the files for free. *Note:* Each child can be accompanied by up to two adults only.

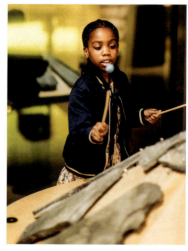

Kids perform at the "On Stage" interactive exhibit at Philharmonie des Enfants.

In the Cité de la Musique, 221 av. Jean-Jaurès, 19th arrond. philharmoniedeparis.fr/en/philharmoniedesenfants. © **01-44-84-44-84.** Admission 15€ adults and kids 12 and above, 12€ ages 4–10, free for visitors 3 and under. Tues and Thurs–Fri 9:30am–12:45pm and 1:30–5:30pm; Wed and Sat–Sun 10am–1pm and 2–6pm. Métro: Porte de Pantin.

THE LEFT BANK
Latin Quarter (5th & 13th Arrondissements)

For several hundred years, the students who flocked to this quarter spoke Latin in their classes at the **Sorbonne** (founded in the 13th c.). Today students still abound around the Sorbonne, and even though classes are taught in French, the name stuck. This youth-filled neighborhood is a lively one, with lots of cinemas and cafes. History is readily visible here, with remains dating back to the Roman occupation: The **rue St-Jacques** and **boulevard Saint-Michel** mark the former Roman *cardo* (main street), and you can explore the remnants of the **Roman baths** at the **Cluny Museum** (p. 210).

Jardin des Plantes ♥♥ GARDEN   Created in 1626 as a medicinal plant garden for King Louis XIII, in the 18th century, it became an internationally famed scientific institution thanks to naturalist, mathematician, and biologist Georges-Louis Leclerc, Count of Buffon, with the help of fellow naturalist Louis Jean-Marie Daubenton. Today the museums are still part academic institutions, but you don't need to be a student to appreciate these lush grounds.

The Jardin des Plantes.

The delightful botanical garden also harbors a small but well-kempt zoo, the **Ménagerie, le Zoo du Jardin des Plantes** (mnhn.fr; ⓒ **01-40-79-56-01;** 13€ adults, 10€ ages 3–25, free for children 2 and under; daily 10am–6pm). Created in 1794, this is the second-oldest zoo in the world (after the Tiergarten Schönbrunn in Vienna). Because of its size, the zoo showcases mostly smaller species, in particular birds and reptiles. But the healthy selection of mammals includes rare species like red pandas, Przewalski horses, and even Florida pumas. If you're interested in tropical plant life, don't miss the park's **Grandes Serres** (ⓒ **01-40-79-56-01;** 9€ adults, 7€ children and students ages 3–25, free for children 2 and under; daily 10am–6pm)—four magnificent 19th-century greenhouses that take you on a botanical journey from the jungle to the desert via a prehistoric plant section. It's fascinating if you've got a green thumb, and a good bet on a cold day.

Rue Geoffroy-St-Hilaire, 5th arrond. jardindesplantesdeparis.fr. ⓒ **01-40-79-56-01.** Free admission to gardens. Daily 8am–dusk. Métro: Gare d'Austerlitz.

Tapestry in progress at the Manufacture Nationale des Gobelins workshop.

Left Bank Attractions

Les Catacombes 17
Cimetière du Montparnasse 7
Eiffel Tower 1
Hôtel des Invalides/ Napoleon's Tomb 4
Jardin des Plantes 22
Jardin du Luxembourg 14
Maison Gainsbourg 9
Manufacture Nationale des Gobelins 24
Monnaie de Paris 10
Musée Bourdelle 6
Musée de l'Institut du Monde Arabe 21
Musée des Egouts de Paris 3
Musée d'Orsay 8
Le Musée de la Libération de Paris–Musée du Général Leclerc–Musée Jean Moulin 16
Musée du Quai Branly 2
Musée de Cluny/ Le Monde Médiéval 18
Musée National Eugène Delacroix 11
Musée Rodin 5
Musée Zadkine 15
Muséum National d'Histoire Naturelle 23
Panthéon 19
St-Etienne-du-Mont 20
St-Germain-des-Prés 12
St-Sulpice 13

Manufacture Nationale des Gobelins ♥♥ TAPESTRY FACTORY TOUR
In the 17th century, Louis XIV purchased this famed tapestry factory with the aim of furnishing his new château (Versailles) with the most splendid tapestries around. The workshop's reputation has survived the centuries, and the factory is still active, working with the same materials used in the time of Louis XIV (wool, cotton, silk). Today the factory operates under the auspices of the French Ministry of Culture and produces modern tapestries to hang in some of France's grandest public spaces. This is definitely not a mass-market operation—these tapestries take several years to finish. Highly skilled workers (who study for 4 years at the on-site school) work from paintings by contemporary artists to create enormous works of art. There are frequent temporary exhibitions, or you could book a tour (in French only), during which you'll watch weavers in action at their giant looms (purchase tickets online).

42 av. des Gobelins, 13th arrond. mobiliernational.culture.gouv.fr. ✆ **08-25-05-44-05** (0.15€/min). Tours 17.50€ adults, 9.90€ students; exhibitions 14€ adults, 8€ students. Check website for tour times; exhibitions Tues–Sun 11am–6pm. Métro: Gobelins.

Musée de Cluny (Le Monde Médiéval) ♥♥♥ MUSEUM
Ancient Roman baths and a 15th-century mansion set the stage for a terrific collection of medieval art and objects at this museum. Built somewhere between the 1st and 3rd centuries, the baths (visible from bd. St-Michel) are some of the best existing examples of Gallo-Roman architecture. They are attached to what was once the palatial home of a 15th-century abbot, whose last owner, Alexandre du Sommerard, amassed a vast array of medieval masterworks. When he died in 1842, his home was turned into a museum and his collection put on display. Of the several magnificent tapestries, the biggest draw is the ***Lady and the Unicorn*** series, one of only two sets of complete unicorn tapestries in the world (the other is at the Met Cloisters in New York City). In five of these late-15th-century tapestries, the lady, her unicorn, a lion, and various other symbolic representations of the animal and vegetable kingdoms illustrate the five senses. In the sixth, she stands before a tent bearing the inscription "To My Only Desire" while placing a necklace in a case held by her servant. The meaning of this last tapestry remains an enigma—the mystery merely adds to its beauty.

6 pl. Paul Painlevé, 5th arrond. musee-moyenage.fr. ✆ **01-53-73-78-00**. Admission 12€ adults, 10€ ages 18–24, free for children 17 and under. Tues–Sun 9:30am–6:15pm. Métro/RER: Cluny–La Sorbonne or St-Michel.

Musée de l'Institut du Monde Arabe ♥♥ MUSEUM
While it harbors a substantial collection, one of the biggest draws to this museum/library/research center is the building itself, designed by architect Jean Nouvel in 1987. The south facade is covered by a metallic latticework echoing traditional Arab designs, with 30,000 light-sensitive diaphragms that open and close according to how bright it is outside. The airy museum space presents a collection that emphasizes the diversity of peoples and cultures in the Middle East, reminding us, among other things, that it was the birthplace of all three major Western religions. While the collection is intellectually stimulating, if

The paleontology gallery at MNHN.

art is what you are after, the Islamic Art section of the Louvre will be more satisfying. Still, there's a terrific view of the Seine and Notre-Dame from the panoramic terrace (open 10am–6pm), plus an interesting cycle of concerts.

1 rue des Fossés St-Bernard, 5th arrond. imarabe.org. © **01-40-51-38-38.** Admission 9€, free for ages 25 and under. Tues–Fri 10am–6pm; Sat–Sun 10am–7pm. Métro: Jussieu, Cardinal Lemoine, Sully-Morland.

Muséum National d'Histoire Naturelle (MNHN) ♥♥ MUSEUM Originally (and still) an academic research institution, this temple to the natural sciences, established in 1793, contains a series of separate museums, each with a different specialty. The biggest draw is the **Grande Galerie de l'Evolution,** where a sort of Noah's ark of animals snakes its way around a huge hall filled with displays that trace the evolution of life and man's relationship with nature. It also has a virtual reality room that lets you get up close and personal to all sorts of animals (5€). One intriguing hall, the **Galerie de Minérologie et de Géologie,** includes a room full of giant crystals, and another with eye-popping precious stones from the Royal Treasury. For dinosaurs, saber-toothed tigers, ancient humans, and thousands of other fossilized skeletons, repair to the **Galeries de Paléontologie et d'Anatomie Comparée.** The museum's **Galerie des Enfants** (children's gallery) offers hands-on interactive displays for little tykes. Except for the Grande Galerie, which has a joint ticket deal with the Galerie des Enfants, you'll have to pay for each *galerie* separately, but a ticket to one gives you a reduced rate at the others.

36 rue Geoffrey, 5th arrond. mnhn.fr. © **01-40-79-54-79.** Admission to each galerie 10€–16€ adults, free for visitors 26 and under. Wed–Mon 10am–6pm. Métro: Jussieu or Gare d'Austerlitz.

Panthéon ♥♥ CHURCH/MAUSOLEUM High atop the "montagne" (actually a medium-size hill) of St-Geneviève, the dome of the Panthéon is one of the city's most visible landmarks. This erstwhile royal church has been transformed into a national mausoleum—the final resting place of luminaries such as Voltaire and Rousseau, Marie and Pierre Curie, World War II heroes of the

Résistance, and (since 2021) the American-born entertainer and activist Josephine Baker, the first Black woman to be given a place in the monument. Initially dedicated to St-Geneviève, the church was commissioned by a grateful Louis XV, who attributed his recovery from a serious illness to the saint. The vast interior was clearly created with a higher power in mind. However, during the Revolution its sacred mission was diverted toward a new god—the Nation—and it was converted into a memorial and burial ground for notable citizens of the Republic. The desired effect was achieved—the enormous empty space, lined with huge paintings of great moments in French history, resembles a cavernous tomb. The star attraction in the nave is a **Foucault's Pendulum** (named after the French physicist Léon Foucault, who invented it in 1851), a simple device—a heavy ball suspended on a long wire above markers—that proves the rotation of the Earth. Visitors can climb the Panthéon's lofty dome between April and October to see the city unfurl in a sprawl of gray rooftops.

pl. du Panthéon, 5th arrond. paris-pantheon.fr. © **01-44-32-18-00.** Admission 13€ adults, free for children 16 and under; dome 3.50€ extra. Apr–Sept daily 10am–6:30pm; Oct–Mar daily 10am–6pm; dome Apr–Oct only. Métro: Cardinal Lemoine. RER: Luxembourg.

St-Etienne-du-Mont ♥♥ CHURCH   One of the city's prettiest churches, this gem is a joyous mix of late Gothic and Renaissance styles. The 17th-century facade combines Gothic tradition with a dash of classical Rome; inside, the 16th-century chancel sports a magnificent **rood screen** (an intricately carved partition separating the nave from the chancel) with decorations inspired by the Italian Renaissance. A pilgrimage site, the church was once part of an abbey dedicated to St-Geneviève (Paris's patron saint), and stones from the saint's original sarcophagus lie in an ornate shrine here. That's about all that is left of her—the saint's bones were burned during the Revolution, and her ashes were thrown in the Seine. The remains of two other great minds, Racine and Pascal, are buried here.

1 pl. St-Geneviève, 5th arrond. saintetiennedumont.fr. © **01-43-54-11-79.** Free admission. Tues–Fri 10am–1pm and 2–7:30pm; Sat–Sun 8:30am–1pm and 2–8pm; Mon 2:30–7:30pm (times vary during school holidays). Métro: Cardinal Lemoine. RER: Luxembourg.

Gothic and Renaissance interiors at St-Etienne-du-Mont.

St-Germain-des-Prés & Luxembourg (6th Arrondissement)

In the 20th century, the St-Germain-des-Prés neighborhood became associated with writers like Jean-Paul Sartre, Simone de Beauvoir, Albert Camus, and the rest of the intellectual bohemian crowd that gathered at **Café de Flore** (p. 154) or **Les Deux Magots** (p. 155). But back in the 6th century, a mighty abbey was founded here that ruled over a big chunk of the Left Bank for almost 1,000 years. The French Revolution put a stop to that, and most of the original buildings were pulled down. You can still find remains of both epochs in this neighborhood, notably at the 10th-century church **St-Germain-des-Prés** and the surviving bookstores and publishing houses that surround it. After your tour, relax at the delightful **Jardin du Luxembourg** nearby.

Jardin du Luxembourg ♥♥♥ GARDEN   Out of the many parks and gardens in Paris, this is my personal favorite. Rolling out like an Oriental carpet before the Italianate Palais du Luxembourg, this vast expanse of fountains, flowers, lush lawns, and shaded glens is the perfect setting for a leisurely stroll, a relaxed picnic, or a serious make-out session, depending on who you're with. At the center of everything is a fountain with a huge basin, where kids can sail toy wooden sailboats (3€ for 30 min.) and adults can sun themselves on the green metal chairs at the pond's edge. The most splendid waterworks is probably the **Medici Fountain** (most easily reached via the entrance at Place Paul Claudel behind the Odéon), draped with lithe Roman gods and topped with the Medici coat of arms, in honor of the palace's first resident, Marie de Médicis.

In 1621, the Italian-born French queen, homesick for the Pitti Palace of her youth, bought up the grounds and existing buildings and had a Pitti-inspired palace built for herself as well as a smaller version of the sumptuous gardens. She relocated here in 1625, only to be banished in 1630 for taking the wrong side against powerful Cardinal Richelieu. The palace passed on to various royals until the Revolution, when it was turned into a prison. After the Revolution, the palace and grounds stayed in government hands up until today, with the exception of the Orangerie, which now holds the **Musée du Luxembourg,** 19 rue de Vaugirard, 6th arrond. (museeduluxembourg.fr; ✆ **01-40-13-62-00;** admission 14€ adults, 10€ ages 16–25, free for children 15 and under; hours vary with exhibits; Métro: Odéon, RER: Luxembourg), which is only open during its excellent temporary exhibits.

Entry at pl. Edmond Rostand, pl. André Honnorat, rue Guynemer, or rue de Vaugirard, 6th arrond. jardin.senat.fr. ✆ **01-42-34-20-00.** Free entry to the park; charges for playgrounds. Daily 7:30am–dusk (from 8:15am in winter). Métro: Odéon. RER: Luxembourg.

Maison Gainsbourg ♥♥ MUSEUM   As the only place in the world dedicated entirely to chanson legend, Serge Gainsbourg, this place, his former home (a historical landmark, smothered in fan graffiti), is a must for music fans. It's a hybrid space that includes a museum, his actual home (looking pretty much as Gainsbourg left it when he died in 1991), a shop, and a piano bar with regular concerts. Serge's house will take about 30 minutes to get around, thanks to an immersive audio guide, while the museum will take you through his works and life, showing lots of hitherto unseen material. ***Note:*** The museum can be visited separately and doesn't have a waiting list, but the house can only be accessed via a joint museum/house ticket for which (at time of writing) there was a 3-month wait, so book well ahead!

14 rue de Verneil, 7th arrond. maisongainsbourg.fr. **01-42-34-20-00.** Admission museum 12€ adults, 6€ ages 7–25, free for kids 6 and under; joint museum and house 29€ adults, 16€ ages 7–25, free for kids 6 and under. Tues, Thurs, Sat–Sun 10am–8pm; Wed and Fri 10am–10:30pm. Métro: Saint-Germain-des-Près.

Monnaie de Paris ♥♥ MUSEUM   The former royal mint, a Republican mint since the Revolution, makes for a fascinating hour's visit, showcasing the history of France's coinage as well as the history of money in general and the industrial process behind it all. Collectors will revel in the rare coin displays: One interactive area contains an écu—France's currency until the Revolution—from the reign of Louis XVI (the story goes it was partly because of his recognizable profile on the coin—Louis had a rather large nose—that he was caught while trying to escape during the Revolution). Other areas let you glimpse into the factory and try your hand at pressing your own coin. The visit ends in the boutique, which brims with collector's coins and jewelry. Don't leave without looking at the contemporary art displays dotted around the building: They contrast beautifully with the factory's palacelike neoclassical architecture, which dates from 1775.

11 quai Conti, 6th arrond. monnaiedeparis.fr. **01-40-46-56-66.** Admission 12€ adults, free for ages 25 and under. Tues–Sun 11am–6pm (until 9pm on Wed). Métro: Pont Neuf or Mabillon.

Musée National Eugène Delacroix.

Musée Zadkine.

Musée National Eugène Delacroix ♥♥ MUSEUM   Housed in what was once the painter's apartment and studio, this small museum is dedicated to Eugène Delacroix, one of the greatest artists of the Romantic period. Delacroix was old and sick when he moved here in 1857 to be closer to the church of St-Sulpice, where he was decorating a chapel. He managed to finish the paintings 3 years before his death here in 1863. "It takes great fortitude to be yourself," he once said, and he certainly had it: At his death, he left behind some 8,000 paintings, drawings, and pastels. Though none of his major works are in the museum, several smaller paintings decorate the walls, including the mysterious *Mary Magdalene in the Wilderness*. Furniture, mementos, and other personal items are displayed, including the artist's palette and paint box. The museum is on the exquisitely beautiful rue de Furstenberg, a small, leafy square. *Note:* You can buy a joint ticket for the Louvre (p. 166) here too for 22€, which is the price of the Louvre's ticket alone.

6 rue de Furstenberg, 6th arrond. musee-delacroix.fr. ✆ **01-44-41-86-50.** Admission 9€ adults, free for children 17 and under, and visitors age 25 and below from Europe. Wed–Mon 9:30am–5:30pm. Métro: St-Germain-des-Prés or Mabillon.

Musée Zadkine ♥♥ MUSEUM   You could easily miss the alleyway that leads to this tiny museum in the small but luminous house where Ossip Zadkine lived and worked from 1928 until his death in 1967. A contemporary and neighbor of artists such as Brancusi, Lipchitz, Modigliani, and Picasso, this Russian-born sculptor is closely associated with the Cubist movement; he was also influenced by the art of Greece and Africa. His sober, elegant sculptures combine abstract geometry with deep humanity. Dozens of examples of his best works are displayed in small, light-filled rooms. Be sure to visit the artist's workshop, tucked behind the tranquil garden. *Note:* Because of the museum's small size, during temporary exhibits you'll have to pay to enter even the permanent collection (which is usually free).

100 bis rue d'Assas, 6th arrond. zadkine.paris.fr. ⓒ **01-55-42-77-20.** Free admission to permanent collections. Tues–Sun 10am–6pm. Métro: Notre-Dame des Champs or Vavin.

St-Germain-des-Prés ♥♥♥ CHURCH

The origins of this church stretch back over a millennium. First established in 543 by King Childebert, who constructed a basilica and monastery on the site, it was built, destroyed, and rebuilt several times over the centuries. Nothing remains of the original buildings, but the bell tower dates from the 10th century and is one of the oldest in France. Most of the rest of the church was built in the 11th and 12th centuries and is Romanesque in style. The church and its abbey became a major center of learning and power during the Middle Ages, remaining a force to be reckoned with up until the eve of the French Revolution. Once the monarchy toppled, however, all hell broke loose: The abbey was destroyed, the famous library burned, and the church vandalized. Restored in the 19th century, though the complex is a fraction of its original size.

The church St-Germain-des-Prés dates to the 10th century.

The first thing you'll notice on entering is that much of the interior is painted in a dazzling range of greens and golds—one of the few Parisian churches to retain a sense of its original facade. The heart of King Jean Casimir of Poland is buried here, as are the ashes of the body of René Descartes (his skull is in the collections of the Musée de l'Homme). On the left as you exit, you can peek inside the **chapel of St-Symphorien,** where during the Revolution over 100 members of the clergy were imprisoned before being executed on the square in front of the church.

Classical music concerts are regularly held in the church (tickets and information are at fnactickets.com). On the last Sunday of the month, afternoon organ recitals are free.

3 pl. St-Germain-des-Prés, 6th arrond. eglise-saintgermaindespres.fr. ⓒ **01-55-42-81-10.** Free admission. Tues–Fri 7:30am–8pm; Sat 8:30am–8pm; Sun 9:30am–8pm. Métro: St-Germain-des-Prés.

St-Sulpice ♥♥ CHURCH

The facade of this enormous edifice looms over an entire neighborhood. Construction started in the 17th century over the remains of a medieval church; it took over 100 years to build, and one of the towers was never finished. Inside, several important works of art are tucked into the church's chapels. The most famous are **three masterpieces by Eugène Delacroix:** *Jacob Wrestling with the Angel, Heliodorus Driven from the Temple,* and *St-Michael Vanquishing the Devil* (on the right just after you enter the church). Jean-Baptiste Pigalle's statue of the *Virgin and Child* lights up the Chapelle de la Vierge at the farthermost point from the entrance. A bronze line runs north–south along the floor; this is part of a **gnomon,** an astronomical device set up in the 17th century to calculate the position of the sun in the sky. A small hole in one of the stained-glass windows creates a spot of light on the floor; every day at noon it hits the line in a different spot, climbing up to the top of an obelisk and lighting a gold disk at the winter equinox. Because of their size, churches were an ideal spot for this type of measurement, making for a rare collaboration between science and religion.

pl. St-Sulpice, 6th arrond. paroissesaintsulpice.paris. © **01-42-34-59-98.** Free admission. Daily 8am–7:45pm. Métro: St-Sulpice.

Eiffel Tower & Les Invalides (7th Arrondissement)

The Iron Lady towers above this stately neighborhood stuffed with embassies and ministries, where the very buildings seem to insist that you stand up straight and pay attention. You'll see lots of elegant black cars with smoked glass cruising the streets, as well as many a tourist eyeing the **Eiffel Tower** or the golden dome of **Les Invalides,** and scurrying in and out of some of the city's best museums, like the **Musée du Quai Branly, Musée d'Orsay,** and **Musée Rodin.**

Eiffel Tower ♥♥♥ MONUMENT   In his wildest dreams, Gustave Eiffel probably never imagined that the tower he built for the 1889 World's Fair would become the ultimate symbol of Paris, and for many, of France. The Eiffel Tower is one of the most visited sites in the nation. No fewer than 50 engineers and designers worked on the plans, which resulted in a remarkably solid structure that, despite its height (324m/1,063 ft., including the antenna) does not sway in the wind.

When the project for the tower was announced, a group of artists and writers, including Guy de Maupassant and Alexandre Dumas *fils,* published a manifesto that referred to it as an "odious column of bolted metal." Others

---

Get a Workout & a Bargain at the Eiffel Tower

No need to go to the gym after marching up the 704 steps that lead you to the first and second floors of the Eiffel Tower. Not only will you burn calories, but you'll save money: At 14.20€ for adults, 7.10€ ages 12 to 24, and 3.60€ ages 4 to 11, this is the least expensive way to visit. Extra perks include an up-close view of the amazing metal structure and avoiding the long lines for the elevator. If you do decide to go to the top, buy a combined stairs and lift ticket (26.90€ adults, 13.50€ ages 12–24, and 6.80€ ages 4–11); as an adult, it'll save you 8.40€ from the lift-only price.

were less diplomatic: Novelist Joris-Karl Huysmans called it a "hole-riddled suppository." Despite the objections, the tower was built—over 18,000 pieces of iron, held together with some 2.5 million rivets. In this low-tech era, building techniques involved a lot of elbow grease: The foundations, for example, were dug entirely by shovel, and the debris was hauled away in horse-drawn carts. Construction dragged on for 2 years, but finally, on March 31, 1889, Gustave Eiffel proudly led a group of dignitaries up the 1,665 steps to the top, where he unfurled the French flag for the inauguration.

Over 130 years later, the tower has become such an integral piece of the Parisian landscape that it's impossible to think of the city without it. Over time, even the artists came around—the tower's silhouette can be found in the paintings of Seurat, Bonnard, Duffy, Chagall, and especially those of Robert Delaunay, who devoted an entire series of canvases to the subject. It has also inspired a range of stunts, from Pierre Labric riding a bicycle down the stairs from the first level in 1923, to Philippe Petit walking a 700m-long (2,296-ft.) tightrope from the Palais de Chaillot to the tower during the centennial celebration in 1989.

The most dramatic view of the tower itself is from the wide terrace at the Palais de Chaillot (Métro: Trocadéro) across the Seine. From there, it's a short walk through the gardens and across the Pont d'Alma to the base. Though several elevators whisk visitors skyward, they do take time to come back down, so be prepared for a wait. Personally, I think the view from the second level is the best; you're far enough up to see the entire city, yet close enough to clearly pick out the monuments. But if you are aching to get to the top, an

View of Palais de Chaillot from the Eiffel Tower.

airplanelike view awaits. The third level is, mercifully, enclosed, but thrill-seekers can climb up a few more stairs to the outside balcony (entirely protected with a grill). The base of the tower is surrounded by bulletproof glass walls as part of a plan to protect visitors from terror attacks. Don't be alarmed, but do build in at least 20 minutes of extra time for passing the checkpoints. *Note:* For all access, you now need to book a time-stamped e-ticket in advance online so you can spend as little time as possible in lines. The line time without a slot can easily climb to 4 hours or more.

Champ de Mars, 7th arrond. toureiffel.paris. **01-44-11-23-23.** Lift to 2nd floor 22.60€ adults, 11.30€ ages 12–24, 5.70€ ages 4–11; lift to 2nd and 3rd floors 35.30€ adults, 17.70€ ages 12–24, 8.90€ ages 4–11; stairs to 2nd floor 14.30€ adults, 7.10€ ages 12–24, 3.60€ ages 4–11; stairs to 2nd floor and lift to the top 26.90€ adults, 13.50€ ages 12–24, 6.80€ ages 4–11. Free admission children ages 3 and under. Daily 9:15am–10:45pm (but times may vary with season so check the website). Métro: Trocadéro or Bir Hakeim. RER: Champ de Mars–Tour Eiffel.

Hôtel des Invalides/Napoleon's Tomb ♥♥ MUSEUM   Military history rules at this grandiose complex, which houses a military museum, church, tomb, hospital, and military ministries, among other things (including some very cute wild rabbits who roam the lawns in spring). Over the entryway, LUDOVICUS MAGNUS is inscribed in huge letters, in homage to the builder of this vast edifice, otherwise known as Louis XIV. Determined to create a home for wounded soldiers, Louis commissioned architect Libéral Bruant to design a monumental structure with formal gardens on what was then the outskirts of the city. The first war veterans arrived in 1674—between 4,000 and 5,000 soldiers would eventually move in, creating a mini-city with its own governor. An on-site hospital, constructed for the severely wounded, is still in service today.

As you cross the main gate, you'll find yourself in a huge courtyard, the *cour d'honneur,* which was once the site of military parades. At the far end on the second story is a statue of "The Little Corporal" (Napoleon I) that once topped the column in Place Vendôme. The surrounding buildings house military offices and the **Musée de l'Armée,** one of the world's largest military museums, with a vast collection of objects testifying to humankind's capacity for self-destruction. A huge wing covers the exploits of everyone from **Louis XIV to Napoleon III;** another wing the two **World Wars.** Also on-site is the **Musée des Plans et Reliefs,** a somewhat dusty collection of scale models of fortresses and battlefields, and the **Musée de l'Ordre de la Libération,** which retraces the history of the Liberation (1940–45).

The **Eglise des Soldati,** or the "Soldier's Church" is lovely and light-filled, decorated with magnificent chandeliers and a collection of flags of defeated enemies.

The **Tomb of Napoléon** lies under one of the most splendid domes in France. Designed by Hardouin-Mansart and constructed from 1679 to 1706, the interior soars 107m (351 ft.) up to a skylight, which illuminates a brilliantly colored cupola fresco by Charles de la Fosse. Ethereal light filters down to an opening in the center of the room, where you can look down on the huge porphyry sarcophagus that holds the Emperor's remains, encased in five successive coffins (one tin, one mahogany, two lead, and one ebony). Surrounding the sarcophagus are the tombs of two of Napoleon's brothers, his son, and several French military heroes. Don't blame the over-the-top setting on Napoleon; the decision to transfer his remains to Paris was made in 1840, almost 20 years after his death. Tens of thousands of people crowded the streets to pay their respects as the coffin was carried under the Arc de Triomphe and down the Champs-Élysées to Les Invalides.

Statue of Napoleon Bonaparte in the Hôtel des Invalides.

Pl. des Invalides, 7th arrond. musee-armee.fr. © **01-44-42-37-72.** Admission to all the museums, the church, and Napoleon's Tomb 15€ adults (10€ from 6pm on late-night opening), free for children 17 and under. Daily 10am–6pm (1st Fri month until 10pm). Métro: Latour-Faubourg, Varenne, or Invalides. RER: Invalides.

Musée des Egouts de Paris ♥♥ MUSEUM If you want to get a better idea of Jean Valjean's underground ordeal in *Les Misérables*, take a trip through Paris's sewer museum. Though you won't actually get on a boat, you will be able to walk through a short stretch of the city's 2,400km (1,490 miles) of sewers (don't worry, you'll be on a raised sidewalk), which should give you a pretty good idea of the different types of passageways and equipment that exist in this underground domain. Interactive circuits of displays explain the history of the city's water supply and waste disposal issues (this was no joke; for centuries, the lack of a proper sewage system helped spread diseases like the Black Plague), as well as technical aspects of this stinky world. Because it's underground and part of the working system, the museum closes when the Seine is high, and can get chilly, so bring a sweater.

Pont de lama, in front of 93 quai d'Orsay, 7th arrond. musee-egouts.paris.fr. © **01-53-68-27-81.** Admission 9€ adults, 7€ students and children 6–16, free for children 5 and under. Tues–Sun 10am–5pm. Métro: Alma-Marceau. RER: Pont de lama.

Musée d'Orsay ♥♥♥ MUSEUM What better setting for a world-class museum of 19th-century art than a beautiful example of Belle Epoque architecture? The magnificent Gare d'Orsay train station, built to coincide with the 1900 World's Fair, has been brilliantly transformed into an exposition space for a collection of treasures that were once scattered among the Louvre and the Musée National d'Art Moderne collections.

The collection spans the years 1848 to 1914, a period that saw the birth of many artistic movements, such as the Barbizon School and Symbolism, but today it is best known for the emergence of Impressionism. All the epoch's superstars are here: Monet, Manet, Degas, Renoir, Cézanne, and Van Gogh.

The top floor is the home of the most famous Impressionist paintings, like Edouard Manet's masterpiece, *Le Déjeuner sur l'Herbe.* Though Manet's composition of bathers and friends picnicking on the grass draws freely from those of Italian Renaissance masters, the painting shocked its 19th-century audience, which was horrified to see a naked lady lunching with two fully clothed men. Manet got into trouble again with his magnificent *Olympia,* a seductive odalisque stretched out on a divan. There was nothing new about the subject; viewers were rattled by the unapologetic look in her eye—this is not an idealized nude, but a real woman, and a tough cookie, to boot.

The middle level is devoted to the post-Impressionists with works by artists such as Gauguin, Seurat, Rousseau, and Van Gogh, like the latter's *Church at Auvers-sur-Oise,* an ominous version of the church in a small town north of Paris where he moved after spending time in an asylum in Provence. This was one of some 70 paintings he produced in the 2 months leading up to his suicide.

A few other standouts:

o **Renoir's *Dance at Le Moulin de la Galette, Montmartre:*** The dappled light and the movement of the crowd in this joyous painting are such that you wonder if it's not going to suddenly waltz out of its frame.
o **Monet's *La Gare St-Lazare:*** The metallic roof of the station frames an almost abstract mix of clouds and smoke; rather than a description of machines and mechanics, this painting is a modern study of light and color.
o **Gauguin's *The White Horse:*** The horse isn't even really white, but you don't care when you gaze at Gauguin's Tahitian version of paradise. Not everyone was charmed by the artist's use of vibrant color: The pharmacist who commissioned the painting refused it because the horse was too green.

Sculptures and decorative arts are also on display here, including a remarkable collection of Art Nouveau furniture and objects. Photo fans will appreciate the fine examples of early photography, including Félix Nadar's portrait of Charles Baudelaire; there

Musée d'Orsay's central hall, in the former Gare d'Orsay train station.

are also some interesting works by nonphotographers like Edward Degas and Emile Zola. If you plan to see the Musée Rodin (p. 222), buying a dual ticket (25€) will save you 5€.

1 rue de la Légion d'Honneur, 7th arrond. musee-orsay.fr. ✆ **01-40-49-48-14.** Admission 16€ adults, 13€ ages 18–25, free for children 17 and under. Tues–Wed and Fri–Sun 9:30am–6pm; Thurs 9:30am–9:45pm. Métro: Solférino. RER: Musée d'Orsay.

Musée du Quai Branly—Jacques Chirac ♥♥♥ MUSEUM   Just a few blocks from the Eiffel Tower, this museum's wildly contemporary design has forever changed the architectural landscape of this rigidly elegant neighborhood. Its enormous central structure floats on a series of pillars, under which lies a lush garden, which is separated from the noisy boulevard out front by a huge glass wall. However you feel about the outside, you cannot help but be impressed by the inside: The vast space is filled with exquisite examples of the traditional arts of Africa, the Pacific Islands, Asia, and the Americas. It makes an ideal showcase for a category of artwork that has too often been relegated to the sidelines of the museum world.

Delicately carved headrests from Papua New Guinea in the form of birds and crocodiles vie for attention with intricately painted masks from Indonesia. There's a selection of "magic stones" from the island nation of Vanuatu, Australian aboriginal paintings, an extensive Asian art section, and an African collection that includes embroidered silks from Morocco, geometric marriage cloths from Mali, and wooden masks from the Ivory Coast. The Americas collection includes rare Nazca pottery and Inca textiles, as well as an intriguing assortment of North American works, such as Haitian voodoo objects, Sioux beaded tunics, and a huge totem pole from British Columbia, Canada. Though some documentation is translated in English, **audio guides** (5€) are a big help for non-French speakers.

37 quai Branly and 206 and 218 rue de Université, 7th arrond. quaibranly.fr. ✆ **01-56-61-70-00.** Admission 14€ adults, free for children 17 and under. Tues–Wed and Fri–Sun 10:30am–7pm; Thurs 10:30am–10pm. Métro: Alma-Marceau. RER: Pont d'Alma.

Musée Rodin ♥♥♥ MUSEUM   Behind the Hôtel Biron, which houses the museum, is a formal garden with benches, fountains, and even a little cafe (no picnics allowed, unfortunately). Of course, it would be foolish not to go inside and drink in some of the 6,600 sculptures of this excellent collection (don't worry, not all are on display), but it would be equally silly not to take the time to admire the large bronzes in the garden, which include some of Rodin's most famous works. Take, for example, *The Thinker.* Erected in front of the Panthéon in 1906 during an intense political crisis, Rodin's first public sculpture soon became a Socialist symbol and was quickly transferred to the Hôtel Biron by the authorities, under the pretense that it blocked pedestrian traffic. Other important sculptures in the garden include the *Burghers of Calais, Balzac,* and the *Gates of Hell,* a monumental composition that the sculptor worked on throughout his career.

The most famous of the marble works is *The Kiss,* which was originally meant to appear in the *Gates of Hell.* In time, Rodin decided that the lovers were too happy for this grim composition, and he explored it as an independent work. The sculpture was inspired by the tragic story of Paolo and Francesca, in which a young woman falls in love with her husband's brother. Upon their first kiss, the husband discovers them and stabs them both. As usual with Rodin's works, the critics were shocked by the couple's overt sensuality, but not as shocked as they were by the large, impressionistic rendition of *Balzac,* exhibited at the same salon, which critic Georges Rodenbach described as "less a statue than a strange monolith, a thousand-year-old menhir." Hundreds of works are here, many of them legendary, so don't be surprised if, after a while, your vision starts to blur. That'll be your cue to head outside and enjoy the

Sculpture of the Three Shades at Musée Rodin.

garden. *Note:* The audio guide costs 6.50€, but does offer excellent extra insight into the pieces you're seeing. Also, if you plan to visit the Musée d'Orsay, buy a joint ticket for 25€, which will save you 5€.

79 rue de Varenne, 7th arrond. musee-rodin.fr. **01-44-18-61-10.** Admission 14€ adults, free for children 17 and under. Tues–Sun 10am–6:30pm. Métro: Varenne or St-Francois-Xavier.

Montparnasse (14th & 15th Arrondissements)

Even though its heart was ripped out in the early 1970s, when the original 19th-century train station was torn down and the **Tour Montparnasse,** an ugly skyscraper, was erected, this neighborhood still retains a redolent whiff of its artistic past. Back in the day, artists such as Picasso, Modigliani, and Man Ray hung out in cafes like **Le Dôme, La Coupole, La Rotonde,** and **Le Sélect,** as did a "Lost Generation" of English-speaking writers like Hemingway, Fitzgerald, Faulkner, and James Joyce. Today the cafes are mostly filled with tourists, but the neighborhood still has quiet corners and even artists' studios. Amazingly, **La Ruche,** the legendary artists' studio from the Golden Years, is still standing (laruche-artistes.fr). And of course, if you don't want to look at the Tour Montparnasse you could take the lift to its panoramic bar/restaurant, Le Ciel de Paris (p. 150).

Cimetière du Montparnasse ♥♥ CEMETERY   This quiet cemetery is the final resting place of many French celebrities. A map to the left of the main gateway will direct you to the gravesite of its most famous couple, Simone de Beauvoir and Jean-Paul Sartre. Others resting here include Samuel

Beckett, Guy de Maupassant, Capt. Alfred Dreyfus, auto tycoon André Citroën, sculptors Ossip Zadkine and Constantin Brancusi, composer Camille Saint-Saëns, photographer Man Ray, poet Charles Baudelaire, and American intellectual and activist Susan Sontag, who was interred here in 2005. You can download a map on the municipal website.

3 bd. Edgar-Quinet, 14th arrond. paris.fr/equipements/cimetiere-du-montparnasse-4082. ℭ **01-44-10-86-50.** Mon–Fri 8am–5:30pm; Sat 8:30am–6pm; Sun 9am–6pm. Métro: Edgar-Quinet.

Le Musée de la Liberation de Paris—Musée du Général Leclerc—Musée Jean Moulin ♥♥♥ MUSEUM

The museum with the longest name in Paris opened in 2019 in time for the 75th anniversary of the Liberation of Paris and is a must for anyone interested in World War II history. Housed in brand-new buildings at Denfert-Rochereau, the museum retraces the history of the Résistance and the figures who helped liberate France—notably Général Leclerc de Hautclocque (who famously joined De Gaulle's government-in-exile in Britain and furthered the Allied cause in Africa) and Jean Moulin, the head of the Résistance. The museum leads you through wartime events, with displays of around 300 items, including official documents and rare film archives. Part of the visit takes you through the underground bunker where Colonel Rol-Tanguy planned the Liberation of Paris.

pl. Denfert-Rochereau, 14th arrond. museesleclercmoulin.paris.fr. ℭ **01-71-28-34-70.** Free admission except to temporary exhibitions. Tues–Sun 10am–6pm. Métro/RER: Denfert-Rochereau.

Musée de la Libération.

Les Catacombes ♥ CEMETERY/HISTORIC SITE   Definitely not for the faint of heart, the city's catacombs are filled with the remains of millions of Parisians whose bones line the narrow passages of this mazelike series of tunnels. In the 18th century, the Cimetière des Innocents, a centuries-old, overpacked cemetery near Les Halles, had become so foul and disease-ridden that it was finally declared a health hazard and closed. The bones of its occupants were transferred to this former quarry and were later joined by those of other similarly pestilential Parisian cemeteries. In 1814, the quarry stopped accepting new lodgers, and the quarry inspector had a novel idea. Rather than leaving just a hodgepodge of random bones, he organized them in neat stacks and geometric designs, punctuating the 1.5km (1 mile) tunnels with sculptures and pithy sayings carved into the rock. The one at the entrance sets the tone: STOP—HERE IS THE EMPIRE OF DEATH. The visit is fascinating for some, terrifying for others; not a good idea for claustrophobes or small children (there are 243 steps). The lighting is appropriately eerie, so you should bring a flashlight if you really want to see. Explanations are in English, French, and Spanish. It's cool down here (around 12°C/54°F) and damp, so a jacket or sweatshirt and rubber-soled shoes are indispensable. Buy an e-ticket with a time slot online—you'll still have to wait in line, but hopefully not for more than 10 minutes.

1 av. du Colonel Henri Rol-Tanguy, 14th arrond. catacombes.paris.fr. © **01-43-22-47-63.** Admission 31€ adults, 25€ ages 18–26, 5€ ages 5–17, free age 4 and under. Tues–Sun 9:45am–8:30pm (last entry 7:30pm). Métro and RER: Denfert-Rochereau.

Musée Bourdelle ♥ MUSEUM   Recently renovated and expanded (to include a lovely cafe), this museum is a testament to the sculptor Antoine Bourdelle (1861–1929), whose work went far beyond the 10 years he spent as Rodin's assistant. A renowned teacher who influenced an entire generation of sculptors, including Alberto Giacometti and Aristide Maillol, Bourdelle was one of the pioneers of 20th-century monumental sculpture. Proud, muscular centaurs, gods, and goddesses stride across these rooms, as well as monuments to famous people. You can also visit the sculptor's studio. **Audio guides** in English (5€) are a big help here.

18 rue Antoine-Bourdelle, 15th arrond. bourdelle.paris.fr. © **01-49-54-73-73.** Free admission to the permanent collection. Tues–Sun 10am–6pm. Métro: Montparnasse-Bienvenüe.

ORGANIZED TOURS & CLASSES

If you've only got a couple of days and you just don't have the stamina to do the research, an organized tour can provide good background information on the city and help you get your bearings. Here are a few ideas for getting to know Paris in an easy and different way.

Boat Tours

The famed **Bateaux-Mouches** (bateaux-mouches.fr; © **01-42-25-96-10;** Métro: Alma-Marceau) cruises leave from Pont de l'Alma on the Right Bank of the Seine, and last for a little over an hour. They tend to be touristy but can be a worthwhile way to enjoy the beauty of the Seine's sites. Tickets cost 17€ for adults, 8€ for kids 4 to 11, and are free for children 3 and under; the recorded commentary is in French, English, and up to three other languages. Lunch, and dinner cruises are also available (ranging 85€–165€).

On the other side of the river, in front of the Eiffel Tower, the **Bateaux Parisiens** (bateauxparisiens.com; ✆ **01-76-64-14-45;** Métro: Bir Hakeim, RER: Champ de Mars–Tour Eiffel) offers similar 1-hour tours (recorded commentary), but in smaller boats. Tickets cost 19€ for adults, 9€ children 3 to 12, and are free for children 2 and under. Bateaux Parisiens also runs a tour departing from Notre-Dame, but the service is less regular. Gourmet lunch and dinner cruises start at 75€ for lunch, and 95€ for dinner.

A little less touristy, **Vedettes du Pont Neuf** (vedettesdupontneuf.com; ✆ **01-46-33-98-38;** Métro: Pont Neuf) runs 1-hour cruises with live guides in French and English from the Square du Vert Galant at the tip of the Île de la Cité. Tickets cost 15€ for adults, 10€ children ages 4 to 12, and are free for children 3 and under. They also offer "happy hour" and champagne cruises from 25€ to 35€ (including plates of charcuterie).

Canauxrama (canauxrama.com; ✆ **01-42-39-15-00;** Métro: Jaurés or Bastille) tours both the Seine and the picturesque Canal St-Martin. For the canal, boats leave from either the Bassin de la Villette or the Bassin de l'Arsenal (near the pl. de la Bastille); tickets start at 18€ and are free for children 4 and

Bateaux-Mouches sightseeing boat tour.

> ### Tour & Ticket Websites vs. Booking Direct
>
> Such websites as **GetYourGuide.com, Viator.com, ToursByLocals.com, TakeWalks.com,** and **Airbnb.com/experiences** are undeniably convenient to use. In just a few minutes you can have advance reservations and/or tickets for tours, museums, historic sites, cooking classes, guided walks, and more. Sometimes they'll offer discounts on high-volume products like bus and boat tours.
>
> Because these websites take a significant commission from these tour providers and attractions, sometimes the price charged will be higher than it would have been had you gone directly to the source. I recently purchased a cooking class in Paris for $85. At the class, I learned that a fellow student had paid $135 to one of the above companies—for the same experience. The chef needed to make ends meet and so charged those who didn't book with her directly significantly more. She did so quietly—the web company she works with has a price guarantee—but her actions are not uncommon.
>
> As well, many of these companies sell priority access for a bit extra, allowing their customers to get on the "reserve line" rather than the regular one. But just **one small warning:** Many travelers have been reporting, especially at such sites as the Eiffel Tower, that so many folks were anteing up for VIP treatment that the "reserve line" moved just as slowly as the regular one.

under. There are two cruises: a shorter one that takes about 1¼ hours, and a longer cruise of about 2½ hours. The first part, which runs through a tunnel under the Place de la Bastille, is eerie (in a fun way), and afterward, you'll enjoy a lovely ride through locks and under pretty, arched bridges. Tours daily from May to September; less frequent service the rest of the year. The company also offers tours that leave the canal and enter the Seine (25€), as well as bistrot-like cruises with champagne and snacks from 30€.

The city's only Michelin-starred fine-dining boat is the *Don Juan II* (p. 115). But multi-Michelin-starred chef Alain Ducasse offers a similar experience at **Ducasse sur Seine** (ducasse-seine.com; Métro: Trocadéro), a 180-person vessel offering 90-minute cruises and contemporary seasonal cuisine. It's docked at Port Debilly on the Right Bank opposite the Eiffel Tower. Lunch and dinner cruises start at 110€ and 280€.

Marin d'Eau Douce, Bassin de la Villette, 37 quai de Seine, 19th arrond. (boating-paris-marindeaudouce.com; ⓒ **09-70-71-40-60;** Métro: Stalingrad or Jaurès), has a fleet of electric self-guide vessels (for up to 5, 7, or 11 people) that don't require licenses, leaving you free to whoosh up and down the Canal de l'Ourcq to see little-known parts of the city. If you opt for the 1-hour cruise (from 45€ depending on the size of your boat), you have to stick to the Bassin de la Villette, a 1km (.6-mile) lake-like stretch of water; the 2-hour (from 80€), 3-hour (from 110€), half-day (from 180€), and full-day (from 220€) routes let you zip along the canal past Parc de la Villette and out of Paris into Pantin, an up-and-coming area that has been (somewhat optimistically) coined the Brooklyn of Paris.

Big Bus Paris hop-on, hop-off tour.

Bus Tours

Yes, they're touristy, and yes, Paris is easy to navigate without an organized bus tour, but hop-on, hop-off buses are worth considering if (1) you're in a hurry and want to see all the main sights in 1 or 2 days, and (2) you don't want to use the public transportation system. There are two main companies to choose between—**Big Bus Paris** and **Toot Bus**—and both offer similar pickings (though Toot Bus is slightly cheaper and offers a few nonstop tours in addition to its hop-on, hop-offs).

The **Big Bus Paris** company has 1- and 2-day tickets (bigbustours.com/en/paris/paris-bus-tours; ⓒ **01-53-95-39-53;** 1-day adult ticket 7€, 2-day adult ticket 78€ [including a river cruise], 25€ children 4–12; prices cheaper online) and one route—the Classic Red Route—which stops at 10 top sites. It also offers Night Tour packages that add a 2-hour evening tour to your daytime hop-on, hop-off package (from 33€ adults, 22€ children 4–12).

TootBus's passes go up to 3 days (tootbus.com; ⓒ **01-42-66-56-56;** 1-day adult pass from 45€, 2-day 53€, 3-day 58€; from 25€ children 4–15), and their Must-See Paris tours include a river cruise (from 59€).

Whichever tour you choose, multilingual audio guides are provided (you can switch them off if you just want to look at the city).

Cycling Tours

Fat Tire Bike Tours (fattiretours.com/paris; ⓒ **01-82-88-80-96,** or 866/614-6218 in North America; Métro: Dupleix) offers a 3½-hour day-tour of Paris by bike in English (from 42€). Kid-size bikes and toddler trailers are available, and the morning tour includes a break in a cafe (food and drinks not included), so this is a good one to choose if you're traveling with your family. They also offer night tours and tours of Versailles and Monet's Garden in Giverny.

If you'd like to see Paris like a local, pick **Paris à Vélo,** 22 rue Alphonse Baudin, 11th arrond. (parisavelo.fr; ⓒ **01-48-87-60-01;** Métro: Richard Lenoir). In addition to their "Heart of Paris" tour (which covers the Marais and the Louvre area), they offer four other themed 3-hour bike tours—Unusual Paris, Iconic Paris, Feminist Paris, and Paris Contrasts—the latter two take you into areas tourists don't usually get to see. The first, for instance, goes to the southern 13th and 14th arrondissements, home to cobbled lanes and artists' workshops; the second is to northern Paris, along the canals and on to futuristic Parc de la Villette. Tickets cost 37€ per person (children minimum height 130cm). They also rent bikes. Tours are in French and English.

Bike About Tours (bikeabouttours.com; no phone) offers 3½-hour tours in small groups, led by knowledgeable, fluent-English speakers for 45€ per person (20€ children). All tours leave from Le Peleton Café (17 rue du Pont Louis-Philippe, 4th arrond.; lepelotoncafe.cc) and cover all the main sights via the city's atmospheric back streets. They also include a pit stop in a Left Bank bakery (food not included) and a few quirky stop-offs, like at Jim Morrison's house and places where famous movies were shot.

Walking Tours

Sight Seeker's Delight (sightseekersdelight.com; ⓒ **06-22-52-57-90**) offers a range of walking tours in English, including Paris Along the Seine, Sweet and Savory Tour, and Secrets of the Night. Tours last from 2½ to 4 hours and

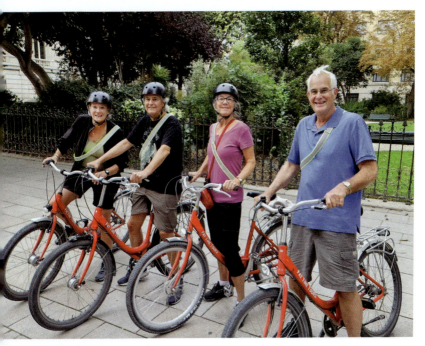

Fat Tire Bike Tours.

prices vary between 50€ and 150€ per person (half-price for ages 4–10, free for children 3 and under).

Paris Walks (paris-walks.com; ⓒ **01-48-09-21-40**) organizes 2-hour walks of the city, based on either a theme or a neighborhood. Most of the walks cost 25€ for adults, 10€ ages 15–20, 8€ children 14 and under; special small-group themed tours (chocolate, the Louvre, fashion) range from 20€ to 50€ per adult. Reservations are only necessary for special tours.

Paris Greeters (greeters.paris) arranges free tours for one to six people with local volunteers. There's no catalog of specific tours; your walk is pretty much up to the greeter, who will choose a neighborhood. Register online and request a specific day and language; you'll then be contacted with the tour details.

Entrée to Black Paris (entreetoblackparis.com) runs a few good tours, from gourmet walks to art-themed visits (for around 25€ for adults, 15€ ages 20 and under). But where it really stands out is with its tours covering themes such as Black history around the Jardin du Luxembourg (scheduled roughly once a week) and Josephine Baker. These walks highlight the life and works of Black figures such as American authors Richard Wright and Chester Himes, and French writer Alexandre Dumas (famed for—among other works—*The Count of Monte Cristo* and *The Three Musketeers*), whose grandmother was an enslaved person of African descent. Tours usually last 2 hours.

An art-themed tour with Entrée to Black Paris.

SEE THE PARIS OF emily in paris

Who hasn't seen, or at least heard of, Darren Starr's Netflix phenomenon *Emily in Paris*? The Parisian life of Emily Cooper (played by Lily Collins) has been such a hit that fans of the show have been flocking to the City of Light in hope of visiting the places featured onscreen. And it's had such an influence on Paris's tourist industry that in 2024 President Macron said he'd "fight hard" to persuade the show to stay in Paris rather than move to Rome. If you would like to follow in her footsteps (albeit minus the stilettos), I have good news: Many settings are in public places and therefore accessible to normal people (with or without designer wardrobes). Here are my top three spots for a large dose of Emily nostalgia, the first one being in Montmartre.

1. **Rue de l'Abreuvoir,** 18th arrond.: One of the show's most memorable scenes has to be the Hästens bed sequence, where Emily sets up an outdoor marketing campaign in front of a statue of Dalida. This street is also where you'll find the **Maison Rose** restaurant (at no. 2), where Emily has dinner in the fifth episode (lamaisonrose-montmartre.com).

2. **Place de l'Estrapade,** 5th arrond.: You can kill three Emily birds with one stone on this pretty little square. Not only is it where Emily shared an apartment with Gabriel (played by Lucas Bravo), but it's also the setting for the bakery where she tastes her first croissant (today's **Boulangerie Moderne**, 16 rue des Fossés Saint-Jacques) and, next door, the *Deux Compères* restaurant where Gabriel worked (today's **Terra Nera**, an Italian eatery).

3. **Café de l'Homme,** 16th arrond.: Inside the **Musée de l'Homme** (p. 189) and with the Eiffel Tower as its iconic backdrop, this posh restaurant is where Emily goes to the launch of the perfume De l'Heure. For the same view, ask for a table on the balcony outside.

Or, if you'd like to see even more places with a guide, try the **Emily in Paris Tour** (emilyinparistour.fr; 32€ per person). Led by Fabien Buonavia, it takes you around multiple sights, mixing Emily trivia with information about Paris life and the architecture you see around you.

Other Guided Tours

4 Roues Sous 1 Parapluie (4roues-sous-1parapluie.com; ✆ **01-58-59-27-82**) offers chauffeur-driven themed rides around Paris in its colorful fleet of electric Citroën 2CV, the tiny, low-cost, and now classic French car that was jokingly referred to as "4 wheels under an umbrella." If there are three people in the car, prices start at 63€ per person for a 90-minute tour; the price of the car is the same, it's simply a question of how you divvy up the bill.

Paris and perfume also go hand in hand, but while most people can name perfume brands, few can actually accurately describe what they're smelling. Cue **Rendez-Vous Parfum** (rendezvousparfum.fr; ✆ **06-35-53-40-47**), an olfactory tour created by Sophie Irles, who—as a perfume developer for major companies like Burberry and Lancel—is to perfume what a sommelier is to wine. The tour, which usually takes place in the Marais, teaches you about things like the groups of scent, how they interact, and the history of perfume, and of course, where to buy some to take home. It's a fascinating 90 minutes to 2 hours and prices start at 350€ for a private group tour.

Cooking Classes

Several cooking schools in Paris offer short-term or 1-day courses. The most famous is **Le Cordon Bleu** (cordonbleu.edu; ✆ **01-85-65-15-00**), which has two sites in Paris, one along Quai André Citroën in the 15th arrond., and the other inside the Hôtel de la Marine (p. 185) in the 8th arrond., at Concorde. Most notably this school is where Julia Child mastered the art of French cooking. Well-known for its professional cooking courses, it also offers short courses for lay food enthusiasts, with prices starting at 80€ for its "Demonstration – The Art of Cooking like a Chef" workshop, showcasing the best of France's cooking techniques and 290€ for lessons on Burgundy cuisine. Classes are translated into English and fill up fast; reserve ahead.

At **Le Foodist** (lefoodist.com; ✆ **06-71-70-95-22;** Métro: Place Monge), over the course of several hours, students don't just master recipes—they learn techniques that they'll be able to use in numerous situations. Since this is delivered with brio and wit by owner Fred and his charming wife, Amanda, the classes are never dull. A range of options is offered, from croissant- and macaron-baking to wine tasting (129€–229€). The highlight, however, is the market visit and class, during which students accompany Fred through the lively Latin Quarter to an open-air market and sample scrumptious cheeses. After cooking together, everyone sits down to a delicious meal with wine (229€).

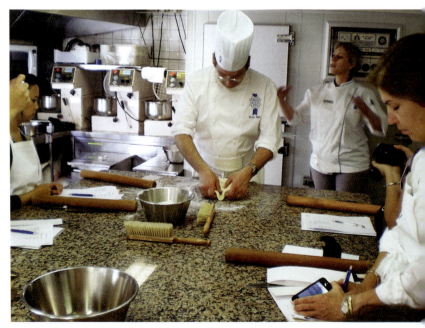

A cooking class at Le Cordon Bleu.

Equally enjoyable are the classes offered by **La Cuisine Paris** (lacuisine paris.com; ⓒ **01-40-51-78-18**; Métro: Hôtel de Ville), a friendly school set up by a Franco-American team. It offers market tours and small classes by professional chefs in both French and English, including the popular French macaron class. Prices range from 119€ for 2 hours to 189€ for half a day.

Similarly, **Les Secrets Gourmands de Noémie** (lessecretsgourmandsde noemie.com; ⓒ **06-64-17-93-32**; Métro: La Fourche or Brochant) offers a range of individual and small-group classes, the most popular of which is the fabulous pastry class. All classes are taught in English by Noémie, who trained at the prestigious Le Nôtre cooking school. Prices start at 120€ for a 2½-hour class. There's are kids' classes too for 45€.

Language Classes

The **Alliance Française** (alliancefr.org; ⓒ **01-42-84-90-00**) has been offering quality French-language classes for over a century. Depending on how many hours and what kind of course you take, courses cost around 190€ to 1,400€ for 4 weeks depending on your level and your needs; rates go down the more weeks you attend. There may be a joining fee.

ESPECIALLY FOR KIDS

Paris is not a particularly kid-friendly city, but it's not kid-unfriendly, either. For one, Parisians generally like kids, as long as they are not running wild. If you visit in the summer, in addition to the suggestions below, just about any age child (including grown-up ones) will have a blast at **Paris Plage** or along the reopened banks of the Seine, **Les Berges,** between Musée d'Orsay and Pont d'Alma, and the **Rives de Seine,** between Bastille and Tuileries (see box, p. 236). Here are some attractions that children may enjoy:

- **Bois de Boulogne** (p. 237)
- **Bois de Vincennes** (p. 239)
- **Centre Pompidou** (p. 186)
- **Château de Vincennes** (p. 239)
- **Choco Story Paris** (p. 203)
- **Cité des Sciences et de l'Industrie** (p. 202)
- **Coulée verte René-Dumont** (formerly Promenade Plantée; p. 198)
- **Eiffel Tower** (p. 217)
- **Jardin d'Acclimatation** (p. 235)
- **Jardin des Plantes** (p. 206)
- **Jardin des Tuileries** (p. 166)
- **Jardin du Luxembourg** (p. 213)
- **L'Hippodrome en Famille** (p. 51)
- **Musée des Arts et Métiers** (p. 181)
- **Musée des Egouts de Paris** (p. 220)
- **Musée Grévin** (p. 175)
- **Muséum National d'Histoire Naturelle** (p. 211)
- **Palais de Tokyo** (p. 192)
- **Parc de Bercy** (p. 198)
- **Parc de la Villette** (p. 203)
- **Parc des Buttes Chaumont** (p. 205)
- **Parc Floral** (p. 239)
- **Parc Zoologique de Paris** (p. 198)
- **Philharmonie des Enfants** (p. 269)

FOR TINY TOTS (0–5 YEARS OLD): Paris has many nice **playgrounds** with safe equipment. For precise locations, visit en.parisinfo.com (search "playground"), ask at your hotel, or just follow the strollers. The Jardin du Luxembourg (p. 213) has multiple activities and a large fountain where you can **rent wooden toy sailboats** (for around 8€) and push them around with a long stick. Most large gardens or parks in this book have a **merry-go-round;** visit offi.fr/enfants/maneges-a-paris-4713.html. The **Jardin d'Acclimatation** (see below) also has plenty of attractions for tiny ones (you just have to be over 80cm tall to go on most of the rides).

FOR THE MIDDLE YEARS (6–9 YEARS OLD): This is when it's time to turn to attractions like **Choco Story** (p. 203), the **Cité des Enfants** (p. 203), the **Philharmonie des Enfants** (p. 269), and the **Jardin d'Acclimatation** (see below), and if you are really desperate, there's always **Disneyland Paris** (p. 304), or even better, **Parc Astérix** (p. 306). The **Parc Zoologique de Paris** (p. 198) is a good bet, as is another, smaller **zoo** at the Jardin des Plantes (the **Ménagerie,** p. 206). The revamped Les Halles district has an adventure playground, the **Jardin Nelson Mandela** (1 rue Pierre Lescot), with a trampoline and swings.

FOR THE TWEENS (10–13 YEARS OLD): At this age, the scale can tip both ways, between "not another museum!" and actually getting interested in some of the cultural offerings. A few museums are particularly suited to this age, like the **Musée des Arts et Metiers** (p. 233), and, in particular, the **Cité des Sciences et de l'Industrie** (p. 202). **Boat** or **bike tours** (p. 225) also work for this crew.

Wooden toy sailboats for rent at the Jardin du Luxembourg.

invader: A FAB STREET-ART APP FOR KIDS (AND GROWN-UPS . . .)

Ever heard of anonymous French street artist, Invader? He's famous for sticking his tile-made depictions of pop-culture icons from the 1970s and '80s on monuments, street corners, and curbs all over the world (thus "liberating art from its usual alienators": museums and institutions). The subjects he chooses cover everything from video game characters like Pac-Man, Mario, and Space Invaders (hence the name), to comics heroes like Spiderman and Batman, and famous artists like Picasso. And because it all started in Paris, there are currently over 4,000 of his works in the city's streets, just waiting for you to flash with a fun app called **Flash Invaders** (space-invaders.com/flashinvaders). If your kids are anything like mine, it'll keep them occupied for hours as you walk between attractions. The way it works is this: You download the app, then whenever you see what looks like a space invader creation in the street, you flash it and (if it's made by Invader) get points. The art is all over the city. There's even one on the Eiffel Tower (at the summit on the outdoor platform). There are currently over 400,000 app users around the world, so every time you flash, you get to see where you stand on the scoreboard. If you live in NYC, Miami, San Diego, or LA in the U.S., or in London, Newcastle, or Manchester in the U.K., you can even continue the hunt back home. It's quite addictive and offers whole new ways to see the city.

Jardin d'Acclimatation ♥ AMUSEMENT PARK/GARDEN   You'll see plenty of grandmothers in designer coats at this elegant amusement park, which is adjacent to the swank suburb of Neuilly. There's a farm with some animals, but the main attractions here are the rides, which include bumper cars, merry-go-rounds, and small roller coasters. You have two types of ticket here: Single Ticket entry (Billets Unitaires), which costs just 7€ to get in, but you pay as you go for the rides (*manages;* around 4.50€ each time), which can add up quickly. You may want to point your offspring in the direction of the huge playground, which includes an area where kids can run around under giant sprinklers in the hot weather. Or opt for the all-inclusive Unlimited Pass (Pass Illimité; from 15€ to 39€, depending on the season) which lets you ride everything without paying extra (except for the ponies). In the same area, you'll find a puppet theater (Wed, Sat–Sun, and school holidays 3 and 4pm) where the French puppet Guignol's adventures are presented free of charge. To reach the park from Porte Maillot, take the *Petit Train* (little train; ticket 3.50€) from Allée de Longchamp at the entrance to the Bois de Boulogne.

Bois de Boulogne. jardindacclimatation.fr. **01-40-67-90-85.** Admission 7€ adults and children 80cm and up, 5€ seniors, free for children under the height of 80cm; attractions 4.50€/ticket, 55€ book of 15 tickets. Mon–Tues and Thurs–Fri 11am–6pm; Wed and Sat–Sun and school holidays 10am–7pm. Métro: Sablons or Porte Maillot.

The New Banks of the Seine & Paris Plage

In a bid to make Paris more environmentally and visitor-friendly, portions of the Seine's banks have been turned into pedestrian- and bike-only stretches. The first part covers the area between the Musée d'Orsay to the Pont d'Alma (known as **Les Berges,** or "the embankments"), and since 2017, the quays between Bastille and the Tuileries Gardens have also been embellished with promenades, gardens, cultural spaces, cafes, sports facilities, and picnic areas along a stretch known as the **Rives de Seine.** This is great news for walkers, as it's now possible to stroll between Bastille and the Eiffel Tower (across bridges) without meeting a single car! You can also eat, drink, flirt at one of the bars, walk, or even take a tai chi class at various points along the route. You'll find kids' activities here, too.

Another hugely successful riverside event is now into its second decade: **Paris Plage.** Every year from mid-July to mid-August, tons of sand is shipped in and dumped on the riverbanks to create a fun and funky "beach," complete with beach volleyball, tea dances, concerts, drink stands, and all sorts of excellent silliness. Success has been such that the beach can be found not only on the Voie Georges Pompidou (near the Hôtel de Ville, 4th arrond.) but also along edges of the Bassin de la Villette (19th arrond.), where you can rent electric boats, paddleboats, and canoes. The number of activities and events swells every season; for a complete rundown, visit the city's **Que Faire à Paris (What to Do in Paris)** website: paris.fr/quefaire (then type "Paris Plage").

ACTIVE PARIS

"Working out" is now an important part of Parisian life, with gyms cropping up all over the place. The problem is that nearly all require an annual fee, so they're hard to access as a visitor. However, any enterprising sports enthusiast can easily find places to bike, in-line skate, or run.

Cycling

You can **rent a bike** by the hour in the **Bois de Vincennes** at Lac Daumesnil or Lac des Minimes and in the **Bois de Boulogne** (in front of the Jardin d'Acclimatation or next to the Lac Inferieur [lower lake]). If you are up to the challenge of Parisian traffic and want to cycle around the city, you can try **Vélib'** (the city's wildly popular self-service bike program) and other similar programs (p. 331). For longer-term rentals, try **Paris à Vélo** (parisavelo.fr) or **Bike About Tours** (bikeabouttours.com), also in our Cycling Tours section (p. 228).

Ice Skating

Two **indoor ice-skating rinks** are open to the public: **Espace Glace** at the Espace Sportif Pailleron, 32 rue E. Pailleron, 19th arrond. (pailleron19.com/patinoire; ✆ **01-40-40-27-70;** Métro: Bolivar), open year-round, and **Patinoire AccorHotels Arena,** 222 Quai de Bercy, 12th arrond. (accorarena.com/fr/le-faubourg/patinoire; ✆ **01-58-70-16-75;** Métro: Bercy), open September to

Ice skating at Champs de Mars park.

May. The latter has DJ–hosted soirées until midnight Fridays and Saturdays. In addition, every year **outdoor rinks** are set up from December through February in public spaces; some of the best are often found on the **Champs de Mars** park, at **Trocadéro,** where you can fill up on Eiffel Tower views as you glide, and under the glorious glass roof of the **Grand Palais** (p. 185).

Parks

Bois de Boulogne ♥♥ PARK   In the 7th century, Dagobert, King of the Francs, used to go hunting in the woods that we now know as the Bois de Boulogne; it remained a hunting domain for the kings of France up until Louis XVI, who finally opened it up to the public. Thick stands of trees, broken up by grassy knolls, manicured gardens, and even a lake or two plus several posh restaurants are tucked into this verdant spread. There is even a nice spot for tiny urbanites to unwind: The **Jardin d'Acclimatation** (see above), a large children's garden/amusement park, is a delight for kids of all ages.

Once Louis XVI was beheaded, and the Revolution got underway, the park was ravaged. It wasn't until Napoleon III decided to remodel the entire city in the mid-1800s that the Bois de Boulogne was attended to. Inspired by the English public parks that he had visited during his years of exile, the emperor gave the command to rebuild the park. Over 400,000 trees were planted, and dozens of chalets, pavilions, snack stands, and restaurants were built. A network of roads and trails was laid down totaling 95km (59 miles). Here are a few of its most popular areas:

o The **Parc de Bagatelle** is a park-within-a-park, with a lush **garden,** a small **château** that hosts concerts in the summer (check listing magazines for details), and a **rose garden** with over 1,000 varieties. New varieties are introduced every year in June, during an international rose competition. The

Rowing on lower lake in Bois de Boulogne.

version of the garden you see today was designed by Forestier, a friend of Monet, who was inspired by Impressionism, which is evident in the artfully placed clusters of flowers and plants.

o The **Pré Catelan** is most famous for its elegant and extremely pricey restaurant, but there are plenty of other reasons to come here. This green enclave includes lush lawns, playgrounds, and flowerbeds, as well as the **Jardin Shakespeare,** which attempts to re-create settings from the Bard's plays. Here you'll find the heaths of Macbeth, the Forest of Arden, and the pond where Ophelia meets her watery death.

o The **Jardin d'Acclimatation** is an old-fashioned amusement park, with lots of grassy areas and nifty playgrounds (see above).

In addition to walking, in-line skating, and cycling (**bike rentals** at the edge of the Lac Inferieur and at the Jardin d'Acclimatation), you can **rent a boat** on the lake, **go fishing** in some of the ponds, or take in a horse race at the Longchamp and Auteuil hippodromes (france-galop.com). The spectacular **Fondation Louis Vuitton** (p. 184) is in the park, right next to the Jardin d'Acclimatation.

16th arrond. paris.fr/pages/les-bois-parisiens-4900. Métro: Porte d'Auteuil, Les Sablons, Porte Maillot, or Porte Dauphine.

Bois de Vincennes ♥♥ PARK   This park doesn't have as many gardens and restaurants as its western counterpart, but there is more of a sense of wilderness in this vast patch of greenery on the eastern end of Paris. Endless paths and alleys wind through woods and open fields; this is a great place for a long bike ride or a hike (though stick to the paths; people without homes have set up tents in some parts of the woods). Not that there are just trees here—if rambling isn't your game, there are plenty of other things to do as well. For starters, there is the **Parc Zoologique de Paris** (p. 198), a state-of-the-art zoo. Then there are the remains of a medieval castle, the **Château de Vincennes,** and a large garden in the park, as well as theaters and a hippodrome for those who prefer to sit back and watch the action. In short, Bois de Vincennes has almost as many pleasures as the Bois de Boulogne, if not as much elegance.

A few of the park's high points:

- The **Parc Zoologique de Paris** (aka the Paris Zoo; p. 198).
- The **Parc Floral:** Created in 1969, this modern mix of **flower beds, ponds, picnic areas,** and a fabulous **playground** is a very pleasant place to spend the afternoon, particularly between May and September when the open-air theater holds free music and theater performances (parcfloralde paris.com/fr). In July, the Paris Jazz Festival takes off for 3 weeks, and in most of August and September, the Festival Classique au Vert cooks up a great program of classical music. For the kids, **Guignol puppet shows** (guignolparcfloral.blogspot.com; 4.50€ adults and children) play most Wednesdays, Saturdays, and Sundays at 3 and 4pm, and daily during school holidays.
- The **Château de Vincennes:** It took 12 years to restore this former royal castle (the heart of France's monarchy until Louis XIV decided to move to Versailles in 1682), and the result—an ivory-colored compound with gracious, turreted ramparts—is truly beautiful. You can visit the imposing

Picnicking in Bois de Vincennes.

Château de Vincennes, a medieval castle in Bois de Vincennes.

gracious, turreted ramparts—is truly beautiful. You can visit the imposing **castle keep,** a **Gothic chapel** with 16th-century stained-glass windows, and the multi-turreted **ramparts.** Bring ID and you can borrow an augmented reality pad that shows you what the castle would have looked like in each room in medieval times. For the best views, opt for a guided tour of the keep's upper floors, usually closed to the public (Sun 11am only), though be prepared for a 250-step climb (av. de Paris, 12th arrond.; chateau-vincennes. fr; ✆ **01-48-08-31-20;** 13€ adults, free for children 17 and under; mid-Sept to mid-May daily 10am–5pm, mid-May to mid-Sept daily 10am–6pm; Métro: Château de Vincennes).

You can **rent bikes** in front of either of the two large lakes or on the esplanade by the château or **rent boats** for rowing around the lake. There are several **playgrounds** and you can go on a pony ride. Thoroughbred racing fans can also check out the **Hippodrome Paris-Vincennes** (vincennes-hippodrome.com), famed for French Trotters, who race in harnesses.

Bois de Vincennes, 12th arrond. paris.fr/pages/les-bois-parisiens-4900. Free admission to main park. Metro: Porte Dorée or Château de Vincennes.

SHOPPING

7

Paris has always been the capital of *luxe*. As early as the 16th century, the city was known as the place to go for luxury goods. Over the centuries an entire industry grew up around the whims and whimsies of the French aristocracy. To keep up appearances, nobles spent outrageous amounts of money on sumptuous clothing, opulent homes, and lavish dinner parties for dozens of similarly well-heeled aristocrats. By the 18th century, thousands of merchants and artisans were working full-time to fill the voluminous orders of some 150 grand families, not to mention Louis XIV and his court in Versailles. It's no wonder that even today, the high and mighty, or just plain rich, come here for the best of the best.

Yet there is so much more shopping to explore than those big-name luxury stores. You'll discover boutiques by up-and-coming designers, lesser-known but fab chocolate stores, and wonderful home decoration shops that sell everything from kitchenware to antique knickknacks. Paris is shopaholic heaven, if you know where to go to find your *bonheur* (happiness).

SHOPPING BY AREA

In Paris, each neighborhood has its own personality, and each personality imposes itself on one or two main shopping streets. Aim for the areas with the highest concentration of your kind of store.

The Right Bank

LOUVRE & ÎLE DE LA CITÉ (1ST ARRONDISSEMENT)
The east side of this arrondissement includes the subterranean shopping mall **Forum des Halles** (covered by a *canopé*, a vast metal canopy covering shops like Lego), which is a short stroll from a major shopping strip on the **rue de Rivoli.** Both feature a wide range of affordable international clothing chains. Rue de Rivoli is also home to the revamped **La Samaritaine** department store, which reopened (after being closed for 15 years) with much pomp and circumstance in 2021. As you move west, the atmosphere shifts dramatically. **Rue St-Honoré** is lined with pricey, sophisticated stores, and prices go through the roof at **Place Vendôme,** which probably has the city's highest density of gemstones per square meter. Even if you are too shy to enter Chaumet or Boucheron, you can happily drool over the window displays.

OPÉRA & GRANDS BOULE-VARDS (2ND & 9TH ARRONDISSEMENTS)

Boulevard Haussmann cuts through this neighborhood like a steamship's wake, drawing hordes of shoppers toward the city's two most famous department stores, **Galeries Lafayette** and **Printemps**. These two behemoths have spawned an entire neighborhood full of mass-market shops just north of the boulevard on **rue de Provence, rue de Mogador,** and **rue Caumartin.** To the south and east of the boulevard lies a maze of **19th-century covered shopping arcades** (see "Arcades," p. 243), as well as a market street filled with enticing food stores, **rue de Montorgueil.** If you're still hungry, get your teeth into the glorious food shops along **rue des Martyrs** in trendy SoPi (South Pigalle, just below Montmartre in the 9th).

The grand interior of Samaritaine department store.

THE MARAIS (3RD & 4TH ARRONDISSEMENTS)

Rue des Francs-Bourgeois is crammed with hip boutiques, and you'll find trendy clothing on all the streets around it, even crowding out the kosher restaurants on **rue des Rosiers,** the historic Jewish quarter. Not as pricey as the luxury boutiques to the west, these stores have stylish duds at vaguely attainable prices (and they are open on Sun, a rarity in this city). The streets around **rues de Bretagne** and **Charlot** in the northern Marais are a hotbed of independent French designers.

CHAMPS-ÉLYSÉES, TROCADÉRO & WESTERN PARIS (8TH, 16TH & 17TH ARRONDISSEMENTS)

Dozens of chic and designer boutiques dot the **rue du Faubourg St-Honoré,** but this shopping street pales in comparison to ultra-exclusive **avenue Montaigne.** Paris's most glamorous shopping street is lined with fancy shops, where you float from Dior to Chanel and everything in between. Teens, tourists, and other young things flock to the neighboring **Champs-Élysées** to crowd into hot mass-market flagships and a "concept" version of the **Galeries Lafayette** department store (p. 245). High-end food shops (Maille, Maison de la Truffe) live in the area around the **Madeleine.**

MONTMARTRE (18TH ARRONDISSEMENT)

Small, fairly affordable design, fashion, jewelry, and gourmet food shops fill the winding streets around Montmartre's **Place des Abbesses.** Wander along **rue des Abbesses,** down **rue Houdon,** and up **rue des Martyrs** and discover

arcades: 19TH-CENTURY SHOPPING MALLS

Paris is filled with covered arcades, primarily in the 2nd arrondissement. These lovely iron and glass galleries are 18th- and 19th-century antecedents of today's shopping malls—each one is lined with shops, eateries, and even the occasional hotel.

Built in 1825, the city's longest arcade, **Passage Choiseul,** 40 rue des Petits Champs, 2nd arrond. (Métro: Pyramides), runs from rue des Petits Champs to rue de Saint Augustin and shelters everything from bargain shoe shops to used bookstores to art galleries. The **Passage des Panoramas,** 11 bd. Montmartre, 2nd arrond. (Métro: Grands Boulevards), intersects with several other short arcades (**Feydeau, Montmartre, Saint-Marc,** and **Variétés**), making an interesting warren of bookshops, antiquary shops (stamps, coins, postcards, engravings), and increasingly, trendy restaurants. Across the street is the entrance to **Passage Jouffroy,** 10 bd. Montmartre, 9th arrond. (Métro: Grands Boulevards), lined with collectors' shops featuring figurines, dollhouses, and cinema memorabilia. Pricier gifts are to be found at **Passage Verdeau,** across the street from the back end of Jouffroy, 31 bis rue du Faubourg Montmartre, 9th arrond. (Métro: Grands Boulevards), a particularly atmospheric arcade with stores selling rare books, antique engravings, and vintage photos.

Farther south, near the Palais Royal, is the chic **Galerie Vivienne,** 4 rue des Petits Champs, 2nd arrond. (galerie-vivienne.com; Métro: Bourse), a beautifully restored arcade with a mosaic tile floor and neoclassical arches. Stores here sell high-end clothes, handbags, textiles, and *objets d'art.* **Legrand Filles et Fils** (p. 261) has tons of fine bottles of wine, as well as a wine school and bistro. Toward Les Halles is the very stylish **Passage du Grand Cerf,** 10 rue Dussoubs, 2nd arrond. (Métro: Etienne Marcel), filled with flashy designer jewelry, clothing stores, and interior design agencies.

---

hidden treasures. Part of **rue Lepic** is a fabulous foodie street, brimming with open shop fronts hawking roast chicken, fresh seafood, and wine. Around rue d'Orsel, below Sacré-Coeur, is a collection of fabric markets, the most famous of which, **Marché Saint Pierre,** has lent its name to the entire area.

RÉPUBLIQUE, BASTILLE & EASTERN PARIS (11TH & 12TH ARRONDISSEMENTS)

As **rue du Faubourg St-Antoine** heads east from the Place de la Bastille, you'll find a number of chain stores. The choices get much more interesting along **rue de Charonne,** home to indie clothing brands and goodies. A great place to window-shop is the **Viaduc des Arts,** along avenue Daumesnil: A collection of about 30 specialist craft stores occupies a series of vaulted arches under the **Coulée verte René-Dumont** (formerly Promenade Plantée; p. 233).

BELLEVILLE, CANAL ST-MARTIN & LA VILLETTE (10TH, 19TH & 20TH ARRONDISSEMENTS)

TThe **Canal St-Martin** is a bastion of local bohemian charm, and you can find interesting shops along neighboring streets such as **rue de Marseille, rue Beaurepaire,** the **quai de Valmy,** and **quai de Jemmapes.** Belleville is an interesting place to explore specialty shops from the city's various immigrant communities. Set in the Cité des Sciences museum building (p. 202), **Boom Boom Villette** in Parc de la Villette is a vast modern food hall with stalls and bars (p. 247) and entertainment spots like **iFly** (iflyfrance.com), a free-falling experience in a transparent cylinder.

The Left Bank
LATIN QUARTER (5TH & 13TH ARRONDISSEMENTS)
Chain stores have taken over much of **boulevard St-Michel,** formerly known for its cafes and bookstores. Opposite Notre-Dame, **Shakespeare and Company** (p. 253) draws hordes to its higgledy-piggledy bookshelves, while food enthusiasts flock to the shops at the southern end of **rue Mouffetard. Chinatown** is also here, home to Pan-Asian stores including the famous **Tang Frères** supermarkets (tang-freres.fr), as is Paris's main city-center **IKEA** (on Place d'Italie).

ST-GERMAIN-DES-PRÉS & LUXEMBOURG (6TH ARRONDISSEMENT)
Even if it's technically in the 7th arrondissement, the shopping nerve center of this neighborhood is **Le Bon Marché** (p. 246), the city's most stylish department store. Radiating eastward is a network of streets with delightful shops, ranging from bargain-oriented **rue St-Placide** to chain stores and shoe heaven on **rue de Rennes** to cute boutiques on **rue St-Sulpice, rue du Cherche Midi,** and **rue du Vieux Colombier.** Down toward the Seine, **rue Bonaparte** and **rue Jacob** tempt with classy, if pricey, offerings; you can stop in at the hip **Taschen** (p. 254) bookstore just off **boulevard St-Germain** for gorgeous coffee-table books on pop culture, photography, and architecture.

EIFFEL TOWER & NEARBY (7TH ARRONDISSEMENT)
Most of this area is more focused on culture than shopping, but along its eastern edge, around the **rue du Bac** and **rue du Grenelle,** you'll find expensive

---

Taxes, *Detaxe* & Refunds

Most items purchased in stores are subject to a 20% Value Added Tax (VAT), which is included in the price you pay (and not tacked on at the end like in the U.S.). The good news is that non–E.U. residents who are 16 and over and stay in France less than 6 months can get a refund of VAT (TVA in French) if they spend over 100€ in a single shop offering tax-free shopping over a maximum of 3 days. Ask the retailer for a *bordereau de vente à l'exportation* (export sales invoice, also called a duty-free slip), which will have a bar code. Both you and the shopkeeper sign the slip, and you then choose how you will be reimbursed (credit on card, bank transfer, or cash). At the airport, before you check your luggage, scan the code in one of the "Pablo" terminals (if your airport doesn't have one, just go to the "*détaxe*" or customs counter). Once the form has been approved, head to the reimbursement counter to immediately claim your money. For more info, visit the **Paris Tourist Office** website (paris jetaime.com), and type "detaxe" into the search bar. Or call ✆ **08-00-84-94-40-40** or +33 (0)1-72-40-78-50 from outside mainland France or abroad.

> ### Shopping Hours
>
> In general, shops are open from 9 or 10am to 7 or 8pm. Many larger stores and most supermarkets are open until at least 8:30pm, often 9pm. Many shops close on Monday, and most close on Sunday, which is still considered a day of rest in this country. This is great for family get-togethers but hard on working shoppers, who have only Saturday to get to the stores. Don't shop on Saturday if you can avoid it; the crowds are annoying, to say the least. If you do want to shop on a Sunday, head to the **Champs-Élysées,** the **Marais,** where pretty much every boutique stays open, or the **Carousel du Louvre,** a chic mall below the Louvre museum.
>
> The French tradition of closing for lunch is vanishing in Paris (although it is still very common elsewhere in France). However, smaller, family-run operations still sometimes close between 1 and 3pm.
>
> *Final note:* Many shops close down for 2 or 3 weeks during July or August, when a mass vacation exodus empties out major portions of the city.

designer shops and **Beaupassage** (p. 143), a chic, open-air food arcade. The market street of **rue Cler** also has dozens of food shops.

MONTPARNASSE & NEARBY (14TH & 15TH ARRONDISSEMENTS)

An ugly shopping center in the Tour Montparnasse complex is filled with the usual chain stores, but the more interesting draw here is **rue Daguerre,** a lovely market street filled with food shops that is as cute as rue Cler but less famous. Farther south in the 15th, **rue de Commerce** buzzes with high-street shops and restaurants, and **Beaugrenelle** (p. 247) is a contemporary mall south of the Eiffel Tower, with curated French fashion brands, hip pop-up stores, and a reduced version of Galeries Lafayette.

DEPARTMENT STORES & MALLS
Les Grands Magasins

Known as the *grands magasins* ("big stores"), the great Parisian department stores were born in the late 19th century and have become landmarks. Over the last few years, the city has also adopted another shopping model: the mall. I've listed the best two here, but you could also check out the underground **Forum des Halles** in Châtelet-les-Halles.

Galeries Lafayette ♥♥   This, the most famous of the *grands magasins,* was a humble haberdasher shop when it opened in 1895. Success inspired architectural excess, like the sumptuous Belle Epoque dome under which fashionable goodies are displayed. Here you'll find everything from luxury labels to kids' stuff to stationery. A separate building is just for men (**Lafayette Homme**), and another across the street has housewares (**Lafayette Maison**) as well as a wine and gourmet shop/food court (**Lafayette Gourmet**). A satellite on the Champs-Élysées (no. 60; galerieslafayette.com/m/magasin champs-elysees; ✆ **01-83-65-61-00**) is set up like a huge concept store, with

Pens, stationery, and books for sale at Le Bon Marché.

hundreds of hand-picked fashion labels and an army of stylists ready to help you. 40 bd. Haussmann, 9th arrond. galerieslafayette.com. *©* **01-42-82-34-56.** Métro: Chausée d'Antin-Lafayette.

Le Bon Marché ♥♥♥ Founded by an enterprising milliner in the mid-1800s, this was one of the world's first department stores. Despite its name (*bon marché* means "affordable"), this is one of the most expensive of Paris's *grands magasins*. But it's also one of the best, with beautiful displays and fabulous clothes of every imaginable designer label, both upscale and mid-range. Right next door is its humongous designer supermarket, **La Grande Epicerie Rive Gauche** (p. 260). 24 rue de Sèvres, 7th arrond. ebonmarche.com. *©* **01-44-39-80-00.** Métro: Sèvres–Babylone.

Printemps ♥♥ The glistening domes of this 19th-century building bring to mind a grand hotel on the French Riviera. High fashion gets priority here; four of the seven floors of women's fashion are devoted to designer labels. If you can't handle the crowds inside, you can always enjoy the famed *vitrines,* or **window displays,** which are usually creative and original. Better yet, ride to the top of Printemps Homme (menswear) and munch your way around the food court (Le Printemps du Goût), where every item, from the vodka to the

Les Soldes: Sale Mania

In the name of fair competition, the French government has traditionally put controls on sales. Two times a year, around the second week in January and the second week in July (official dates are posted a couple of weeks in advance on advertisements and store websites, and sales usually last 5 weeks), retailers are allowed to go hog wild and slash prices as far as they want. Recently, free-market forces have loosened the laws, and smaller sales with less drastic reductions can happen year-round. The result is that while many still breathlessly await the seasonal sales, opening day is both mobbed and anticlimactic, and often, the good stuff has already gone. If you must go, unless you're a dedicated masochist, don't shop on a weekend during sale season; you'll be trampled on in crowded, stuffy stores.

truffles, is French; the views over the city's rooftops are more than Instagrammable there, too. 64 bd. Haussmann, 9th arrond. printemps.com. ⓒ **01-71-25-26-01.** Métro: Havre-Caumartin or St-Lazare.

Samaritaine ♥♥   After almost 2 decades of renovations, the famous riverfront department store reopened in 2021 to include a fashion concept store, the biggest beauty studio on the European continent (only Harrods in London has a bigger one), a spa, and even a luxury hotel (Cheval Blanc Paris; p. 60). To differentiate Samaritaine (still lovingly called La Samaritaine by Parisians who remember its iconic pre-renovated incarnation) from the city's other department stores, many brands by French creators are exclusive to the store. 19 rue de la Monnaie, 1st arrond. dfs.com. ⓒ **01-56-81-28-40.** Métro: Hôtel de Ville.

Malls

Beaugrenelle ♥♥   Shopping lovers will enjoy perusing this mall's 100-plus boutiques, pop-up stores, and multiple restaurants in a contemporary structure close to the Eiffel Tower and the Seine. You'll find the usual international suspects (Zara, H&M, and so forth), plus plenty of French and Parisian fashion brands and a Galeries Lafayette outpost. There's also a 10-screen Pathé movie theater. And it's open on Sundays. 12 rue Linois, 15th arrond. beaugrenelle-paris.com. ⓒ **01-53-95-24-00.** Métro: Charles Michel or Bir-Hakeim.

Boom Boom Villette ♥   This mall's about two things only: food and entertainment. Grub-wise expect lots of street food, with dozens of restaurants and pop-up stalls. As for entertainment, there's iFLY, a transparent indoor skydiving tunnel (ifly france.com); a Pathé movie theater; and France's biggest escape game, based on Batman's Gotham City. 30 av. Corentin Cariou, 19th arrond. boom boomvillette.com. ⓒ **01-49-70-83-30.** Métro: Porte de la Villette.

iFLY indoor skydiving tunnel in Boom Boom Villette.

MARKETS: FOOD & FLEA
Food Markets

Marchés (open-air or covered markets) are small universes unto themselves where nothing substantial has changed for centuries. The fishmonger trumpeting the wonders of this morning's catch probably doesn't sound a whole lot different than their ancestor in the Middle Ages (although their dress has changed), and people no doubt assessed the goods in the stalls with the same pitiless stares that they do today. Certainly, hygiene and organization have improved, but the essence of the experience remains the same—a bustling, joyous chaos where you can buy fresh, honest food.

Even if you don't have access to cooking facilities, *marchés* are great places to pick up picnic goodies or just a mid-morning nosh; along with fruit and vegetable vendors, you'll find bakeries, *charcutiers* (sort of like a deli, but better), and other small stands selling homemade jams, honey, or desserts. Some of the covered markets have small cafes and restaurants.

A few marché rules: Unless you see evidence to the contrary, don't pick up your own fruits and vegetables with your hands. Wait until the vendor serves you and point. Also, don't be surprised if the line in front of the stand is an amorphous blob of people; this is the French way. Surprisingly, fistfights are rare; somehow everyone seems to be aware of who came before them, and if they aren't, no one seems to care.

Every arrondissement in the city has a *marché*. Below is a selective list of the best; you can find hours and locations of all on the municipal website (paris.fr/lieux/marches-alimentaires/tous-les-horaires) in French only, or just ask at your hotel.

- **Le Food Market,** street food stalls along bd. de Belleville, 10th arrond. (one Thurs evening per month from 6–10:30pm; lefoodmarket.fr; Métro: Ménilmontant or Couronnes)
- **Marché d'Aligre,** aka Marché Beauvau, with food and antiques; pl. d'Aligre, 12th arrond. (outdoor market Tues–Fri 7:30am–1:30pm, Sat–Sun 7:30am–2.30pm, covered market Tues–Fri 8am–1pm and 4–7:30pm, Sat 8am–7:30pm, Sun 8am–1:30pm; Métro: Ledru Rollin or Gare de Lyon)
- **Marché Bastille,** bd. Richard Lenoir btw. rue Amelot and rue St-Sabin, 11th arrond. (Thurs 7am–1:30pm, Sun 7am–2:30pm; Métro: Bastille)
- **Marché Batignolles,** organic; bd. Batignolles btw. rue de Rome and pl. Clichy, 17th arrond. (Sat 9am–3:00pm; Métro: Rome)
- **Marché Grenelle,** bd. Grenelle btw. rue Lourmel and rue du Commerce, 15th arrond. (Wed 7am–1:30pm, Sun 7am–2:30pm; Métro: Dupleix)
- **Marché Monge,** pl. Monge, 5th arrond. (Wed and Fri 7am–1:30pm, Sun 7am–2:30pm; Métro: Place Monge)
- **Marché Raspail,** bd. Raspail btw. rue de Cherche-Midi and rue de Rennes, 6th arrond. (Tues and Fri 7am–1:30pm, organic Sun 7am–2:30pm; Métro: Rennes)
- **Marché Saxe-Breteuil,** av. du Saxe near pl. de Breteuil, 7th arrond. (Thurs 7am–1:30pm, Sat 7am–2:30pm; Métro: Ségur)

Antiques Fairs & Brocantes

You've probably heard of the famous *marché aux puces,* or **flea market,** at Clignancourt (see below), and if you're an inveterate browser, it's probably worth the visit. But the better deals are to be had at the ***brocantes,*** antiques or jumble sales, held periodically around the city. Though most of what you will find at these sales is sold by professional *brocanteurs* who scout estate sales and other insider sources, your selection will be much wider and the chances

Shopping for antiques at Marché aux Puces de Paris St-Ouen–Clignancourt.

of finding a postwar ceramic pastis pitcher or heirloom lace curtains at affordable prices are much higher than at some of the more overpopulated flea markets. To find out where and when the *brocantes* are happening, a good site to try is paris.fr/pages/brocantes-et-vide-greniers-chiner-a-paris-18730.

Flea Markets

Marché aux Puces de la Porte de Vanves ♥♥ This weekend event is easily the best flea market in Paris—dealers swear by it. There's little in terms of formal antiques and furniture. It's better for old linens, vintage Hermès scarves, toys, costume jewelry, perfume bottles, and bad art. Sadly, dealers tend to up the prices when they hear a foreign accent. Don't be shy; haggle them down. Get there early—the best stuff goes fast. av. Georges-Lafenestre, 14th arrond. pucesdevanves.fr. No phone. Sat–Sun 7am–2pm. Métro: Porte de Vanves.

Marché aux Puces de Paris St-Ouen–Clignancourt ♥ Engulfing the Porte de Clignancourt area at the northern edge of the city, this claims to be the world's largest antiques market. Split into 15 specialty markets, the sprawling, trendy mini-city is visited by thousands of visitors. Although it was once a bargain-hunter's dream, prices now often rival those of regular antiques dealers. Still, hardcore browsers may turn up a treasure. **Note:** Beware of pickpockets. Also, to avoid the tatty markets surrounding Les Puces, get off at Métro Garibaldi. Porte de Clignancourt, 18th arrond. pucesdeparissaintouen.com. No phone. Fri 8am–noon; Sat–Sun 10am–6pm; Mon 11am–5pm. Métro: Porte de Clignancourt or Garibaldi.

RECOMMENDED STORES
Antiques, Art & Collectibles

Drouot ♥♥ This auction house sells a bit of everything, from fine art to vintage and reproduction decorative objects, jewelry, and housewares—many

Antiques shopping at Drouot.

of them affordable. It has been an institution since it opened in 1852, with 15 rooms dedicated to art, as well as collectibles and furniture. Artworks are usually displayed the day before the auction. Anyone can bid; just raise your hand or shout out a price. L'Hôtel Drouot, 9 rue du Drouot, 9th arrond. drouot.com. ✆ **01-48-00-20-00.** Métro: Richelieu-Drouot.

59 Rivoli ♥♥♥ Want some Parisian art to take home? This delightful and quirky artists' studio is a must. Every inch of it—from the frescoed ceilings to the graffiti-clad stairwell—is devoted to creation, with each room devoted to a different artist (there are over 30 of them!). You can find everything from hand-engraved skateboards to sculptures. There are sometimes free concerts Saturday and Sunday evening (Sept–June). There's no other place quite like it in Paris. 59 rue de Rivoli, 1st arrond. 59rivoli.org/homepage. No phone. Métro: Châtelet.

Village St-Paul ♥♥ When you pass through an archway on rue St-Paul, you come upon a lovely village-like enclosure, the remnant of a centuries-old hamlet that was swallowed up by the city. Today, it's a quiet village of antiques dealers and design shops, selling everything from old bistro chairs to vintage lingerie to Iranian kilim rugs. Check the website for the periodic antiques and design fairs. rue St-Paul, 4th arrond. https://parisjetaime.com/eng/culture/le-village-saint-paul-le-marais-p1368. No phone. Métro: St-Paul.

Artist's studio at 59 Rivoli.

Beauty & Perfume

At the airport, you'll be assaulted with **duty-free shops** carrying loads of tax-free perfume; another colony of similar shops is near the Opéra, usually with lines of people waiting outside. But you will most likely get the same tax rebate no matter where you go (p. 244). If you're short on time, seek out one of two huge perfume and makeup chains: the ubiquitous **Marionnaud** (marionnaud.fr) and the user-friendly **Sephora** (sephora.fr). For something more original, try one of the shops listed below.

Village St-Paul in an antiques shopping enclave.

Detaille 1905 ♥ Founded by the Countess of Presle in 1905, this handsome, old-fashioned store offers its own elegant line of *eau de toilette* and other beauty products for both men and women, such as its signature *Baume Automobile,* developed by the countess when she realized (even back then) what pollution can do to your skin. These unique products can only be purchased at the wood-paneled boutique or ordered by phone or online through the shop's website. 10 rue St-Lazare, 9th arrond. detaille.com. ✆ **01-48-78-68-50.** Métro: Notre-Dame-de-Lorette.

Wood-paneled boutique Detaille 1905.

La Station by The Different Company ♥♥ Indeed, something *is* different about this perfume company. This independent operation, founded in 2000, makes its own unique fragrances with mostly natural materials. Signature scents include Osmanthus, Sel de Vétiver, and Rose Poivrée. 10 rue Ferdinand Duval, 4th arrond. lastationtdc.fr. ✆ **01-42-78-19-34.** Métro: St-Paul.

Editions de Parfums Fréderic Malle ♥♥ Master perfumer Fréderic Malle's chic temple to the nose offers a superb range of original fragrances. In his Marais store, evocative-sounding aromas like Noir Epices and Lipstick Rose are displayed in ultramodern wooden structures that look like floating clouds. There are stands at Galeries Lafayette (p. 245), Printemps (p. 246), and Le Bon Marché (p. 246), as well as stores in three other locations: 140 av. Victor Hugo in the 16th arrondissement, 83 rue de Passy in the 16th, and 10 rue Cambon in the 1st. 13 rue des Francs Bourgeois, 4th arrond. fredericmalle.com. ✆ **01-40-09-25-85.** Métro: St-Paul.

Books
ENGLISH BOOKSTORES

Paris's English-language bookshops tend to double as cultural meeting places. Those that have survived the ongoing bookshop crisis are good places to pick up English-language newsletters, chat in English, and attend readings (sometimes by famous authors).

The Abbey Bookshop ♥ Canadians will be happy to find a cozy store that specializes in Canadian authors, as well as other English-language literature. You'll have to squeeze in between the piles of books, but this is a relaxed, welcoming place with good readings and events. 29 rue de la Parcheminerie, 5th arrond. abbeybookshop.org. **01-46-33-16-24.** Métro: St-Michel.

The Abbey Bookshop specializes in Canadian authors.

San Francisco Book Company ♥♥ Centrally located, this shop has a few new books and an excellent stock of used books, including hardback classics, paperback airplane reading, and rare and out-of-print editions. 17 rue Monsieur Le Prince, 6th arrond. sfparis.com. **01-43-29-15-70.** Métro: Odéon.

Sylvia Whitman, owner of Shakespeare and Company.

Sylvia Beach: Mother of the Lost Generation

Born in Baltimore in 1887, **Sylvia Beach** fell in love with Paris early in life and moved there at the end of World War I. A few years later, with the encouragement of her companion, bookshop owner Adrienne Monier, Beach opened **Shakespeare and Company**, a bookstore and lending library specializing in English and American books. For the next 20 years, the shop at 8 rue Dupuytren served as an unofficial welcome center for American and English visitors, particularly literary ones, and specifically those who would later come to be known as members of **"The Lost Generation"**: T. S. Eliot, Ezra Pound, F. Scott Fitzgerald, Gertrude Stein, and Ernest Hemingway. But the one who made the biggest impression, literally, was James Joyce. After his novel Ulysses was banned in both the U.S. and England and no publisher would touch it, Beach courageously published it herself. In February 1922, after endless proofs and corrections by the author, the 1,000 copies arrived in the store and were all snapped up instantaneously. Later, the book became a modern classic, making a mint for its publisher, Random House. Beach never saw a penny but claimed that she didn't mind because she'd have done anything for Joyce and his art. In 1941, during the Nazi occupation of Paris, the contents of the entire bookstore "vanished" overnight (hidden in a vacant apartment in the same building) to avoid confiscation by the Nazis. The books were saved, but Beach spent 6 months in an internment camp. After the war, she returned to Paris, but the bookshop's doors never reopened. The store's memory lives on in its more recent incarnation at 37 rue de la Bûcherie (see Shakespeare and Company).

Shakespeare and Company ♥♥♥ The venerable literary shrine is so popular with tourists that you may have to wait to get in because of the store's limited capacity. Run by the late George Whitman for some 60 years, it's now helmed by his daughter, Sylvia, who was named after Sylvia Beach (she founded the original bookshop in 1919; see box, above). Many legendary writers have stopped in over the decades for a cup of tea; many an aspiring author has camped out in one of the back rooms. Check the website for readings and events. A coffeeshop run by the same people behind **Bob's Juice Bar** (p. 111) is next door and serves wonderful cakes. 37 rue de la Bûcherie, 5th arrond. shakespeareandcompany.com. ✆ **01-43-25-40-93.** Métro/RER: St-Michel–Notre-Dame.

Smith & Son ♥♥♥ Formerly the Paris branch of the English chain, WH Smith, it's now the biggest indie bookstore in the city, and has been around since 1870. Along with its huge range of English-language books and magazines, it hosts signings by famous authors, and harbors a lovely tearoom next to the children's' section, where scones with English cream draw locals and visitors alike. Look out for the shop's stunning fireplace and Domestic Revival–style reliefs. There's even a period stained-glass window of George Washington's coat of arms, and no one really knows why it's there. A second branch is in the Marais now too at 20 rue des Rosiers, 4th arrond. 248 rue de Rivoli, 1st arrond. smithandson.com. ✆ **01-53-45-84-40.** Métro: Concorde.

Smith & Son is Paris's biggest independent bookstore.

The Red Wheelbarrow Bookstore.

The Red Wheelbarrow Bookstore ♥♥♥   In a glorious location opposite the Jardin du Luxembourg, this venerable bookshop shines, not only for its collections (which range from the classics to the best of today's contemporary literature), but also for the knowledge of its staff, who is incredibly well read and enjoys making recommendations. If you're travelling with kids, make a beeline for The Red Balloon, their beautiful bilingual children's bookstore just next-door at no. 9. 11 rue Medicis, 6th arrond. theredwheelbarrowbookstore.com. ✆ **01-42-01-81-47.** RER: Luxembourg.

FRENCH & ENGLISH BOOKSTORES

Galignani ♥♥♥   The oldest English-language bookstore in Paris, this shop has thrived since 1810. Owned by the literary Galignani family, whose ancestor used one of the first printing presses back in 1520, the store is filled with a terrific range of both French and English books, with emphasis on French classics, modern fiction, sociology, and fine arts. 224 rue de Rivoli, 1st arrond. galignani.com. ✆ **01-42-60-76-07.** Métro: Tuileries.

Les Mots à la Bouche ♥   It may have moved from the Marais, but this is still Paris's best-stocked LGBTQ+ bookstore. You can find French- and English-language books as well as gay-info magazines, such as *Têtu*. 37 rue St-Ambroise, 11th arrond. motsbouche.com. ✆ **01-42-78-88-30.** Métro: Rue St-Maur or St-Ambroise.

Taschen ♥   This hip bookstore sells tomes in French and English about art, architecture, fashion, pop culture, and design, catering to those who love coffee-table books and beautiful pictures. The section at the back features framed photos from the books. 2 rue de Buci, 6th arrond. taschen.com. ✆ **01-40-51-79-22.** Métro: Odéon or Mabillon.

Clothing & Shoes

Balibaris ♥♥   Kick-started by a young Parisian fashion entrepreneur, this is where Parisian men go for cool, smart outfits that work just as well on a

Galignani is the oldest English-language bookstore in Paris.

night out as in the office. You'll find classically cut pants and chinos, and denim and suede jackets, along with a spattering of cotton and leather bags. The city has multiple branches (including in Galeries Lafayette [p. 245] and Printemps [p. 246]). 21 rue St Sulpice, 6th arrond. balibaris.com. ✆ **01-43-21-95-79.** Métro: Mabillon or Odéon.

French Trotters ♥   This emporium is the flagship store for this temple of urban chic for men and women. While the original store (30 rue de Charonne, 11th arrond.) features both hot local French labels and the store's own brand of relaxed *branchitude* (hipness), this one sells all that plus housewares, books, and shoes. 128 rue Vieille du Temple, 3rd arrond. frenchtrotters.fr. ✆ **01-44-61-00-14.** Métro: St-Sébastien-Froissart or Files du Calvaire.

Kiliwatch ♥   At this institution for fashion lovers who like to mix vintage garb with brand-new clothes, whole sections are dedicated to anything from the 1960s to the 1990s, as well as a host of hip French men's and women's brands you won't usually find back home. 64 rue Tiquetonne, 2nd arrond. kiliwatch.paris. ✆ **01-42-21-17-37.** Métro: Etienne Marcel.

Make My Lemonade ♥♥   Despite the English name, this independent, affordable women's fashion house is resolutely French. It feels like an urban boudoir and offers beautiful clothes cut to fit women with real curves (think velvet jackets and long flowing floral dresses). Sewing or nail art workshops are sometimes held in the front room. 61 Quai de Valmy, 10th arrond. makemylemonade.com. ✆ **09-67-42-23-97.** Métro: Jacques Bonsergent.

Zadig & Voltaire ♥   I don't know what the philosopher would make of this trendy young French brand, but Voltaire might have appreciated its rock-'n'-roll spirit. Look for perfectly distressed jeans, comfy cashmeres, biker boots, and more, for men, women, and children. Dozens of branches are open around Paris. 1 rue du Vieux Colombier, 6th arrond. zadig-et-voltaire.com. ✆ **01-43-29-18-29.** Métro: St-Sulpice.

CHILDREN'S CLOTHING

Botoù ♥♥ If you're looking for something funky for your children's feet, this is where to start. These cool and colorful shoes will make your kids look like they live in this fun and hip neighborhood (SoPi), with options from goldfish-print sneakers to tiger-print ankle boots. 20 rue Milton, 9th arrond. botou.fr. ✆ **09-83-82-06-58.** Métro: Notre-Dame-de-Lorette.

L'Île aux Fées ♥♥ This boutique's exquisite dresses for little girls are all handmade in Madagascar (the owner's birthplace) and embroidered according to local techniques with pretty flowers and bows. You'll find gorgeous outfits for baby boys, too—mostly 1920s-inspired sailor outfits with puffy shorts and wide-collared tops. Prince Louis, eat your heart out! 66 rue Notre-Dame des Champs, 6th arrond. lileauxfees.com. ✆ **01-43-25-07-59.** Métro: Vavin.

Marie Puce ♥♥ You can dress everyone—from babies to tweens to mums—here. Marie offers easy elegance—especially for tots who need to dress up (at least a little) but can't stand frills. Much of the clothing is 100% made in France. 60 rue du Cherche Midi, 6th arrond. mariepuce.com. ✆ **01-45-48-30-09.** Métro: Sèvres-Babylone or St-Placide.

Handmade girl's clothes at L'Île aux Fées.

Elegant baby clothes at Marie Puce.

LINGERIE

Judging from the number of lingerie stores in even the smallest French towns, it's safe to say that French women *love* underwear. And for good reason—French lingerie is often exquisite.

ERES ♥♥♥ A two-story temple to undies? *Mais oui!* This light-filled bi-level flagship store (with big windows overlooking the Madeleine church; p. 187) is the place to go for slick underwear, swimwear, and lacy home-wear. Prices are steep, but the lingerie is utterly wearable—nay, showoff-able! There are multiple boutiques across Paris, so check the website. 2 rue Tronchet, 8th arrond. eresparis.com. ✆ **01-47-42-28-82.** Métro: Madeleine.

Saint Germain des Slips ♥♥ This is a Left Bank outpost of Le Slip Français, a quirky company (*slip* means "underpants") that makes every undergarment it sells—from men's boxer shorts to women's bras—in France. You can accessorize with bags and T-shirts to match your undies, too. See the website for more locations. 20 rue du Vieux Colombier, 6th arrond. leslipfrancais.fr. ✆ **01-45-38-90-56.** Métro: St-Sulpice.

VINTAGE CLOTHING

Some Parisian vintage shops sell designer clothing; others scour the U.S., U.K., and other European countries for the everyday retro garb they sell. Unless you aim for the designer category, it can be hit-and-miss. The Marais has several excellent vintage boutiques, so it's a good place to start.

Didier Ludot ♥ An homage to the haute couture of yesteryear has fancy frocks created between 1900 and 1980. This swank boutique has been around for over 50 years and is more of an antiques shop than a clothing store. 24 galerie de Montpensier, in the arcades of the Palais Royal, 1st arrond. instagram.com/didierludot. ✆ **01-42-96-06-56.** Métro: Palais-Royal–Musée du Louvre.

Free'p'Star ♥ Vintage hunters will delight in terrific finds at this trendy store in the heart of the Marais, which specializes in funky fashions from yesteryear. Some of it is tatty, but real bargains can certainly be had. There are five branches, two of the best being 52 and 61 rue de la Verrerie, also in the 4th arrondissement. 20 rue de Rivoli, 4th arrond. freepstar.fr. ✆ **01-42-77-63-43.** Métro: St-Paul.

Lapin Boutique ♥♥ This vintage store is for lovers of the 1960s and '70s, featuring everything from upcycled 1970s strapless dresses and leather satchels to 1960s hats, and lacey tops and blazers. It carries some accessories too. 9 rue Oberkampf, 11th arrond. lapinboutique.com. No phone. Métro: Filles du Calvaire or Oberkampf.

Concept Stores

Trendiness oozes from the walls of all of Paris's concept stores—basically one-stop boutiques selling curated items by different designers and brands. Some have a cult following; most include a hip coffee shop for perusing your purchases post-splurge.

Bü ♥ A cross between IKEA and an upscale hardware store, this Ali Baba's cave of treasures, this enigmatically named store (it's French, not

Lapin Boutique.

Scandinavian) has shelves upon shelves of reasonably priced housewares, stationery, leather handbags, luggage, and toys, as well as regional edibles. 45 rue Jussieu, 5th arrond. www.bu-store.com. ✆ **01-40-56-33-22.** Métro: Jussieu or Cardinal-Lemoine.

European-made housewares and gifts at Landline.

Empreintes ♥♥ French arts and crafts take center stage in this glorious, four-story space that showcases handmade jewelry, tableware, furniture, lighting, and *objets d'art*. Prices start under 70€, with some items as low as 20€. A projection room shows arts and crafts–themed movies. 5 rue de Picardie, 3rd arrond. empreintes-paris.com. ✆ **01-40-09-53-80.** Métro: Filles du Calvaire or Temple.

Landline ♥♥♥ If you only have a chance to go to one boutique in Paris, make it this gorgeous general supply store in the Boho 11th arrondissement. Created by Franco-American Caroline Morrison, it's the place to find exquisite, built-to-last items from Europe to use at home (pans, knives, terra cotta ceramics by Parisian artist Katherine Oh) and on your body (organic face creams, artisan wool vests, Venetian velvet slippers). There are toys, too—glorious wooden ones that will last a lifetime. And a whole section on brushes—including a special wooden brush just for dusting bookcases. Who'd have thought? I can't stress how wonderful this place is! 107 ave Parmentier, 11th arrond. landlineparis.com. ✆ **01-43-55-83-61.** Métro: Parmentier or Goncourt.

Merci ♥♥ Set in a former factory on the edge of the Marais, Merci offers hand-picked designer brands mixed with vintage one-offs on the second floor, with cool kitchenware in the basement. Jewelry, linen, and stationery are other favorites here. Sip coffee in one of the cafes. 111 bd. de Beaumarchais, 3rd arrond. merci-merci.com. ✆ **01-42-77-00-33.** Métro: Filles du Calvaire.

Food & Drink
CHOCOLATE & GATEAUX
A La Mère de Famille ♥ Founded in 1761, this piece of Parisian history has committed its soul to candies and chocolates à l'ancienne. You'll find classic chocolates as well as old-fashioned bonbons like *berlingots,* lemon drops, caramels, and jellied fruits. Eleven other locations are around the city. 35 rue du Faubourg Montmartre, 9th arrond. lameredefamille.com. ✆ **01-47-70-83-69.** Métro: Grands Boulevards.

François Pralus ♥♥♥ Pralus owns a cacao plantation in Madagascar, ensuring the extraordinary quality of every bean that goes into his chocolate, which comes in "crus" (vintages), rather like wine, each wrapped in colorful paper like exquisite parcels. Be sure to try the *barre infernale—*melt-in-your-mouth bars of dark chocolate–encased praline. The pink-dotted *Praluline* is the most delicious, buttery brioche you may ever taste. This is one of three boutiques in Paris. 35 rue Rambuteau, 4th arrond. chocolats-pralus.com. ✆ **01-57-40-84-55.** Métro: Rambuteau.

Patisserie Mélilot ♥♥ Off the beaten tourist track in the 20th arr. Patisserie Mélilot is an absolute find —a tiny shop run by Sabrina, who does everything herself, from baking in the morning to selling her wares in the afternoon (hence the boutique's only open from 4–7pm), Everything she makes—from the gem-like choux pastries filled with pistachio cream to the chocolate-peanut tarts and sweetclover flan (custard tart) is out of this world, and made with locally sourced products to boot. Be prepared to line up. 50 rue de la Réunion, 20th arrond. patisseriemelilot.fr. ✆ **01-82-28-14-35.** Métro: Buzenval.

Cream-filled pastries at Patisserie Mélilot.

Patrick Roger ♥♥ Is that a life-size chocolate orangutan in the window? Oh yes, it is. Not only is Patrick Roger a master chocolatier, but he is also a sculptor who uses his medium to convey his message. One year he found inspiration in elephants, and in the past, he's tackled subjects as challenging as a 4m-tall (13-ft.) chocolate version of Rodin's *Balzac*. He has seven Parisian shops. 108 bd. St-Germain, 6th arrond. patrickroger.com. ✆ **01-43-28-38-42.** Métro: Odéon.

Candies and chocolates at historic A La Mère de Famille.

259

SPECIALTY GROCERIES

Eataly ♥♥♥   France and Italy have a mutual admiration for each other's cuisine, and nowhere is this more obvious than in this fabulous, three-story emporium of Italian food. Artisanal products made both in France and Italy line the shelves, alongside market counters of cheese and cold meats, and multiple restaurants, where you can pull up a chair and sample the food with a glass of Italian wine. 37 rue Sainte-Croix de la Brettonerie, 4th arrond. eataly.fr. ✆ **01-83-65-81-00.** Métro: Hôtel-de-Ville.

La Grande Epicerie Rive Gauche ♥♥   This huge gourmet grocery mecca, an outgrowth of Le Bon Marché department store (p. 246), stocks every gourmet substance you could possibly imagine, and many that you couldn't. Sculpted sugar cubes, designer mineral waters, truffle-balsamic vinegar, pink salt from the Himalayas—need we go on? It also has an excellent (if expensive) takeout department if you are looking for picnic items. A second address is at 80 rue de Passy in the 16th. 38 rue de Sèvres, 7th arrond. lagrandeepicerie.fr. ✆ **01-44-39-81-00.** Métro: Sèvres-Babylone.

Maille ♥   True, you can find Maille gourmet mustard all over the place, but you can only get it hand-pumped here in the official boutique. Pumped fresh into a stoneware pot and sealed with a cork, it has an altogether different taste, and it is delicious. Choose from mustard made with a dash of Chablis, Chardonnay, Sauternes, or splurge on Chablis with truffle bits. 6 pl. de la Madeleine, 8th arrond. maille.com. ✆ **01-40-15-06-00.** Métro: Madeleine.

La Cave at La Grande Epicerie Rive Gauche.

WINES

Wine in France is stunningly cheap. In Paris you can buy a bottle of something extremely pleasant for as little as 5€ or 6€. But before you start planning to stock your wine cellar back home, consider this sad truth: Most non-E.U. countries won't let you bring back much more than a bottle or two (p. 335). Wine stores abound, and even the humblest of them are generally staffed by knowledgeable wine lovers who will be glad to help you find the perfect bottle to celebrate your Parisian adventure.

Cave des Abbesses ♥ This small wine shop/wine bar has been serving residents of Montmartre since 1986. Not only will the staff help you muddle through excellent vintages, but you can also sample a few and nibble on cheese and charcuterie (open until 10:30pm). 43 rue des Abbesses, 18th arrond. cavesbourdin.fr. ⓒ **01-42-52-81-54.** Métro: Abbesses.

Legrand Filles et Fils ♥♥ More than just a wine store, this is a place where you can learn everything there is to know about the sacred grape. The store has a dedicated, well-informed staff and a huge stock of wines; hosts wine tastings and classes; and also sells books and paraphernalia. It's in the glamorous Galerie Vivienne (p. 243). 1 rue de la Banque, 2nd arrond. caves-legrand.com. ⓒ **01-42-60-07-12.** Métro: Bourse.

Wine shopping at Legrand Filles et Fils.

Les Domaines Qui Montent ♥♥♥ French wine drinkers know that you'll get the best prices when you buy direct at a vineyard. In an attempt to make these prices available to urbanites, this association of wine producers offers a vast selection of *vins du producteur*, wines that come from small vineyards where the emphasis is on quality, not quantity. Prices are very good, and if you come by at lunchtime, you can open a bottle and eat a meal at their *table d'hôte* (18.90€ for two courses). They have five other locations across the city. 22 rue Cardinet, 17th arrond. lesdomainesquimontent.com. ⓒ **01-42-27-63-96.** Métro: Courcelles or Wagram.

Gifts & Souvenirs

Arty Dandy ♥♥ Dedicated to selling French and European brands (especially when they're eco-friendly), this chic shop has a stock that might include sheepskin wine coolers, handmade ceramics and jewelry, funky clothes, and all sorts of accessories you never knew existed. There's another branch in the Marais at 43 rue de Turenne, 3rd arrond. *1 rue Furstemberg, 6th arrond. artydanydyofficiel.com. ℂ **01-43-54-00-36.** Métro: Mabillon.*

Fnac ♥   A huge chain that sells a combination of books, music, electronics, and tickets to shows and museums, Fnac (pronounced "fnack") has branches all over the city. This is an ideal spot if you need something for your computer, smartphone, or camera. *136 rue de Rennes, 6th arrond. fnac.com. ℂ **09-69-32-43-34.** Métro: St-Placide.*

Galerie Portfolio ♥   Tucked in a delightful covered passage, this hybrid gallery-cum-boutique is the place to come for stunning Paris-themed photos. Some of them are old black and white; others are quirky and contemporary. There are vintage posters too. Everything would look good on a wall at home. *55 passage Jouffroy, 9th arrond. galerieportfolio.com. ℂ **01-56-92-04-47.** Métro: Grands Boulevards.*

Housewares, Kitchen & Decoration

E. Dehillerin ♥♥♥   This venerable store near Les Halles is where chefs come to buy their kitchen material. E. Dehillerin sells everything from copper pans and ergonomic zesters, fish-bone tweezers, whipped cream siphons, and plenty of other things you never knew you needed. Keep track of what you want to buy on a piece of paper, then pay at the till, where you'll be handed your order. Prices are displayed without VAT, which is added when you pay. *18 and 20 rue Coquillère, 1st arrond. edehillerin.fr. ℂ **01-42-36-53-13.** Métro/RER: Les Halles.*

Fleux ♥♥♥   Bold linens and bright tableware are sold in this household store (next-door to Eataly p. 260), along with anything else gorgeous that may embellish your home—lamps, mirror, clocks, platters, and vases. The beautiful tea towels, placemats, and tablecloths here make great gifts and pack easily. Two other boutiques on the same street (nos. 40 and 52) cover everything from art and crafts to kids toys and accessories. *39 rue Sainte-Croix de la Bretonnerie, 4th arrond. fleux.com. ℂ **01-89-97-66-34.** Métro: Hôtel de Ville.*

Copper pans at E. Dehillerin.

Jewelry & Accessories

Bijoux Burma ♥   Pretend you are a princess with these excellent copies of the kind of spectacular pieces you could never afford. These famous, high-quality synthetic jewels, set in gold, silver, or vermeil, are some of the best fakes around. All four branches are strategically placed in the fanciest shopping neighborhoods. 50 rue François 1er, 8th arrond. bijouxburma.com. ⓒ **01-47-23-70-93.** Métro: Franklin-D-Roosevelt.

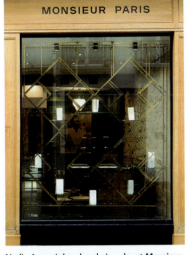

Monsieur ♥♥   Unique jewelry at reasonable prices handmade in an atelier in the Marais—who could ask for more? Nadia Azoug is known for her beautiful, delicate Art Deco–inspired pieces, made with gold, silver, semiprecious stones, and the occasional set of diamonds. The designs are very light and elegant, and many are unisex. Prices start at a very affordable 80€. 53 rue Charlot, 3rd arrond. monsieur-paris.com. ⓒ **06-50-02-01-75.** Métro: Filles du Calvaire.

Nadia Azoug's handmade jewelry at Monsieur.

WHITE bIRD ♥♥   If you are looking for a unique engagement ring or present for your sweetheart, this is a good bet. The low-key store offers a terrific selection of jewelry made by talented independent craftspeople and

WHITE bIRD jewelry store.

designers. A second store is at 7 bd. des Filles du Calvaire, and a third at 62 rue des Saint-Pères. 38 rue du Mont Thabor, 1st arrond. whitebirdjewellery.com. ✆ **01-58-62-25-86.** Métro: Concorde.

Toys & Games

Au Nain Bleu ♥ The venerable "Blue Dwarf" has been selling children's toys since 1836. You won't find anything plastic or electronic here—just hand-picked European cuddly teddies, dolls, pirate ships, trucks, costumes, and wooden puppets. 14 rue St. Roch, 1st arrond. aunainbleu.com. ✆ **09-75-89-28-43.** Métro: Tuileries.

La Cabane Enchantée ♥♥ This vintage-style establishment is a marvelous example of the quintessential

La Cabane Enchantée is an old-school toy store.

French toy store. Wooden toys, scale models, musical instruments, dolls, board games, stuffed animals, costumes—in short, everything that delights and enchants and doesn't need batteries. 20 av. Félix Faure, 15th arrond. facebook.com/lilibullelafeequifabulle. ✆ **01-45-58-17-44.** Métro: Félix Faure.

ENTERTAINMENT & NIGHTLIFE

Paris blooms at night. Its magnificent monuments and buildings become even more beautiful when they're cloaked in their evening illuminations. Simply walking around town can be an excellent night out, but the city is also a treasure trove of rich nightlife offerings. Choose from bars and clubs from chic to shaggy, sublime theater and dance performances, top-class orchestras, and scores of cinemas and art-house movie theaters.

While Paris isn't a 24-hour town like some international capitals, and many neighborhoods may seem pretty quiet after sundown, you will still have plenty of places to go if you are ready for a night out. Below is a selection of some of the better entertainment options, from drinking hot spots to sports venues.

GETTING TICKETS Many hotels will help you get tickets, and most venues offer reservations online, some with apps to download your ticket onto your phone. The tourist office also runs an online ticket service for a selection of shows (parisjetaime.com/eng/tickets). Otherwise, one of the easiest ways to buy tickets is at **Fnac** (p. 262), the giant bookstore/music chain (follow the signs to the "Billeterie"). You can also **order your tickets online** in English at fnactickets.com or **by phone** at ⓒ **01-41-57-32-19. Ticketmaster.fr** offers a similar service.

Discount hunters can stand in line at one of the city's two **half-price ticket booths,** run by Le Kiosque Théâtre (kiosqueculture.com). The main one is on the west side of the Madeleine (facing 15 pl. de la Madeleine, exit rue Tronchet from the Madeleine Métro stop; Tues–Sat 12:30–2:30pm and 3–7:30pm, Sun 12:30–3:45pm). The second is close to the Eiffel Tower (101 quai Jacques Chirac, exit Bir-Hakeim Métro stop, then facing the Seine turn right; Tues–Sat 12:30–6:30pm; Sun 12:30–3:45pm). Plenty of ticket discounts can also be had at **BilletRéduc,** billetreduc.com (in French).

THEATER

Paris has dozens of theaters, most of which have something going on almost every night. The catch here is, almost all of it is in French. But even if you can't spit out much more than *bonjour*, you

> **Finding Out What's On**
>
> **Sortir à Paris** (sortiraparis.com) lists everything from plays and festivals to concerts and movie screenings in English. If you can read French, two other websites to try are **l'Officiel des Spectacles** (offi.fr) and **Télérama** (telerama.fr). Or for the latest info about live music, try **Lylo** (lylo.fr), also in French. By the way, if you see a sign at a theater or on an events website that says *location*, that means "box office," not location.

have options, including musicals at the **Lido 2 Paris** (the new incarnation of the former Lido cabaret; p. 267) and a few English-language shows (see "Shows in English," p. 268). Alternatively, you can opt for one of the many avant-garde offerings at theaters like **Théâtre National de Chaillot** (p. 268) or **Théâtre de la Ville** (p. 267), where the shows combine dance, theater, and images, and often don't really need translation.

Comédie-Française ♥♥ In 1680, Louis XIV announced the birth of a company of actors, chosen by himself, with the aim of "making theater productions more perfect." More than 300 years later, it is still considered the crème de la crème of the French theater scene. In addition to the gorgeous main theater (**Salle Richelieu**), the company presents its offerings in two other theaters: **Théâtre du Vieux Colombier,** 21 rue du Vieux Colombier, 6th arrond. (Métro: St-Sulpice or Sèvres–Babylone), and the smaller **Studio-Théâtre,** Galerie du Carrousel du Louvre, under the Pyramid, 99 rue de Rivoli, 1st arrond. (Métro: Palais Royal–Musée du Louvre). pl. Colette, 1st arrond. comedie-francaise.fr. ⓒ **01-44-58-15-15.** Métro: Palais-Royal–Musée du Louvre.

Odéon, Théâtre de l'Europe ♥ Less venerable and more modern, this grand theater presents both new plays and old classics, but even the classics usually get a modern twist. You can see lots of cutting-edge pieces here, including several from other European countries (hence the moniker "Théâtre de l'Europe"). Foreign productions are supertitled, in French, always, but sometimes also in English. The Odéon's second space, **Ateliers Berthier,** 1 rue André Suarès, 17th arrond. (Métro: Porte de Clichy), presents smaller-scale productions. pl. de l'Odéon, 6th arrond. theatre-odeon.eu. ⓒ **01-44-85-40-40.** Métro: Odéon.

LANDMARK MULTIUSE VENUES

La Seine Musicale ♥♥♥ This architectural marvel sits on an island next to the western suburb of Boulogne-Billancourt like a futuristic cruise ship. The complex includes recording studios, restaurants, a garden, and multiple top-notch concert spaces catering to classical music, dance, pop, musical comedies, and other events. The classical music hall is encased in a huge, globe-shaped structure protected by an enormous photovoltaic sail that slowly rotates around the globe, screening it from the sun and producing solar energy. It's a bit of a trek to get here, but it will be a concert experience you won't soon forget. Ile de Seguin, Boulogne-Billancourt. laseinemusicale.com. ⓒ **01-74-34-54-00.** Métro: Pont de Sèvres, then a 10-min. walk.

Lido 2 Paris ♥♥♥ The Lido on the Champs-Élysées was once one of the city's most famous cabarets—a kitschy place of lip-syncing, feather-clad girls and fancy footwork. Today, the fancy footwork remains, but the rest has been replaced by a different art form: musical theater. In English! Lido is now the place to see raucous shows that have previously included *Cabaret, A Funny Thing Happened on the Way to the Forum,* and the *Rocky Horror Picture Show* and *Hello Dolly.* Book well ahead for tickets, and expect to get to know your neighbors well: The room still has an intimate cabaret feel, with small, round tables packed tightly together on raised platforms. 116 ave des Champs-Élysées, 8th arrond. lido2paris.com. ⓒ **01-55-33-45-50.** Métro: George V.

The performing arts venue La Seine Musicale, located on Seguin Island.

Stade de France ♥♥♥ In the nearby suburb of Saint-Denis, this vast stadium is first and foremost for sports, hosting national and international soccer and rugby games. But it's also one of France's most prestigious concert venues, drawing megastars like Bruno Mars, Ed Sheeran, Beyoncé, and Linkin Park. If you're with sports-mad kids, the daytime guided tours run by Cultival (some in English; cultival.fr) are worth the 90 minutes, taking you into the locker rooms and other places usually off-limits (from 16€ adults, 11€ children 5–18, free for children 4 and under). stadefrance.com. ⓒ **01-73-03-60-03.** Métro: Saint-Denis Porte de Paris. RER B: La Plaine Stade de France.

A Funny Thing Happened on the Way to the Forum at Lido 2 Paris.

Théâtre de la Ville ♥♥ It's hard to say which lineup is the most impressive here: theater (new and recent authors), dance (modern dance companies, such as Anne Teresa De Keersmaeker and Lucinda Childs), or music (mostly young stars of the classical music scene). A lot of international productions

> **Shows in English**
>
> English-language performances are rare (although see **Lido 2 Paris** on p. 267 and Odéon, Théatre de l'Europe p. 266), but there are a few comedy nights that are worth a detour. One of the best stand-up performers is **Paul Taylor** (paultaylorcomedy.com) who plays at numerous theaters and even fills up big concert venues like the Zenith (le-zenith.com). Another excellent one is **Sebastien Marx** (sebmarx.com/en), who performs in both English and French (check his website for details of when and where), sometimes alongside multiple local comics and the occasional international star. Also look out for *How to Become a Parisian in One Hour* (at Théatre des Nouveautés; reservations at oliviergiraud.com), a one-person show written by Olivier Giraud, a Frenchman who spent several years in the U.S., and **Sarah Donnelly** (sarahdcomedy.com) whose stand-up show plays at multiple theaters. For open-mic nights, check the **Comedy in Paris** website (comedyinparis.com). And if you're looking for "theater" proper, an excellent English-language box-office service is **Theatre in Paris** (theatreinparis.com), with tickets to multiple shows offering English supertitles.

stop by here on tour. There are two more addresses: at 31 rue des Abbesses, 18th arrond., and Espace Cardin, 1 av. Gabriel, 8th arrond. 2 place du Châtelet, 4th arrond. theatredelaville-paris.com. ☏ **01-42-74-22-77.** Métro: Châtelet.

Théâtre du Châtelet ♥♥   Specializing in all that is big and splashy, this lovely 19th-century theater hosts international orchestras and contemporary dance companies, as well as revivals of musical-theater classics (usually in their original language). Previous biggies have included *West Side Story* and *Les Misérables*. 1 pl. du Châtelet, 1st arrond. chatelet.com. ☏ **01-40-28-28-40.** Métro: Châtelet.

Théâtre National de Chaillot ♥♥   Dance and theater are on equal footing at this beautiful Art Deco theater in the Palais de Chaillot, where contemporary choreographers and theater directors share a jam-packed program. Dance programs often include video and text, and theater productions often incorporate the abstract. 1 pl. du Trocadéro, 16th arrond. theatre-chaillot.fr. ☏ **01-53-65-30-00.** Métro: Trocadéro.

OPERA & CLASSICAL MUSIC

Opéra Comique/Salle Favart ♥♥   For a lighter take on opera, try this architectural puff pastry filled with operettas. Created in 1714 for theatrical performances that included songs, the Opéra Comique endured several fires before finally settling down in a beautiful 19th-century theater. It's an excellent opportunity to enjoy both history and music in a splendid setting. Works by 19th-century composer Jacques Offenbach are nearly always on the program. 5 rue Favart, 2nd arrond. opera-comique.com. ☏ **01-70-23-01-31.** Métro: Richelieu–Drouot or Quatre-Septembre.

Opéra de Paris ♥♥♥   This mighty operation includes both the **Palais Garnier,** pl. de l'Opéra, 9th arrond. (an attraction in itself; p. 176) and the

Ben Duke dance company at Théâtre de la Ville.

Opéra Bastille, pl. de la Bastille, 12th arrond., a slate-colored behemoth that has loomed over the Place de la Bastille since 1989. In theory, more operas are performed at Bastille, which has more space and supposedly better acoustics. The Garnier, home of the **Ballet de l'Opéra National de Paris,** focuses more on dance, but you can see either at both. The opera program sticks pretty much to the classics, while the ballet offerings are becoming more adventurous. Subtitles are often in English. operadeparis.fr. © **08-92-89-90-90** (.35€/min.); from outside France, +33 (0)1-71-25-24-23.

Philharmonie de Paris ♥♥♥   Hovering over La Villette like a visiting spaceship, this mega venue seats 2,400 spectators and serves as the home of the Orchestre de Paris. Yet another creation of uber-architect Jean Nouvel, this silvery apparition also encompasses a music museum and other performance spaces in the adjacent **Cité de la Musique** building, as well as a nifty cafe and restaurant. In keeping with La Villette's policy of making culture accessible to all, the season includes symphonic and choral concerts, as well as

---

Dance Performances

Paris is the nation's dance capital, and most of the country's best companies are based here, including the phenomenal **Ballet de l'Opéra National de Paris** (see "Opéra de Paris," p. 268). Top French choreographers like Angelin Preljoçaj, Blanca Li, and José Montalvo have produced here, as well as other European stars like Sidi Larbi Cherkaoui and Mats Ek. Two of the biggest dance venues are **Théâtre National de Chaillot** (p. 268) and **Théâtre de la Ville** (p. 267).

performances for young people, families, and audiences that don't usually find themselves in concert halls (these book up fast). The Cité de la Musique complex offers a wide range of music options from classical to contemporary to jazz, and a good dose of the offbeat and unexpected. Highlights include young musicians and rising stars; small orchestras and chamber musicians also show up on the program. 221 av. Jean-Jaurès, 19th arrond. philharmoniedeparis.fr. ⓒ **01-44-84-44-84.** Métro: Porte de Pantin.

CABARET & CHANSON

At the end of the 19th century, cabarets and music halls opened in Montmartre, frequented by oddballs and artists, as well as aristocrats and bourgeoisie looking for a good time. These nightclubs offered an offbeat reflection of the times: Singers like Aristide Bruand would sing about the life of the destitute, and sharp political satire would share the stage with cheeky dancing girls dancing that new step, the can-can. Those days are long gone. There is nothing particularly Parisian, or even French, about cabarets anymore. Today's audiences are likely to arrive in tour buses, and contemporary shows are more Vegas than Paris. What you will see here is a lot of scenic razzmatazz and many sublime female bodies, mostly *torse nue* (topless).

If music's your thing, try "chanson" instead—those peculiarly melody-challenged songs that Edith Piaf sang. If you don't understand the words, it can be hard to understand why so many French people get all misty-eyed when they listen to this music. Each song is a poem set to music; in fact, some lyrics are the works of famous French authors. Whether it's cabaret or chanson you're looking for, these places will tick your boxes, albeit with a large dose of cliché.

Moulin Rouge ♥ When it opened in 1889, the Moulin Rouge was the talk of the town, and its huge dance floor, multiple mirrors, and floral garden inspired painters like Toulouse-Lautrec. In later decades, legendary French singers like Charles Trenet and Charles Aznavour regularly wowed the crowds. Times have changed. Today's Moulin Rouge, with its *Féerie* show, relies heavily on lip-syncing and prerecorded music, backed by dozens of be-feathered long-legged Doriss Girls. Be prepared for plenty of glitz and not a whole lot else. Though its rooftop bar, Le Toit, set behind the iconic windmill (part of its Machine du Moulin Rouge

The Moulin Rouge, a Montmartre icon.

nightclub p. 278), is an atmospheric spot for a glass or two (p. 281). 82 bd. Clichy, pl. Blanche, 18th arrond. moulinrouge.fr. ⓒ **01-53-09-82-82.** Show only 118€–158€; show with dinner 255€–270€. Métro: Blanche.

The Crazy Horse ♥   This temple to "The Art of the Nude" presents an erotic dance show with artistic aspirations. Be advised that unlike the other shows, this one is known for what the girls *aren't* wearing. The performers, who slither, swagger, and lip-sync with panache, have names like Zula Zazou and Nooka Karamel. *Note:* While it has no dining on-site, it has honestly-priced dinner-show packages with nearby Asian fusion restaurant Ginger (11 rue de la Tremoille, 8th arrond.; ginger-paris.com). For instance, an average three-course meal at Ginger costs around 70€. The show alone is 115€. Separately, you'd pay 185€, whereas the dinner and show packages start at 180€. 12 av. George V, 8th arrond. lecrazyhorseparis.com. ⓒ **01-47-23-32-32.** 119€ show only; from 139€ show and champagne; show plus dinner packages 185€–365€. Métro: George V or Alma Marceau.

MOVIES

With over 400 movie screens and hundreds of films on offer every week, Paris is the cinephile capital of the world. The art-house cinemas specialize in rare films, old classics, and independent works. You can find listings of both mainstream and art-house theaters online at **Allocine** (allocine.fr). Many of the mainstream movies shown in the big chain movie theaters are dubbed in French (v.f., or *version française*). If you want to see a mainstream English-language film, make sure you find one in VOST (*version orginale sous-titrée*, subtitled); cinema companies **MK2** (mk2.com) and **UGC** (UGC.fr) will nearly always be showing an English-language movie. Or check out **Lost in Frenchlation** (lostinfrenchlation.com), a film society that organizes three to four monthly screenings of French movies with English subtitles.

Some of the most famous art houses include **Le Champo, Reflet Medecis,** and **Ecoles Cinéma Club,** all in the Latin Quarter. The most scandalous is **Studio 28,** 10 rue Tholozé, 18th arrond. (cinema-studio28.fr; ⓒ **01-46-06-47-45;** Métro: Blanche or Abbesses), where Luis Buñuel's polemical 1930 movie, *L'Age d'Or,* was censored after only two showings here. One of the best-looking art-house theaters is the **Louxor,** 170 bd. Magenta, 10th arrond. (cinemalouxor.fr; ⓒ **01-44-63-96-96;** Métro: Barbès-Rochechouart), a gorgeous restored, neo-Egyptian 1920s movie palace.

In addition to regular movie theaters, two giant **cinema archives** have their own theaters and programs. The first is the **Forum des Images,** Forum des Halles, Porte St-Eustache, 1st arrond. (forumdesimages.fr; ⓒ **01-44-76-63-00;** Métro: Châtelet–Les Halles), which has a bank of over 7,500 films, including thousands that feature Paris as either the subject or the setting. The other is the **Fondation Jérôme Seydoux-Pathé,** 75 av. des Gobelins, 13th arrond. (fondation-jeromeseydoux-pathe.com; ⓒ **01-83-79-18-96;** Métro: Place d'Italie), which specializes in film history and regularly screens silent films accompanied by live pianists.

LIVE ROCK, JAZZ, ELECTRO & MORE

Paris has a wide range of places to hear live music, from tiny medieval basements to huge modern concert venues. Whatever your musical tastes, you are bound to enjoy your outing: Not only do many of the world's greatest musicians swing through the city on a regular basis, but you can't beat the walk to the nightclub/bar/theater with the lights of Paris twinkling in the background.

Live Music
JAZZ CLUBS

Paris has been a fan of jazz from its beginnings, and many legendary performers like Sidney Bechet and Kenny Clark made the city their home. Still a haven for jazz musicians and fans of all stripes, Paris boasts dozens of places to duck into and listen to a good set or two. Some of the best are listed here.

Baiser Salé ♥♥   Some of the biggest Franco-African jazz stars, like Richard Bona and Angelique Kidjo, got their start here, and the program still highlights the best in African, Caribbean, and Asian jazz, as well as French jazz. Regular jam sessions are on Sundays. 58 rue des Lombards, 1st arrond. lebaisersale.com. ⓒ **01-42-33-37-71.** Cover free–25€. Métro: Châtelet.

Caveau de la Huchette ♥   This temple of swing has seen business boom since it was re-created in a scene in the 2016 hit film *La La Land*. Legends like Count Basie and Lionel Hampton once graced this basement club,

Franco-African jazz at Baiser Salé.

> **Heaven-Sent Music Venues: Concerts in Churches**
>
> Many of Paris's most beautiful churches and cathedrals, including St-Eustache and Sainte-Chapelle, host organ and other classical music concerts. Not only is the setting delightful, but the acoustics are generally otherworldly. Concerts are usually listed in the weekly listings website l'Officiel des Spectacles (offi.fr), under concerts. Most churches print monthly schedules, which they display near the entrance to the sanctuary (and sometimes on their websites). Ticket prices are reasonable; sometimes concerts are free, and if they aren't, you likely won't pay more than 30€.

and some excellent musicians still play here. The first part of the evening is usually for enjoying the music. After that, there's often swing and Lindy Hop until 2 or 4am. 5 rue de la Huchette, 5th arrond. caveaudelahuchette.fr. ⓒ **01-43-26-65-05.** Sun–Thurs cover 14€; Fri–Sat 16€; students 24 and under 10€. Métro/RER: St-Michel.

Le Duc des Lombards ♥♥ This is one of the most renowned jazz clubs in Paris, where famous names come to play in a small, intimate space. That said, it's a relatively low-key place, and tickets aren't too hard to get. Reserve your ticket in advance, then get here early if you want to sit up front. Platters of cheese and charcuterie are served. Free jam sessions take place on Fridays and Saturdays after midnight 'til 4am. 42 rue des Lombards, 1st arrond. ducdeslombards.com. ⓒ **01-42-33-22-88.** Cover free–41€; dining options available. Métro: Châtelet.

Le Sunset/Le Sunside ♥♥ Yes, this is another famous jazz club on the rue des Lombards, but what sets this one off is its split personality. Le Sunset Jazz is dedicated to electric jazz and international music, whereas Le Sunside is devoted to acoustic jazz for the most part. Some of the hottest names in French jazz appear here regularly (Jacky Terrasson and Pierre-Yves Plat, to name a couple), along with a crop of international stars. 60 rue des Lombards, 1st arrond. sunset-sunside.com. ⓒ **01-40-26-46-60.** Tickets free–35€. Métro: Châtelet.

New Morning ♥♥♥ Big names and hot acts? Look no further. This place has terrific lineups, including virtuosos like Avishai Cohen, and a long list of fusion upstarts and world music stars. There's history too: Chet Baker, Dexter Gordon, and Didier Lockwood all once graced its stage. This relatively large club fills up quickly, and it's no wonder: This is one of the best jazz venues in town, but the top ticket price is only around 35€. 7 rue des Petites-Ecuries, 10th arrond. newmorning.com. No phone. Cover free–30€. Métro: Château-d'Eau.

CONCERT VENUES

Cabaret Sauvage ♥♥ Is it a cool club or a circus tent? The answer is not clear at this space, where you are just as likely to encounter Brazilian samba, electro funk, or trapeze artists. Blues bands from the Balkans and Vietnamese jazz musicians share the calendar with avant-garde circus acts and Algerian

Performers at New Morning club.

acrobats. Although this big-top cabaret is essentially a performance space with an accent on world music and dance, it also hosts dance parties, where you can boogie to jungle and techno, as well as *raï* (Algerian folk music), mambo, samba, and so forth. Parc de la Villette, entrance at 59 bd. MacDonald, 19th arrond. cabaretsauvage.com. **01-42-09-03-09.** Métro: Porte de la Villette.

La Cigale ♥♥ This 19th-century music hall draws some of the biggest artists working in music today—playing everything from indie rock to hip-hop to jazz. Balcony seating is available for those who arrive early, and there's plenty of open floor space for those who want to dance. 120 bd. de Rochechouart, 18th arrond. lacigale.fr. **01-49-25-89-99.** Métro: Pigalle or Anvers.

Le Petit Bain ♥♥ Small and intimate, this cool music boat floating on the Seine is a place to see emerging bands, mostly of the rock, pop, and electro variety. There's a waterside restaurant and a rooftop bar for those who want to make a night of it. In summer, the fun spreads onto the riverbank, with dining and more music outside. 7 port de la Gare, 13th arrond. petitbain.org. No phone. Métro: Quai de la Gare or Bibliothèque François Mitterrand.

Olympia ♥♥♥ For French musicians, playing the Olympia is a little like reaching the golden heaven of the Greek gods. Legends like Georges Brassens, Edith Piaf, Louis Armstrong, and Aretha Franklin have all appeared at this cavernous hall, which draws French and international pop, rock, and jazz stars like Juliette Greco, Diana Krall, and Sting. 28 bd. des Capucines, 9th arrond. olympiahall.com. **01-47-42-94-88.** Métro: Opéra or Madeleine.

Zenith Paris ♥♥ Tucked away in a corner of Parc de la Villette (p. 203), this 6,785-seater behemoth is the place to see both big international performers (Kylie Minogue, Stereophonics, Weezer…) and French stars. While you won't find a restaurant per se, outside the main doors are the Zen Eat stands (food-truck-like spots), which hawk hot dogs and burgers à la americaine—enough to soak up the wine and beer (which are also sold there), and keep you going through the show. 211 avenue Jean Jaurès, 19th arrond. le-zenith.com. No phone. Métro: Porte de Pantin (then walk through the park; it's well-lit at night).

MUSIC BARS

Whether you're into rock, pop, or electro, Paris has bars aplenty to choose from. Many have stages for live shows, while others are the realms of DJs big and small. In the 1990s Paris and Versailles were the hubs of a new sound, *La French Touch,* electronic music that drew inspiration from disco and added its own beats. The trend took the world by storm, creating groups and artists like Daft Punk, Saint Germain, Kavinsky, and Justice. While these groups are more likely to be headlining stadiums nowadays, Paris's music bar scene is still creative. Keep your eyes and ears open, and you might just hear the next big sound.

L'Alimentation Générale ♥   Despite its name (which means "grocers"), not a food shelf is in sight at this funky music bar-cum-nightclub. Instead, you'll find a grungy, concrete-floored space with a small stage and crowds of Gen Z and millennials moving to the sound of jazz, funk, rock, and (in the club area) electro-rock and disco. Drinks are cheap and when you need something to soak them up with, pop into its adjacent pizzeria, **Alimentari**. 64 rue Jean-Pierre Timbaud, 11th arrond. alimentation-generale.net. ℂ **09-81-86-42-50.** Métro: Parmentier.

Les Disquaires ♥♥   In party HQ (aka the Bastille area), this is the place to come early for the happy hour, then stay for the live jazz, soul, hip-hop, funk, and pop concerts. Once the show's over, it's DJ time until 2am (5am Fri–Sat). 4–6 rue des Taillandiers, 11th arrond. lesdisquaires.com. No phone. Métro: Bastille or Ledru Rollin.

Supersonic ♥   In a cool industrial building at Bastille, this temple to the independent spirit is free and promotes unknown stars of tomorrow. Live

Discover up-and-coming bands at Supersonic.

bands play anything from garage and electro to post-punk and psych, and there's a specialist indie music record shop (order online and pick up your purchase when you go). 9 rue Biscornet, 12th arrond. supersonic-club.fr. ⓒ **01-46-28-12-90.** Métro: Bastille.

CATEGORY-DEFYING VENUES

An increasing number of venues are so multifunctional they defy any attempt to fit them under the usual headings. Sure, you can enjoy music and dance in these places, but you can also check out a poetry lounge, visit an art expo, happen in on a lecture/demonstration, and of course, eat, drink, and be merry. Many are all-day affairs, where the activities change as the sun goes down, while others are purely for night owls. With so many variables, checking the venue's program online is the best way to find out what's on.

La Bellevilloise ♥♥ This 19th-century building was the home of the city's first workers' cooperative, offering cultural activities and meeting spaces to the downtrodden. Today the structure has been transformed, but the mission is still a cultural one. Dedicated to "light, night, and creativity," the lofty space has been divvied up into art galleries, performance spaces, a concert hall, a club, and a restaurant with a lovely outdoor terrace. The program ranges from film festivals to fashion shows, with a good dose of contemporary music. On Sundays, there's a popular brunch (reservations recommended) with live jazz and an all-you-can-eat buffet. 19–21 rue Boyer, 20th arrond. labellevilloise.com. ⓒ **01-46-36-07-07.** Métro: Gambetta.

La Gare-Le Gore ♥♥ A edgier spot in Paris you will not find: This former squat in the abandoned, graffiti-clad Flandres train station (not far from LaVillette, p. 200) looks as dodgy as can be. But don't be fooled. Inside you'll find one of the city's most exciting jazz clubs, where you're just as likely to listen to international biggies as you are graduates from local Conservatoire. And after midnight, the vaulted basement opens as a hip nightclub where electro plays 'til 6am. There's also a snack bar (think fries and sandwiches) and a vast track-side garden to eat and drink in. There's just one rule: No talking when the musicians play! 1 avenue Corentin Cariou, 19th arrond. facebook.com/LaGareLeGore. No phone. Métro: Corentin Cariou.

La Recyclerie ♥♥♥ Describing itself as an "eco-responsible place of experimentation," this converted train station by Porte de Clignancourt and the St-Ouen flea market in northern Paris is part restaurant, part bar, part urban farm, and part furniture repair shop. Bees produce honey in rooftop hives, chickens lay eggs in open-air pens, and vegetables grow in lovingly tended patches. In nice weather, a suitably downscale-hip **bar and restaurant** sprawls out onto the former rail lines, where everyone from cool 20-somethings to families with kids tuck into weekly changing menus that might include Lebanese mezes or handmade burgers. 83 bd. Ornano, 18th arrond. la recyclerie.com. ⓒ **01-42-57-58-49.** Métro: Porte de Clignancourt.

La Bellevilloise is an eclectic events space.

Le Centquatre ♥♥♥ What was once the municipal morgue is now a vast space dedicated to all things artistic and fun. You'll find food for both the soul and the stomach here: theater, dance, music, and visual arts, as well as a Saturday food market, cafes, and restaurants. Along with concerts and dance parties for grown-ups are activities for families and little ones. If that's not enough, you can also shop in the Emmaüs shop (a charitable organization that sells wonderful used knickknacks and furniture) or browse the bookstore. 5 rue Curial, 19th arrond. 104.fr. **01-53-35-50-00.** Métro: Riquet.

Machine du Moulin Rouge ♥♥ A heck of a lot hipper than its historic next-door neighbor (the Moulin Rouge, p. 270), this three-story multitasker has dance floors, concert space, and bars—basically, everything you need for a rollicking night out. The music-savvy crowds come for electronic everything: rock, funk, pop, dubstep, glitch, drum'n'bass, house—not to mention live music by rising stars. There's also a seasonal rooftop and a champagne bar that serves a popular brunch. Set just below the famous windmill sails, its terrace is great for photos too. 90 bd. de Clichy, 18th arrond. lamachinedumoulinrouge.com. **01-53-41-88-89.** Métro: Blanche.

An art exhibit at Le Centquatre.

Alfresco: Summer Terraces with a View

From May to October, Parisians head outdoors, sharpening their elbows to vie for the best rooftop, riverboat, and sidewalk terraces. And you should, too: Many spots offer some of the best views the city has to offer. For dreamy vistas onto Île-Saint-Louis, try **Les Maqueraux** river barge, Quai de l'Hôtel de Ville, Parc Rives de Seine, 4th arrond. (lesmaquereaux.com; ✆ **01-73-78-36-41;** Métro: Hôtel-de-Ville), where those in the know sit on the tree-shaded quayside to indulge in crisp rosé and oysters. Or hit the bar at the soaring **TOO Hôtel** (p. 88) for panoramic vistas over the entire city. It's particularly good on Bastille Day (July 14) and New Year when you can see the fireworks exploding all over the city (book early to claim your spot). For a more plebian view over the city's rooftops and the Eiffel Tower, try **Moncoeur Belleville,** 1 rue des Envierges, 20th arrond. (moncoeurbelleville.com; ✆ **01-43-66-38-54;** Métro: Pyrénées), which sits on a hill above Parc de Belleville. The interior and food are nothing to shout about, but the terrace is lovely.

Outdoor dining at Moncoeur Belleville.

THE BAR SCENE

For a city that does not seem to have a particularly feisty nightlife at first sight, Paris has an astounding assortment of bars. There are cafes galore, of course, but a cafe is not necessarily a bar. Though both serve alcohol, cafes offer a laid-back place to sip at any time of day or night, whereas anything that calls itself a bar usually has an edgier feel and gets going after dark. Bars generally stay open until around 2am. *Tip:* If you want to mingle with Parisians, hit the hotel bars. Trendy ones like at **The Hoxton** (p. 72), **L'Hôtel** (p. 90), **Hôtel Particulier** (p. 74) and **Hôtel des Grands Voyageurs** (p. 90) all have brilliant bars, coveted by locals for their plush, intimate settings.

Bars & Cafes

Café Charbon ♥   A turn-of-the-20th-century beauty, this cafe has been around for years and still somehow manages to draw hordes of happy (and hip) night owls into its arched-ceilinged dining/drinking area. The door in the back leads to the nightclub, **Le Nouveau Casino** (nouveaucasino.fr), where live bands and DJs shake it up until the wee hours. You can come here any time of day for coffee, a drink, or a decent meal. 109 rue Oberkampf, 11th arrond. lecafecharbon.fr. ⓒ **01-43-57-55-13.** Métro: Parmentier or Ménilmontant.

La Palette ♥   Cézanne, Picasso, and Braque once hung out in this old-world Left Bank bar, and you'll still find a spattering of artists, students, and gallery owners today. The front room's where the regulars prop themselves up; the beautiful back room is where the romantics go to sip wine amid original frescoes and old mirrors. 43 rue de Seine, 6th arrond. instagram.com/lapalette.officiel. ⓒ **01-43-26-68-15.** Métro: St-Germain-des-Prés.

Lavomatic ♥♥   This fun joint can only be accessed by a hidden door inside a working laundromat. Once you find it (try the washing machine door in the corner opposite the entrance), you're in for a night of funky electro sound and regressive cocktails. Try the Nuage Rose (pink cloud), a gin drink with red-fruit syrup, lemon juice, hibiscus tonic, and mini-marshmallows. Bring your clothes for a spin in the washer while you have fun upstairs. Lavomatic opens at 6pm. 10 rue René Boulanger, 10th arrond. lavomatic.paris. No phone. Métro: République, Temple, or Jacques Bonsergent.

Le Perchoir ♥♥♥   Take in a fabulous view of eastern Paris from this rooftop bar, which has been so successful it has spawned a passel of other quirky nightspots—one of which is on the roof of the Porte de Versailles exhibition center in the middle of an urban farm. Sip a cocktail on an outdoor sofa and gaze at Sacré-Coeur, or flirt at the tented bar. It's popular, so reserve at least a week ahead. 14 rue Crespin du Gast, 11th arrond. leperchoir.fr. ⓒ **01-89-71-14-62.** Métro: Ménilmontant.

Tiger ♥♥   A must if you're into gin. This ultra-cool bar has a hundred varieties to try (not in one sitting!), which—with all the different tonics—equates to a colossal 1,040 possible drink combinations! Fancy making your own? The friendly bartenders run regular gin cocktail-making masterclasses from 69€. 13 rue Princesse, 6th arrond. tiger-paris.com. ⓒ **01-84-05-81-74.** Métro: Saint-Germain-des-Près.

Bartenders at Tiger, a gin bar.

Wine Bars

Wine fans can lose their heads in this city, not because they drink too much but because Paris has so many tempting wine bars to choose from. Not only can you sample all sorts of delightful fruits of the vine at a *bar à vin*, but you can also usually nibble something salty and delicious (generally cheese, charcuterie, or oysters) to complement what's in the glass.

The view from Le Perchoir rooftop bar.

La Cave à Michel ♥♥   This long, narrow bar in gritty Belleville is standing-only—which is part of the fun. Snag a spot at the bar and watch the locals kiss cheeks as they greet each other and chat over the impressive collection of natural wines (mostly French and Italian) and some of the best tasting plates in northern Paris (think marinated sea bass ceviche, black pig ham, and beef tataki, all excellently prepared). 36 rue Ste-Marthe, 10th arrond. instagram.com/lacaveamichel/. ✆ **01-42-45-94-47.** Métro: Belleville.

Le Baron Rouge ♥♥   This neighborhood institution spills out onto the pavement steps from the Marché d'Aligre. It has only a few tables, so most people stand at the counter or outside, especially during market hours. Huge vats of wine are stacked up inside, and you can fill up if you bring a bottle. In season (Sept–Apr), oysters accompany your wine; otherwise, the menu is limited to cheese and charcuterie. It's a little rough and tumble getting in your drink order at the bar, but that's half the fun. 1 rue Théophile Roussel, 12th arrond. lebaronrouge.net. ✆ **01-43-43-14-32.** Métro: Ledru-Rollin.

Poupée ♥♥   This place, named after the doll museum and hospital that used to inhabit the street (a stone's throw from the Pompidou Center), is the realm of Flo, the bar's passionate manager, who talks about wines as if they were his family. Almost every bottle has been personally sourced from vineyards across mainland France and Corsica. Soak it up with one of the huge cheese and meat platters. On a warm day, the leafy terrace is a gorgeous spot. 2 Impasse Berthaud, 3rd arrond. instagram.com/poupee.marais. ✆ **06-32-99-63-97.** Métro: Rambuteau or Hôtel-de-Ville.

Simone La Cave ♥   This lovely wee spot has a few small tables, but the locals usually prop themselves up at the bar for liquid delights like Grololo, red from the Loire with a cheeky name (*Grololo* means "big boobs," a play on words of the Grolleau grape variety), and platters of cheese, meats, and oysters (when in season). For a full-blown sit-down treat, its sister restaurant, Simone (at no. 33), awaits with inventive bistro cuisine. 13 boulevard Arago, 13th arrond. simonelerestolacave.com/la-cave. ✆ **01-43-37-82-70.** Métro: Les Gobelins.

Cocktail Bars

Over the last few years, Paris has become a mixology powerhouse, with fabulous cocktail bars opening in all sorts of places across town, from speakeasies hidden behind unmarked doors to tapas joints where cocktails steal the show from the wine. Hotel bars are some of the loveliest spots for cocktails too, especially the palaces where each drink (albeit expensive—around 35€) comes with free nibbles (p. 71). Elsewhere, expect to pay between 10€ and 20€.

Flo, the affable bar manager at Poupée.

Candelaria ♥♥♥ Concealed at the back of a Mexican taqueria, this place kick-started the speakeasy trend in 2011, and it's still one of the best. The bar is tiny, so reserve ahead, then sip delights like Las Ciguapas (gin, rum, violet, and citrus jam) in intimate, candlelit surrounds. When the munchies set in, the tacos out front are scrumptious. 52 rue Saintonge, 3rd arrond. candelaria-paris.com. ✆ **01-42-77-98-37.** Métro: St-Sébastien-Froissart.

Experimental Cocktail Club ♥♥♥ This sophisticated bar is known for its gourmet cocktails and has the feel of a neo-baroque speakeasy. DJs play on weekends, though the music is never cranked up to a wild party level. Things stay cool and refined as you sip delightful creations like Misu (Nikka whiskey, coffee liqueur, vermouth, orange and chocolate bitter) and Experience No. 1 (vodka, elderberry, lemon, and basil). 37 rue St-Sauveur, 2nd arrond. experimentalcocktailclub.com/paris. ✆ **01-45-08-88-09.** Métro: Sentier.

Candelaria, a cozy speakeasy.

Harry's Bar ♥♥ It may be filled with expats, but there's something truly Parisian about Harry's. Its history is so intrinsically linked to the city: Hemingway drank here, Gershwin composed much of *An American in Paris* here, and the Bloody Mary was allegedly created here in 1921. If you're here after 10pm, head straight to the basement piano bar for the live music. 5 rue Danou, 2nd arrond. harrysbar.com. ✆ **01-42-61-71-14.** Métro: Opéra or Quatre-Septembre.

Le Mary Celeste ♥♥ Though it's not a cocktail bar per se—the wine, oysters, and excellent small plates shout out "restaurant"—the drinks at this coveted Marais address are wonderfully mixed and slide down easy. The Rain Dog (whiskey, fern syrup, mint, and lemon) goes wonderfully with the oysters, which—incidentally—sometimes get their own happy hour. 1 rue Commines, 3rd arrond. lemaryceleste.com. ✆ **01-42-77-98-37.** Métro: St-Sébastien–Froissart.

Moonshiner ♥ Another speakeasy–style joint, this one is hidden at the back of a small, red-fronted pizzeria (Pizza da Vito). Nibble on pies laden with Parma ham and spicy sausage, then step through the fridge door into an Art Deco boudoir where vintage jazz plays as you sip wonderful, offbeat creations like the Eau de Parfum: champagne, peach, olibanum, and cognac. 5 rue Sedaine, 11th arrond. moonshinerbar.fr. ✆ **09-50-73-12-99.** Métro: Bréguet-Sabin.

Beer Bars

The French are famous for their wine, but they've always loved their beer. King Charlemagne granted monks the monopoly of its production as far back as the 9th century, and in the 1800s, Paris had over 60 breweries. Though two World Wars took the fizz out of the industry (and Stella Artois became the cafe staple), dozens of microbreweries have recently opened to rekindle the city's love of ale. Parisian craft brews tend to have telling names like La Parisienne and Parisis, and are often served (like wine) with cold meats and cheese.

Au Trappiste ♥♥ This busy brasserie-style pub on edgy rue St Denis offers 120 bottled beers and 20 on tap—all to be soaked up with lip-smacking grub like mussels and fries, and sauerkraut laden with sausages. It's a great spot if you're into rugby: TV screens show almost every game of the season. 4 rue St Denis, 1st arrond. facebook.com/autrappisteparis. ✆ **01-46-59-04-28.** Métro: Châtelet.

La Binouze offers 600 types of beer.

Paname Brewing Company on the Bassin de la Villette.

La Binouze ♥♥   You'll find wine and cider here, but the star of the show is the *bière*! (Its name, Binouze, is even slang for beer.) There are some 600 types to choose from—twelve on tap, the rest lining the walls in bottles and cans. It's a chill place to try local brews like the Faubourg (a grassy pilsner by the BAPBAP company) and the Mosaic—light, pale with notes of mango—by La Superbe. There's a second address at 11 rue du Paradis in the 10th arrond. 72 rue Rochechouart, 9th arrond. labinouze.fr. ✆ **09-53-17-23-10.** Métro: Anvers.

Paname Brewing Company ♥♥   A 19th-century warehouse overlooking the Bassin de la Villette canal holds this hip joint. Six beers are brewed on-site, from the refreshing, amber-hued Barge du Canal to the Bête Noire (aka "Black Beast"), a delicious dark ale with a licorice/caramel finish. Soak it all up with international street food along the lines of pizza and burgers. 41 bis quai de la Loire, 19th arrond. panamebrewingcompany.com. No phone. Métro: Laumière or Ourcq.

THE GAY & LESBIAN SCENE

Paris has a vibrant gay nightlife scene, primarily centered around the Marais. Gay dance clubs come and go so fast that even the magazines devoted to them, like **Qweek** (qweek.fr), have a hard time keeping up. *Têtu* magazine (tetu.com), sold at most newsstands, has special nightlife inserts for gay bars and clubs. Both publications are in French.

Bonjour Madame ♥   A fab spot for dining, drinking "margayritas," debating, and attending concerts and exhibitions, this isn't a lesbian bar per se, but it has a definite feminist slant and a desire to welcome the LGBTQ community. To find out what's on, check out the Instagram page instagram.com/bonjourmadame_paris. 40 rue de Montreuil, 11th arrond. ✆ **09-83-51-61-33.** Métro: Faidherbe-Chaligny or Rue des Boulets.

La Champmeslé ♥   This low-key and colorful dive bar is one of the Marais' stalwart lesbian hangouts. The nights tend to start off quietly, but don't be fooled: Several potent mojitos later, and there's dancing on the bar and loud music until 4am. On most Tuesdays from 8pm, tarot card readers come by to read fortunes. 4 rue Chabanais, 2nd arrond. No website. ✆ **01-42-96-85-20.** Métro: Pyramides.

283

Chez Moune ♥♥   With its leopard-print carpet, red lighting and velvet banquettes, and glam photos of female bodies, this SoPi (South Pigalle below Montmartre) institution is where the ladies (lesbian and straight) and a handful of their male friends come to party. Known for its mix of pumping music and an open-minded ethos, it's a favorite nightspot with the glam crowd. Make sure you dress up to get in; the dress code is 'chic' and the doormen often turn people away. 54 rue Jean-Baptiste Pigalle, 9th arrond. chezmoune.paris. No phone. Métro: Pigalle

Le Tango (aka La Boîte à Frissons) ♥   This wacky hetero-friendly gay and lesbian dance hall plays all sorts of cheesy pop and accordion music. Arrive early and practice dancing the foxtrot and tango, or come later for the DJ who'll play everything except techno. 13 rue au Maire, 2nd arrond. tangoparis. com. ☏ **01-42-72-17-78.** Métro: Arts et Métiers.

Raidd Bar ♥   This wild place offers hunky bartenders, a spacious dance floor, go-go dancers, and male strippers who take it all off under an open shower. On weekends you might have to get past the *selectionneur* at the door who decides who's cool enough to enter. 23 rue du Temple, 4th arrond. raiddbar. com. ☏ **01-53-01-00-00.** Métro: Hôtel-de-Ville or Rambuteau.

SPECTATOR SPORTS

For inveterate sports fans who need a good dose of athletic adrenaline, Paris can supply an ample fix. The French go crazy for soccer, rugby, tennis, and horse racing, among other sports.

Horse Racing

Race information is available in newspapers like **L'Equipe,** sold at Paris kiosks, and online at france-galop.com (in English).

The epicenter of Paris horse racing is the **Hippodrome de Longchamp,** in the Bois de Boulogne, 16 arrond. (francegalop-live.com; ☏ **01-44-30-75-00;** RER or Métro: Porte Maillot, and then a free shuttle bus on race days; otherwise, bus 244 to the Les Moulins–Camping stop). Established in 1855 during the autocratic and pleasure-loving reign of Napoleon III, it's the most prestigious track, boasts the greatest number of promising thoroughbreds, and awards the largest purse in France. The most important event at Longchamp is the **Qatar Prix de l'Arc de Triomphe** in early October. Sports aside, it's also the venue for some of the city's biggest music festivals.

Another racing venue is the **Hippodrome d'Auteuil,** also in the Bois de Boulogne (francegalop-live.com; ☏ **01-40-71-47-47;** Métro: Porte Auteuil), known for its steeplechases and obstacle courses. On most weekends between April and November, the city's racecourses host **L'Hippodrome en Famille,** day-long racing fiestas that include races by both professionals and amateurs, shows, games, and of course, pony rides. Visit evenements.france-galop.com. Also see **Hippodrome de Vincennes** (p. 240), famed for its harness racing.

A football match at Parc des Princes Stadium.

Soccer (Football)

Known throughout France as *le football,* or just *le foot,* soccer is one of France's most popular national sports. The Paris team is **Paris Saint-Germain,** also known as **PSG.** They play their home matches at the **Parc des Princes,** 24 rue du Commandant Guilbaud, 16 arrond. (psg.fr; Métro: Porte de St-Cloud), a stadium with a capacity of almost 49,000 spectators. The season runs from September to May; tickets start at 20€ and go through the roof. *Note:* A very small but nasty segment of PSG fans can get violent at games, particularly when the match is against a rival team like Marseille. National games, played at the **Stade de France** (p. 267) in the nearby suburb of Saint-Denis are generally much calmer.

Tennis

France's version of Wimbledon, the **French Open** (or as it's known here, **Roland Garros;** rolandgarros.com) takes place over 2 weeks between late May and early June in the Roland Garros Stadium in the 16th arrondissement (Métro: Porte d'Auteuil). Tickets should be purchased online well in advance for this world-scale tennis event.

DAY TRIPS FROM PARIS

Paris is at the heart of a vast, new-fangled region known as the *Métropole du Grand Paris* (or Greater Paris)—an eclectic sprawl of 131 municipalities that is inhabited by more than 7 million people and dotted with wonderful cultural and historical treasures. You'll find everything from majestic palaces to picturesque artistic villages, and all are only a short train ride from the city center.

If you've never been there, your first choice should probably be the château and gardens of **Versailles.** They're close by, easily accessible by train, and truly not to be missed. **Chartres** (though just outside Grand Paris) would be my second choice, for its breathtaking Gothic cathedral, its winding streets and its half-timbered houses, which will give you a taste of something completely different from Paris. After that, it's a toss-up. If castles are your game, **Fontainebleau** should be high on your list. Fans of Claude Monet love exploring the gardens at **Giverny** (in Normandy), and families with kids in tow tend to pick **Disneyland Paris,** though would get more for their buck at France's answer to Disney, **Parc Astérix.** All these sites are reachable by train from Paris (except Parc Astérix, which requires a shuttle); train tickets do not require reservations and can be bought the day you travel.

VERSAILLES ♥♥♥

21km (13 miles) SW of Paris, 71km (44 miles) NE of Chartres

The grandeur of the Château of Versailles is hard to imagine until you are standing in front of it. Immediately, you start to get an idea of the power (and ego) of the man who was behind it, King Louis XIV. One of the largest castles in Europe, it is also forever associated with another, less fortunate king, Louis XVI, and his wife, Queen Marie Antoinette, who were both forced to flee when the French Revolution arrived at their sumptuous doorstep. The palace's extraordinary gardens, designed by the legendary landscape architect André Le Nôtre, are worth the visit on their own.

Don't feel you have to see everything. For many, a visit to the palace is enough culture, and a nice, relaxing stroll/picnic/nap in the park is a great way to finish off the day. To escape the hordes

Métropole du Grand Paris

(and they're intense at Versailles), my favorite spot is Marie Antoinette's Estate, where—hidden from the palace—you'll get a more bucolic taste of life during the Ancien Régime, thanks to the quaint garden, the pretty Trianons (mini-palaces), hamlet, and other small buildings. You won't be alone, but you won't be elbow-to-elbow with crowds either.

Essentials

GETTING THERE Take the **RER C** (transilien.com; about 30–40 min. from the Champs de Mars; Pont d'Alma, Invalides, St-Michel, or Musée d'Orsay stations) to **Versailles-Château–Rive Gauche.** Make sure the final destination for your train is Versailles-Château–Rive Gauche and *not* Versailles Chantier, which is a 25-minute walk from the palace. Assuming you've taken the right train, it's about a 5-minute walk from the Versailles–Rive Gauche train station to the château—don't worry, you can't miss it. Versailles has a second station, **Versailles–Rive Droite,** accessed from Gare St-Lazare station in Paris (5€ one-way). This is a great option if you plan to picnic in the

287

The majestic approach to the Palace of Versailles.

palace grounds, as you'll go down rue du Maréchal Foch, past a U Express supermarket (no. 45) and **Marché Notre-Dame** (daily 7:30am–1:30pm and 3–7:30pm; outdoor stalls in the center of the square Tues, Fri, and Sun 9am–2pm), the town's main market, where you can fill up on French delights. Glass is permitted in the park, so don't feel you have to skimp on wine!

Unless you have a **Paris Visite** or other pass that includes zones 1 to 5 (p. 329), you'll need to buy a special ticket for the RER C (one-way fare 4.15€ adults, 2.05€ children 4–10, free for children 3 and under); a regular Métro ticket will not suffice. You can buy a ticket from any Métro or RER station; the fare includes a free transfer on the Métro (ratp.fr). Note: While some tickets can now be bought via the RATP or IDF Mobilités (for Greater Paris) apps, you will still have to get your tickets to Versailles at a Métro or RER station counter or machine.

VISITOR INFORMATION Château de Versailles: chateauversailles.fr; ✆ **01-30-83-78-00. Palace:** Apr–Oct Tues–Sun 9am–6:30pm; Nov–Mar Tues–Sun 9am–5:30pm. **Marie Antoinette's Estate:** Tues–Sun noon–5:30pm. **Garden and park:** Apr–Oct daily 7am–8:30pm; Nov–Mar daily 8am–6pm. **Versailles Tourist Office:** Place Lyautey (opposite the Versailles–Rive Gauche station); versailles-tourisme.com; ✆ **01-39-24-88-88**).

TICKETS If you are made of tough stuff and want to see everything in a day, you can buy the all-inclusive 1-day **Château Passeport,** which grants you access to the main château, the gardens, the Trianon palaces, Marie Antoinette's Estate, and temporary exhibitions (Nov–Mar 24€ adults; Apr–Oct 32€ adults, including Les Grandes Eaux Musicales). If you have limited time and energy, buy a **ticket to just the Palace** (21€, free for children 17 and under) or **just the Trianons and Marie Antoinette's Estate** (12€).

Important note: You will have to reserve a time slot for your visit. This should be done online when you purchase your ticket.

EVENING SHOWS Spectacular **fountain night shows** are held from mid-June to mid-September (32€ adults, 28€ ages 6–17), where you stroll around the gardens and enjoy illuminated fountains, music, and fireworks.

Versailles

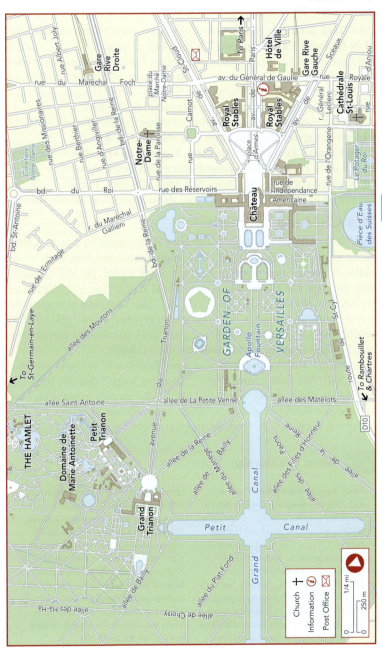

Big names in classical music, theater, and dance fill the stage at the magnificent **Opéra Royal** in the palace; reserve well in advance and expect royal ticket prices (40€–150€).

DAYTIME SHOWS From April to October on most Fridays and Tuesdays, **"Les Grandes Eaux Musicales"** (depending on your ticket, this could be included; otherwise, 10.50€ adults, 9€ ages 6–17) play throughout the gardens closest to the castle. This consists of baroque music playing as a backdrop to the fountains. While it's pleasant, you won't miss anything essential if your ticket does not offer you entrance to this part of the gardens.

Tickets: You can purchase tickets to all shows mentioned above at the château at chateauversailles-spectacles.fr (⁀ **01-30-83-78-89**).

Les Grandes Ecuries: The **Académie Equestre de Versailles** (bartabas.fr) is housed in the **royal stables,** a palatial edifice immediately opposite the château. On weekend afternoons (Sat 6pm, Sun 3pm; 22€–30€), you can watch their "equestrian ballet" in full swing. After the shows, visitors can tour the stables.

The Château of Versailles

Back in the 17th century, after having been badly burned by a nasty uprising called Le Fronde, Louis XIV decided to move his court from Paris to Versailles, a safe distance from the intrigues of the capital. He also decided to have the court move in with him, so he could keep a close eye on them and nip any new plots or conspiracies in the bud. This required a new abode that was not only big enough to house his court (anywhere from 3,000 to 10,000 people would be palace guests on any given day), but also one that would be grand enough to let the world know who was in charge.

A château was already on the site when Louis came to town; his father, Louis XIII, had built a small castle, "a hunting lodge," there in 1623. This humble dwelling simply would not do for the so-called Sun King, who brought in a flotilla of architects, artists, and gardeners to enlarge the castle and give it a new look. In 1668, the king's architect, Louis Le Vau, began work

---

Sleep Like Royalty

Fancy a night in the palace? You're in luck. You can sleep like the Sun King at Versailles' Airelles Château de Versailles, Le Grand Contrôle hotel, set in three palatial 17th-century buildings on the château's grounds. Each of the 14 rooms costs a pretty packet (from around 2,200€/night), but boy, are they special: busy French country–style decor with bold patterns, chandeliers, antique furniture, palatial bathrooms, and views over the Orangerie (the royal citrus grove). Food-wise, expect French classics with a modern twist, courtesy of celebrated French chef Alain Ducasse. There's also a sumptuous spa by Valmont (famed for their cellular cosmetics). The most exciting part, perhaps, is that guests get daily private after-hours tours of the palace, so you can walk its endless gilded chambers and really get a feel for what royal life would have been like without the crowds (airelles.com; ⁀ **01-85-36-05-50**).

The Queen's Apartments in Versailles with a secret door used by Marie Antoinette.

on the enormous "envelope," which literally wrapped the old castle in a second building. From the front, you can see the remnants of the old castle; the buildings that surround the recessed central courtyard (called the **Marble Court**) are what's left of that structure.

Construction, which involved as many as 36,000 workers, ground on for years; in 1682 Louis XIV and his court moved in, but construction went on right through the rest of his reign and into that of Louis XV. Louis XVI and his wife, Marie Antoinette, made few changes, but history made a gigantic one for them: On October 6, 1789, an angry mob of hungry Parisians marched on the palace, and the royal couple was eventually forced to return to Paris. Versailles would never again be a royal residence.

The palace was ransacked during the Revolution, and in the years after, it fell far from its original state of grace. Napoleon and Louis XVIII did what they could to bring the sleeping giant back, but by the early 1800s, during the reign of Louis-Philippe, the castle was slated for demolition. This forward-thinking king decided to invest his own money to save Versailles, and in 1837 the vast structure was made into a national museum. Precious furniture and art objects were retrieved or re-created; paintings, wall decorations, and ceilings were restored. Restoration is ongoing, but even if a few areas are closed, the place is so huge that you can still tour yourself into a 17th-century stupor.

TOURING THE PALACE

The rooms in the "envelope," or the newer part of the building, were designed to impress. They include the **Grand Apartments,** the **Queen's Apartments,** and the **Galerie des Glaces.** These, along with the **King's Apartments** and the **Chapel,** are must-sees.

Each room in the **Grand Apartments** ♥♥♥ is dedicated to a different planet (that circles around the sun, as in the Sun King), and each has a fabulous ceiling fresco depicting the god or goddess associated with said heavenly sphere. The first and probably the most staggering, painting-wise, is in the **Salon d'Hercule** ♥♥. It holds an enormous canvas by Paolo Veronese, *Christ at Supper with Simon,* as well as a divinity-bedecked ceiling by François Lemoyne that portrays Hercules being welcomed by the gods of Olympus. At 480 sq. m (5,166 sq. ft.), it is one of the largest paintings in France. The **Salon d'Apollon** ♥, not surprisingly, was the Sun King's throne room.

The ornate **Salon de Guerre** ♥ and **Salon de Paix** ♥ bookend the most famous room, the **Galerie des Glaces (the Hall of Mirrors)** ♥♥♥. Louis XIV commanded his painter-in-chief, Charles Le Brun, to paint the 12m-high (40-ft.) ceiling of this 73m-long (240-ft.) gallery. This masterwork is illuminated by light from the 17 windows, which are matched on the opposite wall by 17 mirrored panels. Add to that a few enormous crystal chandeliers and the effect is dazzling. This splendid setting was where, in 1919, World War I officially ended with the signing of the Treaty of Versailles.

The **Queen's Apartments** ♥♥ include a gorgeous bedroom with silk hangings printed with lilacs and peacock feathers. It looks exactly as it did in 1789, when Marie Antoinette was forced to flee revolutionary mobs through a secret door (barely visible in the wall near her bed). The **King's Apartments** ♥♥♥ are even more splendiferous, though in a very different style: Here, the ceilings have been left blank white, which brings out the elaborate white and gold decoration on the walls. The **King's Bedroom** ♥♥♥, hung from top to bottom with gold brocade, is fitted with a banister that separated the king from the 100 or so people who would watch him wake up in the morning. If you have the fortitude, you can take a **guided visit** to the king's private apartments (an additional 10€; some in English) to get a more intimate look at castle life (note that some passageways are just 80cm wide).

The **Chapel** ♥♥♥, a masterpiece of light and harmony is where the kings attended Mass. This lofty space reflects both Gothic and baroque styles.

TOURING THE DOMAINE DE MARIE ANTOINETTE

Northwest of the Apollo Fountain lies the **Domaine de Marie Antoinette** ♥♥♥ (if you don't have a Château passport, you'll need a separate ticket to get in). It was here that the young queen sought refuge from the strict protocol and infighting at the castle. Her husband gave her the **Petit Trianon** ♥♥, a small manor that Louis XV used for his trysts, which she transformed into a stylish haven. When the queen had finished decorating the manor in the latest fashions, she set to work creating an entire world around it, including a splendid **English garden** ♥, several lovely pavilions, a jewel-like **theater** ♥♥, and even a small **hamlet** ♥, complete with a working farm and a dairy, where she and her friends would play cards and gossip, or take a stroll in the "country." Although the **Grand Trianon** ♥ is not linked to the story of Marie Antoinette, it is worth a brief visit. Built by Louis XIV as a retreat for himself and his family, this small palace consists of two large wings connected by an open columned terrace that has a delightful garden **view** ♥.

Old hamlet on the Domaine de Marie Antoinette estate.

TOURING THE GARDENS & PARK

The entire 800-hectare (2,000-acre) park is laid out according to a precise symmetrical plan. From the terrace behind the castle is an astounding **view** ♥♥♥ that runs past two parterres, down a central lawn (the Tapis Vert), down the **Grand Canal** ♥♥, and seemingly on into infinity. A solar theme is reflected in the statues and fountains along the main axis of the perspective; the most magnificent is the **Apollo Fountain** ♥♥♥, where the sun god emerges from the waves at dawn on his chariot. On the sides of the main axis, near the castle, are a set of six groves, or **bosquets** ♥, leafy mini-gardens hidden by walls of shrubbery; some were used as small outdoor ballrooms for festivities, others for intimate rendezvous out of reach of the prying eyes of the court. Today, you can **picnic, bicycle** (bikes can be rented next to the restaurant La Flottille; 23€/day, plus shorter time options), rent a *petit véhicule* (golf cart) next to the bike area (from 42€/hr.; only for visitors 25 and over with a driver's license), or even **row a boat** (from 16€/30 min.). The **Little Train** ferries you between the chateau and the garden (9€; or you can buy a combined Passport and Little Train ticket for 31€; the trip include a free, downloadable audioguide app for the journey).

CHARTRES ♥♥♥

97km (58 miles) SW of Paris, 76km (47 miles) NW of Orléans

You'll spot it long before you see the actual town: the spire of the cathedral of Chartres rising above a sea of wheat fields. This stunning edifice and its inspiring stained-glass windows are easy to tour, and you'll still have time to wander through the narrow streets of the ancient (and beautiful) town.

Essentials

GETTING THERE From Paris's Gare Montparnasse, **trains** run directly to Chartres, taking about 1 hour. Tickets cost around 19.60€ one-way; for more information and reservations, see sncf-connect.com or call ⓒ **36-35**. If **driving,** take A10/A11 southwest and follow signs to Le Mans and Chartres. (The Chartres exit is marked.)

VISITOR INFORMATION The **Office de Tourisme** is in the Maison du Saumon, 8 rue de la Poissonerie (chartres-tourisme.com; ⓒ **02-37-18-26-26**).

Exploring the Cathedral

This magnificent UNESCO-protected Gothic cathedral, with its carved portals and three-tiered flying buttresses, would be a stunning sight even without its legendary **stained-glass windows.** These ancient glass panels are truly glorious: a kaleidoscope of colors so deep, so rich, and so bright, it's hard to believe they are some 700 years old. Meant as teaching devices more than artwork, the windows functioned as a sort of enormous cartoon, telling the story of Christ through pictures to a mostly illiterate populace. From the church's beginnings, pilgrims came to see a piece of cloth that believers say was worn by the Virgin Mary during Christ's birth. The **relic** is still here, but these days it's a different sort of pilgrim who is drawn to Chartres: More than 1 million tourists come here every year to admire the magnificent edifice.

The 12th-century south transept rose window of Chartres Cathedral.

A Romanesque church stood on this spot until 1194, when a fire burnt it virtually to the ground. All that remained were the towers, the Royal Portal, and a few remnants of stained glass. The locals were so horrified that they sprang into action; in a matter of only 3 decades a new cathedral was erected, which accounts for its remarkably unified Gothic architecture. This was one of the first churches to use buttresses as a building support, allowing the architect (whose name has been lost) to build its walls at twice the height of the standard Romanesque cathedrals and make space for its famous windows. The new cathedral was dedicated in 1260 and has survived the centuries with relatively little damage. The French Revolution somehow spared the

Chartres Cathedral

cathedral. During World War I and World War II, the precious windows were dismounted piece by piece and stored in a safe place in the countryside.

Before you enter the church, take in the **facade** ♥♥, a remarkable assemblage of religious art and architecture. The base of the two towers dates from the early 12th century. The tower to your right (the **Old Tower,** or South Tower) is topped by its original sober Romanesque spire; that on your left (**New Tower,** or North Tower) was blessed with an elaborate Gothic spire in the early 1500s, when the original burned down. Below is the **Royal Portal** ♥♥♥, a masterpiece of Romanesque art. Swarming with kings, queens,

The labyrinth on the floor of Chartres Cathedral.

prophets, and priests, this sculpted entryway tells the story of the life of Christ. The rigid bodies of the figures contrast with their lifelike faces; it is said that Rodin spent hours here contemplating this stonework spectacle.

Once you're inside the cathedral, the radiant colors of the **stained-glass windows** ♥♥♥, which shine down from all sides, pierce the dim interior. Three windows on the west side of the building, as well as the beautiful rose window to the south called **Notre Dame de la Belle Verièrre** ♥, date from the earlier 12th-century structure; the rest are mostly of 13th-century origins. You will soon find yourself wondering how in the world medieval artists, with such low-tech materials, managed to create such vivid colors. The blues, in particular, seem to be divinely inspired. In fact, scientists have finally pierced at least part of the mystery: The blue was made with sodium and silica compounds that made the color stand up to the centuries better than glass made with other colors.

Another indoor marvel is the **chancel enclosure** ♥♥♥, which separates the chancel from the ambulatory. Started in 1514 by Jehan de Beauce, this intricately sculpted wall depicts dozens of saints and other religious superstars in yet another recounting of the lives of the Virgin and Christ. Back in the ambulatory is the Chapel of the Martyrs, where the cathedral's cherished **relic** resides: a piece of cloth that the Virgin Mary supposedly wore at the birth of Christ, which was a gift of Charles the Bald in 876.

Chartres also harbors a rare **labyrinth** ♥, traced on the floor of the cathedral near the nave. The large circle is divided into four parts with a winding path that leads to the center. In the Middle Ages, these labyrinths represented the symbolic path that one must follow to get from Earth to God; pilgrims would follow the path while praying, as if they were making a pilgrimage to

Jerusalem. *Note:* The cathedral asks that visitors not talk or wander around during Mass, which is generally held in the late morning and early evening. You are welcome to sit in on services, of course.

16 Cloître Notre-Dame. cathedrale-chartres.org. 📞 **02-37-21-75-02**. Free admission. Daily 8:30am–7:30pm.

Exploring the Old Town

Give yourself a little time to explore the medieval cobbled streets of the **Vieux Quartier (Old Town)** ❤❤. The narrow lanes near the cathedral have some gabled houses, including the colorful facades of **rue Chantault.** Seek out **rue du Bourg,** where you'll find the famous **Salmon House** (which houses the tourist office) and some lovely sculptures. In the lower town, you can stroll along the picturesque **Eure River** with its stone bridges and ancient washhouses. If you go on a Saturday morning, a farmers market takes over **Place Billard** (8am–2pm). Between April and January, also look out for **Chartres en Lumières,** a fabulous sound-and-light show (chartresenlumieres.com; free; daily dusk–1am), which turns the facades of city's monuments into beautiful, rippling screens of color.

Centre International du Vitrail ❤ Get the stained-glass backstory at this international center devoted to the glory of this luminous art form. The permanent collection focuses on Renaissance stained glass, while the

The Salmon House and tourist office in Chartres.

temporary shows highlight contemporary works. The center also offers workshops, classes, and training for both professionals and amateurs.

5 rue du Cardinal Pie. centre-vitrail.org. 02-37-21-65-72. Admission 7€ adults, 5.50€ students and children 14–18, free for children 13 and under. Mon–Fri 10:15am–12:15pm and 2–5:30pm; Sat–Sun 2–5:30pm.

Musée des Beaux-Arts de Chartres ♥ Housed in an impressive former episcopal palace, this museum of fine arts boasts a collection covering the 16th to 20th centuries, including works from Zurbarán, Watteau, and Soutine.

29 Cloître Notre-Dame. chartres.fr/musee-beaux-arts/horaires-et-animations. 02-37-90-45-80. Free admission. Admission to temporary exhibitions 7€ adults, 3.50€ children 18 and under. Tues–Sat 10am–12:30pm and 2–6pm (until 8pm Thurs); Sun 2–6pm.

GIVERNY ♥♥

74km (46 miles) NW of Paris

For this trip, a lot depends on the weather. If you luck out and the sun is shining, it's worth the schlep by train or car to bask in the glory of this stunning garden, which bears the artistic stamp of its genius creator, Claude Monet. The painter and his family moved to this tiny town in 1883, and Monet spent the rest of his life here, painting views of the dreamlike garden that he created out of the grassy slope behind his house. Today, the **Fondation Claude Monet** is open to the public April to October, and for a fee, you too can wander about the brilliant flower beds, lush bowers, and water-lily ponds that inspired this Impressionist master. After the garden, sample the bucolic joys of the village, which manages

The village of Giverny.

> ### Where to See Impressionist Paintings in Giverny
>
> While you won't see any original paintings at the Fondation Claude Monet, you will see plenty of Impressionist art at the **Musée des Impressionismes**, 99 rue Claude Monet (mdig.fr); ✆ **02-32-51-94-65**; 12€ adults, free for children 17 and under; May through mid-Nov and late Dec through early Jan daily 10am–6pm, mid-Nov through mid-Dec and early Jan through mid-Jan Fri–Sun 10am–6pm; advance online reservation required). Housed in a sleek modern building with yet another lovely garden, this airy museum offers temporary exhibits that explore the movement, both in France and abroad. English-language audioguides are available for 4€.

to stay charming despite the seasonal tourist infestation. You can also take in one of the excellent temporary exhibits at the **Musée des Impressionismes.** On the other hand, if it is raining or truly dreary out, you'll be better off staying in Paris and getting your Monet fix at the **Musée Marmottan Monet** (p. 190) and/or visiting the water lilies at the **Orangerie** (p. 166).

Essentials

GETTING THERE   Trains (SNCF; for schedules, visit sncf-connect.com or call ✆ **36-35**) leave roughly every hour from the Gare St-Lazare train station to Vernon, the closest stop to Giverny, which is about 7km (4½ miles) away. The trip takes between 50 minutes and just over an hour (depending on the train), and costs 16.80€. From Vernon, you can either take a shuttle bus (10€ round-trip) or rent a bike (electric and pedal) at Givernon Rental Station, right by the train station (39 rue Emile Steiner, 27200 Vernon; location-velo-vernon.fr; ✆ **07-66-42-82-22**; from 10€/day; reserve in advance online) and pedal there on the marked bike path.

If you're **driving,** take the Autoroute A14 to the A13 toward Rouen. Take exit 16 for Vernon and follow the D181 across the Seine into the town. From Vernon, take the D5 to Giverny. Expect it to take about an hour from Paris; try to avoid weekends.

TICKETS   Advance reservations are not mandatory at the Fondation Claude Monet, but they're highly recommended. Numbers are limited, so this way you're sure to get in. You can buy your tickets online at the Maison et Jardins Claud Monet site (see below), at a Fnac ticket office, or on the Fnac site (in English, fnactickets.com). Tickets are 12€ for adults (2€ more via Fnac), 7€ for ages 7 to 17 and students, and free for children 6 and under.

Exploring Giverny: The Fondation Claude Monet

When you enter this kingdom of color, you'll quickly realize that Monet wasn't just a brilliant painter, he was also a gifted gardener—his dual talents complemented each other completely. If you have visited the Orangerie in Paris and seen Monet's magical *Nympheas,* or water lilies, spread across huge canvases in two oval-shaped rooms, in a way you have already visited this garden; they were painted here, with the aim of faithfully re-creating the feeling you would have if you were looking at the same flowers at Giverny.

The first and closest garden to the house is the **Clos Normand** ♥♥, an ostensibly French-style garden that is a glorious riot of color depending on the season. Gladioli, larkspur, phlox, daisies, and asters, among other flowers, clamor for your attention; irises brighten the small lawn. In the midst of it all is **Monet's house** ♥, where you can admire his **Japanese print collection**.

The painter's most famous works, the endless water-lily series, were born in the **Water Garden** ♥♥♥, farther down the slope. Here, Monet's intention was to build a garden that resembled those in the Japanese prints he collected, including a **Japanese bridge** ♥ that figures prominently in several of his canvases. Today the garden looks much as it did when Monet was immortalizing it. Willows weep quietly into the ponds; heather, ferns, azaleas, and rhododendrons carpet the banks; and frogs croak among the water lilies. This garden was a sanctuary for the painter to explore one of his favorite subjects: the interplay of water and light.

This is an extremely popular outing for both individuals and tour groups, so your best bet is to come on a slower day like Monday or Wednesday, and/or to arrive at the opening or after 3pm, when the groups have left. The museum has a cafe or you can lunch at the **Restaurant Baudy** in the village, an old inn where many an Impressionist used to stay when they visited Claude (81 rue Claude Monet; restaurantbaudy.com; ✆ **02-32-21-10-03**).

84 rue Claude Monet. https://claudemonetgiverny.fr. ✆ **02-32-51-28-21.** Admission 12€ adults, 7€ students and ages 7–17, free for children 6 and under. Apr–Oct daily 9:30am–6pm. Closed Nov–Mar.

Monet's house in Giverny.

FONTAINEBLEAU ♥♥♥

60km (37 miles) S of Paris, 74km (46 miles) NE of Orléans

Napoleon called it "the house of the centuries; the true home of kings," and he had a point: Fontainebleau was a royal residence for over 700 years. Elegant and dignified, this grand château of 1,500 rooms carries the architectural imprint of many a monarch. Dense forest and verdant countryside surround the château, making a day here a relaxing green interlude to your Parisian trip.

GETTING THERE Trains to Fontainebleau leave from the Gare de Lyon (schedules and info at transilien.com). The 40-minute trip costs 5€ for adults and 2.50€ for children 4 to 10 one-way. Get off at Fontainebleau–Avon and take the local bus (line 1), direction Lilas, to the Château stop; use a regular Métro ticket for this. The buses are timed to meet the train from Paris. If you're **driving,** take A6 south from Paris, exit Fontainebleau.

VISITOR INFORMATION The **Office de Tourisme** is at 4 bis place de la République (fontainebleau-tourisme.com; ✆ **01-60-74-99-99**).

Exploring Fontainebleau

Though kings were already living here by the 12th century, it was during the Renaissance that Fontainebleau really took on its regal allure. In 1528, inveterate castle-builder King François I decided to completely rebuild Fontainebleau and make it into a palace that would rival the marvels of Rome. He brought in two renowned Italian artists, Il Rosso and Primaticcio, to decorate his new home. Their style of work came to be known as the School of Fontainebleau, characterized by the use of stucco (moldings and picture frames) and frescoes that depicted various allegories and myths. This school was highly influenced by the Mannerist style of Michelangelo, Raphael, and Parmigianino.

François I was also an art collector: His vast accumulation of Renaissance treasures included Da Vinci's *Mona Lisa* and *The Virgin of the Rock,* both of which once hung here. After François' death his descendants continued work on the castle, but it wasn't until the 17th century and the arrival of Henri IV on the scene that there were any major transformations. Henri added several wings and a courtyard (the **Cour des Offices** ♥♥), and made major changes to the decor, inviting a new clutch of artists, who established a second School of Fontainebleau. This time, the artists were of French and Flemish origin and used oil paint and canvas instead of frescoes. Napoleon was very fond of this palace and made a lasting imprint on the castle's interior. Fontainebleau made an imprint on the emperor as well: On April 20, 1814, he abdicated here, before being sent off to exile on the island of Elba.

TOURING THE CHÂTEAU

The visit to the chateau includes the **Grands Appartements** and the Napoleon I museum (Musée Napoleon 1er).

Your first encounter with the château will take place in the **Cour du Cheval Blanc** ♥♥♥ at the entrance to the palace. It was in this grand square,

The Cour du Cheval Blanc, Fontainebleau Palace.

surrounded by wings of the castle on three sides, that Napoleon said adieu to his faithful imperial guards. "Continue to serve France," he pleaded. "Her welfare was my only concern." The main building before you dates from François I's era; the sumptuous **horseshoe staircase** ♥♥ was added by Henri II. One of the first things you'll see during your visit is the **Chapelle de la Trinité** ♥. This is where Louis XV married Polish princess Marie Leczinska and where the future Napoleon III was baptized. Linking the chapel with the royal apartments is the **Gallery of François I** ♥♥♥, a stunning example of Renaissance art and decoration. Overseen by Il Rossi, a team of artists covered the walls with exceptional frescoes, moldings, and *boiseries* (carved woodwork). Throughout the gallery you will see the salamander, François' official symbol.

The other major must-see is the **Salle de Bal** ♥♥♥. This 30m-long (98-ft.) ballroom is a feast of light and color; the frescoes by Primaticcio and Nicolo dell'Abate have been completely restored, and their rich hues radiate as if they were painted yesterday. Huge windows let in light; the monumental fireplace at the far end was designed by 16th-century architect Philibert Delorme.

The **Royal Apartments** ♥♥ have been redecorated by successive monarchs. Louis XIII was born in the **Salon Louis XIII** ♥, a fact that is

Hiking Trails Left by French Kings

The Fontainebleau Forest is riddled with *sentiers* (hiking trails) made by French kings and their entourages who hunted here. In 1842, a forest-loving veteran of Napoleon's army, Claude François Denecourt, created the first official public walking trails, some 150km (93 miles) of pathways called the *sentiers bleus*. A "Guide des Sentiers" is available at the tourist information center (p. 301). Bike paths also cut through the forest. You can rent bikes at **A La Petite Reine,** 14 rue de la Paroisse, in the center of town (alapetitereine.com; ✆ **01-60-74-57-57**), for 10€ per hour and 20€ for a full day (helmets can be hired for 3€ and kids' seats for 5€). You'll also find route suggestions on the website.

symbolized in the ceiling mural showing Love riding a dolphin. Though several different queens slept in the **Chambre de l'Impératrice** ♥♥, its current setup reflects the epoch of Empress Joséphine (Napoleon's first wife). The sumptuous bed, crowned in gilded walnut and covered in embroidered silk, was made for Marie Antoinette. The queen would never see it; the Revolution exploded before she could arrange a visit to the château. Napoleon transformed the Kings' bedroom into the **Salle du Trône** ♥, or Throne Room. Because several centuries of kings, from Henri IV to Louis XVI, slept here, the decor is a mashup of styles: The throne is Empire, the folding chairs are Louis XVI, and the ceiling murals date from the 17th and 18th centuries.

You can learn more about the emperor at the **Musée Napoléon 1er** ♥, in the Louis XV wing, where you'll see historic memorabilia and artwork relating to his reign.

TOURING THE GARDENS

The lush and quiet **Garden of Diane** ♥, on the castle's north side, was created during the time of François I and centers around a statue of the goddess surrounded by four dogs. The **English Garden** ♥, complete with an artificial stream and lush groves of tall trees, was added by Napoleon. The vast **Carp Pond** ♥, which extends directly from the south side of the **Cour de la Fontaine.** Surrounding the gardens and park is **Fontainebleau Forest** ♥♥, which, if you have the time, is worth the visit (see box, p. 302).

pl. du Général-de-Gaulle, 77300 Fontainebleau. chateaudefontainebleau.fr. ✆ **01-60-71-50-70.** Grands Appartements and Musée Napoléon 1er 14€ adults, 12€ students 18–25, free for children 17 and under. Apr–Sept Wed–Mon 9:30am–6pm; Oct–Mar Wed–Mon 9:30am–5pm.

Salle de Bal at Fontainebleau.

DISNEYLAND PARIS ♥

41km (25 miles) E of Paris

This giant resort has two parks: the classic Disneyland, complete with the Buzz Lightyear Laser Blast and Star Wars rides, like Hyperspace Mountain; and Disney Studios, which in addition to the Marvel Avengers Campus and the brand new "Frozen" land (which at time of writing was set to open in 2026) has thrill rides and exhibits themed around Disney animation techniques and films. Outside the parks, there's also a golf course, a spa, tennis courts, and **Disney Village,** with its boutiques, restaurants, disco, and IMAX theatre.

However, unless you're a diehard Disney fan in search of the classics, don't expect your mind to be blown in or out of the parks: Only Marvel brings anything particularly new to the table. If you're an unequivocal Disney fan, you may still find some enjoyment. But if you're not, see Parc Astérix (p. 306), where you get the theme park thrills in a much more pleasant environment—plus a bit of French culture for good measure.

The **Disney Premier Access** offers two skip "skip the line" options: the **Disney Premier Access One,** whereby you have to fork out yet more money for the privilege of fast-track lines (about 8€–15€, depending on the attraction's popularity) and the **Disney Premier Access Ultimate,** whose high price (about 90€ to over 140€ per person, depending on the season) allows for unlimited direct access to all rides without a long line. For up-to-date information, check disneylandparis.com on the day of your visit or download their app.

Essentials

GETTING THERE By far the easiest way to get to the parks from central Paris is by **RER A** (RATP; ratp.fr; 45 min.; 5€ adults, 2.50€ children 4–10 one-way). Get on at any of its downtown stations and take it all the way to its terminus at Marne-la-Vallée–Chessy (just make sure that this is the terminus—the RER A has multiple destinations). When you get out, you'll be a 5-minute walk from the entrance. By **car,** head east on the A4 and take the Parcs Disney exit. By train, from outside Paris, you could arrive by **TGV** (the French railway's high-speed train); see sncf-connect.com/en-en/. From Paris's Roissy–Charles de Gaulle (CDG) and Orly airports, you could also catch the **Magic Shuttle** (magicalshuttle.co.uk; 24€ adults, 11€ children 3–10, free for children 2 and under), a direct shuttle to the parks and Disney hotels.

VISITOR INFORMATION Disneyland Paris Guest Relations Office is in City Hall on Main Street U.S.A. (disneylandparis.com; ⓒ **09-69-32-60-61**). For general regional tourist information, visit the **Point Information Tourisme** between the train station and Disney Village (visitparisregion.com).

TICKETS Admission varies depending on the season. In peak season, a date-stamped 1-day, 1-park ticket (for either the main park or Walt Disney Studios) costs about 67€ adults, 56€ children 3 to 11, and free for children 2 and under; a 2-day park-hopper ticket is roughly 152€ adults, 142€ kids; and a 3-day park-hopper ticket is around 216€ adults, 200€ kids. Special offers can include transportation to and from Paris; check the website.

HOURS Hours vary throughout the year, but most frequently they are daily 10am to 7:30pm. Check the website for exact hours during your stay.

Exploring Disney
DISNEYLAND PARK
When you enter the park, you'll step right into **Main Street U.S.A,** that utopian rendition of early-20th-century America, complete with horse-drawn buggies and barbershop quartets. Here, in City Hall, you'll find the **information center** as well as a train that leaves from Main Street Station. In **Frontierland,** you'll find Big Thunder Mountain, Phantom Manor, the *Thunder Mesa* paddle-wheel steamboat, and the Lucky Nugget saloon. Next is **Adventureland,** with the Swiss Family Robinson treehouse and Pirates of the Caribbean. Onward toward **Fantasyland,** with Sleeping Beauty's Castle, whizzing teacups, flying Dumbos, and "It's a Small World." Last stop: **Discoveryland,** home of *Star Wars* Hyperspace Mountain and Star Tours: The Adventure Continues. Parades course down Main Street every afternoon, and around closing time there's a spectacular light and fountain show.

WALT DISNEY STUDIOS PARK
Walt Disney Studios is now the go-to park for Marvel fans, thanks to the recent **Marvel Avengers Campus,** replete with Iron Man– and

A daily parade at Disneyland Paris.

> **Medieval Provins: Straight Out of Disney**
>
> If Disney's re-created medieval towns were real, they would undoubtedly look like Provins. This quaint, fairy tale–like settlement of half-timbered houses, medieval ramparts, spooky underground passages, and cobbled streets was once the Count of Champagne's capital, famed across medieval France for its *foires*, or fairs. Today it's just over an hour from Paris (by train from Gare de l'Est; transilien.com; 5€) and Disneyland Paris (by bus no. 50; 2.50€) and is a great place for a family-themed day out, with falconry and jousting shows, and pleasant strolls along age-old streets lined with UNESCO-protected medieval buildings. For more information, visit provins.net.

Spider-Man–themed attractions, and an after-dark drone light show. Split into four worlds—Pixar, Marvel, Toon Studio, and Production Courtyard—the Studios Park is also the place for films and parades and yet more musical shows. Fun rides here include *Ratatouille:* **A Recipe for Adventure,** a 4D ride where you get a rat's-eye view of the restaurant kitchen in the movie of the same name, and **Crush's Coaster,** which plunges you into the world of *Finding Nemo*. Smaller visitors can try the **Toy Soldiers Parachute Drop** or the *Cars* ROAD TRIP ride, where they can speed along Route 66 on the lookout for popular characters like Mater and Lightning McQueen.

PARC ASTÉRIX ♥♥♥

41km (25 miles) E of Paris

While Disney is all about transposed Americana, **Parc Astérix** is all about France—well, a comical vision of France, at least, as seen through the eyes of Roman bashers, Astérix the Gaul and his best friend Obélix, comic-book/cartoon characters, beloved to the French. Astérix, the main character, is a wily Gaul who lives in the last remaining Gaulish village of the Roman Empire. Thanks to a magical strength potion, he and Obélix (who fell in the potion as a baby and displays extra-human strength) defend their village from the Romans, and frequently go on adventures around the world.

Even if you don't speak French, the theme park (40 km north of Paris) is a fun place to visit, with some 50 attractions and shows, including France's fastest roller coaster. You can easily make a night of it, with three themed hotels to choose between, all within walking distance of the park.

Essentials

ARRIVING From Paris, the easiest option is to take the **RER B** (ratp.fr; 30 min.; 11.80€ adults, 7.90€ ages 4–10 one-way) to Aeroport Charles-de-Gaulle Terminal 3 (the first airport stop). Inside the RER building (upstairs), look for the Parc Astérix desk, where you will be directed to the shuttle bus to the park (10€ adults return, 9€ children 3–11). By **car,** head north on the A1 (direction Lille) and take the Parc Astérix exit (between exits 7 and 8).

VISITOR INFORMATION Check parcasterix.fr (⊘ **09-86-86-86-87**). There's an info point at the park entrance. You should download the app for waiting times for the rides, show schedules, and restaurant reservations.

ADMISSION Admission varies upon the season and whether you buy tickets online, but generally, a 1-day ticket costs around 60€ for adults and 52€ for children ages 3 to 11 (free for children 2 and under). Seasonal offers can include nights in a hotel and the park's line-jumping **Filotomatix pass** (check the website).

HOURS Hours vary throughout the year, but are usually 10am to 7pm with later closings in the summer, Halloween, and Christmas. Check the website for details.

Exploring Parx Astérix

Split into seven of the comics' "worlds"—**Gaul,** the **Vikings, Egypt, Ancient Greece,** the **Roman Empire, Time Travel,** and the druid **Festival Toutatis**—there are big and small rides throughout the park, along with eating places and live performance spots, including the popular outdoor high-diving pool—**Les Plongeons d'Olympe**—in Ancient Greece. You can defy gravity on genuinely thrilling roller coasters in most worlds, like on **Goudurix** (a play on words for *gout du risque,* as in "a taste for risk"), which has no less than five loops in the Vikings zone; and on **Festival Toutatis** (in its same-named world), which aside from being fast, holds the world record for air times (the number of times your bottom leaves the seat), at 23. There are numerous water rides too, from **Le Grand Splatch** to the **Menhir Express** (both in Gaul; for the Menhir Express, wear a rain poncho. Seriously!), as well as meet-and-greets with the characters, and gentle rides and play areas for smaller ones.

Where to Stay and Eat

Parc Astérix is doable as a day trip from Paris, but for full immersion, think about spending the night. Online packages usually combine park entry, breakfast, a Filotomatix pass, and a night in one of the three themed hotels: the **Trois Hiboux** (decked out like a wood cabin), **La Cité Suspendue** (a cluster of quaint, stilted forest cabins linked by bridges), and **Les Quais de Lutèce** (dressed up like a Roman town, complete with its own waterway). Staying in any of the hotels gets you 30 minutes of access to the park before opening. To reserve by phone, call ⊘ **09-86-86-86-87.** Or reserve online at parcasterix.fr.

Restaurant-wise, the park is strewn with multiple places, hawking everything from croissants and burgers (ubiquitous now all over France) to pizza and fries. For a sit-down meal with waiter service, reserve ahead (on the app or online at parcasterix.fr) for one of two restaurants: the **Restaurant du Lac,** which serves Obélix's favorite, wild boar; or outdoor **Le Patio** in the Roman Empire, which offers Italian fare. The hotels also have buffet restaurants serving an array of classic French cuisine (around 35€–50€ per person).

WALKING TOURS OF PARIS

You simply won't be able to fully appreciate the flavors and moods of Paris if you don't explore the streets and absorb the sights, sounds, and even smells that make up its sensory identity. A mere city block can encompass several centuries' worth of history. Below are tours of two of the city's best areas for ambling about.

WALKING TOUR 1: **MONTMARTRE**

START:	**Place des Abbesses (Métro: Abbesses)**
FINISH:	**Sacré-Coeur (Métro: Abbesses)**
TIME:	**About 1½ hours**
BEST TIME:	**Weekdays, when stores are open and the crowds are smaller**
WORST TIME:	**Weekends, when the area around Sacré-Coeur looks like the Métro at rush hour**

Montmartre has become forever linked with a certain image of Paris: quaint cobblestoned streets, accordion serenades, and the Sacré-Coeur hovering in the background. Or maybe it's the Moulin Rouge and can-can girls whooping it up on the Place Blanche. Although the area around Sacré-Coeur is probably the most tourist-clogged in the capital and the Moulin Rouge is a tour-bus trap, the *butte* (as it's called) still has its own magic and it's not hard to find. Though legendary artists like Picasso and Utrillo are gone, new ones have taken their place, and they aren't the ones hawking portraits in the Place du Tertre. In fact, within a couple blocks of the mobs on the *place* are quiet cobbled streets lined with lovely vine-trimmed houses, cute cafes, and shops.

1 Place des Abbesses

The first thing you'll notice when you are coming out of the Métro (take the lift; there are 176 steps) is the exit itself: This lovely Art Nouveau confection of glass and metal is one of two surviving Métro entrances by Hector Guimard with a glass roof (the other is at Porte Dauphine in the 16th arrond.). Look around the leafy plaza. Back in 1134, King Louis *Le Gros* (the Fat, otherwise known as Louis VI) founded an abbey up here,

Montmartre Walking Tour

1. Place des Abbesses
2. Bateau Lavoir
3. Moulin de la Galette and the Moulin du Radet
4. Allée des Brouillards
5. Place Dalida
6. Clos Montmartre Vineyard
7. Au Lapin Agile
8. Musée de Montmartre
9. Rue St-Rustique
10. Place du Tertre
11. Basilique du Sacré-Coeur
12. Cimetière de Montmartre

and this square is named after the various abbesses who ran it. As most of them came from wealthy, aristocratic families, they did not fare well during the Revolution. In 1794, the 43rd abbess, Louise de Montmorency-Laval, who was 71 years old and both blind and deaf, was guillotined, and the abbey was pillaged. Her crime? She was found guilty of "blindly and deafly plotting against the Revolution."

Walk west on rue des Abbesses to rue Ravignan, where you will make a right uphill. At the top of the street is Place Emile Goudeau. At no. 11 bis–no. 13 is the:

2 Bateau Lavoir

This building started out as a piano factory but later was home to artists, actors, and poets, who stayed here when they were all young and struggling. In 1889, this odd edifice—constructed on different levels to accommodate the steep slope it was built on—was divided into artists' studios. By 1904, a young man named Pablo Picasso was living and working here, as well as Juan Gris and Amadeo Modigliani, not to mention the poets Max Jacob and Guillaume Apollinaire, among others. It was here

309

that Picasso painted *Les Demoiselles d'Avignon,* a painting that signaled the birth of Cubism. Unfortunately, this fertile artistic breeding ground, which was dubbed the **Bateau Lavoir,** or the Floating Laundry, by Jacob, burned down in 1970. All that's left of the original structure is one facade on the small plaza. The rest was rebuilt in 1978 and today still houses a few artists' studios, though none are open to the public.

The original Art Nouveau entrance at Abbesses Métro.

Turn left on tiny rue d'Orchampt, a quiet cobbled street, which curves up to an intersection with rue Lepic. Take a short detour left down rue Lepic to the:

3 Moulin de la Galette & Moulin du Radet

More than 30 windmills once dotted Montmartre's vineyard-covered slopes. Here are the last two that still exist: the **Moulin du Radet** (on the corner of rue Girardon), which is now a swank restaurant called the Moulin de la Galette, and—somewhat confusingly—the "real" **Moulin de la Galette,** of Renoir painting fame, located down the street at no. 75, also known as the Moulin Blute-Fin. Whatever its name, this old mill, which was owned by the same family of millers since the 17th century, was a witness to tragedy. In 1814, it had the misfortune of being attacked by a garrison of Cossacks, who were in town because the Allies (Germany, Prussia, and Russia, among a host of others) had come to Paris to stop French attacks on the rest of Europe and put Napoleon in his place. The miller tried valiantly to defend his property but ended up hacked to pieces and nailed to the blades of his windmill. Years later, the miller's son turned the farm into an outdoor music hall, the famous Moulin de la Galette depicted in a legendary painting by Renoir (you can see the painting at the Musée d'Orsay; p. 220). Other painters who frequented these

---

Montmartre for the Weary: Bus No. 40

The actual distance on the walk described below is not long, but the terrain will make it seem a lot longer. Montmartre is up on a high hill (*butte*) overlooking the city, so be prepared for some steep ups and downs. Visitors with reduced mobility (or who are simply tired) might replace parts of this walk with **bus line 40** that makes a wide circuit of the *butte.* The bus, which costs a regular Métro ticket, leaves Place Pigalle every 12 to 15 minutes. For information and a map, visit ratp.fr.

bucolic dance parties included Toulouse-Lautrec, Van Gogh, and Utrillo. Today the mill is private property.

Return to rue Girardon and turn left, then left again on av. Junot, walking past some of Montmartre's most elegant homes. Follow av. Junot as it curves to the right, making a sharp right on rue Simon Dereure. The street ends at Place Casadesus; climb the stairs to the footpath called:

4 Allée des Brouillards

This tranquil path leads past a number of massive houses, set back in large gardens, most of which are at least partially shielded from prying eyes by tall fences. The largest garden surrounds a white country manor known as the **Château des Brouillards,** or Fog Castle. Built in 1772, this romantic dwelling most likely got its name from the mist that crept up from a nearby spring when the water contacted the cold morning air. Gérard de Nerval lived here in 1854, and surely this was the ideal writer's haven for this quintessential Romantic-era poet. Painter Pierre-Auguste Renoir lived and worked in one of the houses behind the château; his son, filmmaker Jean Renoir, was born there.

Moulin du Radet windmill.

Continue down the path to its end, at:

5 Place Dalida

This small crossroads is graced with a bust of one of Montmartre's most beloved residents, Yolanda Gigliotti, aka Dalida. This Egyptian-born singer, of Italian ancestry, was one of France's biggest stars, recording hundreds of hits and winning 70 gold records. The blonde bombshell moved to the *butte* in 1962, where she lived out the rest of her stormy life in a four-story mansion that her fans dubbed "Sleeping Beauty's Castle." After a series of unfortunate love affairs, two of which ended with her partners' suicides, she took her own life in 1987. Her **statue** looks out on one of the most prototypical views of Montmartre: a cobbled lane leading up a hill with Sacré-Coeur in the background.

Walk up rue de l'Abreuvoir and turn left on rue des Saules:

6 Clos Montmartre Vineyard

As you make your way down rue des Saules, you will notice an unlikely vineyard on the right-hand side of the street. This is in fact the last of Montmartre's vineyards; for centuries, vineyards covered the *butte*. Back

Place Dalida square in the Montmartre neighborhood.

in the 16th century, winemaking was the primary industry in the area—though nobody ever bragged about the high quality of the product. A ditty about Montmartre wine went thus: "The wine of Montmartre—whoever drinks a pint, pisses a quarte." By the way, in those days, a "quarte" equaled 67 liters (70 quarts). Whatever its merits, this tiny vineyard still produces. The harvest is celebrated with a raucous street party every year (p. 56), and rare bottles of Clos Montmartre are auctioned off with the proceeds benefiting local public projects.

Continue down rue des Saules to the intersection with rue St-Vincent:

7 Au Lapin Agile

The story goes that André Gill, a habitué of this rowdy corner cabaret—which was then called the Cabaret des Assassins—painted a sign for the place showing a rabbit (*lapin*) jumping out of a stockpot. The cabaret became known as the Lapin à Gill (Gill's Rabbit), which in time mutated into Au Lapin Agile (the Agile Rabbit). The singer Aristide Bruant (immortalized in a poster by Toulouse-Lautrec) bought the inn in 1902 and asked Frédé, a local guitar legend, to run it. Under Frédé's guidance, the cabaret thrived, and the best and the brightest of the Montmartre scene were drawn to its doors, including Picasso, Verlaine, Renoir, Utrillo, and Apollinaire. Today Au Lapin Agile is still a cabaret, though a much calmer one, showcasing traditional French chanson (p. 270). The shows are heavy on nostalgia and cheesy sing-alongs, but they can be good, kitschy fun when you're in the mood.

Turn right on rue St-Vincent, then right on rue Mont Cenis. Climb the stairs and turn right on rue Cortot:

8 Musée de Montmartre

At 12 rue Cortot lies the peaceful **Musée de Montmartre** (p. 196), which offers an overview of neighborhood history and is housed in the former residence of Rosimond, a famous 17th-century actor who was in

Molière's troupe. In another century, Renoir painted here (this is where he created the *Bal du Moulin de la Galette*), as did Utrillo, who lived here with his mother, the model and painter Suzanne Valadon, and her lover André Utter. The Jardins Renoir (gardens) make for some wonderful downtime, with views over the vineyards and the northern side of the city. At the seasonal cafe, chairs are sprawled out toward the lawns on hot days, and young kids can run around safely (just watch out for the pond).

Continue to the end of rue Cortot and turn left on rue des Saules; walk up to rue St-Rustique and turn left:

9 Rue St-Rustique

By now you'll have noticed the crowds thickening and a change in the atmosphere toward the Disneyesque and tacky. Trinket shops appear on every corner, and "artists" badger you to draw your portrait. Dive quickly into rue St-Rustique, a narrow channel of calm. Not only does the noise die down, but you'll be rewarded with an excellent photo op of the bulb-like tops of Sacré-Coeur sprouting above the end of the street. This is one of the oldest streets in Montmartre, with a medieval-style gutter in its center and no sidewalks.

Walk to the end of rue St-Rustique and turn right. On your right is the entrance to:

10 Place du Tertre

Now there's no avoiding it: the most tourist-drenched, mob-swamped spot in Paris. A quick walk down the hill toward the Place des Abbesses will lead you to plenty of nice restaurants and cafes. You will probably be approached by people begging to do your portrait—these "artists"

Cabaret Au Lapin Agile.

may do decent caricatures, but if you think you're looking at the next Picasso, you're kidding yourself.

Duck back out of Place du Tertre and continue down rue du Mont Cenis until it curls around to the left and becomes rue Azaïs. Keep walking until you're in front of:

11 Basilique du Sacré-Coeur

After you've looked up at the gleaming white basilica and its odd, pseudo-Byzantine domes, turn around and admire the stunning view from the esplanade, or parvis, in front of the church; on a clear day you can see as far as 50km (31 miles). Though you won't be able to see the Eiffel Tower (it's too far over on the right, though you can see it if you walk to the corner of rues Azaïs and Saint-Eleuthère just below), you will take in a majestic panorama that includes the Pompidou Center, St-Eustache, the Opéra, and the Louvre. What you are mainly looking at here is eastern Paris, the more plebian (and hip) side—an entirely appropriate view from this historically working-class, low-rent neighborhood. The view actually gets better as you walk down to the bottom-most level of the esplanade; from here you can also take in the lovely gardens below, which had a starring role in the classic Montmartre movie, *Amélie,* by Jean-Pierre Jeunet (2001). Also see p. 194.

View of Sacré-Coeur from rue St-Rustique.

Montmartre Cemetery: Where the VIPs RIP

When it comes to strolling through historic cemeteries (a favorite Parisian pastime and a surprisingly lovely way to spend a peaceful hour), the Cimetière du Père-Lachaise in the 20th arrondissement steals the show with the graves of legends such as Jim Morrison, Oscar Wilde, and Edith Piaf. But overlook **Montmartre's cemetery** at the foot of the *butte* and you'll miss more than just a tranquil stroll. This is where the tombs of famous artists such as Edgar Degas, ballet dancer Vaslav Nijinsky, and the New Wave movie director François Truffaut lie along higgledy-piggledy alleys. It's like walking through history, and a great spot for some downtime on a sunny day. Tag it onto the end of your tour by heading back to Place des Abbesses and following rue des Abbesses westward. When it turns into rue Lepic, take rue Joseph Maistre on the left, and turn left again onto rue Caulaincourt. As you walk over the bridge, look for the staircase down to avenue Rachel on the left; the entrance is on your left.

WALKING TOUR 2: **THE MARAIS**

START:	**Village St-Paul (23–27 rue St-Paul; Métro: St-Paul)**
FINISH:	**Place des Vosges**
TIME:	**1½ hours, not including shops, restaurants, or museums**
BEST TIME:	**During the week, when the streets are full of life, and Sundays, when unlike other parts of the city, many shops and restaurants are open**
WORST TIME:	**Saturdays, when shoppers flood most of the neighborhood and the Jewish quarter completely shuts down**

The Marais is one of the few areas that Baron Haussmann largely ignored when he was tearing up the rest of the city in the 19th century; for that reason, it still retains a medieval feel. Though very few buildings actually date from the Middle Ages, this warren of narrow streets and picturesque squares is layered with a rich history, which is apparent in the pleasing hodgepodge of architectural styles. The neighborhood's glory days date from the 16th and 17th centuries, when anyone who was anyone simply had to build a mansion or a palace here. Though the area fell from grace in the 18th and 19th centuries, many of the grand *hôtels particuliers* (private mansions) were reborn as museums and public archives. Today, the Marais is a fascinating mix of hip gentrification and the remnants of a working-class neighborhood. It is at once the center of the city's gay life, as well as the historic Jewish quarter. Some of the city's best museums and boutiques are in the Marais, so you could easily spend an entire day here.

1 Village St-Paul

Many centuries ago, a small hamlet sat on this spot when the area was still mostly marshland (*marais* means "swamp"). While the neighborhood has transformed many times since, a small reminder of this village lives on, hidden behind an ordinary row of buildings on rue St-Paul. Pass through the entryway and you'll come into a kind of large interior courtyard that dates from the 14th century, when it was part of the gardens of Charles V's royal residence. At one point the houses and buildings built over and around the gardens were slated for demolition; a neighborhood committee saved them, and in the 1970s the village was restored and turned into a sort of antiques center, with stores and art galleries (see levillagesaintpaul.com and "Shopping," p. 242). The village hosts seasonal *déballages,* or outdoor arts and antiques fairs. Today the commercial emphasis has shifted from antiques to design.

Exit the village on rue des Jardins St-Paul. On one side of this street is a playground that runs along a huge stone wall, the:

2 Rampart of Philippe Auguste

Before you (beyond the local basketball court) is the best-preserved stretch of the city walls built by Philippe Auguste, King of France. Before leaving town on a crusade in 1190, Philippe decided to beef up security. The result was a mighty rampart that defined the city limits. The wall in front of you once ran in a semicircle from the Seine, up to around rue Etienne Marcel, and curved over to protect the Louvre and back down to the Seine (a similar semicircle was built 20 years later on the Left Bank). Aside from this stretch, only small fragments can be found here and there on both banks, so you'll have to imagine the rest; you'll also have to imagine the towers and the six massive portals that once were the only land access into the city.

Turn left down rue des Jardins St-Paul and right on rue de l'Avé Maria. Just where it branches off to the right on rue du Figuier is:

3 Hôtel de Sens

Built between 1475 and 1519, this splendid fortress/mansion is a rare example of medieval urban architecture. When Paris came under the jurisdiction of the Bishop of Sens back in the 15th century, he promptly built himself a suitably fabulous home in the city. Later, Henri IV briefly used it to house his wife, Queen Margot, whose many love affairs were causing him ceaseless headaches. The bishops stopped coming to the Hôtel de Sens altogether in 1622, preferring to rent it out. By the time the city bought it in 1911, it was in a pitiful state; the building's restoration—which started in 1929—wouldn't be completed until 1961. The Hôtel now houses the **Bibliothèque Forney,** a library dedicated to the

Medieval Hôtel de Sens.

The Marais Walking Tour

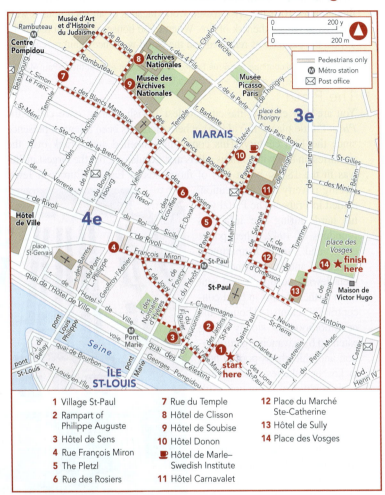

1 Village St-Paul
2 Rampart of Philippe Auguste
3 Hôtel de Sens
4 Rue François Miron
5 The Pletzl
6 Rue des Rosiers
7 Rue du Temple
8 Hôtel de Clisson
9 Hôtel de Soubise
10 Hôtel Donon
⌾ Hôtel de Marle–Swedish Institute
11 Hôtel Carnavalet
12 Place du Marché Ste-Catherine
13 Hôtel de Sully
14 Place des Vosges

decorative arts. Take a minute to admire the turrets and towers in the courtyard.

Follow the side of the building up rue du Figuier and turn left onto the path that leads around to the back of the Hôtel and its pretty French gardens. The path leads to rue des Nonnains d'Hyères, where you'll turn right, then walk left on rue de Jouy to where it intersects with:

4 Rue François Miron

Walk left down rue François Miron to the corner of rue Cloche Perce. You will notice two multi-storied half-timbered houses: the **Maison à l'Enseigne du Faucheur** (no. 11) and the **Maison à l'Enseigne du**

317

Mouton (no. 13). Pre-Haussmann, houses like these were once all over the city; now they are extremely rare. These two date from the 14th century, though after 1607 the crisscrossed wood facades of all such houses were covered to reduce the risk of fire. When these houses were restored in the 1960s, the plaster was removed and the wood was once again revealed.

Double back and continue down rue François Miron until it ends at the St-Paul Métro station. Cross the rue de Rivoli and continue left up rue Pavée to:

5 The Pletzl

You are now entering the city's oldest Jewish quarter, once called the *Pletzl* ("little place" in Yiddish), where there has been a Jewish presence since the 13th century. This community swelled and shrank over the centuries, in line with various edicts and expulsions, but the largest influx was in the 1880s, when tens of thousands of Eastern European Jews, fleeing poverty and persecution, settled in France. The Pletzl was hit hard during the infamous roundups of 1942, when police came and emptied apartment buildings and even schools of their Jewish occupants and sent them to their deaths in Nazi concentration camps. Though the neighborhood is slowly being eaten up by advancing gentrification and chic shops pop up next to kosher bakeries, a small and fairly traditional community still lives here. At no. 10 is the unusual **Synagogue de la rue Pavée,** designed by Hector Guimard, the Art Nouveau master who created the famous Métro entrances. This is the only existing religious edifice by Guimard, whose wife was Jewish. In 1940, on Yom Kippur, the Germans dynamited the synagogue; it was eventually restored and is now a national monument (open for religious services only).

Synagogue de la rue Pavée in the Pletzl.

Continue up rue Pavée to where it crosses:

6 Rue des Rosiers

Rumor has it that this street got its name from the rose bushes that once lined its edges, back in the days when it ran along the exterior of the city walls. Up until recently, it was the main artery of the Jewish quarter; today, all that's left are a few kosher restaurants and a bookstore or two.

Great falafel can still be found here (**L'As du Fallafel;** p. 113); if you happen to be in the area around lunchtime, you might get handed a free sample from one of the competing restaurants.

Turn left on rue des Rosiers and continue to the end, where you'll turn right on rue Vieille du Temple. You are now in the trendier (and gay) part of the neighborhood. Take the first left at rue des Blancs Manteaux and follow this pretty street all the way to where it ends at:

7 Rue du Temple

By the time you hit this street you'll notice that the neighborhood has changed from trendy to workaday; rue du Temple is lined with jewelry and clothing wholesalers. But this street—which back in medieval times led to the stalwart fortress of the Knights Templar—also harbors some lovely examples of 17th-century *hôtels particuliers* (private mansions). Turn right and walk to no. 71, the **Hôtel de St-Aignan,** otherwise known as the **Musée d'Art et d'Histoire du Judaïsme** (p. 180). This exercise in 17th-century grandeur includes a sneaky architectural trick: One of the three facades facing the courtyard, which seems to be the front of an enormous building, is really just a facade. Despite the presence of carefully curtained windows, on the other side of the wall is merely another wall, yet another chunk of Philippe Auguste's ramparts.

Façade of Hôtel de St-Aignan, otherwise known as the Musée d'Art et d'Histoire du Judaïsme.

Continue up to rue de Braque and turn right. Walk to the end where the street intersects with rue des Archives. Across the street is the:

8 Hôtel de Clisson

The vaulted archway is what is left of the **Hôtel de Clisson,** a magnificent mansion that was built in 1380 and for centuries housed some of the grandest of the grand, including dukes of Guise, who hung out there for 135 years. Well, it may have been good enough for them, but by 1700, when François de Rohan, the Prince of Soubise, got his hands on it, he decided the time had come for a change (see below).

Turn right and walk down rue des Archives to rue des Francs Bourgeois and turn left. First thing you'll see on your left is the sumptuous gateway to the:

9 Hôtel de Soubise

The enormous *cour d'honneur,* a huge horseshoe-shaped courtyard, is edged with open galleries holding 56 pairs of double columns. These lead

Interior of 17th-century Hôtel de Soubise.

to a largely 17th-century palace, which now holds the National Archives. This jaw-dropping sight was the creation of architect Pierre Alexis Delamair, who was hired by the Prince of Soubise to build onto the courtyard and overhaul the building. Later, the prince's son, the future Cardinal de Rohan, asked Delamair to build him his own palace next door, the adjoining **Hôtel de Rohan-Strasbourg.** A part of the Hôtel de Soubise houses the **Musée des Archives Nationale** (60 rue des Francs-Bourgeois, 3rd arrond.; archives-nationales.culture.gouv.fr; ✆ **01-40-27-60-96;** free admission; Mon and Wed–Fri 10am–5:30pm, Sat–Sun 2–5:30pm), which displays items from the vast National Archives, as well as temporary exhibitions. You can also visit the **apartments of the Prince and Princess of Soubise.** Though just a few rooms, they retain the opulent decor of the period and give a sense of how the other half lived in the 18th century. The Hôtel de Rohan also displays sumptuous decor taken from the former **Chancellerie d'Orléans,** a palatial 18th-century mansion demolished in the early 20th century.

Continue down rue des Francs Bourgeois and window-shop (or just plain shop) in the stylish boutiques that line this street. Turn left onto rue Elzevir, and head to the:

10 Hôtel Donon

This sumptuous 16th-century mansion houses the **Musée Cognacq-Jay** (p. 179), a small but fabulous and free museum dedicated to 18th-century art. Originally built in 1575, the *hôtel* got its name from its first owner, Médéric de Donon. By the early 20th century, the building had become commercial premises. Fortunately, it was acquired by the City of Paris in 1974 and restored to its former glory. Architecturally, the building is typical of other 16th-century Marais *hôtels*—symmetrical design, with wings set around a rectangular courtyard—but it stands out for its stonework, which is much less ornate than that of other grand mansions in the Marais.

Go back and turn left back onto rue des Francs Bourgeois, then left again to the intersection with rue Payenne for a short detour, about half a block down:

Take a Break ☕

The Hôtel de Marle, the home of the **Institut Suédois,** Swedish Institute (11 rue Payenne, 3rd arrond.; paris.si.se; ⓒ **01-44-78-80-20;** Tue–Sun noon–7pm), has the lovely **Café FIKA** (open 10am to 7pm) with tables in the courtyard in the summer. Nibble a vanilla-scented *kanelbulle* while you take in the exterior of this 16th-century mansion. If you still need a rest, sprawl out on a bench in the Square Georges Cain, a small, leafy park just across the street.

Walk back down rue Payenne, turn left onto rue des Francs Bourgeois, then left again onto rue Sévigné to:

11 Hôtel Carnavalet

If you're interested in learning about the history of Paris, the **Musée Carnavalet** (p. 178) is a must. Not only does it cover thousands of years of the city's past, but it also has beautiful gardens. Originally built in 1548, the *hôtel* got its name from its second owner, the widow of a Breton nobleman named François Kernevenoy, whose surname no one could pronounce. The mangled Parisian pronunciation, "Carnavalet," stuck. In 1660, a new owner gave François Mansart the job of enlarging and modernizing his lodgings: The result was so pleasing that in 1677, Madame de Sévigné, famed letter-writer and woman of the world, rented the building and lived there until her death. There are superb sculptures

Eighteenth-century paintings and decor in the Musée Cognacq-Jay.

in the garden courtyards, including a **bronze statue of Louis XIV** in the **Cour d'Honneur.**

Follow rue de Sévigné south, then turn left onto rue d'Ormesson to:

12 Place du Marché Ste-Catherine

The name speaks to the open-air market that once stood here; today, this shaded plaza remains a lovely oasis of green and quiet in this busy neighborhood. Thankfully, no cars are allowed on the square, and the cafes on its edges all have outdoor seating in nice weather.

Continue to rue St-Antoine and turn left without crossing the street to no. 62:

Gardens of Musée Carnavalet.

Detail of Hôtel de Sully.

The Chinese Lounge in the Maison de Victor Hugo.

13 Hôtel de Sully

The most splendiferous of the many splendiferous mansions in the Marais, the **Hôtel de Sully** was built by a rich 17th-century businessman, Mesme-Gallet. While his version was quite sumptuous, the mansion really came to life when it was bought by the Duc de Sully, who hired architect François Le Vau to give it a makeover. After his death, the palacelike edifice was sold, divided, and built upon—like so many mansions in the Marais. The building was completely restored in the 1970s to Le Vau's version; you can now stroll through the courtyard and admire the sculpted exterior in its virtually pristine state. Though the building is closed to the public, you can traipse through the front courtyard to a second one with a peaceful **garden** filled with sparrows.

Go through the door in the back of the garden to the:

14 Place des Vosges

Officially inaugurated in 1612, this exquisite **Renaissance square,** bordered by 36 virtually identical stone and brick town houses, was the idea of King Henri IV, who unfortunately didn't live to see it finished. After a stroll under the arcades, which run below the town houses, take a seat on a bench in the square and admire the tall trees and elegant symmetry of the landscaping, as well as the huge **statue** in the middle of Louis XIII astride his horse. The square has seen a number of illustrious tenants over the centuries: The most famous inhabitant, no doubt, was writer Victor Hugo, who lived at no. 6 from 1832 to 1848; his house is now the free-to-visit **Maison de Victor Hugo** (p. 178) and has a lovely courtyard cafe.

| 11 |

PLANNING YOUR TRIP TO PARIS

Not all roads lead to Paris, but getting there is a pretty straightforward affair. Once you arrive, you'll need to know how to get around and how to take care of practical matters. Below I supply all the nitty-gritty details you need to have a comfortable, safe, and affordable stay in Paris.

GETTING THERE

By Plane

Paris has two international airports: **Aéroport d'Orly,** 18km (11 miles) south of the city (mostly European flights), and **Aéroport Roissy-Charles-de-Gaulle** (**CDG;** mostly long-haul carriers), 30km (19 miles) northeast. The contact information for both airports is parisaeroport.fr; ⓒ **00-33-1-70-36-39-50** from abroad, and ⓒ **39-50** from France (.35€/min.). Before you fly, check this website for up-to-date airport information.

If you are taking Ryanair or another discount airline to **Beauvais airport** (see below), be advised that that airport is about 80km (50 miles) from Paris.

ROISSY-CHARLES-DE-GAULLE (CDG) AIRPORT CDG has three terminals that are some distance from one another. A free train called the **CDGVAL** connects all three to the two train stations.

The quickest way into central Paris from the airport is the fast **RER B** (ratp.fr; ⓒ **34-24**) suburban trains, which leave every 10 to 15 minutes between roughly 4:50am and 11:50pm. It takes about 40 minutes to get to Paris, and RER B stops at several central Métro stations, including Châtelet-Les-Halles and Saint-Michel–Notre-Dame. A single ticket, which can be bought at the machines in the stations at the terminals, as well as on the Bonjour RATP app, costs 13€ adults, 6.50€ children ages 4–10, free for children 3 and under. (Also see "Getting Around by Public Transport," p. 328, for more information on prices.)

The **Roissybus** (ratp.fr; ⓒ **34-24**) departs every 20 minutes from the airport daily from 6am to 12:30am and costs 13€ for the 70-minute ride. The bus leaves you in the center of Paris, at the corner of rue Scribe and rue Auber, near the Opéra.

The **taxi** rate from Roissy into the city is now a fixed rate of 56€ to the Right Bank and 65€ to the Left Bank, not including supplements (4€ for immediate reservation, 7€ for advance reservation, 5.50€ for a fifth person). Taxi stands are outside each airport terminal. If you're approached by anyone offering you a taxi, please politely turn them down. Alternatively, Uber functions in France and costs about 50€ to 70€ in an UberX car (uber.com; p. 333) depending on traffic and distance. Prices increase when demand is high.

ORLY (ORY) AIRPORT Orly has four terminals, numbered 1 to 4. Since June 2024, the fastest and cheapest option to get to Paris is now the new extension of **Métro line 14,** which links Orly airport in the south to Saint-Denis Pleyel station in the northern suburb of Saint-Denis (for the Stade de France, p. 267) via the town center. This single train ride (with automated trains leaving every 3 to 5 min.) will get you to the Châtelet stop in the center in roughly 25 minutes; the one-way fare is 13€ adults, 6.50€ children ages 4 to 10. This is much cheaper, faster, and more pleasant than the alternative route: taking the 8-minute monorail **OrlyVal** (orlyval.com), which gets you to the **RER** station "Antony," from where you catch RER B into the center. Combined travel time for this journey is about 45 minutes; the one-way fare for the OrlyVal plus the RER B is 13€ adults, 6.50€ children ages 4 to 10, free for children 3 and under. (Also see "Getting Around by Public Transport" for information on prices.) For both journeys, trains run roughly between 5:30am and 11:30pm (11:50pm for line 14).

The **Orlybus** (ratp.fr; © **34-24**), which leaves every 15 minutes between 5am and 12:30am, links the airport with Place Denfert-Rochereau, a 30-minute trip that costs 13€ for both adults and children.

A **taxi** from Orly to central Paris costs a fixed price of 36€ for a Left Bank destination, and 44€ for the Right Bank, not including supplements (4€ for immediate reservation, 7€ for advance reservation, 5.50€ for a fifth person). Uber costs around 35€ to 40€ in an UberX car (uber.com; p. 333). Prices increase during high demand.

BEAUVAIS (BVA) AIRPORT Beauvais airport (aeroportparisbeauvais.com; © **08-92-68-20-66;** .45€/min.) is around 80km (50 miles) from Paris and is served by budget airlines such as Ryanair and Wizz Air. Buses leave about 20 minutes after each flight has landed and, depending on the traffic, take about 1 hour and 15 minutes to get to Porte Maillot on the western edge of Paris. To return to Beauvais, you need to be at the bus station at least 3 hours before the departure of your flight. A one-way ticket costs 16.90€ (29.90€ return ticket) if you purchase it online in advance.

By Train

One of best ways to get around France and Europe is by train. The French railway agency, the **SNCF** (**Société Nationale des Chemins de Fer Français;** sncf-connect.com), has a vast network that connects most major cities and quite a few smaller towns, though you will often have to pass through Paris to get from one place to another. The cheapest tickets are sold online at ouigo.com, which is part of SNCF, but the on-board service (which usually includes a buffet car or trolley service and lets you travel with as many bags as you need) is different and Ouigo doesn't cover as many destinations. On Ouigo trains no food or drink is sold (bring your own or starve), and as with low-cost airlines, you pay extra (from 3€ to 7€) if you want to choose your seat, and you are allowed one item of size-restricted hand luggage, plus a shoulder bag. Any extra/larger items are charged from 5€ each way upon reservation. If you are caught with more luggage than you reserved, you will be asked to pay 20€ extra per bag as you go through the ticket gate (aka the cattle-herd gate, as people line up untidily as they wait their turn). As a result, travelers must arrive 30 minutes before departure.

If you're traveling with kids 3 and under, they are allowed to sit on your knees and travel for free. Seats for kids ages 4 to 11 cost from 5€, but they have the same bag allowance as you.

With a standard (non-discounted) Oui SNCF ticket, you can carry as much luggage as you need, and it is recommended that you arrive 15 minutes in advance (some trains are very long, and it can take almost that amount of time to walk to your carriage; train platforms are typically displayed on the '*Departs*' screens 15 to 20 minutes before departure).

The SNCF connects to railways in neighboring countries, including the U.K., Germany, Holland, and Belgium. **Eurostar** (eurostar.com), which passes under the channel for 20 minutes, will get you from Paris's Gare du Nord to St. Pancras Station, London, in just 2¼ hours. If London is your destination, know that even though the regular ticket price can be high (around 200€ one-way!), scads of discounts are available (from as little as around 44€ one-way) on the website, especially if you purchase in advance and/or are flexible about times. Since the closure of Thalys in 2023, Eurostar now also covers its former destinations—cities like Brussels (just 1¼ hr. from Paris), Amsterdam (3½ hr.), Rotterdam (2 hr. 40 min.), and Cologne (3 hr. 20 min.). Tickets range anywhere from 49€ to 200€ depending on what deal you get. For rail passes that you can use throughout Europe, visit **Rail Europe** (raileurope.com).

Paris has seven major train stations: **Gare d'Austerlitz** (13th arrond.), **Gare de Lyon** (12th arrond.), **Gare de Bercy** (12th arrond.), **Gare Montparnasse** (14th arrond.), **Gare St-Lazare** (8th arrond.), **Gare de l'Est** (10th arrond.), and **Gare du Nord** (10th arrond.). Stations can be reached by bus or Métro. *Warning:* I have never had trouble, but as in many cities, stations and surrounding areas can be seedy and are frequented by pickpockets. Be alert, especially at night.

By Bus

You can travel to and from Paris from other European countries by bus via two main companies: **Flixbus** (global.flixbus.com), which has over 1,000 routes, and tickets starting for as little as 5€ (buy online, via the app, or in Paris go to the FlixShop at Gare-Bercy, 208 quai de Bercy, 12th arrond.), and **BlaBlaCar Bus** (thetrainline.com/bus-companies/blablabus; reserve online or via the app), offering 400 routes with even cheaper tickets starting at 2.99€. The main bus stop for both of these companies is Bercy-Seine (210 quai de Bercy, 12th arrond.)

By Car

I wouldn't recommend driving in Paris to my worst enemy, but renting a car and driving around France can be a lovely way to see the country. All the major car-rental companies have offices here, though you'll often get better deals if you reserve before you leave home. **AutoEurope** (autoeurope.com) is an excellent source for discounted rentals. Even better may be **AutoSlash.com,** which applies discount codes to rentals from all the major multinational firms; this can mean big savings. It also monitors prices, so if a rate drops, it re-books you automatically. You pay for the rental at the counter, not in advance. Also check out **Avis** (avis.com), **Hertz** (hertz.com), and **Europcar** (europcar.com). If you don't want to traipse across town to a car-hire shop, try **Carlili** (carlili.fr/en), which delivers and collects your car, at the address of your choice, 7 days a week.

Before you step on the gas, at the very least, try to get a list of international road signs; your car rental agency should have one. Driving in France is not substantially different from driving in most English-speaking countries (although British travelers will have to get used to driving on the "wrong" side of the road). However, you'll have to contend with French drivers, who tend to zoom around with what the more timid among us would call reckless abandon (particularly look out for motorcyclists, who can be daredevils). Truthfully, since the installation of radar a few years ago, drivers have become much more well-behaved; you, too, should pay attention to speed limits or risk a steep fine. The two biggest driving differences: *priorité à droite,* which means priority is always given to vehicles approaching from the right at intersections, unless otherwise indicated; and the fondness for **roundabouts** (traffic circles). Rule number one regarding the latter: The person entering the roundabout does *not* have priority. Rule number two: Look at the sign posted *before* the roundabout that indicates which exit goes in what direction so that you'll be prepared when it's time to get off. The good news is that if you miss your turnoff, you can just circle around until you figure out where it is. In Paris, certain large roundabouts, like Place Charles de Gaulle at the top of the Champs-Élysées, don't have marked lanes, so it can seem like a free-for-all. The key here is not to hesitate, and to look around you at all times.

GETTING AROUND

Finding an Address

The river Seine divides Paris into the **Rive Droite (Right Bank)** to the north and the **Rive Gauche (Left Bank)** to the south. You can figure out which is which if you face west. (Figuring out which way is west is another problem.) Paris is divided into 20 municipal districts called **arrondissements,** which spiral out clockwise starting with the 1st, which is the geographical center of the city. It's not easy to figure out without a map or an app, so I strongly suggest that you invest in a booklet called *Paris Pratique par Arrondissement*, which has a bus and Métro map for each arrondissement. You can buy one for about 6€ in most *Presse*—newspaper—stands and at Fnac stores (p. 262), or on Amazon.com beforehand for considerably more. The only thing is that at time of writing, the current edition is old, so the bike lanes and Vélib' stand info is not up-to-date. The city layout won't have changed, though. Or there are, of course, dozens of good map apps for Paris if you prefer—though Wi-Fi doesn't always work as well as it should in public spaces, and it's still near impossible to get good 4G or 5G coverage on the Métro. Also note that in April 2023, Parisians voted to ban self-serve electric scooters (called *trottinettes*), considering them too dangerous to keep on the streets, so you can no longer rent them to get around town (though you'll still notice a few people with their own).

By Public Transport

For everything you ever wanted to know about the city's public transport, visit the **RATP** (ratp.fr; ✆ **34-24**) or the app Bonjour RATP (ratp.fr/apps/bonjour ratp). Paris and its suburbs are divided into five travel zones, with zones 1 and 2, covering the city itself, and the outer zones covering places like Versailles and the airports.

Single RATP tickets are valid on the Métro, bus, tram, and RER, and now (as of 2025) have standardized prices—2.50€ for the Métro and RER, and 2€ for buses and trams (children 4 to 9 years old pay half-price; kids 3 and under ride free)—no matter where you travel within the five zones (except for the main airports tickets, which cost 13€, see p. 324).

All paper tickets were phased out in 2025, so to use the public transport system, you will need to purchase a plastic pass known as a **Navigo** Card (which costs 2€). You can get these from the machines or windows in Métro stations, or directly on your telephone via the app Bonjour RATP. Once you have your card, you charge it (either on your phone with the app or at a machine) with your required tickets. Children 4 to 9 years old pay half-price for tickets; kids 3 and under ride free.

By far the easiest way to get tickets is via the app. If the ticket you need is not displayed, it is probably because it is incompatible with the tickets already present on your card. For instance, if you need an airport ticket, you will need to generate a separate card on the app, as (somewhat annoyingly) the system can't tell whether you're travelling within the city or to the airport when you go through the turnstiles. Without the app, you can buy tickets (via the plastic Navigo card) at the window or from machines at most Métro entrances. The machines take coins, notes and chip-enabled credit cards only. Bear in mind that the RATP has now also phased out the once ubiquitous *carnet* (a pack of 10 tickets sold at a discounted rate), so you can only buy individual tickets, or daily, weekly or monthly passes (see below). The downside to the disappearance of the *carnet* is the price; ten carnet tickets would previously have cost 17.50€ (though they were only valid for zones 1 and 2), now ten individual tickets cost 25€, and cannot be shared between people. Each person will need their own card. If necessary, you can have multiple people's cards on one phone.

Tourists can benefit from a **Paris Visite** pass, which offers unlimited travel in all zones on bus, Métro, and RER, as well as access to the airports. But, think hard about how much you are going to use your pass however, as you'll probably end up walking a lot, and, if you're here for a few days, a weekly Navigo pass might do the trick. It all comes down to the math. For instance, a Paris Visite adult pass costs 29.90€ for 1 day, 44.45€ for 2 days, 62.30€ for 3 days and 76.25€ for 5 days, and though they include airport tickets (which alone would cost 13€ each way), it might be cheaper for you to get the **Navigo weekly pass,** which can be bought on the app at the ticket booth or ticket machines for 2€, then charged for 31.60€. That includes going to and from the airports (via line 14 for Orly) and transport for day trips such as Versailles or Fontainebleau, so it could quickly pay off. If your trip fits into a Friday-to-Thursday schedule, this 7-day card is substantially cheaper than a 5-day, 76.25€ Paris Visite card. On the other hand, of you get a 1-day Navigo card, which costs 12€, it doesn't include the airports, so you'd need to add your return journey to the airport (which would cost 26€), and would end up costing 8.10€ more than the 1-day Paris Visite card.

BY MÉTRO (SUBWAY)

The city's first Métro, or subway, was at the apex of high tech at its inauguration on July 19, 1900, and over a century later, it still functions very well. The lack of cleanliness and wheelchair/stroller access are its greatest downfalls and somewhat embarrassing for the city that hosted the 2024 Paralympics. There is, however, an ongoing push to render the city more accessible, so don't be surprised to find some stations closed between certain hours. Another problem is not technical, but political: Subway workers are fond of strikes (*grèves*) and periodically instigate slowdowns or complete shutdowns of a few lines. Usually, strikes are merely annoying and most of the time your route will not be affected, though your trip might take a little longer than normal. If you see the words *Movement Social* on the TV monitor as you enter the station, or notice little traffic cones in the bottom right-hand corner of the icon for the metro line you need, your line is probably involved (low groans and cursing by ticket holders are also good indicators of strike activity). You can also check your line on the app, which is updated in real time.

Strikes aside, the Métro is usually efficient and civilized, especially if you avoid rush hour (7:30–9:30am and 6–8pm). It's generally safe at night, and you don't need to worry about taking it at 3am because you can't. Alas, when people dolefully talk about "the Last Métro," they're usually not discussing a movie by François Truffaut. Instead, they're referring to a fact of Parisian life: Your evening out must be carefully timed so that you can run to the station before the trains shut down between midnight and 1am. To ease your pain, the transit authority added an extra hour on weekends, so now the Métro closes around 2am on Friday, Saturday, and pre-holiday evenings. The suburban trains (the RER; see below) close down around the same time (without the weekend bonus hour). Buses, known as Noctaliens, then take over until the Metro reopens in the morning (see p. 330).

A map covering the whole Paris region is essential (use the one on the RATP app (ratp.fr/apps/bonjour-ratp) or Île-de-France Mobilités app (iledefrance-mobilites.fr), or pick one up at any ticket window. There's also one on the inside back cover of this book. The key is to know both the number of the line and its final destination. If you are on the no. 1 line (direction La Défense) and you want to transfer at the enormous Châtelet station to get to St-Michel, at Châtelet you'll need to doggedly follow the signs to the no. 4, direction Bagneux Lucie Aubrac.

> **Transit Price Check**
>
> With so many new options, deciding on how to get around can be brain busting. If price is your only criteria, here's a quick comparison based on a 30- or 45-minute ride:
> **Vélib':** 3€
> **Métro:** 2.50€
> **Vélib' electric:** 3€

BY RER

Your only underground express choice is the **RER** (pronounced "ehr-euh-ehr"), the suburban trains that dash through the city making limited stops. The down sides are (a) they don't run as often as the Métro, (b) they're a lot less pleasant, and (c) they're hard to figure out since they run on a different track system and the same lines can have multiple final destinations. *Important:* You'll need to scan your ticket to get out of the turnstile on the way out. To check your destinations, check the departure boards (or screens) on the quays: The stops served by the next train are either listed or lit up.

BY BUS

Thanks to a network of dedicated bus lanes, buses can be an efficient way to get around town, and you'll get a scenic tour to boot. The majority start running around 6am and stop anywhere from 9:30pm to midnight; service is reduced on Sundays and holidays. You can use Métro passes on the buses, or you can buy a special (and cheaper) bus ticket on the app for 2€ directly from your mobile phone.

Another option is to buy a SMS ticket. All you have to do, when you see your bus approaching, is send an SMS to ⓒ 93100 with the word *BUS,* followed by the number of the route (with no gaps between the two). For instance, if you're on route 86, type *BUS86;* if you're on route 2 of the Noctalien night bus, write *BUSN02*. You'll immediately receive an SMS in return, with your ticket. This costs 2.50€, and is valid for 1 hour.

Just to complicate things, you cannot, alas, reuse a ticket you've used on the Métro on the bus. Neither can you reuse an SMS bus ticket on a tram. You can, however, reuse the same app or plastic Navigo card ticket you've used on the bus on a tram (and vice versa) within a 90-minute limit. Tickets and passes need to be validated in the machine next to the driver's cabin. Or, if you have an SMS one on your phone, show the driver as you board.

BY TRAM

Over the past few years, Paris has added 11 new tramway lines, with extensions and new lines in progress. These tramways connect Paris with its suburbs;

within Paris they run along the outer circle of boulevards that trace the city limits. Tickets are 2€ if bought via the app, or you can use a 2.50€ Métro ticket.

By Bicycle

With over 1,000km (620 miles) of bike lanes, Paris has become a veritable cyclists' city—aided, undoubtedly by the hugely successful **Vélib'** (vel-*LEEB*) self-serve bike rental scheme launched in 2007 (the name comes from *vélo*, meaning "bicycle," and *liberté*, meaning "freedom"). Vélib' is still going strong, and with over 1,400 bike stands, now also includes electric bikes (colored blue; around 40% of the 19,000-strong fleet; the pedal bikes are green), so you can get around even faster.

For Vélib', you have several subscription options (online, via the Vélib app or through the RATP Bonjour app): Buy a single-journey ticket for 3€ for a 45-minute journey on a pedal bike or an electric bike; get a 1-day pass for 5€ (pedal bike) or 10€ (electric), which gives you the right to multiple 30-minute (45-min. for electric) rides as often as you'd like for 24 hours (and, for the 10€ pass, even includes a free hour on a pedal bike); and purchase the 3-day pass for 20€ (which includes 60 min. on pedal bikes and 45 min. on electric). If you want to go over 30 minutes, you pay 1€ for your extra 30 minutes on a pedal bike, and 2€ for 30 minutes on an electric bike. The bikes are fitted with a V-Box, a computer system set between the handlebars, which enables you to lock and unlock the bikes. It also lets you leave your bike in an otherwise full station; follow the instructions and park it top-to-tail with another bike.

The English version of the website (velib-metropole.fr/en_GB) explains how everything works; the assistance phone number is ✆ **01-76-49-12-34.** Ideally, you should buy your subscription ahead of time online or via the Vélib app (make sure you have your secret code to punch in on the stand). Helmets are not provided, so if you're feeling queasy about launching into traffic, bring one along. *Note:* Cyclists no longer always have the right to ride in the bus lanes; check for road signs. *One more tip:* Download the Vélib' and Bonjour RATP app on your phone, so you don't waste precious time looking for a place to check in or check out.

Other self-serve bike companies include **Lime** (li.me) and **Dott** (ridedott. com, which has a fleet of e-bikes).

If you don't want to self-serve, you can still rent a bike from **Paris à Vélo!,** 22 rue Alphonse Baudin (parisavelo.fr; ✆ **01-48-87-60-01;** Métro: St-Sébastien-Froissart or Richard Lenoir). Rentals for a regular bicycle cost 19€ for half a day and 22€ for a full day, but they do require a safety deposit of at least 250€, depending on the type of bike you rent. If you're feeling extra lazy, electric bikes are available from 38€ for half a day and 45€ for a full day.

One Word About Driving in Paris

Don't. Even if you are a Formula 1 racecar driver with years of experience, you'll be alternately outraged and infuriated by the aggressive tactics of your fellow drivers and the inevitable *bouchons* (literally, a bottle stopper or cork), or jams, which tie up traffic and turn a simple jaunt into a harrowing nightmare. To make matters worse, it's easy to believe that the street and direction signs were cunningly placed by someone who gets kicks out of watching hapless drivers take wrong turns.

Your troubles are not over once you get to your destination, because then you will have to park, which is a whole other trauma. Spots are elusive, to say the least, and you'll probably find yourself touring the neighborhood for at least 15 minutes until you find one. By then you'll have figured out why it is that Parisians park on pedestrian crossings: Often, there's nowhere else to park.

One final hurdle: feeding the **parking meter.** All parking is *payant*—that is, you must pay (Mon–Sat 9am–8pm). And you can't use coins in the *horodateur* (parking meter) anymore—you must either pay with a chip-enabled credit card or via the following apps: **paybyphone.fr**, **flowbird.fr**, **easypark.fr**, or **indigoneo.fr**. If you pay by card at the parking meter, you'll probably get a print-out ticket that you must put on your dashboard. If you pay via one of the apps, you don't have to do anything except state where you are parked (and sometimes give the car license plate); the traffic police have a device linked to the apps and can see that you've paid from the car's license plate. Paris is a polluted city, so the city is trying to reduce traffic, largely with dissuasive parking prices. Today in the most central arrondissements (1–11), parking costs 6€ for the first hour, then increases incrementally to a whopping 75€ for 6 hours; in the outer arrondissements (12–20), it's 4€ per hour, up to 50€ for 6 hours. What's more, you can't stay in the same spot for more than 6 hours—and fines have increased to 75€ in zones 1 to 11, and 50€ in zones 12 to 20. Mercifully, on Sundays and from 8pm to 9am the rest of the week, all street parking is free. If you are not up to the challenge, try one of the many **underground parking lots,** indicated by a sign with a white P on a blue background; parking in one of these is between 2.60€ and 4€ per hour, or between 26€ and 35€ for 24 hours. As well as letting you pay your parking meter, **Indigno Neo** (indigoneo.fr) handily has a map of underground parking, with a real-time reservation system.

If, despite this rant, you still feel compelled to rent a car and drive around the city, or are forced to do so due to extenuating circumstances, at the very least get your hands on a basic explanation of international street signs (this should be available at your car-rental agency) and a good street map or app. Taxi drivers nowadays use the app Waze (waze.com), which works like a GPS using real-time traffic info to guide you to your destination using the fastest, least traffic-clogged route. Finally, try to keep your cool, because no matter how sure you are that you are following the rules of the road, at some point, someone in another car will curse you. Good luck—you're going to need it.

By Boat

The **Batobus** (batobus.com; ✆ **01-76-64-79-12**) is a fleet of boats that operates along the Seine, stopping at nine points of interest, including the Eiffel Tower, the Musée d'Orsay, the Louvre, Notre-Dame, and the Hôtel de Ville. Much like the hop-on, hop-off buses (see "Bus Tours," p. 228), these boats are more about sightseeing and less about getting quickly from place to place, though they will get you up and down the Seine. Unlike the Bateaux-Mouches (p. 225), the Batobus has the advantage of not providing cheesy, recorded commentary.

The only fare option is a day pass valid for either 1 or 2 days, or a year, each allowing as many entrances and exits as you want. At time of writing, the 1-day passes cost 23€ for adults and 13€ for children 4 to 11, while the 2-day passes cost 27€ for adults and 17€ for 4 to 11s, and the yearly passes cost 73€ for adults and 48€ for 4 to 11s. You'll save a euro or two if you reserve online. Boats operate daily from around 10am; boats come by every 25 to 40 minutes, depending on the season. Last call is anywhere from 5pm during the week in the winter to 7pm in the summer; see the website for exact intervals and closing hours.

By Taxi

Nowadays, there's not much difference in either price or reservation method between ride-hailing companies such as Uber, and traditional Parisian taxi companies like G7. If anything, Uber's disruptive presence has made the more traditional companies pull their socks up, making them more reliable and pleasant to use than some the newer ride-hailing enterprises (Yes, Uber, that's you!). Generally speaking, whether you decide to use traditional taxis or one of the ride-hailing apps listed below, you should download the smartphone app and enter your credit-card details. Once you're logged on, you enter your location and your destination. No cash changes hands, and the cost of your journey is either estimated (in the case of classic Parisian taxis), or pre-calculated according to its "real" distance (in the case of ride-hailing companies like Uber) so you're not penalized if you have to make a detour. With either type of ride, the screen shows the whereabouts of your taxi in real time, as well as the car's number plate, the driver's name, and (sometimes) their photo. When traveling abroad (especially if you're a woman), it's reassuring to know who will be driving your cab, and for central Paris, you rarely have to wait more than 5 minutes for a taxi to arrive.

For ride-hailing apps, both **Uber** (uber.com) and **Bolt** (bolt.eu) offer services in English, while reliable **Heetch** (heetch.com) and **LeCab** (lecab.fr), provide ridesharing in French—and sometimes at a lower price.

To hail a cab from the street, try for those with a full green or white light (red light or a single white bulb means they're taken), or look for a taxi stand, which resembles a bus stop and usually sports a blue TAXI sign. If you don't have the app, it can be easier to call a cab than to hail one: **Taxi G7** (g7.fr; ✆ **36-07;** .45€/min.) is the main company; **Alpha Taxis** is another (reservation.alphataxis.fr; ✆ **01 45 85 85 85**).

Calculating taxi fares is a complicated business. When you get in, the most the meter should read is 4.40€. Then, the maximum basic rate for Paris *intra-muros* is 1.27€ (depending on the day of the week and the hour this may be lower). The minimum fare is 8€; if you have more than four people in your party, you'll be charged an extra 5.50€ for the fifth person, too. If you reserve a taxi for immediate pickup, the extra charge is 4€; to reserve in advance costs 7€. The saving grace here is that the distances are usually not huge, and barring excessive traffic, your average crosstown fare should fall between 15€ and 25€ for two. Tipping is not obligatory, but rounding up or a .50€ to 1€ tip is customary. Almost all taxis these days accept card payments, but if you don't use the app, then double check before you climb in.

On Foot

If you have the time and the energy, the best mode of transport in this small and walkable city is your own two feet. You can cross the center of town (say from the Place St-Michel to Les Halles) in about 20 minutes. This is the best way to see and experience the city and take in all the little details that make it so wonderful.

[Fast FACTS] PARIS

Area Codes The country code for France is 33, and the area code for Paris is 01.

Business Hours Opening hours in Paris are erratic. Most museums close 1 day a week (usually Mon or Tues) and some national holidays. Museum hours tend to be from 9:30am to 6pm, and some museums (like the Louvre, p. 166) have late-night openings. Generally, **offices** are open Monday to Friday from 9am to 6pm, but don't count on it—always call first. **Banks** tend to be open from 9am to 5pm Monday to Friday, but some branches are open on Saturday instead of Monday. **Large stores** are open from around 10am to 7 or 8pm. Some **small stores** still have a lunch break that can last for up to 2 hours, from 1 to 3pm, but this is becoming increasingly rare. Most shops, except those in the Marais or on the Champs-Élysées, are closed on Sunday. Restaurants are typically closed on Sunday evenings and/or Mondays, and many businesses across the city are closed for 2 weeks in August and sometimes between December 25th and January 1st.

Cell Phones The three letters that define much of the world's wireless capabilities are **GSM** (Global System for Mobile Communications), a big, seamless network that makes for easy cross-border mobile phone use throughout Europe and dozens of other countries worldwide. You can use your mobile phone in France provided it is GSM and 3G, 4G, or 5G; just confirm this with your operator before you leave.

Using your phone abroad can be expensive, and you usually have to pay to receive calls, so it's a good idea to get your phone "unlocked" before you leave. Then you can buy a SIM card from one of the three main French providers: **Bouygues Télécom** (bouyguestelecom.fr), **Orange** (orange.fr), or **SFR** (sfr.fr). A temporary SIM card (*carte prépayée*) costs anywhere from about 5€ to 40€, depending on the number of minutes bundled with it. Alternatively, if your phone isn't unlocked, you could buy a cheap mobile phone in Paris. To top up your phone credit, buy a prepaid card (*carte prépayée*) from *tabacs*, supermarkets, and mobile phone outlets. Prices range from 5€ to 100€.

A final (probably better) strategy? Use FaceTime, Messenger, or WhatsApp for free phone calls. Make sure you have the app before you get to Europe and then use it whenever you have a signal.

Customs What you can bring into France: Citizens of E.U. countries can bring in any amount of goods as long as the goods are

WHAT YOU CAN take out OF FRANCE

Australian Citizens The **Australian Customs Service** (abf.gov.au/entering-and-leaving-australia/duty-free; ⓒ **131-881** in Australia, or 612/6196-0196 from abroad) has complete customs information on its website. The duty-free allowance in Australia is A$900 or, for those 17 and younger, A$450. Those 18 and over can bring home up to 2.25 liters of alcoholic beverages.

Canadian Citizens For a clear summary of Canadian rules, visit the **Canada Border Services Agency** (cbsa-asfc.gc.ca; ⓒ **800/461-9999** in Canada, or 204/983-3500 from abroad). Canada allows its citizens a C$800 exemption. You can also bring back up to 1.5 liters of wine, 1.14 liters of other alcoholic beverage, or up to 8.5 liters of beer.

New Zealand Citizens The answers to most questions regarding customs can be found on the website of the **New Zealand Customs Service** under "duty and allowances" (customs.govt.nz; ⓒ **0800/428-786,** or 64-9/886-4651 from outside New Zealand). The duty-free allowance for New Zealand is NZ$700. You are allowed to bring back 4.5 liters of wine or beer, and not more than 3 bottles of spirits (each bottle not exceeding 1.125 liters).

U.K. Citizens Post-Brexit, there are now limits on what you can bring back to the country from France: You can bring 42 liters of beer, 18 liters of non-sparkling wine, 4 liters of spirits over 22% alcohol by volume or 9 liters of alcohol up to 22% (including sparkling wine). For information, contact **HM Revenue Customs** (gov.uk/bringing-goods-into-uk-personal-use/arriving-in-Great-Britain; ⓒ **44/300-200-3700**).

U.S. Citizens For specifics on what you can bring back and the corresponding fees, click on "Know Before You Visit" at **www.cbp.gov**. Or, contact the **U.S. Customs & Border Protection** (**CBP;** ⓒ **877/227-5511** in the U.S., or 202/325-8000 from outside the U.S.). Returning U.S. citizens who have been away for 48 hours or more are allowed to bring back, once every 31 days, $800 worth of merchandise duty-free. Included in your allowance is 1 duty-free liter of alcoholic beverage; after that, it depends what state you live in, so check with your state customs office for amounts.

---

intended for their personal use and not for resale. Non–E.U. citizens are entitled to 200 cigarettes, 100 small cigars, 50 cigars, or 250g of tobacco duty-free. You can also bring in 4 liters of non-sparkling wine, 16 liters of beer, 2 liters of alcoholic beverages less than 22% alcohol, and 1 liter of spirits more than 22% alcohol. (Also see the box "What You Can Take Out of France," above.)

Dentists & Doctors

Doctors are listed in the **Pages Jaunes** (French equivalent of the Yellow Pages; pagesjaunes.fr) under "Médecins." Online, type "medecin generaliste" in the central search box and "Paris" in the right-hand one; names (and even photos) will appear. You'll also find a list of doctors and specialties on the **Doctolib** website (doctolib.fr). The standard fee for a consultation with a general practitioner (*médecin generaliste*) is 25€. **SOS Médecins** (ⓒ **36-24,** .15€/min., and ⓒ **01-47-07-77-77;** sosmedecins.fr) makes house calls that cost around 90€ to 130€ (prices quoted are for people without French social security). Or you can request an online appointment. There are also five walk-in surgeries open until midnight (listed on the website). Find a list of English-speaking dentists and doctors in Paris on the U.S. Embassy website: fr.usembassy.gov/services/medical-assistance. See also "Emergencies" and "Health," below.

11

Drinking Laws
Supermarkets, grocery stores, and cafes sell alcoholic beverages. The legal drinking age is 18. Wine and liquor are sold every day of the week, year-round. Cafes generally open around 7am and serve until closing (between midnight and 2am). Bars and nightclubs usually stay open until 2am (sometimes 5am), but they must stop serving alcohol 1½ hours before closing. You can drink in public, but you cannot be drunk in public.

The law regarding drunk driving is tough. A motorist is considered legally intoxicated if his or her blood-alcohol content exceeds .05%. If it is between .05% and .08%, the driver faces a fine of 750€. Over .08% and it could cost 4,500€ or up to 2 years in jail.

Electricity
Electricity in France runs on 220 volts AC (60 cycles); the U.S. runs on 120 volts AC. Adapters for plugs (Type E is most useful in France) or transformers are needed to fit sockets; you can buy these in branches of Fnac (p. 262). You can also buy them at many electronics stores before your trip. Check if your appliance can handle 220 volts; fortunately many today are dual voltage. If your appliance isn't, though, you risk frying it. In such cases, use a transformer. If the appliance is dual voltage, you need only an adapter so you can plug into a socket.

Embassies & Consulates
If you have a passport, immigration, legal, or other problem, contact your consulate. Many require you to fill in an online form to explain your situation. Otherwise, call before you go—they often keep odd hours and observe both French and home-country holidays.

The Embassy of **Australia,** 4 rue Jean-Rey, 15e (france.embassy.gov.au; ✆ **01-40-59-33-00;** Métro: Bir Hakeim), is open Monday to Friday 9am to 5pm except public holidays. The Consular section is open Monday to Friday from 9am to noon and 2 to 4pm. Both are accessible by appointment only.

The Embassy of **Canada,** 130 rue du Faubourg Saint-Honoré, 8e (international.gc.ca/country-pays/france; ✆ **01-44-43-29-00;** Métro: Franklin-D-Roosevelt or Alma-Marceau), is open Monday to Friday 9am to 5pm by appointment only.

The Embassy of **Ireland,** 12 av. Foch, entrance 4 rue Rude, 16e (ireland.ie/en/france/paris; ✆ **01-44-17-67-00;** Métro: Argentine), is open without an appointment Monday to Friday 9:30 to 11:30am; to request an appointment, you must fill in an online form.

The Embassy of **New Zealand,** 103 rue de Grenelle, 7e (mfat.govt.nz/en/countries-and-regions/europe/france/new-zealand-embassy; ✆ **01-45-01-43-43;** Métro: Solferino), is open Monday 10:30am to 1pm and 2 to 5pm; Tuesday to Friday 9am to 1pm and 2 to 5pm.

The Embassy of the **United Kingdom,** 35 rue du Faubourg St-Honoré, 8e (gov.uk/world/france; ✆ **01-44-51-31-00;** Métro: Concorde or Madeleine), is open Monday to Friday 9:30am to 1pm and 2:30 to 5pm.

The Embassy of the **United States,** 2 av. Gabriel, 8e (fr.usembassy.gov; ✆ **01-43-12-22-22;** Métro: Concorde), is open Monday to Friday 9am to 6pm. Appointment required for passport and other services; you can schedule online on the website.

Emergencies
In an emergency, call ✆ **112,** or the fire brigade (Sapeurs-Pompiers; ✆ **18**), who are trained to deal with all kinds of medical emergencies, not just fires. For a medical emergency and/or ambulance, call ✆ **15.** For the police, call ✆ **17.**

Etiquette & Customs
Parisians like pleasantries and take manners seriously: Say bonjour, madame/monsieur, when entering an establishment and au revoir when you depart. Always say pardon when you accidentally bump into someone. With strangers, people who are older than you, and professional contacts, use vous rather than tu (vous is the polite form of the pronoun you).

Health
For travel abroad, non–E.U. nationals should consider buying medical travel insurance. For U.S. citizens, Medicare and Medicaid do not provide coverage for medical

costs incurred abroad, so check what medical services your health insurance covers before leaving home. That said, medical costs are a fraction of what they are in the U.S. (for example, a visit to a GP costs 25€), so you may even decide to do a little medical tourism (be sure to bring your prescriptions). U.K. nationals need a U.K. Global Health Insurance Card (GHIC) or a **European Health Insurance Card (EHIC)** to receive free or reduced-cost medical care during a visit to a European Union (E.U.) country, Iceland, Liechtenstein, Norway, or Switzerland (go to nhs.uk, then type GHIC into the search box).

If you suffer from a chronic illness, consult your doctor before your departure. Pack prescription medications in your carry-on luggage and carry them in their original containers, with pharmacy labels—otherwise they might not make it through airport security. Carry the generic name of prescription medicines, in case a local pharmacist is unfamiliar with the brand name.

For further tips on travel and health concerns, and a list of local English-speaking doctors, contact the **International Association for Medical Assistance to Travelers** (**IAMAT;** iamat.org; © **716/754-4883** in the U.S., or 416/652-0137 in Canada). You can also consult a list of English-speaking dentists and doctors in Paris at the U.S. Citizen Services page on the U.S. embassy website (fr.usembassy.gov). See also "Dentists & Doctors," "Emergencies," "Hospitals," and "Pharmacies" in this section.

Hospitals Most Parisian hospitals have 24-hr. emergency rooms, and some have a specialty (Hôpitals Necker and Trousseau are two of the best children's hospitals in France, for example). For addresses and information on all Paris public hospitals, visit aphp.fr.

Two private hospitals in nearby suburbs have English-speaking staff and operate 24 hours a day (and cost much more than the public ones): the **American Hospital of Paris,** 55 bd. du Château, 92200 Neuilly-sur-Seine (americanhospital.org; © **01-46-41-25-25;** Métro: Pont de Levallois; 15-min. walk from station; bus: 82, 93, 163, and 174); and the **Hôpital Franco-Britannique,** 3 rue Barbès or 4 rue Kleber, Levallois (hopitalfrancobritannique.org; © **01-47-59-59-59;** Métro: Anatole-France; bus 93, 164, 174).

Hotlines S.O.S. Help is a hotline for English-speaking callers in crisis (soshelpline.org; © **01-46-21-46-46;** daily 3–11pm).

Internet & Wi-Fi Many Parisian hotels and cafes have Internet access, and Wi-Fi (pronounced wee-fee here) is increasingly common in public spaces. Cybercafes are few and far between nowadays, but the huge **Milk** location in Les Halles (31 boulevard de Sébastopol, 1st arrond.) is reliably open 24/7 (milklub.com).

LGBTQ+ Travelers France is known for being a particularly open country when it comes to the LGBTQ+ community. "Gay Paree" boasts a large LGBTQ+ population, and had an openly gay mayor, Bertrand Delanoë, for over a decade. The center of gay and lesbian life is in the Marais. The annual Gay Pride March (also called La Marche des Fiertés—March of Pride—to include all LGBTQ+ people) usually takes place on the last Sunday in June (p. 53). Information and resources can be found in Paris's largest, best-stocked gay bookstore, **Les Mots à la Bouche,** 37 rue Saint-Ambroise, 11th arrond. (motsbouche.com; © **01-42-78-88-30;** Métro: Rue Saint-Maur), which carries publications in both French and English. To find listings and events, try **Qweek** (qweek.fr), a website focused on Paris (French only).

Lost & Found If you lose an important belonging, contact the police's **Bureau des Objets Trouvés,** 36 rue des Morillons, 15 arrond. (objetstrouves prefecturedepolice.franceobjetstrouves.fr/en). If you left something on the bus, Métro, or RER, consult ratp.fr/en and search for "lost and found," or if that doesn't work (the RATP's website has flaws), type

"RATP lost & found" in your standard search engine. If your object is found (including on the RATP network), the police bureau will contact you by SMS.

Mail Every arrondissement has a post office (**La Poste;** laposte.fr; ⓒ **36-31**). Most are open Monday to Friday 9am to 7pm, Saturday 9am to 1pm; the Louvre post office (50 rue du Louvre; Métro: Louvre-Rivoli) is open Monday to Saturday 8am to midnight and Sunday 10am to midnight. Stamps are also sold in *tabacs* (tobacconists).

Money & Costs Frommer's lists exact prices in the local currency. The currency conversions quoted below were correct at press time. However, rates fluctuate, so before departing consult a currency exchange website such as oanda.com or xe.com to check up-to-the-minute rates.

ATMs are widely available in Paris, but if you're venturing into rural France, it's always good to have cash in your pocket. Be sure you know your personal identification number (PIN) and daily withdrawal limit before you depart. Many banks impose a fee when you withdraw money abroad, and that fee can be higher for international transactions than for domestic ones. In addition, the bank from which you withdraw cash may charge its own fee. For currency exchanges, always use a bank (you'll get a better exchange rate that way).

Visa is the most common credit card in France, but with the exception of American Express, which is sometimes refused, international credit cards are widely accepted. Foreign credit cards, particularly those without an embedded chip, do not always work in machines. At time of writing, most shops allow you to flash your card (without inputting the pin number) up to 50€. Payments from mobile phone apps are also accepted and don't cap at 50€. Check for hidden fees when using your card abroad—some bank charges can be up to 3% of the purchase price. Some family-run shops, restaurants, and bars don't accept credit or debit cards; check in advance and have cash on hand.

Traveler's checks are no longer accepted.

Passports Citizens of New Zealand, Australia, Canada, the U.K., and the United States need a valid passport to enter France. The passport is valid for a stay of 90 days. All children must have their own passports.

Allow plenty of time before your trip to apply for a passport; at time of writing, processing time in the U.S. was 4 to 6 weeks, plus 2 to 3 weeks for expedition. Even an emergency request can take up to 2 weeks. You may also have to be prepared to fly across the country to get the requisite in-person appointment. (Check travel.state.gov for the most updated information.) Keep in mind that if you need a passport in a hurry, you'll pay a higher processing fee.

Pharmacies You'll spot French *pharmacies* by looking for the green neon cross above the door. If your local pharmacy is closed, there should be a sign on the door indicating the nearest one open. Pharmacists give basic medical advice and can take your blood pressure. *Parapharmacies* sell medical products and toiletries, but they don't dispense prescriptions. Pharmacies open 24/7 include: **Pharmacie Européene,** 6 pl. de Clichy (pharma-europenne.fr; ⓒ **01-48-74-65-18;** Métro: Place de Clichy); and **Pharmacie de la Place de la République,** 5 Pl. de la République, 11th arrond (lapharmaderepu.com; ⓒ **01-47-00-18-08;** Métro République; 8am–2am). **Pharmacie Bastille,** 6

THE VALUE OF THE EURO VS. OTHER POPULAR CURRENCIES

€	US$	C$	£	A$	NZ$
1	1.03	1.48	0.83	1.66	1.84

WHAT THINGS COST IN PARIS	€
Taxi from the airport to downtown Paris (Orly or CDG)	36.00–65.00
Métro ticket	2.50
Double room, expensive	320.00 and up
Double room, moderate	171.00–319.00
Double room, inexpensive	85.00–170.00
Three-course dinner for one without wine	30.00–60.00
Glass of beer, 25cl	3.50–6.00
Espresso	1.00–3.00
Admission to most museums	9.00–22.00

boulevard Richard-Lenoir, 11th arrond (pharmacie bastille.com; ⓒ **01-47-00-49-44**; Métro: Bastille). See also "Emergencies" and "Health," above.

Police In an emergency, call ⓒ **17** for the police, or ⓒ **112,** the European Union–wide toll-free emergency number. The Préfecture de Police has stations all over Paris. To find the nearest one, call ⓒ **34-30.** See also "Emergencies," above.

Safety In general, Paris is a safe city, and it is safe to use the Métro late at night. However, certain Métro stations (and the areas around them) are best avoided at night: Châtelet-Les Halles, Gare du Nord, Barbès Rochechouart, and Strasbourg St-Denis. The RER can feel dodgy late at night; try to find alternative transport to and from the airport (such as buses or taxis) late at night or early in the morning.

The most common crime problem in Paris is pickpockets. They prey on tourists around popular attractions such as the Louvre, the Eiffel Tower, the Champs-Élysées, Notre-Dame, St-Michel, Centre Pompidou, Versailles, and Sacré-Coeur, in the major department stores, and on the Métro. Take precautions and be vigilant at all times: Don't take more money with you than necessary, keep your passport in a concealed pouch (if you must carry it), and ensure that your bag is firmly closed at all times. Also, around the major sites it is quite common to be approached by a young girl or boy and asked if you speak English. Another technique it to approach you with a survey to sign. It's best to avoid these situations and any incident that might occur, by shaking your head and walking away.

In cafes, bars, and restaurants, it's best not to leave your bag under the table or on the back of your chair. Keep it between your legs or on your lap to avoid it being stolen. Never leave valuables in a car.

In times of heightened security concerns, the government mobilizes police and armed forces, so don't be surprised to see soldiers strolling around transport hubs and carrying automatic weapons. Also see "Terrorism," below.

Paris is a cosmopolitan city and most nonwhite travelers shouldn't experience any problems. Although there is a significant level of discrimination against West and North African immigrants, harassment of African-American and Asian tourists is exceedingly rare. **S.O.S. Racisme,** 51 av. de Flandre, 19th arrond. (sos-racisme.org; ⓒ **01-40-35-36-55**), offers legal advice to victims of prejudice and will even intervene to help with the police.

Female travelers should not expect any more hassle than in other major cities, and the same precautions apply. French men tend to stare a lot, but it's generally harmless. Avoid walking around the less safe neighborhoods (Barbès

Rochechouart, Strasbourg St-Denis, and the Rue St-Denis side of Châtelet-Les-Halles) alone at night and never get into an unmarked taxi. If you are approached in the street or on the Métro, it's best to avoid entering into conversation and walk away. If you feel threatened, enter the nearest cafe, restaurant, or bar.

Senior Travel Many discounts are available to men and women 60 and over. Although they often seem to apply only to residents of E.U. countries, discounts can be had by announcing at the ticket window of a museum or monument that you are 60 years old or more. You may not receive a discount, but it doesn't hurt to ask. "Senior," incidentally, is pronounced *seenyore* in France. Senior citizens do not get a discount for traveling on public transport in Paris, but the national trains do offer them. Check sncf-connect.com for details.

Smoking Smoking is now banned inside all public places, including cafes, restaurants, bars, and nightclubs; it is still rife on cafe terraces, however.

Student Travel Student discounts are less common in France than in other countries, simply because young people 26 and under are usually offered reduced rates and even free entry to some museums and attractions. Some discounts only apply to residents of E.U. countries, who will need to prove this with a passport, ID card, or driver's license, but if you're not from the E.U. it's worth carrying an ID to prove your age and announcing it when buying tickets. If you're 27 or under and are planning multiple train journeys across France, consider buying the SNCF's Carte Avantage Jeune (young person's advantage card) for 49€, which offers 30% off on national trains and limits ticket prices (sncf-connect.com).

Taxes As a member of the European Union, France routinely imposes a value-added tax (VAT in English; *TVA* in French) on most goods. The standard VAT is 20% and is already included in virtually all prices for consumer goods and services (you'll know for sure when you see TTC, which means *toutes taxes comprises*, "all taxes included"). If you're over 16 and not an E.U. resident, you can get a VAT refund if you're spending less than 6 months in France and you purchase goods worth at least 100€ over a maximum of 3 days, at a retailer offering tax-free shopping (*vente en détaxe*) in the same brand or group of brands. Give them your passport and ask for a *bordereau de vente à l'exportation* (export sales invoice), which must have a barcode. Both you and the shopkeeper sign the slip, and you choose how you want to be reimbursed (credit on card, bank transfer, or cash). Once you get to the airport, scan the code in one of the "Pablo" terminals (if your airport doesn't have one, just go to the "detaxe" counter). Once the form has been approved, head to the reimbursement counter to immediately claim your refund. If all of this is too confusing, visit the French customs website, douane.gouv.fr/fiche/eligibility-vat-refunds-pablo, or search for "duty free" at the tourist office: parisjetaime.com.

Telephones France no longer has public telephone booths. Instead, you should look at mobile phone options (see "Cell Phones," above).

The country code for France is 33. To make a local or long-distance call within France, dial the 10-digit number of the person or place you're calling. Mobile numbers begin with 06 or 07. Numbers beginning with 0 800, 0 805, and 0 809 are free in France; most other numbers beginning with 08 are not. Many public service numbers are now four digits, and some are toll-free.

To make international calls from Paris, first dial 00 and then the country code (U.S. and Canada 1, U.K. 44, Ireland 353, Australia 61, New Zealand 64). Next dial the area code and number. For example, if you want to call the British Embassy in Washington, D.C., you would dial
✆ **001 202/588-6500.**

Terrorism France has reinforced its domestic security measures following the terror attacks of 2015 and 2017. But don't let the fear of terrorism dissuade you from traveling here. Just be vigilant and follow the advice of the local authorities. When you enter a new place, familiarize yourself with the emergency exits. If you see something untoward or notice an abandoned bag or package on public transport, get off the train/bus/tram or move away, and alert either a member of staff or the **police** (🕾 **17** or 112). Elsewhere, if you see anything suspicious, call the police or go to the nearest police station. In the unlikely event that you find yourself in danger, the words to remember are "escape, hide, alert." Move away from the danger, help others to move away, and alert the people around you. If you need to hide, turn off both the ring and vibration mode on your telephone. If you see security forces, do not run toward them or make sudden movements, and keep your hands up or open.

Time France is on **Central European Time,** which is 1 hour ahead of Greenwich Mean Time. French daylight saving time lasts from the last Sunday in March to the last Sunday in October. France uses the 24-hr. clock. So 13h is 1pm, 14h15 is 2:15pm, and so on.

Tipping By law, all bills in cafes, bars, and restaurants say *service compris,* which means the service charge is included. Waiters are paid a living wage and do not expect tips. However, they certainly won't mind if you leave one, and if you are planning on frequenting a certain cafe, it's a good investment to leave 1€ or 2€ after a meal. Taxi drivers usually appreciate a 5% to 10% tip, or for the fare to be rounded up to the next euro. The French give their hairdressers a tip of about 15%.

Toilets Paris is full of gray-colored street-toilet kiosks, which are a little daunting to the uninitiated, but free, and are automatically washed and disinfected after each use (though still smelly). If you're in dire need, you can duck into a cafe or brasserie to use the toilet but expect to make a small purchase (coffee standing at the bar will do) if you do so (or ask nicely). If you're pregnant or with small children and ask, the cafe workers will usually let you use the facilities for free.

Travelers with Disabilities While the city still won't win any prizes for accessibility (narrow, tortuous sidewalks, few ramps at public facilities, endless stairways in Métro stations, despite the Olympics and Paralympics being held here in 2024), slow and steady progress is being made (though not enough in my eyes). However, there are over 60 wheelchair-accessible bus lines and several RER stations; in addition, all stations on Métro line 14 are accessible. Access to all tram lines is flush with the ground, though you might have to navigate a curb to get to the station. To find the closest accessible stations, maps, and more, visit iledefrance-mobilites.fr/en/the-network/easy-access-transports or call 🕾 **09-70-81-83-85** (in French). Many classic Parisian taxis are now accessible. You can request one via telephone or via the apps. Most museums are now accessible too; visit their websites for details. Several art museums even offer tactile visits for people who are visually impaired. Many hotels with three or more stars (under the French national rating system, not ours) have at least one wheelchair-accessible room. Hotels that are particularly sensitive to the subject may bear the "Tourisme & Handicaps" label. The **Paris Tourist Office** (paris jetaime.com) has a good listing of accessible hotels on its site, as well as plenty of other info and links for travelers with disabilities. Click on the English flag, then click "Plan your stay," followed by "Paris for people with disabilities." One other good resource is Sage Traveling (sagetraveling.com/paris-accessible-holiday), which organizes wheelchair-accessible tours and offers a goldmine of tips for navigating the city. Bear in mind that if you drive in Paris and have a disabled display card, you can park for free and for an unlimited amount of time in any parking space.

Visas E.U. nationals don't need a visa to enter France. Nor do U.S., British, Canadian, Australian, New Zealand, or South African citizens for trips of up to 3 months. As of May 2025, however, U.S. nationals coming to some countries in the E.U. may require authorization through a system similar to the U.S.'s ESTA. Europe's version is the "European Travel Information and Authorization System," or **ETIAS** for short, and is available online. For more information and updates on the system's implementation, see the website travel europe.europa.eu/etias_en.

If non–E.U. citizens wish to stay longer than 3 months, they must apply to a French embassy or consulate for a long-term visa.

Visitor Information

The main **Office du Tourisme et des Congrès**, is now in a place called **Spot 24** (named after the 2024 Olympics), at 105 Quai Jacques Chirac, 15th arrond. (parisjetaime.com), is open daily 10am to 6pm. You will find a list of other smaller tourist information points, known as kiosks, here: parisjetaime.com/eng/article/welcome-centres-a936. Or there's a visitor's Réception at the **Carousel du Louvre**, 99 rue de Rivoli, 4 arrond. (Wed–Mon 11am–7pm), which works as a sort of tourist office.

Water Drinking water is safe, if not particularly tasty. To order tap water in a restaurant, ask for *une carafe d'eau*. Drinking fountains—like the iconic, green Wallace fountains—are dotted all about the city, and you'll find drinking water taps in almost every park. Paris even has fizzy water fountains in certain green spaces (like the Jardin de Reuilly), designed to persuade people to ditch polluting plastic bottles and fill up from taps instead. You can find a map of drinking fountains on the following website: fontaine.eaudeparis.fr.

USEFUL TERMS & PHRASES

12

It is often amazing how a word or two of halting French will change your hosts' disposition in their home country. At the very least, try to learn a few numbers, basic greetings, and—above all—the life-raft phrase, *Parlez-vous anglais?* (Do you speak English?). Many Parisians speak passable English and will use it liberally if you demonstrate the basic courtesy of greeting them in their language. *Bonne chance!*

BASIC VOCABULARY
THE BASIC COURTESIES

English	French	Pronunciation
Yes/No	Oui/Non	**Wee/Noh**
Okay	D'accord	***Dah*-core**
Please	S'il vous plaît	**Seel voo *play***
Thank you	Merci	***Mair*-see**
You're welcome	De rien	**Duh ree-*ehn***
Hello (during daylight)	Bonjour	**Bohn-*jhoor***
Good evening	Bonsoir	**Bohn-*swahr***
Goodbye	Au revoir	**O ruh-*vwahr***
What's your name?	Comment vous appellez-vous?	**Kuh-*mahn* voo za-pell-ay-*voo*?**
My name is	Je m'appelle	**Jhuh ma-*pell***
How are you?	Comment allez-vous?	***Kuh*-mahn tahl-ay-*voo*?**
So-so	Comme ci, comme ça	**Kum-*see*, kum-*sah***
I'm sorry/excuse me	Pardon	**Pahr-*dohn***

GETTING AROUND & STREET SMARTS

English	French	Pronunciation
Do you speak English?	Parlez-vous anglais?	**Par-lay-voo ahn-*glay*?**
I don't speak French	Je ne parle pas français	**Jhuh ne parl pah frahn-*say***
I don't understand	Je ne comprends pas	**Jhuh ne kohm-*prahn* pah**
Could you speak more loudly/more slowly?	Pouvez-vous parler plus fort/plus lentement?	**Poo-vay voo par-*lay* ploo for/ploo lan-te-*ment*?**
What is it?	Qu'est-ce que c'est?	**Kess kuh *say*?**
What time is it?	Qu'elle heure est-il?	**Kel uhr eh-*teel*?**

English	French	Pronunciation
What?	Quoi?	**Kwah?**
How? or What did you say?	Comment?	**Ko-*mahn*?**
When?	Quand?	**Kahn?**
Where is?	Où est?	**Ooh eh?**
Who?	Qui?	**Kee?**
Why?	Pourquoi?	**Poor-*kwah*?**
here/there	ici/là	**ee-*see*/lah**
left/right	à gauche/à droite	**a gohsh/a drwaht**
straight ahead	tout droit	**too drwah**
Fill the tank (of a car)	Le plein, s'il vous plaît	**Luh plen, seel-voo-play please**
I want to get off at	Je voudrais descendre à	**Jhe voo-*dray* day-*sen* drah-ah**
airport	aéroport	**air-o-*por***
bank	banque	**bahnk**
bridge	pont	**pohn**
bus station	gare routière	**gar roo-tee-*air***
bus stop	arrêt de bus	**ah-*ray* duh boohs**
by means of a car	en voiture	**ahn vwa-*tur***
cashier	caisse	***kess***
cathedral	cathédrale	**ka-tay-*dral***
church	église	**ay-*gleez***
driver's license	permis de conduire	**per-*mee* deh con-*dweer***
elevator	ascenseur	**ah-sahn-*seuhr***
entrance (to a port building or a city)	porte	**port**
exit (from a building or a freeway)	sortie	**sor-*tee***
gasoline	carburant/essence	**car-bur-*ahn*/eh-*sahns***
hospital	hôpital	**oh-pee-*tahl***
luggage storage	consigne	**kohn-*seen*-yuh**
museum	musée	**mu-*zay***
no smoking	défense de fumer	**day-*fahns* de fu-may**
one-day pass	ticket journalier	**tee-kay jhoor-nall-ee-ay**
one-way ticket	aller simple	**ah-*lay* sam-pluh**
police	police	**po-*leece***
round-trip ticket	aller-retour	**ah-lay re-*toor***
store	magasin	**ma-ga-*zehn***
street	rue	**roo**
ticket	billet	***bee*-yay**
toilets	les toilettes/les WC	**lay twa-*lets*/les vay-*say***
I'd like	Je voudrais	**Jhe voo-*dray***
a room	une chambre	**ewn *shahm*-bruh**
the key	la clé (la clef)	**la clay**

NECESSITIES

English	French	Pronunciation
How much does it cost?	C'est combien?/ Ça coûte combien?	Say comb-bee-*ehn*?/ Sah coot comb-bee-*ehn*?
That's expensive	C'est cher/chère	Say share
Do you take credit cards?	Est-ce que vous acceptez les cartes de credit?	Es-kuh voo zaksep-tay lay kart duh creh-*dee*?
I'd like to buy	Je voudrais acheter	Jhe voo-dray ahsh-tay
aspirin	aspirines	ahs-peer-*een*
condoms	préservatifs	pray-ser-va-*teef*
a gift	un cadeau	uh kah-*doe*
a hat	un chapeau	uh shah-*poh*
a map of the city	un plan de ville	uh plahn de *veel*
a newspaper	un journal	uh zhoor-*nahl*
a postcard	une carte postale	ewn carte pos-*tahl*
a road map	une carte routière	ewn cart roo-tee-*air*
some soap	du savon	dew sah-*vohn*
a stamp	un timbre	uh *tam*-bruh

NUMBERS & ORDINALS

English	French	Pronunciation
zero	zéro	zare-oh
one	un	oon
two	deux	duh
three	trois	twah
four	quatre	kaht-*ruh*
five	cinq	sank
six	six	seess
seven	sept	set
eight	huit	wheat
nine	neuf	noof
ten	dix	deess
eleven	onze	ohnz
twelve	douze	dooz
thirteen	treize	trehz
fourteen	quatorze	kah-*torz*
fifteen	quinze	kanz
sixteen	seize	sez
seventeen	dix-sept	deez-*set*
eighteen	dix-huit	deez-*wheat*
nineteen	dix-neuf	deez-*noof*
twenty	vingt	vehn
thirty	trente	trahnt
forty	quarante	ka-*rahnt*
fifty	cinquante	sang-*kahnt*

English	French	Pronunciation
one hundred	cent	**sahn**
one thousand	mille	**meel**
first	premier	**preh-mee-ay**
second	deuxième	**duhz-zee-em**
third	troisième	**twa-zee-em**
fourth	quatrième	**kaht-ree-em**
fifth	cinquième	**sank-ee-em**
sixth	sixième	**sees-ee-em**
seventh	septième	**set-ee-em**
eighth	huitième	**wheat-ee-em**
ninth	neuvième	**neuv-ee-em**
tenth	dixième	**dees-ee-em**

THE CALENDAR, DAYS & SEASONS

English	French	Pronunciation
January	Janvier	**jhan-vee-ay**
February	Février	**feh-vree-ay**
March	Mars	**marce**
April	Avril	**a-vreel**
May	Mai	**meh**
June	Juin	**jhwehn**
July	Juillet	**jhwee-ay**
August	Août	**oot**
September	Septembre	**sep-tahm-bruh**
October	Octobre	**ok-toh-bruh**
November	Novembre	**no-vahm-bruh**
December	Decembre	**day-sahm-bruh**
Sunday	Dimanche	**dee-mahnsh**
Monday	Lundi	**luhn-dee**
Tuesday	Mardi	**mahr-dee**
Wednesday	Mercredi	**mair-kruh-dee**
Thursday	Jeudi	**jheu-dee**
Friday	Vendredi	**vawn-druh-dee**
Saturday	Samedi	**sahm-dee**
yesterday	hier	**ee-air**
today	aujourd'hui	**o-jhord-dwee**
this morning/this afternoon	ce matin/cet après-midi	**suh ma-tan/set ah-preh-mee-dee**
tonight	ce soir	**suh swahr**
tomorrow	demain	**de-man**
summer	été	**aytt-ay**
fall	automne	**aw-tonne**
winter	hiver	**iv-erre**
spring	printemps	**prehn-tawm**

BASIC MENU TERMS

Note: No need to get intimidated when ordering in French. Simply preface the French-language menu item with the phrase *"Je voudrais"* (jhe voo-*dray*), which means, "I would like. . . ." *Bon appétit!*

MEATS

English	French	Pronunciation
beef	boeuf	**buhf**
beef stew	pot au feu	**poht o *fhe***
chicken	poulet	***poo*-lay**
dumplings of chicken, veal, or fish (often pike)	quenelles	**ke-*nelle***
duck breast	magret de canard	**maa-*gray* duh can-*ar***
preserved duck	confit de canard	**con-*fee* duh can-*ar***
fattened goose or duck liver	foie gras	**fwah grah**
ham	jambon	**jham-bohn**
kidneys	rognons	**row-nyon**
leg of lamb	gigot d'agneau	***jhi*-goh dahnyoh**
lamb	agneau	**lahn-*nyo***
lamb chop	cotelette d'agneau	**koh-te-*let* dahn-*nyo***
liver	foie	**fwah**
pork	porc	**pohr**
potted and shredded pork	rillettes de porc	**ree-yet duh pohr**
rabbit	lapin	**lah-*pan***
dried sausage	saucisson	**soh-see-*sohn***
snails	escargots	**ess-car-*goh***
steak	bifteck	**beef-*tek***
steak with pepper sauce	steak au poivre	**stake o *pwah*-vruh**
sweetbreads	ris de veau	**day *ree* duh voh**
veal	veau	**voh**
veal stew with white sauce	blanquette de veau	**blahn-*ket* duh voh**

FISH/SEAFOOD

English	French	Pronunciation
fish	poisson	**pwoss-*ohn***
herring	hareng	**ahr-*rahn***
lobster	homard	**oh-*mahr***
monkfish	lotte	**loht**
mussels	moules	**moohl**
oysters	huîtres	**hoo-*ee*-truhs**
pike	brochet	**broh-*chay***
sea bass	bar	**bar**

347

English	French	Pronunciation
sea bream	dorade	dor-*ahde*
shrimp	crevettes	kreh-*vette*
smoked salmon	saumon fumé	soh-*mohn* fu-*may*
trout	truite	tru-eet
tuna	thon	tohn

SIDES/APPETIZERS

English	French	Pronunciation
bread	pain	pan
butter	beurre	bhuhr
fries	frites	freet
green beans	haricots verts	*ah*-ri-co ver
rice	riz	ree
salad	salade	sa-*lahd*
vegetables	légumes	lay-*goom*

BEVERAGES

English	French	Pronunciation
beer	bière	bee-*aire*
coffee (espresso)	café	ka-*fay*
coffee (decaf)	décaféiné/déca	day-kah-*fay*-nay/day-ca
coffee (with milk)	café crème/café au lait	ka-*fay* krem/ka-*fay* o-*lay*
coffee (long, with hot water)	allongé	al-on-djhay
milk	lait	lay
orange juice	jus d'orange	zhoo dor-*ahnjhe*
soda	soda	so-*da*
tap water	eau du robinet	oh doo rob-in-ay
tea	thé	tay
tea (herbal)	tisane	tee-*zahn*
tea (w/lemon)	thé au citron	tay o see-*tran*
water	eau	oh
wine (red)	vin rouge	vhin *rooj*
wine (white)	vin blanc	vhin *blahn*

SPICES/CONDIMENTS

English	French	Pronunciation
mayonnaise	mayonnaise	may-o-*nayse*
mustard	moutarde	moo-*tard*
olive oil	huile d'olive	weele dol-*eeve*
pepper	poivre	pwah-vruh
salt	sel	sel
sugar	sucre	*sook*-ruh
vinegar	vinaigre	vin-*aigre*

Index

See also Accommodations and Restaurant Indexes
4 Roues Sous 1 Parapluie, 231
59 Rivoli, 250
13th arrondissement neighborhood, 32–33

General Index
A
Abbey Bookshop, 252
Académie Française, 41, 233
Accessories, 263–264
Accommodations, *See also* Accommodations Index
    accessibility, 58
    Adagio, 98
    Airbnb.com, 97
    amenities, 57–58
    aparthotels, 98
    Apartments Actually, 98
    Bastille, 77–81
    bed & breakfasts, 98
    Belleville, 81–82
    best, 5–6
    Canal St-Martin, 81–82
    Champs-Élysées, 67–70
    Citadines, 98
    Eastern Paris, 77–81
    Eiffel Tower, 92–95
    Flipkey.com, 97
    Grands Boulevards, 71–74
    Île de la Cité, 59–64
    La Villette, 81–82
    Latin Quarter, 82–89
    Left Bank, 82–97
    Louvre, 59–64
    Luxembourg, 89–92
    Marais, 64–67
    Montmartre, 74–77
    Montparnasse, 95–97
    Opéra, 71–74
    palace status, 59, 71
    Parc Astérix, 307
    Paris Appartements Services, 98
    Paris Attitude, 98
    Parisian Home, 98
    rentals, short-term, 97–98
    République, 77–81
    reservations, 58
    Right Bank, 59–82
    seasons, 58–59
    star grading, 59
    St-Germain-des-Prés, 89–92
    Trocadéro, 67–70
    Versailles, 290
    Vrbo.com, 97
    Western Paris, 67–70
A La Mère de Famille, 258
A La Petite Reine, 302
Adagio, 98
Addresses, 327–328
Aéroport d'Orly, 324–325
Aéroport Roissy-Charles-de-Gaulle, 324
Air travel, 324–325
Airbnb.com, 97
Antiques fairs, 248
Antiques, arts, 249–250
Apartments Actually, 98
Arc de Triomphe, 3, 16, 44, 183–184
Arcades, 21, 243
Area codes, 334
Arty Dandy, 261–262
Atelier des Lumières, 11, 197
Au Lapin Agile, 312
Au Nain Bleu, 264
Au Trappiste, 282

B
Baiser Salé, 272
Balibaris, 254–255
Ballet de l'Opéra National de Paris, 269
Banlieues Blues, 51
Barbarians, 38
Bars, 278–283
Basilica of St-Denis, 38
Basilique du Sacré-Coeur, 194–195, 314
Bastille Day, 53–54
Bastille neighborhood, 30–31
    accommodations, 77–81
    attractions, 197–200
    dining, 124–129
    shopping, 243
Bateau Lavoir, 309–310
Bateaux Parisiens, 226
Bateaux-Mouches, 225–226
Batobus, 332–333
Beach, Sylvia, 253
Beaugrenelle, 247
Beaupassage, 143, 245
Beauty, 251
Beauvais airport, 324–325
Beer bars, 282–283
Belle Epoque, 45–46
Belleville, 9
    accommodations, 81–82
    attractions, 200–206
    dining, 129–134
    neighborhood, 31
    shopping, 243–244
Bibliothèque National François Mitterrand, 48
Big Bus Paris, 228
Bijoux Burma, 263
Bike About tours, 229
Biking, 3, 331
Boat cruises, 2, 16, 225
Boat tours, 225–227
Boat travel, 332–333
Bois de Boulogne, 10, 45, 184, 233, 237–238
Bois de Vincennes, 5, 10, 233, 238–240
Bonjour Madame, 283
Books, 252–254
Boom Boom Villette, 21, 203, 247
Botoù, 256
Bourse de Commerce—Pinault Collection, 157–160
Bridges, 179
Brocantes, 248
Bü, 257–258
Bus tours, 228
Buses, 8, 326–327, 330
Business hours, 334
Buttes Chaumont, 45, 205

C
Cabaret, 270–271
Cabaret Sauvage, 204, 273–274
Café Charbon, 279
Cafes, 2, 8, 153–156, 279
Canal St-Martin, 204
    accommodations, 81–82
    attractions, 200–206
    dining, 129–134
    neighborhood, 31
    shopping, 243–244
Canauxrama, 204, 226
Candelaria, 11, 281
Capetian dynasty, 39–40
Car travel, 327
Carolingian dynasty, 38–39
Cathédrale de Notre-Dame, 4, 39, 160–162
Cave des Abbesses, 261
Caveau de la Huchette, 272–273
Cell phones, 334
Centre International du Vitrail, 297–298
Centre Pompidou, 4, 48, 177, 186, 198, 233
Champs de Mars, 20
Champs-Élysées, 16, 18
    accommodations, 67–70
    attractions, 183–194
    dining, 114–118
    neighborhood, 28–29
    shopping, 242
Chanson, 270–271
Chartres, 293–298
    Centre International du Vitrail, 297–298
    Chartres Cathedral, 294–297
    Musée des Beaux-Arts de Chartres, 298
    Notre Dame de la Belle Verièrre, 296
    Vieux Quartier (Old Town), 297
Chartres Cathedral, 294–297
Château de Vincennes, 233, 239–240
Château des Brouillards, 311
Château of Versailles, 42, 290–293
Château Passeport, 287
Chez Moune, 284
Children's clothing, 256
Chinatown, 140
Chinese New Year, 51
Choco Story, 21, 203, 233
Church concerts, 273

GENERAL INDEX

Cimetière du Montparnasse, 223–224
Cimetière du Père-Lachaise, 200–202
Cinemas, 271
Citadines, 98
Cité des Sciences et de l'Industrie, 21, 202–203, 233
City layout, 23–24
Classical music, 268–270
Classique au Vert, 54
Clos Montmartre Vineyard, 311–312
Clothing, 254–257
Cocktail bars, 281–282
Coffee, 154
Collectibles, 249–250
College de France, 41
Comédie-Française, 266
Concept stores, 257–258
Concert venues, 273–274
Conciergerie, 163–164, 173
Consulates, 336
Contemporary Paris, 48–50
Continental breakfast, 58
Cooking classes, 232–233
Costs, 338–339
Coulée verte René-Dumont, 10, 198, 233
Cour Carrée, 42
Crazy Horse, 271
Cruises, 2, 225
Customs, 334–336
Cycling tours, 228–229
Cycling, 236

D

Dalí Paris, 19, 195–196
Dance performances, 269
David Lebovitz, 101
Dentists, 335
Department stores, 245–247
Detaille 1905, 251
Didier Ludot, 257
Dining, see also Restaurants Index
 after-hours, 110
 Bastille, 124–129
 Beaupassage, 149
 Belleville, 129–134
 cafes, 2, 8, 153–156
 Canal St-Martin, 129–134
 Champs-Élysées, 114–118
 children, 120
 Chinatown, 140
 closings, 100
 coffee, 154
 continental breakfast, 58
 David Lebovitz, 101
 Eastern Paris, 124–129
 Eiffel Tower, 144–148
 The Fork, 101
 Grands Boulevards, 118–122
 hours, 100
 Île de la Cité, 102–109
 Latin Quarter, 134–141
 Le Fooding, 101

Left Bank, 134–151
Louvre, 102–109
lunch, 106
Marais, 109–114
menu terms, 347–348
Montmartre, 122–124
Montparnasse, 148–151
neo-bistros, 99
Northeast Paris, 129–134
Opéra Bastille, 118–122
outdoor dining, 278
Parc Astérix, 307
pastries, 152
picnics, 101
République, 124–129
reservations, 100–101
Right Bank, 102–134
set-price, 106
St-Germain-des-Prés, 141–144
tearooms, 151–153
tipping, 100
vegetarian, 111
waiters, 106
Disabilities, 341–342
Disneyland Paris, 304–306
Doctors, 335
Domaine de Marie Antoinette, 292
Drinking laws, 336
Driving, 331–332
Drouot, 249–250
Duc des Lombards, 23, 273

E

E. Dehillerin, 262
Eastern Paris, 30–31
 accommodations, 77–81
 attractions, 197–200
 dining, 124–129
 shopping, 243
Eataly, 260
Editions de Parfums Fréderic Malle, 251
Eglise St-Eustache, 167, 173
Eiffel Tower, 2, 4, 12, 16–17, 20, 46, 217–219, 233
 accommodations, 92–95
 attractions, 217–233
 dining, 144–148
 neighborhood, 34–35
 shopping, 244–245
Electricity, 336
Embassies, 336
Emergencies, 336
Emily in Paris, 231
Empreintes, 258
English shows, 268
Enlightenment, 43–44
Entrée to Black Paris, 230
ERES, 256
Espace Glace, 236
Etiquette, 336
European Health Insurance Card (EHIC), 337
Events calendar, 50–56
Experimental Cocktail Club, 281

F

Families, 19–21, 120, 233–236
Fat Tire Bike Tours, 228
Festival Chorus, 51
Festival du Merveilleux, 56
Fête de la Musique, 52
Fête des Tuileries, 53
Flash Invaders, 235
Flea markets, 249
Fleux, 262
Flipkey.com, 97
FlyView, 22
Fnac, 262
Foire du Trône, 51
Fondation Claude Monet, 299–300
Fondation Louis Vuitton, 2, 184–185
Fontainebleau, 41, 301–303
Food markets, 247–248
Food, shopping, 258–260
Forum des Halles, 48, 167
Fountain shows, Versailles, 288
François Pralus, 258–259
Free'p'Star, 257
French Open, 52
French Trotters, 255

G

Galerie Portfolio, 262
Galeries Lafayette, 245–246
Galignani, 254
Gallo-Roman baths, 38
Games, 264
Gardens, 10
Gargoyles, 162
Gay and lesbian scene, 283–284
Gay Pride, 53
Gifts, 261–262
Giverny, 10, 298–300
 Fondation Claude Monet, 299–300
 Musée des Impressionismes, 299
Grand Palais, 46, 185, 192
Grands Boulevards neighborhood, 25–26
 accommodations, 71–74
 attractions, 174–176
 dining, 118–122
 shopping, 242

H

Harry's Bar, 281
Health, 336–337
Hidalgo, Anne, 50
Hippodrome Paris-Vincennes, 240
Horse racing, 284
Hospitals, 337
Hôtel Carnavalet, 321–322
Hôtel de Clisson, 319
Hôtel de la Marine, 185–186, 194, 232
Hôtel de Sens, 316–317
Hôtel de Soubise, 319–320

Hôtel de Sully, 323
Hôtel de Ville, 39, 41, 177–178
Hôtel des Invalides, 219–220
Hôtel Donon, 320
Hotel La Fantaisie, 9, 71
Hotels, *see* Accommodations Index
Hotlines, 337
Housewares, 262

I
Ice skating, 236–237
Île de la Cité, 2, 13
   accommodations, 59–64
   attractions, 157–174
   dining, 102–109
   neighborhood, 24–25
   shopping, 241
Institut du Monde Arabe, 48, 210
International Agricultural Show, 51
International Circus Festival of Tomorrow, 51
Internet, 337

J
Jardin d'Acclimatation, 10, 233, 235
Jardin des Plantes, 9, 20, 32, 206–207, 233
Jardin des Tuileries, 164–165, 233
Jardin du Luxembourg, 8, 10, 17, 20, 213, 233
Jazz clubs, 272–273
Jewelry, 263–264
Journées du Patrimoine (Heritage Days), 55

K
Kiliwatch, 255

L
L'Alimentation Générale, 275
l'Officiel des Spectacles, 266
La Bellevilloise, 276
La Binouze, 283
La Cabane Enchantée, 264
La Cave à Michel, 280
La Champmeslé, 283
La Cigale, 274
La Cité de l'Architecture et du Patrimoine, 186
La Cuisine Paris, 233
La Gare-Le Gore, 276
La Grande Epicerie Rive Gauche, 260
La Madeleine, 3, 187
La Palette, 279
La Recyclerie, 276
La Seine Musicale, 266–267
La Sorbonne, 17
La Station by The Different Company, 275
La Villette, 21, 200
   accommodations, 81–82
   attractions, 200–206
   shopping, 243–244
Landline, 11, 258
Landmark venues, 266–268
Language classes, 233
Lapin Boutique, 257
Latin Quarter, 9, 17, 20, 32–33, 134
   accommodations, 82–89
   attractions, 206–212
   dining, 134–141
   shopping, 244
Lavomatic, 279
Le Baron Rouge, 280
Le Bon Marché, 90, 246
Le Centquatre, 277
Le Cordon Bleu, 232
Le Duc des Lombards, 273
Le Food Market, 130, 248
Le Foodist, 232
Le Kiosque Théâtre, 265
Le Mary Celeste, 282
Le Perchoir, 279
Le Petit Bain, 274
Le Sunset/Le Sunside, 273
Le Tango, 284
Left Bank, 32–36
   13th arrondissement, 32–33
   accommodations, 82–97
   attractions, 206–225
   dining, 134–151
   Eiffel Tower, 34–35
   Latin Quarter, 32–33
   Les Invalides, 34–35
   Luxembourg, 33–34
   Montparnasse, 35–36
   shopping, 244–245
   St-Germain-des-Prés, 33–34
Legrand Filles et Fils, 261
Les Berges, 19, 22, 236
Les Catacombes, 225
Les Disquaires, 275
Les Domaines Qui Montent, 261
Les Grandes Eaux Musicales, 290
Les Grandes Ecuries, 290
Les Halles, 39, 167
Les Invalides, 43–44, 217
   attractions, 217–233
   neighborhood, 34–35
Les Mots à la Bouche, 254
Les Secrets Gourmands de Noémie, 233
L'Hippodrome en Famille, 51, 233
L'Île aux Fées, 256
LGBTQ+ travelers, 337
Lido 2 Paris, 266–268
Lingerie, 256–257
Lollapalooza., 54
Lost & found, 337–338
Louis XIV, 42–43
Louvre, 2, 166; *see also* Musée du Louvre
   accommodations, 59–64
   attractions, 157–174
   dining, 102–109
   neighborhood, 24–25
   shopping, 241
Luxembourg neighborhood, 33–34
   accommodations, 89–92
   attractions, 213–217
   shopping, 244
Lylo, 266

M
Machine du Moulin Rouge, 19, 277–278
MAD, *see* Musée des Arts et Métiers
Mail, 338
Maille, 260
Maison de Balzac, 166, 187
Maison de Victor Hugo, 166, 178
Maison Gainsbourg, 213–214
Make My Lemonade, 255
Malls, shopping, 243, 247
Manufacture Nationale des Gobelins, 9, 89, 210
Marais, 9, 18, 40, 42, 109, 315
   accommodations, 64–67
   attractions, 176–183
   dining, 109–114
   neighborhood, 27–28
   shopping, 242
   walking tour, 315–323
Marché aux Puces de la Porte de Vanves, 249
Marché aux Puces de Paris St-Ouen–Clignancourt, 249
Marché Bastille, 248
Marché Batignolles, 248
Marché d'Aligre, 248
Marche des Fiertés, 53
Marché Grenelle, 248
Marché Monge, 248
Marché Raspail, 248
Marché Saxe-Breteuil, 248
Marché St-Germain, 13
Marie Puce, 256
Marin d'Eau Douce, 9, 21, 204, 227
Markets, 3
Medival times, 40–41
Ménagerie, 20, 207
Menu terms, 347–348
Merci, 258
Merovingian dynasty, 38–39
Metro, 329–330
Modern-day Paris, 48–50
Mona Lisa, 167, 170–171
Money, 338
Monnaie de Paris, 214
Monsieur, 263
Montagne St-Genevieve, 37–38, 211
Montmartre, 8, 19, 38, 308
   accommodations, 74–77
   attractions, 194–196
   cemetery, 314
   dining, 122–124
   neighborhood, 29–30
   shopping, 242–243
   walking tour, 308–314
Montmartre Grape Harvest Fest, 56

351

GENERAL INDEX

Montparnasse neighborhood, 35–36
   accommodations, 95–97
   attractions, 223–225
   dining, 148–151
   shopping, 245
Moonshiner, 282
Mosquée de Paris, 9, 20, 153
Moulin de la Galette, 310–311
Moulin du Radet, 310–311
Moulin Rouge, 19, 270–271
Movies, 271
Musée Bourdelle, 8, 166, 225
Musée Carnavalet, 8, 166, 178–179
Musée Cognacq-Jay, 8, 166, 179–180
Musée d'Art et d'Histoire du Judaïsme, 180
Musée d'Art Moderne de la Ville de Paris, 187–188
Musée d'Orsay, 7, 19, 48, 166, 175, 220–222
Musée de Cluny, 17, 38, 162, 210
Musée de l'Homme, 188–189, 216, 231
Musée de l'Institut du Monde Arabe, 210–211
Musée de l'Orangerie, 16, 166, 299
Musée de la Chasse et de la Nature, 180–181
Musée de la Liberation de Paris—Musée du Général Leclerc—Musée Jean Moulin, 224
Musée de la Musique, 203–205
Musée de la Vie Romantique, 166, 174–175
Musée de Montmartre, 19, 21, 196, 312–313
Musée des Arts Decoratifs, 165, 191
Musée des Arts et Métiers, 181, 233
Musée des Arts Forains, 56, 198
Musée des Beaux-Arts de Chartres, 298
Musée des Egouts de Paris, 220, 233
Musée des Impressionismes, 299
Musée du Louvre, 2, 7, 13–16, 18, 22, 41, 102, 166–170
Musée du Quai Branly, 7, 19, 48, 222
Musée Grévin, 175, 233
Musée Gustave Moreau, 175
Musée Jacquemart-André, 7, 22–23, 152, 189–190
Musée Marmottan Monet, 190, 299
Musée National de la Marine, 188
Musée National des Arts Asiatiques Guimet, 166, 175, 191
Musée National Eugène Delacroix, 166, 215

Musée National Picasso-Paris, 166, 177, 181–182
Musée Nissim de Camondo, 67, 191
Musée Rodin, 22, 166, 222–223
Musée Yves Saint Laurent, 11, 191–192
Musée Zadkine, 20, 166, 215–216
Museum National d'Histoire Naturelle, 20, 211, 233
Music bars, 275–276
Music, live, 272–276

N

Napoleon, 44
Napoleon's Tomb, 219–220
Navigo Card, 328–329
Neighborhoods
   Left Bank, 32–36
      13th arrondissement, 32–33
      Eiffel Tower, 34–35
      Latin Quarter, 32–33
      Les Invalides, 34–35
      Luxembourg, 33–34
      Montparnasse, 35–36
      St-Germain-des-Prés, 33–34
   Right Bank, 24–31
      Bastille, 30–31
      Belleville, 31
      Canal St-Martin, 31
      Champs-Élysées, 28–29
      Eastern Paris, 30–31
      Grands Boulevards, 25–26
      Île de la Cité, 24–25
      Louvre, 24–25
      Marais, 27–28
      Montmartre, 29–30
      Northern Paris, 31
      Opéra, 25–26
      République, 30–31
      Trocadéro, 28–29
      Western Paris, 28–29
New Morning, 273
New Year's Eve, 56
Nightlife, 265–285
   Au Trappiste, 282
   Baiser Salé, 272
   Ballet de l'Opéra National de Paris, 269
   bars, 278–283
   beer bars, 282–283
   Bonjour Madame, 283
   Cabaret Sauvage, 273–274
   cabaret, 270–271
   Café Charbon, 279
   cafes, 279
   Candelaria, 281
   Caveau de la Huchette, 272–273
   chanson, 270–271
   Chez Moune, 284
   church concerts, 273
   cinemas, 271
   classical music, 268–270
   cocktail bars, 281–282
   Comédie-Française, 266
   concert venues, 273–274
   Crazy Horse, 271
   dance performances, 269
   English shows, 268
   Experimental Cocktail Club, 281
   gay and lesbian scene, 283–284
   Harry's Bar, 281
   jazz clubs, 272–273
   L'Alimentation Générale, 275
   l'Officiel des Spectacles, 266
   La Bellevilloise, 276
   La Binouze, 283
   La Cave à Michel, 280
   La Champmeslé, 283
   La Cigale, 274
   La Gare-Le Gore, 276
   La Palette, 279
   La Recyclerie, 276
   La Seine Musicale, 266–267
   landmark venues, 266–268
   Lavomatic, 279
   Le Baron Rouge, 280
   Le Centquatre, 277
   Le Duc des Lombards, 273
   Le Kiosque Théâtre, 265
   Le Mary Celeste, 282
   Le Perchoir, 279
   Le Petit Bain, 274
   Le Sunset/Le Sunside, 273
   Le Tango, 284
   Les Disquaires, 275
   Lido 2 Paris, 266–268
   Lylo, 266
   Machine du Moulin Rouge, 277
   Moonshiner, 282
   Moulin Rouge, 270–271
   movies, 271
   music bars, 275–276
   music, live, 272–276
   New Morning, 273
   Odéon, Théâtre de l'Europe, 266
   Olympia, 274
   Opéra Comique/Salle Favart, 268
   Opéra de Paris, 268–269
   opera, 268–270
   outdoor dining, 278
   Paname Brewing Company, 283
   Philharmonie de Paris, 269–270
   Poupée, 280
   Raidd Bar, 284
   Simone La Cave, 280
   Sortir à Paris, 266
   spectator sports, 284–285
   Stade de France, 267
   summer terraces, 278
   Supersonic, 275–276
   theater, 265–266
   Théâtre de la Ville, 266–269
   Théâtre du Châtelet, 268

Théâtre National de Chaillot, 266, 268–269
tickets, 265
Tiger, 279
wine bars, 280
Zenith Paris, 274
Northeast Paris, dining, 129–134
Northern Paris, 31
Notre-Dame cathedral, 13, 17, 160
Notre Dame de la Belle Verièrre, 296
Nuit Blanche, 50, 53
Nuit Européenne des Musées, 52

O

Odéon, Théâtre de l'Europe, 266
Olympia, 274
One-day itinerary, 12–16
Open-air markets, 3
Opera, 268–270
Opéra Bastille, 48, 269
 accommodations, 71–74
 attractions, 174–176
 dining, 118–122
 neighborhood, 25–26
 shopping, 242
Opéra Comique/Salle Favart, 268
Opéra de Paris, 268–269
Opéra Garnier, 174–176
Opéra Royal, 290

P

Palais de Chaillot, 12, 217
Palais de Tokyo, 192, 233
Palais du Luxembourg, 42
Palais Garnier, 4, 22, 176
Palais Royal, 42–43, 170–171
Paname Brewing Company, 283
Panthéon, 4, 17, 20, 38, 178, 211–212
Parc André Citroën, 9
Parc Astérix, 306–307
Parc de Belleville, 9
Parc de Bercy, 198, 233
Parc de la Villette, 54, 203–205, 233
Parc des Buttes Chaumont, 205, 233
Parc Floral, 8, 10, 233, 239
Parc Monceau, 192
Parc Zoologique de Paris, 10, 80, 198–199, 233, 239
Paris à Vélo, 229
Paris Appartements Services, 98
Paris Attitude, 98
Paris Autumn Festival, 55
Paris Carnival, 51
Paris Commune, 45–46
Paris Greeters, 230
Paris Jazz Festival, 52
Paris Marathon, 51–52
Paris Passlib', 163
Paris Plage, 54
Paris Visite, 329

Paris Walks, 230
Parisian Home, 98
Paris-Versailles Walk, 55
Parks, 10, 237–240
Passerelle Simone de Beauvoir, 179
Passports, 338
Patisserie Mélilot, 259
Patrick Roger, 259
Père-Lachaise, 9, 44, 200
Perfume, 251
Petit Palais, 46, 166, 192–193
Pharmacies, 338
Philharmonie de Paris, 4, 204, 269–270
Philharmonie des Enfants, 205–206, 233–234, 269
Picasso-Paris, 7, 181
Pitchfork Music Festival, 56
Place Dalida, 311
Place Dauphine, 13, 42
Place de la Bastille, 44–45, 199–200
Place de la Concorde, 3, 16, 18, 193–194
Place de la République, 45, 49, 197
Place des Abbesses, 308–309
Place des Victoires, 43
Place des Vosges, 18, 42, 182–183, 323
Place du Marché Ste-Catherine, 322
Place du Tertre, 313–314
Place du Trocadéro, 28
Place Vendôme, 2, 43, 171–172
Pletzl, 318
Police, 339
Pont Alexandre III bridge, 46, 179
Pont des Arts, 22, 179
Pont Marie, 179
Pont Neuf, 2, 13, 41–42, 179
Postwar Paris, 47–48
Poupée, 280
Printemps, 246–247
Promenade Plantée, 10, 198
Public transport, 328–331

Q

Qatar Prix de l'Arc de Triomphe, 56

R

Raidd Bar, 284
Rampart of Philippe Auguste, 315–316
RATP, 328
Red Wheelbarrow Bookstore, 254
Renaissance, 41–42
Rendez-Vous Parfum, 231
République neighborhood, 30–31
 accommodations, 77–81
 attractions, 197–200
 dining, 124–129
 shopping, 243

RER, 324–325, 330
Restaurants, *see also* Dining and Restaurants Index
 best, 4–5
Restoration, 44–45
Right Bank, 24–31
 accommodations, 59–82
 attractions, 157–206
 Bastille, 30–31
 Belleville, 31
 Canal St-Martin, 31
 Champs-Élysées, 28–29
 dining, 102–134
 Eastern Paris, 30–31
 Grands Boulevards, 25–26
 Île de la Cité, 24–25
 Louvre, 24–25
 Marais, 27–28
 Montmartre, 29–30
 Northern Paris, 31
 Opéra, 25–26
 République, 30–31
 shopping, 241–244
 Trocadéro, 28–29
 Western Paris, 28–29
Rock en Seine, 54
Romans, 37–38
Romantics, 22–23
Rue de Menilmontant, 9
Rue des Rosiers, 318–319
Rue du Temple, 319
Rue François Miron, 317–318
Rue St-Rustique, 313

S

Sacré-Coeur, 2, 19, 21, 194
Safety, 339–340
Saint Germain des Slips, 257
Sainte-Chapelle, 4, 40, 164, 172–173
Sales, shopping, 246
Salon du Chocolat, 56
Samaritaine, 247
San Francisco Book Company, 252
Seine, 2, 49, 236
Seine Musicale, 51, 266
Senior travel, 340
Serge Gainsbourg, 92, 213
Shakespeare and Company, 132, 253
Shoes, 254–257
Shopping, 241–264
 accessories, 263–264
 antiques fairs, 248
 antiques, arts, 249–250
 arcades, 243
 Bastille, 243
 beauty, 251
 Belleville, 243–244
 books, 252–254
 brocantes, 248
 Canal St-Martin, 243–244
 Champs-Élysées, 242
 children's clothing, 256
 clothing, 254–257

353

GENERAL INDEX

Shopping (cont.)
collectibles, 249–250
concept stores, 257–258
department stores, 245–247
Eastern Paris, 243
Eiffel Tower, 244–245
flea markets, 249
food, 258–260
food markets, 247–248
games, 264
gifts, 261–262
Grands Boulevards, 242
hours, 245
housewares, 262
Île de la Cité, 241
jewelry, 263–264
La Villette, 243–244
Latin Quarter, 244
Left Bank, 244–245
lingerie, 256–257
Louvre, 241
Luxembourg, 244
malls, 243, 247
Marais, 242
Montmartre, 242–243
Montparnasse, 245
Opéra, 242
perfume, 251
République, 243
Right Bank, 241–244
sales, 246
shoes, 254–257
souvenirs, 261–262
St-Germain-des-Prés, 244
taxes, 244
toys, 264
Trocadéro, 242
vintage clothing, 256
Western Paris, 242
wine, 261
Sight Seeker's Delight, 229
Simone La Cave, 280
Smith & Son, 253
Smoking, 340
SNCF (Société Nationale des Chemins de Fer Français), 325
Soccer (football), 285
Solidays, 52
Sorbonne, 40
Sortir à Paris, 266
Souvenirs, 261–262
Spectator sports, 284–285
Square du Vert Gallant, 13, 22, 160, 179
Stade de France, 51, 267
St-Etienne-du-Mont, 4, 20, 41, 212
St-Eustache, 41, 167, 173–174
St-Germain-des-Prés, 13, 18, 20, 38, 141, 213, 216
accommodations, 89–92
attractions, 213–217
dining, 141–144
jazz festival, 52
neighborhood, 33–34
shopping, 244
St-Germain l'Auxerrois, 41, 174

St-Gervais–St-Protais, 39
St-Sulpice, 18, 216–217
Student travel, 340
Summer terraces, 278
Supersonic, 275–276

T

Taschen, 254
Taxes, 244, 340
Taxis, 333–334
Tearooms, 151–153
Techno Parade, 55
Telephones, 340
Tennis, 285
Terrorism, 340–341
Theater, 265–266
Théâtre de la Ville, 266–269
Théâtre du Châtelet, 268
Théâtre National de Chaillot, 266, 268–269
Three-day itinerary, 18–19
Tiger, 279
Time, 341
Toilets, 341
Toot Bus, 228
Tours, 225–232
4 Roues Sous 1 Parapluie, 231
Bateaux Parisiens, 226
Bateaux-Mouches, 225–226
Big Bus Paris, 228
Bike About tours, 229
boat tours, 225–227
bus tours, 228
Canauxrama, 226
cycling tours, 228–229
Emily in Paris, 231
Entrée to Black Paris, 230
Fat Tire Bike Tours, 228
Paris à Vélo, 229
Paris Greeters, 230
Paris Walks, 230
Rendez-Vous Parfum, 231
Sight Seeker's Delight, 229
tickets, 227
Toot Bus, 228
Vedettes du Pont Neuf, 226
walking tours, 229–230
Toys, 264
Train travel, 325–326
Trams, 33–331
Trocadéro neighborhood, 28–29
accommodations, 67–70
attractions, 183–194
shopping, 242
Tuileries, 10, 16, 164, 166
Two-day itinerary, 16–18

V

Vélib', 3, 22, 50, 236, 331
Vedettes du Pont Neuf, 226
Versailles, 286–293
accommodations, 290
Château of Versailles, 290–293
Château Passeport, 287
Domaine de Marie Antoinette, 292

fountain shows, 288
Les Grandes Eaux Musicales, 290
Les Grandes Ecuries, 290
Opéra Royal, 290
Vieux Quartier (Old Town), 297
Views, 2
Village St-Paul, 250, 315
Villette, 54; see also Parc de la Villette
Vintage clothing, 256
Visas, 342
Visitor information, 342
Vocabulary, 343–346
Vrbo.com, 97

W

Walking tours, 229–230, 308–323
Marais, 315–323
Montmartre, 308–314
Walt Disney Studios Park, 305–306
Water, 342
We Love Green, 53
Western Paris, 28–29
accommodations, 67–70
attractions, 183–194
dining, 114–118
shopping, 242
WHITE bIRD, 263–264
Wi-Fi, 337
Wine bars, 280
Wine, shopping, 261
World Wars, 46–47

Z

Zadig & Voltaire, 255
Zénith, 204, 274
Zoo, see Parc Zoologique de Paris

Accommodations

52 Clichy, 98
Airelles Château de Versailles, 290
Apostrophe, 96
B Montmartre, 75
Bonne Nuit Paris, 98
Cheval Blanc Paris, 6, 60
Deskopolitan House Hotel Paris, 78
Eden Lodge Paris, 6, 78–79
Familia Hôtel, 88
Generator Paris, 82
Grand Hôtel des Balcons, 92
Hôtel 34B, 73–74
Hôtel Aiglon, 96
Hôtel Arvor, 72–73
Hôtel Bachaumont, 72
Hôtel Brighton, 6, 60–61
Hôtel Cabane, 96
Hôtel Caron de Beaumarchais, 66
Hôtel Chopin, 73
Hôtel Clément, 92
Hôtel de L'Empereur, 93

354

Hôtel de la Porte Dorée, 5, 79–80
Hôtel de Londres Eiffel, 93–94
Hôtel de Varenne, 94
Hôtel des Arts Montmartre, 76
Hôtel des Grandes Ecoles, 86–87
Hôtel des Grands Voyageurs, 6, 23, 90
Hôtel des Marronniers, 91
Hôtel Design Sorbonne, 87
Hôtel du Champ de Mars, 94–95
Hôtel du Cygne, 61–64
Hôtel Henriette, 88–89
Hôtel Jeanne d'Arc Le Marais, 6, 67
Hôtel Jules et Jim, 67
Hôtel La Fantaisie, 71–72
Hôtel Lancaster, 6, 68
Hôtel Le Vert Galant, 89
Hôtel Les Jardins du Luxembourg, 87
Hôtel Louison, 91
Hôtel Monte Cristo, 86
Hôtel Muguet, 95
Hôtel Particulier Montmartre, 74–75
Hôtel Passy Eiffel, 69
Hôtel Relais Saint-Germain, 90
Hôtel Saint-Jacques, 87
Hôtel Saint-Louis en l'Isle, 67
Hôtel Signature St-Germain-des-Prés, 92–93
Hôtel Thérèse, 61
Hôtel Verneuil, 91–92
Hoxton, 72
L'Hôtel, 6, 90–91
La Cité Suspendue, 307
La Villa Paris, 98
Le Citizen, 81–82
Le Pavillon des Lettres, 69–70
Le Relais Montmartre, 77
Les Etangs de Corot, 95
Les Quais de Lutèce, 307
Maison Bréguet, 6, 79
Monsieur George, 69
New Orient Hôtel, 70
Pavillon de la Reine, 64–66
The People—Paris Nation, 80–81
Sinner, 66
Solar Hôtel, 97
Terrass" Hotel, 76–77
TOO Hôtel Paris–McGallery, 2, 88
Trois Hiboux, 307

Restaurants
Aki, 22, 108
Aki Café, 108
Angelina, 151
Arnaud Larher, 152
Au Bascou, 111–112
Au Petit Marguery, 139

Au Pied de Cochon, 5, 110
Auberge Etchegorry, 89
Auberge Nicolas Flamel, 109–110
Aux Bons Crus, 127
Benoit, 110–111
BigLove Caffé, 112–113
Bistroy Les Papilles, 139
Bob's Juice Bar, 111, 132
Bouillon Pigalle, 123–124
Bouillon République, 113
Boulangerie, 149
Boutique yam'Tcha, 109
Brasserie du Louvre–Bocuse, 103
Brasserie Martin, 127–128
Café de Flore, 13, 18, 47, 154
Café de la Paix, 154–155
Café des Musées, 112
Café FIKA, 321
Chambelland, 5
Chez Fernand, 13, 142
Chez Georges, 119
Chez Gladines Saint-Germain, 141
Chez Michel, 130
Chez Pippo, 148
Clamato, 5, 125
Closerie des Lilas, 149
Clover Grill, 103
Divellec, 145
Don Juan II, 115
EELS, 130
ELMER, 111
Eric Kayser, 101
Eté en Pente Douce, 155–156
Frenchie Bar à Vins, 5, 120
Fulgurances, 126
Geosmine, 124–125
Ground Control, 11, 120, 128–129
Happy Cow, 111
Higuma, 108
Hôtel du Nord, 132
Huîtrerie Régis, 5, 142
Imperial Choisy, 140
Isakaya Dassai, 149
Jardin des Pâtes, 141
Jules Verne, 4, 145–146
Juveniles, 22, 106
L'As du Fallafel, 113
L'Assiette, 150
L'Ebauchoir, 129
L'Escudella, 147
La Bellevilloise, 23, 276
La Condesa, 119–120
La Coupole, 155
La Ferrandaise, 17, 141–142
La Fontaine de Mars, 146
La Pantruche, 121
La Pâtisserie de Cyril Lignac, 152
La Renomméé, 4, 22, 106–107
La Rotisserie d'Argent, 140
La Tour d'Argent, 4, 134–138
La Tour de Montlhéry–Chez Denise, 108, 110

La Truffière, 138
Ladurée, 153
Laïa, 5, 126–127
Lao Douang Chan, 140
Lazare, 116–117
Le Café du Marché, 148
Le Casse Noix, 147
Le Ciel de Paris, 95, 150
Le Clarence, 116
Le Comptoir, 90, 143
Le Coq & Fils, 122
Le Drugstore (Publicis), 117
Le Grand Restaurant, 115–116
Le Nélie, 152
Le Nemours, 18, 170
Le Patio, 307
Le Petit Cler, 22, 148
Le Petit Josselin, 151
Le Petit Pontoise, 140
Le Petit Rétro, 117–118
Le Potager du Marais, 111, 114
Le Pure Café, 156
Le Relais de l'Entrecôte, 4, 20, 120, 143–144
Le Relais Louis XIII, 142
Le Rostand, 17, 156
Le Tambour, 110
Le Verre Volé, 132–133
Les Arlots, 131
Les Deux Magots, 13, 18, 47, 155
Les Petits Plats, 150
Madame Brasserie, 16, 146
Maison Millie, 21
Marché des Enfants Rouge, 114
Mersea, 149
Michi, 122
MijoT, 131
Monte Carlo, 118
Mosquée de Paris, 153
Musée Jacquemart-André tearoom, 22–23, 152
Naam, 133
Nell'Arte, 121–122
Noglu, 5, 111, 129
Pâtisserie Viennoise, 144
Paul, 101
Pierre Hermé, 152
Pierre Sang In Oberkampf, 127
Poppy, 23, 90
Public House, 121
Restaurant Auguste, 146
Restaurant du Lac, 307
Restaurant Polidor, 144
Rosa Bonheur, 4, 120, 205, 133–134
Sébastien Gaudard, 152
Septime, 5, 125
Stohrer, 152
Udon Jubey, 108
Verjus, 102
Wepler, 122–123
Zerda Café, 131

Photo Credits

Front cover: Songquan Deng / Shutterstock.com; p. i: Goga18128 / Shutterstock; p. iii: NicoElNino / Shutterstock; p. 2: Courtesy of TOO Hotel / Quentin Carnicelli; p. 3: Lembi / Shutterstock; p. 4: E. O. / Shutterstock; p. 5: Courtesy of La Renomméé / Mary Devinat; p. 6: Courtesy of L'Hôtel; p. 7: Courtesy of Musée d'Orsay / Sophie Boegly; p. 8: Page Light Studios / Shutterstock; p. 9: Page Light Studios / Shutterstock; p. 10, top: Courtesy of La Fantaisie / Jerome Galland; p. 10, bottom: Alaattin Timur / Shutterstock; p. 11: Courtesy of Ground Control; p. 13: Courtesy of Eifel Tower / Charlotte Robillard; p. 16: Nadiia_foto / Shutterstock.com; p. 17: Courtesy of Notre Dame / Julio Piatti; p. 20: Courtesy of The Louvre / Erica Russo; p. 21: Courtesy of Jardin des Plantes / MNHN / Bruno Jay; p. 23: EricBery / Shutterstock.com; p. 25: Courtesy of Samaritaine / Matthieu Salvaing; p. 27: Kiev.Victor / Shutterstock.com; p. 28: Maurizio De Mattei / Shutterstock; p. 29: Maximillian Cabinet / Shutterstock; p. 30: Adisa / Shutterstock; p. 32: Mehdi33300 / Shutterstock; p. 33, top: VDB Photos / Shutterstock.com; p. 33, bottom: Valerie2000 / Shutterstock; p. 34: Alex Segre / Shutterstock; p. 35: Courtesy of Les Catacombes de Paris; p. 39: Jean LucIchard / Shutterstock; p. 40: Heracles Kritikos / Shutterstock.com; p. 42: Bensliman hassan / Shutterstock; p. 45: Laurence soulez / Shutterstock.com; p. 46: Kemal Taner / Shutterstock.com+C35; p. 47: Petr Kovalenkov / Shutterstock.com; p. 49: Ilolab / Shutterstock; p. 52: Leonard Zhukovsky / Shutterstock; p. 53: DreamSlamStudio / Shutterstock; p. 54: Elena Dijour / Shutterstock; p. 55: Elena Dijour / Shutterstock; p. 56: Paul Gueu / Shutterstock; p. 60: Courtesy of Hôtel Brighton / Gilles Trillard; p. 61: Courtesy of Hôtel Thérèse; p. 64: Courtesy of Pavillon de la Reine / Jerome Galland; p. 66: Courtesy of Sinner Paris / Nicolas Receveur; p. 68: Courtesy of Hotel Lancaster / Eric Cuvillier; p. 69: Courtesy of Monsieur George / Benoit Linero; p. 70: Courtesy of Le Pavillon des Lettres / David Grimbert; p. 71: Courtesy of Le Bristol / Claire Cocano; p. 72: Courtesy of Hôtel La Fantaisie / Jérome Galland; p. 73: Courtesy of Hotel 34B / Guillaume Grasset for Astotel; p. 74: Courtesy of Hôtel Particulier Montmartre / Yannick Labrousse; p. 76: Courtesy of Terrass" Hotel / Christophe Bielsa; p. 77: Courtesy of Le Relais Montmartre; p. 78: Courtesy of Deskopolitan House Hotel Paris / Frédéric Baron-Morin; p. 79: Courtesy of Eden Lodge Paris / Stephane Frances; p. 80, top: Courtesy of Hôtel de la Porte Dorée / David- Emmanuel Cohen; p. 80, bottom: Courtesy of The People – Paris Nation; p. 81: Courtesy of Le Citizen; p. 82: Courtesy of Generator Hostel / Valentine Tchoukhonine; p. 86: Courtesy of Hôtel des Grandes Ecoles; p. 88: Courtesy of TOO Hôtel / Jerome Galland; p. 89, top right: Courtesy of Hôtel Henriette / Hervé Goluza; p. 89, bottom left: Courtesy of Hôtel Le Vert Galant / David Grimbert; p. 93: Courtesy of Hôtel Signature St-Germain-des-Prés; p. 94, left: Courtesy of Hôtel de Varenne; p. 94, right: Courtesy of Hôtel de Londres Eiffel; p. 96: Courtesy of Hôtel Cabane / PIERRE MUSELLEC; p. 98: Courtesy of 52 Clichy; p. 103, top: Courtesy of Brasserie du Louvre–Bocuse; p. 103, bottom: Courtesy of Clover Grill / Benedetta Chiala; p. 109: Olrat / Shutterstock; p. 110: Courtesy of Au Pied de Cochon / Simon Detraz; p. 111: Courtesy of ELMER / Alban Couturier; p. 112, top: Courtesy of Café des Musées; p. 112, bottom: Courtesy of Big Mamma; p. 113: Theendup / Shutterstock; p. 114: Elena Dijour / Shutterstock; p. 115: Courtesy of Don Juan II; p. 116: Courtesy of Le Grand Restaurant / hanh Renaud; p. 117: Courtesy of Le Clarence; p. 118: Courtesy of Le Drugstore (Publicis) / Natalia Khoroshaieva; p. 119, top: Courtesy of Chez Georges / The Social Food Studio / Shirley Garrier; p. 119, bottom: Courtesy of La Condesa / Laurent Dupont; p. 121: Courtesy of Public House / Benoît Linéro; p. 124, top: Courtesy of Bouillon Pigalle / THE TRAVEL BUDS STUDIO; p. 124, bottom: Courtesy of Geosmine / Laurent Dupont; p. 125: Rodtei / Shutterstock; p. 126, top: Courtesy of Fulgurances / Victoire Terrade x Crea Agency; p. 126, bottom: Courtesy of Laïa; p. 128, top: Courtesy of Brasserie Martin / Lucile Derveaux; p. 128, bottom: Courtesy of Ground Control / Studio 81; p. 129: Courtesy of Noglu; p. 130, top: Kent Wang; p. 130, bottom: Courtesy of EELS / Geraldine Martens; p. 131: Courtesy of MijoT; p. 132: Courtesy of L Avant Comptior Hotel Du Nord Restaurant / Valérie Manikowski; p. 133: Courtesy of Naam / Hipstamatic Photo; p. 134: Courtesy of La Tour D'Argent / Matthieu Salvaing; p. 138: Courtesy of La Truffière; p. 139: Courtesy of Bistroy Les Papilles; p. 140: Courtesy of Rôtisserie d'Argent; p. 143, top: Courtesy of Le Comptoir; p. 143, bottom: Courtesy of Le Relais de l'Entrecôte; p. 145, top: Courtesy of Divellec / Jacques Gavard; p. 145, bottom: Fabulousparis / Shutterstock; p. 147: Petr Kovalenkov / Shutterstock.com; p. 150: Courtesy of Le Ciel de Paris; p. 151, top: Courtesy of Le Petit Josselin; p. 151, bottom: Courtesy of Angelina; p. 152: Courtesy of Le Nélie (Musée

PHOTO CREDITS

Jacquemart-André) / Sofiacome; p. 153: Spatuletail / Shutterstock; p. 155: Courtesy of La Coupole / Simon Detraz; p. 156, top: Mo Wu / Shutterstock; p. 156, bottom: Petr Kovalenkov / Shutterstock.com; p. 160: NicoElNino / Shutterstock; p. 161: Courtesy of Notre Dame; p. 164: Kiev.Victor / Shutterstock; p. 165: Marina99; p. 168: Zhukova Valentyna / Shutterstock; p. 172: Mistervlad / Shutterstock.com; p. 173: Pol. Albarran / Shutterstock; p. 175: Courtesy of Museum of Romantic Life / Pierre Antoine; p. 176: Gilmanshin / Shutterstock.com; p. 178: Pavel Ilyukhin / Shutterstock; p. 180: Courtesy of Musée d'Art et d'Histoire du Judaïsme - MAHJ / Jerome Galland; p. 182: Melissa Baucom; p. 183: Eric Isselee / Shutterstock; p. 185, top left: Erica Russo; p. 185, bottom right: Courtesy of Grand Palais / Simon Lerat; p. 186: Franck Legros / Shutterstock; p. 188: © Musée National de la Marine/N. Krief; p. 189: Courtesy of Musée de l'Homme / Emmanuelle Blanc; p. 190: Courtesy of Culturespaces / Thomas Garnier; p. 193: Courtesy of Petit Palais / Benoit Fougeirol; p. 194: Erica Russo; p. 195: Adisa / Shutterstock; p. 196: Nikolpetr / Shutterstock; p. 197: Courtesy of Culturespaces / Eric Spiller; p. 199: Courtesy of Parc Zoologique de Paris; p. 200: Bert e Boer / Shutterstock; p. 202: Arty Om / Shutterstock; p. 203: Cité des Sciences et de l'Industrie; p. 204: Jerome LABOUYRIE / Shutterstock; p. 205: Anna Linda Knoll / Shutterstock; p. 206: Courtesy of Philharmonie des Enfants / Vincent Leroux; p. 207, top: Courtesy of The Jardin des Plantes / F-G Grandin ; p. 207, bottom right: Courtesy of Manufacture Nationale des Gobelins; p. 211: Danny Ye / Shutterstock; p. 212: Zoran Karapancev / Shutterstock; p. 214: Courtesy of Musée National Eugène-Delacroix © Musée du Louvre / GrandPalaisRmn / Olivier Ouadah; p. 215: Courtesy of Musée Zadkine / Nicolas Borel; p. 216: EQRoy / Shutterstock; p. 218: Courtesy of Eiffel Tower / E.Li; p. 220: Olrat / Shutterstock; p. 221: Melissa Baucom; p. 223: Wjarek / Shutterstock; p. 224: Musée de la Libération / Pierre Antoine; p. 226: Lapas77 / Shutterstock; p. 228: Frantic00 / Shutterstock; p. 229: Erica Russo; p. 230: Courtesy of Entrée to Black Paris; p. 232: Glenn Dettwiler / Flickr; p. 234: Courtesy of Sight Seeker's Delight / Lou Ludbrook; p. 237: Elena Dijour / Shutterstock; p. 238: BERK OZDEMIR / Shutterstock; p. 239: Elena Dijour / Shutterstock; p. 240: Vlastas / Shutterstock; p. 242: Courtesy of Samaritaine / Stéphane ABOUDARAM / WE ARE CONTENT(S); p. 246: Courtesy of Le Bon Marché; p. 247: Courtesy of Boom Boom Villette; p. 249: Stefano Ember / Shutterstock.com; p. 250, top: Courtesy of Drouot / Alain Potignon; p. 250, bottom: Courtesy of 59 Rivoli; p. 251, top: Courtesy of Village Saint-Paul; p. 251, bottom: Courtesy of Detaille 1905; p. 252, top right: Courtesy of The Abbey Bookshop; p. 252, bottom: Craigfinlay; p. 254, left: Courtesy of Smith & Son / Jacques Giral; p. 254, right: Courtesy of The Red Wheelbarrow Bookstore; p. 255: Courtesy of Galignani / David Atlan; p. 256, top: Courtesy of L'Île aux Fées; p. 256, bottom: Courtesy of Marie Puce; p. 257: Courtesy of Lapin Boutique; p. 258: Courtesy of Landline / Francois Goize; p. 259, top: Courtesy of Patisserie Mélilot / Geraldine Martens; p. 259, bottom: Courtesy of A La Mère de Famille; p. 260: Courtesy of La Grande Epicerie Rive Gauche / Virgile Guinard; p. 261: Courtesy of Legrand Filles et Fils / Constantin Mirbach; p. 262: Edsel Little; p. 263, top right: Courtesy of Monsieur; p. 263, bottom: Courtesy of WHITE bIRD; p. 264: Courtesy of La Cabane Enchantée / Yann Maignan; p. 267, top: Olrat / Shutterstock; p. 267, bottom: Courtesy of Lido 2 Paris; p. 269: Courtesy of Théâtre de la Ville / Camilla Greenwell; p. 270: Torfo / Flickr; p. 272: Courtesy of Baiser Salé; p. 274: Courtesy of New Morning / LEO FAVREAU; p. 275: Courtesy of Supersonic / Laure Ghilarducci; p. 277, top: Courtesy of La Bellevilloise; p. 277, bottom right: Jean-Pierre Dalbéra; p. 278: Courtesy of Moncoeur Belleville; p. 279: Courtesy of Tiger / Favaro Cassandre; p. 280: Courtesy of Le Perchoir / Jerome Galland; p. 281, top: Courtesy of Poupée; p. 281, bottom: Courtesy of Candelaria / GUILLAUME BELVEZE; p. 282: Courtesy of La Binouze / Nathalie Roux; p. 283: Courtesy of Paname Brewing Company / Gilles Rivollier / l'Associé; p. 285: Mikolaj Barbanell / Shutterstock; p. 288: Gilmanshin / Shutterstock.com; p. 291: Tanja Djurasevic; p. 293: Stoniko / Shutterstock; p. 294: Jorisvo / Shutterstock; p. 296: El Greco 1973 / Shutterstock; p. 297: Walencienne / Shutterstock; p. 298: Pack-Shot / Shutterstock; p. 300: Marcobrivio.photography / Shutterstock.com; p. 302: Courtesy of Château de Fontainebleau / Thibaut Chapotot; p. 303: Courtesy of Château de Fontainebleau / Lucie Page; p. 305: Chris Smithe / Shutterstock; p. 310: Heracles Kritikos / Shutterstock.com; p. 311: JeanLucIchard / Shutterstock; p. 312: Page Light Studios / Shutterstock.com; p. 313: Kiev.Victor / Shutterstock.com; p. 314: Adisa / Shutterstock; p. 316: Kiev.Victor / Shutterstock; p. 318: Onyshchenko / Shutterstock; p. 319: Courtesy of Musée d'Art et d'Histoire du Judaïsme - MAHJ / Jérôme Galland; p. 320: Isogood_patrick / Shutterstock; p. 321: Courtesy of Musée Cognacq-Jay / Pierre Antoine; p. 322, top right: Lotsostock / Shutterstock; p. 322, bottom: Jmbf / Shutterstock.com; p. 323: Courtesy of Maison de Victor Hugo / Pierre Antoine; back cover: laraslk / Shutterstock.com.

NOTES

NOTES

Before, During, or After your use of a Frommer's guidebook... you'll want to consult
FROMMERS.COM

FROMMERS.COM IS KEPT UP-TO-DATE, WITH:

NEWS
The latest events (and deals) to affect your next vacation

BLOGS
Opinionated comments by our outspoken staff

SLIDESHOWS
On weekly-changing, practical but inspiring topics of travel

CONTESTS
Enabling you to win free trips

PODCASTS
Featuring experts from around the world

DESTINATIONS
Hundreds of cities, their hotels, restaurants and sights

TRIP IDEAS
Valuable, offbeat suggestions for your next vacation

*AND MUCH MORE!

Smart travelers consult Frommers.com